Hohenheim

Hans L. Merkle

Dienen und Führen

ERKENNTNISSE EINES UNTERNEHMERS

Mit Beiträgen von
Henry A. Kissinger
und Hermann Scholl

Hohenheim Verlag
Stuttgart · Leipzig

INHALT

Hans L. Merkle

REMARKS BY HENRY A. KISSINGER

October 2001

It is a great honor to be asked to deliver a speech in memory of one of the most remarkable men I have known. It is a daunting task as well. For those in this room who knew Hans Merkle, nothing I can say will be able to reflect his complexity and inspirational quality. For those who did not have the opportunity to encounter his extraordinary combination of dedication and authority, any description of him will, in this age of standardized norms, seem out of scale.

Hans Merkle was a man of seeming paradoxes. He was my friend, yet he rarely spoke a personal word to me. One knew one could always rely on him, yet he would have considered statements to that effect as an elaboration of the self-evident or a derogation from the nature of friendship. Merkle was an inspiring leader who moved people by his aura without having to insist on the prerogatives of hierarchy. Even while achieving enormous success in business (it is no exaggeration to describe him as the most influential German businessman for two decades), he spent much of his free time reading and developing an astonishing erudition in philosophy, history, even poetry – all without a university degree. He displayed this staggering knowledge only rarely in conversations; Hans Merkle would have considered that as so much unworthy ostentation. "One must never say all one knows," he noted in his speech, "Service and Leadership" *(Dienen und Führen).*

The range of Merkle's interests is reflected in the titles of his speeches and essays: "The Art of Prediction"; "Man, Machines, and Technology"; "Rights and Duties in the Republic"; "Service and Leadership"; "Elites and How to Encourage Them"; "Profession as Experience"; "A Critique of Technology"; "Virtue and Trust", among many others. How many modern managers would have thought of writing an essay on the meaning of Caesar going to the Capitol on the day he was assassinated even though he had received many warnings? Did it reflect the virtue of trust in republican institutions or the sin of arrogant self-confidence challenging republican norms?

Merkle's essentially philosophical essays did not deal with the issues directly related to his company. But they do explain its extraordinary success under his leadership, growing from sales of DM 2 billion in 1964 when he took over the reins, to DM 21.2 billion in 1985, and to DM 60 billion in the year 2000. And the smoothness of the transition after he stepped down as chairman shows that Merkle achieved his highest aim of raising management beyond the personal and imparting to his successors the standard of meticulous attention to detail, insistence on a striving for perfection and, above all, on an ethic of decency and a selection based on character, which I consider the hallmark of Bosch.

I met Hans Merkle 24 years ago at a dinner of Chase Manhattan Bank's International Advisory Board, which took place in a New York museum. Sigmund Warburg had urged Merkle to introduce himself to me. That, however, proved easier said than done. Merkle did not want to impose himself, while I waited for him to approach me. Finally I introduced myself. And Merkle's first words to me were: "You should know that I worked in a responsible position in a military ministry in Berlin. I did not like the Nazis, but I served my country during the war. If that bothers you, you should have nothing to do with me."

That night at the museum laid the basis for permanent respect. For it was clear that Merkle wanted nothing less than to obscure the past. He once said that people who deny their history also reject their future. But the appropriate lessons had to evolve in the realm of conscience of the individual and of his society and not in comments to foreigners. Merkle took many actions to make clear where he stood, including the activities of the Bosch Foundation in Israel. But, true to his signature style, he never publicized them.

Hans Merkle was infinitely solicitous of his friends but became embarrassed when one acknowledged his concern as if that would destroy its moral significance as an act of grace. On the occasion of my being made honorary citizen of Fürth, the town in which I was born, Merkle appeared, having driven over two hours to get there. Only later did I learn that it had been the first day of radiation treatment for the illness that ultimately claimed his life and that he had come straight from this exhausting procedure to a formal ceremony and a boisterous lunch.

So when one writes or speaks about Hans Merkle, one deals with the incarnation of intangibles. To him, the central quality of a society or of any organization was trust *(Zuversicht).* Confidence results less from deliberate policy than from the intuitive acceptance of personalities who inspire by example rather than articulateness. He quoted with approval a line from Alfred Tennyson: "And trust me not at all or all in all." The ultimate requirement of leadership was, as Merkle would quote Peter Drucker, to earn trust: "Trust is the conviction that the leader means what he says."

Merkle always meant what he said. In his view, leadership was service; it avoids self-satisfaction during periods of success and provides inner strength to persist in times of adversity. It consists in equal parts of delegating credit for achievement while assuming responsibility for failure. The chief executive must not only outline a direction but inspire its execution. And he must never rest on what has been achieved. Thus Merkle ended his speech at Bosch's centenary celebration summing up the achievements of the past 100 years with a warning against complacency: "We at Bosch know our worth. But this consciousness does not entitle us to lean back in our chairs in self-satisfaction. We see our challenge not in reaping what we have sown but in sowing what will be reaped tomorrow."

In his style of leadership, Merkle confronted the root dilemma of modern society: how, in a period of rapid change, to bridge the gap between a society's experience and its possibilities, between the preservation of what is valuable and the space needed for the emergence of the new? Societies grow attached to the familiar, but leaders must point toward what does not yet exist. Even if ideas or concepts originate with one or a few individuals, they must be internalized by those who execute them and become, as it were, their own convictions. The role of leadership is, in a sense, lonely, but the execution cannot be solitary; it must reflect a consensus. Democracy is therefore a mandate of modernity. The vitality of a society depends crucially on the interplay between the inspiration of the individual and the translation of it into the commonplace of the society or of the enterprise.

A democracy whose leaders rely only on exploiting the mood of the moment will soon drift without direction and end in dictatorship. But, equally, leadership conceived as the expression of the arbitrary of an individual will turn power into a demonic enterprise. For that reason, a well-conceived concept of national interest is less an assertion of power than a limitation of it.

Hans Merkle feared an unprecedented form of tyranny as potentially inherent in the modern technological world. Permit me to quote from his essay, "The Demonism of Power": "It is conceivable – and perhaps we have an obligation to face it – that the demonism of power in the future cannot be related to the individual any longer. Power becomes increasingly anonymous but no less dangerous for the free evolution of humanity. Falsification of concepts is the first step toward the development of concentrations of power of a new kind – impersonal, intangible, almost ghostly; one is reminded of Kafka. And because society so emasculated will not be able to deal with social processes without some mechanism, social tasks will be assigned to organs of a new kind. The despotism of tyrants will be replaced by the despotism of the apparatus."

Therefore, the individual's fulfillment must not be subordinated to the demands of politics, and politics must not be defined as the sole, or even the principal, purpose of social life. The ultimate goal of political life should not be imposition of a ubiquitous, interchangeable norm but to promote independence in enterprises and for individuals. Wherever it is forgotten that political duties are, in the end, based on political rights and that these rights must be revitalized in each period, politics turns into manipulation.

Real conservatives – among whom Merkle counted himself – are not opposed to progress; on the contrary, they create the condition for progress by preserving the foundations on which to build and by warning of those steps urged in the name of progress that lead into an abyss.

The executive is tested above all when adversity strikes. A prescient quote from Merkle from 1975 may be appropriate: "Too extended periods of unrestrained growth spoil both managers and workers, distort a sense of proportion, erase distinctions, and weaken the sense for the essential, for the necessary, for the possible. They obscure the peril that threatens every society and every economy which prevails too easily without having to prove itself. If the wind changes and storms threaten, the hour of ultimate testing has come; then we will learn who can read the weather map and who is able to navigate against the wind."

This is why for Merkle – as already for Robert Bosch – the fostering of talent was a primary preoccupation. The founder of the company had laid down in the guidelines of the Bosch Foundation, to which he had refused to give his name in keeping with the Bosch tradition of anonymity (it was so named only after his death by Merkle), that one of its principal goals was to prepare society for the adaptation of thought processes and procedures to the changes subtly latent in all societies. Foremost among these was the free and unhindered development of the human personality.

These fragmentary summaries of the thoughts of a remarkable man explain what I would describe as the "Bosch style": total reliability, an unflagging sense of service, a dedication always to function at the frontiers of knowledge, a notion of profit based on energetic enterprise and insistent competitiveness with the proceeds always available to the common good. "To belong to the elite," wrote Merkle, "brings with it duties rather than rights. To be sure, the performance demanded of leaders should not and does not remain unrewarded. But the goal of the effort must never be material reward. Elites should not define themselves by ruling but by serving – or better, they rule best by serving. Those who belong to the real elite do not insist on being called elites. Those who do insist on it do not belong."

This explains the seemingly anonymous, almost impersonal, and yet, in its ultimate sense, deeply individual style of Hans Merkle. For his work to be meaningful, it could not be the expression of a personal preference; this would undermine its moral significance. It had to be a reflection of a higher obligation which evoked the sense of duty. Merkle would quote from Max Planck: "The ultimate good of which no power in the world can deprive us is a pure way of thinking *(reine Gesinnung)* which finds its expression in a conscientious carrying out of one's duties." To which Merkle added: "No more can be expected of us but also no less."

In this spirit, I want to say a few words about the contribution that Hans Merkle and some members of his generation – at least one of whom is here tonight – have made to the rebirth of Germany and its relationship to the international community in the aftermath of the Second World War.

Biographers make much of my German birth. And it is, of course, true that one's environment shapes one's attitudes even in difficult times (which is why I still take an active weekly interest in the four Bavarian football clubs in the *Bundesliga* – although Fürth is regrettably in the second *Bundesliga*). But my real connection with Germany stems from the end of the war. I arrived here with the army of occupation in 1945 after a seven-year absence. Few of you present will remember the devastation, desolation, and spiritual despair of those months; it belongs to the formative experiences of your fathers and grandfathers. There is no time now, and this is not the occasion, to review the political evolution of more than half a century – though it seems like only yesterday to me.

I want to pay tribute to those who had the moral courage to start again, to rebuild their country, and to bring it back to the community of nations by the very qualities I have called the Bosch attributes: reliability, steadiness, enterprise, and an abiding commitment to democratic values. Governments of both major parties established a steady policy tied to the democratic West. In the process, America and Germany together went through two Berlin crises, the building of the Wall, and finally reunification. Occasional disagreements in tactics have never undermined the underlying unity of purpose.

And just when, on both sides of the Atlantic, the end of the Cold War had evoked a seemingly endless debate about the continuing validity of the democratic partnership, the terrorist attack on New York and Washington has returned the democracies to fundamentals. Too many of us had been seduced by the siren song of the end of history, of the reduction of politics to psychiatry and social work, and of the predominance of narrow national concerns. We have learned that there are incompatible values rampant in the world around us and that there are those so eager to destroy our civilization that they will sacrifice their lives to do so and will not recoil before the murder of innocent civilians. It has obliged the West to relearn what it had nearly forgotten: that in its unity and solidarity resides its ultimate strength. So I want to take this opportunity to thank our German friends here for the many expressions of support and compassion that reached us from all over Germany and for the highly appreciated demonstrations of solidarity from the German government.

None of this would have surprised Hans Merkle. He was born in what was then Baden, now Baden-Württemberg, but he incarnated some of the best values of the Prussian ethos. One of these is, "Always be more than you seem to be" *(mehr sein als scheinen).* Applied to Merkle and adapting it to one of the quotes I mentioned earlier, I would rephrase his own basic maxim this way: "Always say less than you know and always do more than you say."

For all I have said, Merkle's posture of aloofness did not reflect a lack of deep feeling. On the contrary, it was wrested from a deeply passionate nature. He obscured this aspect of his personality because he did not wish to impose his sentiments even on his friends. Like one of the heroes of classical drama, Merkle took on himself the battles to which he thought destiny had called him. Those of us whom he honored with his friendship therefore felt as if we had been admitted into a chivalrous order.

The emotions from which Merkle's aristocratic conduct had been wrung can be seen in a letter he wrote in November 1944, when his hometown of Pforzheim had been destroyed in the war: "Fate would not pass this town by. But for me this place is not of brick and mortar; it is founded on quite a different kind of building block that cannot be reduced to rubble so long as the heart does not allow it. And the heart will not acquiesce. It clings to old scenes, to hills and trees, and to the memory of many days which were gifts of God and of youthful dreams. For, in the end, ideas are stronger than men and more long-lasting."

A few months after his death, Merkle's daughter Monika and Dr. Scholl did me the honor of accompanying me to Hans Merkle's grave on a still, verdant hillside, shaded by trees overlooking the city of Pforzheim which had risen from the ashes, rebuilt by men and women whose dreams overcame their reality.

After that occasion, Monika graciously let me see the letter I have just read to you. I thought then how lonely a life this caring man imposed on himself, how much of the travail of others he took on himself, and I wondered whether some of us might have broken through this solitude by an act of grace.

But then I reflected that Hans Merkle lived just as he wanted. Duty was his companion, honor his imperative. He expressed this best in his essay, "Virtue and Trust": "Confidence in the future – that virtue of the soul, as the French put it – must be fought for every day. It involves permanent exertion, a coming-and-going; yet, as we travel a path so strewn with stones, a God occasionally consoles us with a smile."

Hans Merkle inspired many of us in traveling these stony paths and thereby vouchsafed this world an occasional smile from a God.

Hans L. Merkle and the Advance of International Management Practice

BY HERMANN SCHOLL

October 2001

1. **Introduction**

First of all, Ladies and Gentlemen, let me thank Dr. Henry Kissinger for his outstanding contributions last night. Above all Dr. Kissinger, thank you so much for your speech in honor of Hans Merkle, which came from your heart and which showed your deep friendship to Hans Merkle. And thank you for your remarks and the following discussion on the actual scenario which gave many of us strong guidelines for our own activities and responsibilities in the next months.

You honored Hans L. Merkle, both the man and the business leader. Therefore I will only make reference to biographical data or events wherever it is necessary for a better understanding of my topic.

The year 1958 was a lucky year, most certainly for Bosch, but also for Hans Merkle.

In 1935, at the age of 22, Hans Merkle joined a medium-sized textile firm. In doing so he gained broad experiences with international business before and during the war, and especially in the post-war period. However, by the mid '50s his personal development in business and his personality had far exceeded the limited possibilities offered by this company, so in 1958 he accepted an offer to join Bosch.

In 1958, Bosch was in the process of making its third attempt in its history toward internationalization, after two setbacks suffered as a result of the First and Second World Wars.

Hans Merkle decisively influenced the development of the Bosch Group for 35 years – up to 1993 and also beyond that date. Of the 35 years until 93, he was a member of the Board of Management for 26 years, 21 of which he served as chairman. He was also a member of the top controlling body of the Bosch Group for 30 years, 28 of which as chairman, initially in the committee of executors and then later of the holding company which has over 92 % of the voting rights.

From 1993 until his death last year he played a more consultative role regarding all important decisions, and in this manner, also exerted enduring influence. In other words, he had in fact the power in the company for 42 years.

I, myself, have known Hans Merkle for 31 years. I was introduced to him in 1969, after having joined middle management at Bosch. My working relationship with him began when I was appointed to the Board of Management in 1973. Initially we did not have close working contacts, because Merkle discussed the really important subjects primarily with the senior members of the Board of Management, one of whom, of course, I was not at that time. However, I was frequently invited to meetings with the CEOs of big automobile manufacturers whom Merkle invited to our company in Stuttgart. At that time I was primarily responsible for the new technologies at Bosch, and was usually asked by Merkle to give a technical overview of the Bosch Group at such meetings.

A close and trust-based working relationship began in 1993, when I became Chairman of the Board of Management. There was mutual interest in a close exchange: I, on my part, sought advice on important questions relating to business and personnel policy. Hans Merkle, on his side, was always concerned about the future of the

Bosch Group, especially with regard to the automotive group. He paid special attention to the growing predominance of the increasingly more powerful automobile manufacturers, who became fewer and fewer in number because of concentration in the industry. Our last conversation of this nature took place on Sunday, September 17, 2000, five days before his death.

Hans Merkle attached great importance to a clear demarcation of personal responsibilities in the company. He was not a friend of teams.

In private conversations he could be extraordinarily charming and could display a great sense of humor. In business matters, however, he was very strict. There was little laughter during discussions and meetings. He expressed his sense of humor only very rarely. I remember a Board meeting in the early '80s. He was in a good mood and talked about an invitation of business friends to the Bosch hunting ground in Bavaria. Apparently, in his eagerness to hunt, a guest of the hunting party committed a great *faux pas*. He shot repeatedly at a stag from far too great a distance, before the professional hunter accompanying him gave the go-ahead for the shot. I still remember exactly what Hans Merkle said: "Der Hirsch blieb einfach stehen, um sich nicht dem Sperrfeuer des Schützen auszusetzen." – "The stag simply stood still so as not to be exposed to the barrage from the hunter."

*

Ladies and Gentlemen, the following observations are based for the most part on my own experiences. In some instances I have also received valuable information from Monika Merkle, Hans Merkle's daughter, who joined us for this conference. In addition, the Bosch Archive conducted some research, for which I am most grateful.

2. The International Experiences of Hans L. Merkle before Joining Bosch

After a business apprenticeship, Hans Merkle, at the age of 22, joined the Gminder company, a rather small family enterprise in the textile industry, in Reutlingen, close to Stuttgart. The company's activities centered on the processing of cotton into fabric. Two areas of activity in particular were crucial to the success of this company: first, the purchase of raw materials, especially cotton; secondly, the correct assessment of international currency fluctuation, since most purchases were made outside Germany.

By the way, these two areas were well known to me personally – my grandfather was in the international wool business. He and I had frequent conversations about this back in the '50s. Foreign currency changes, and then possible political tensions, were crucial to him. Tensions between states meant to him a risk of war, with an additional high demand for wool for military uniforms, and thus rising prices for wool on the world market.

Hans Merkle worked closely with Louis Gminder, one of the family directors. Louis Gminder told him once: "If you want to work in my company you will have to learn ten new English and ten new French words every day. Both languages are indispensable in international business."

Hans Merkle followed this advice, probably throughout his life, and also applied it to other languages. He spoke English and French fluently, and had a good knowledge of Latin, Greek, Spanish and Russian.

During the Second World War Hans Merkle was assigned to the German army at the start of 1941. As a textile expert, it was his responsibility to coordinate the textile trade and industry with respect to war needs, including in the countries then occupied by the German Army. This required travel to these countries and also to neutral Switzerland.

After the war, Hans Merkle frequently traveled in the service of his company Gminder, where he became a member of its Board of Management in 1950. In addition to numerous trips to neighboring European countries, several trips to North and South America as well as to East Asia should be mentioned in particular.

In 1958, the then-head of Bosch, Hans Walz, was apparently looking for a successor. During Robert Bosch's lifetime Walz had been his closest associate, and after the death of Robert Bosch in 1942, Walz became the second head of Bosch, after the company founder. Hans Merkle was interested in a change, because due to the many family directors at Gminder, there was not enough room for further development. Even though Merkle did not have Bosch-specific knowledge of the industry, he did have optimal qualifications for a leadership position at Bosch, where initially he headed the finance department.

3. **The Bosch Group in 1958**

In 1958, Bosch was intensely concerned with regaining ground lost in the Second World War. At this point I should mention the international activities of the Bosch Group before the First and Second World Wars to provide some background:

The first phase of internationalization had begun in 1898, only 12 years after the establishment of the company, with the first foreign branch office in England. This phase lasted until 1914, the start of the First World War. In this phase, foreign branch offices were set up in all important European countries, as well as in North America, South America, South Africa, Egypt, China and Japan. In addition, there were already two foreign production plants: in France and the U.S. Already at that time, the United States was especially important to Bosch. Before the First World War Bosch had a market share of 80 % in the field of automotive ignition because of the famous high-voltage magneto, a Bosch invention. All foreign operations were lost as a result of the First World War.

The second phase lasted from 1919 until 1939. During this time the lost foreign branch offices and production plants in France and the U.S. were reopened. Two new production plants were also added in England and Italy in the early '30s. The Second World War again resulted in a loss of all operations outside Germany.

The third phase, the reconstruction after the war, lasted until about the middle of the '60s. It is interesting to note that the interruption after the Second World War was considerably more severe than that after the First World War: after the First World War, Bosch began restructuring international positions as early as in 1919. After the Second World War, these activities did not begin before 1950. There were several reasons for this. After the end of the war in 1945, came the Morgenthau Plan, according to which Germany was to be turned into an agrarian country. After that, antitrust proceedings were pursued against Bosch, with the goal of breaking up Bosch's monopoly position in the fuel injection field, similarly to what was done to the German chemical industry after the war. The proceedings were not stopped until the early '50s.

In addition, Germany was initially no longer sovereign. There was a military government. The first German federal government did not begin operating before 1949.

By 1958, the year Merkle joined Bosch, the former foreign branch offices were reopened for the most part. In addition, important new production plants were also added in the '50s: in Argentina, India, Australia, Brazil and Switzerland.

4. The International Development of the Bosch Group under Hans L. Merkle

Merkle took over the chairmanship of the Board of Management from Hans Walz in 1963. He had already been a partner in the holding company since 1961. In 1965, he also became chairman of this body, a position he held until 1993.

Merkle pursued the expansion of the Bosch Group outside Germany very systematically and with great vigor. The resultant expansion was far beyond the level the company had reached before the Second World War. The major steps taken were primarily:

1. The acquisiton of European foreign branch offices in all important countries. Although these had been contract partnerships, they were not in Bosch's possession up until then.
2. The further expansion of production outside Germany with the priority goal of developing those markets, which at that time were inaccessible to exports because of customs barriers or local content regulations.
3. The foreign production bases were primarily oriented towards supplying foreign production plants of German automotive manufacturers, which had meanwhile been set up, for example, in Australia, Brazil, Argentina and Mexico.
4. Establishment of production plants in the U.S. and England and sustained expansion of production in France and Spain. In addition, the first production joint ventures were established in Japan, and cooperation with the Japanese licensees Nippon Denso and Diesel Kiki was strengthened.

5. Management Principles in the Bosch Group under Hans L. Merkle

Right up through the present, the Bosch Group essentially rests on three pillars, which were systematically shaped and strengthened primarily by Hans Merkle:

1. Simple and clear structuring of business data along commercial lines.
2. A strong technology base, capable of innovation.
3. The systematic development of managerial personnel within the company.

The annual business planning has a range of three years, with one plan year and two forecast years. The business data of an ongoing year are monitored monthly by stringent controlling. Before starting the planning process for the subsequent year, the current year is subjected to a very critical target performance comparison.

The strong technological position rests on two pillars: a powerful centralized research and advance development, which also includes in-house development of strategically important production technologies and processes, and the actual product development conducted in a decentralized manner in the various product divisions.

The development of managerial personnel is coordinated on a centralized worldwide basis, starting at the level of the department managers.

The direction of the activities outside Germany is not handled by a separate organization, but is an integral part of the management process of the entire Bosch Group. The designation of the foreign activities is symptomatic of this way of thinking. They are not called "Auslandsgesellschaften" – "foreign or overseas companies", but "Regionalgesellschaften" – "regional subsidiaries", so as not to discriminate against them.

Hans Merkle did not establish general management principles and then adhere to them rigidly. His work as head of the Bosch Group is primarily characterized by the constant evolution of his management methods. Looking back, it can be stated, also in comparison with the development of other companies: Hans Merkle identified changes in basic national and international conditions early on, or even anticipated them; and he oriented the company prospectively towards these changes. For this reason the international organization of the Bosch Group evolved steadily. However, this did not create disruptions. On the contrary, organizational changes, if they are not too frequent, usually lead to a strengthening, because they release new energies.

There was a functional division of labor at Bosch within the Board of Management up to the early '60s. The parent company was not yet subdivided into product divisions or business segments. Organizational boundaries only existed because of the corporate legal structure, which demarcated at that time numerous separate legal entities in Germany and various regional subsidiaries abroad.

In the course of the '60s, product divisions based on the various product areas were formed in several stages. Toward the end of the '60s, there were six product divisions in the automotive equipment field, and approximately ten divisions for other products. Each product division was led by a functionally structured management team, with responsibilities for sales, technology and commercial functions.

The introduction of product divisions also brought about a change in the rules of procedure for the Board of Management of the parent company. In addition to several corporate functions, such as finance, controlling and personnel, the remaining members of the Board of Management were responsible for particular lines of business. The individual product divisions were assigned to the individual members of the Board of Management with respect to all functions. As mentioned earlier, this corresponded to Hans Merkle's way of thinking. He was very much in favor of the personal, undivided responsibility of a manager for a specific field of operation.

Initially, the regional subsidiaries were still under the central direction of one single member of the Board of Management. Up to the early '70s, this was also in line with the largely independent regional activities in markets closed by customs barriers. The international aftermarket was also assigned to a single member of the Board of Management.

A crucial organizational step taken by Merkle was the reorganization of the entire production activities in Europe. A distinction was no longer made between German and other European plants. This means, Bosch already had an integral European production system in the early '80s, long before the formation of the European Union. All European plants were assigned to one of the various product divisions of the parent company depending on their key products. Formally, the plants were part of the regional subsidiaries. However, these only had a coordinating function, for example, with regard to questions involving labor law or wage scales. The line responsibility for production clearly rested with the respective product divisions. In this manner the impact of the Bosch Group in Europe was decisively strengthened.

A very important and personal target of Merkle was the

6. **Expansion of the Market Position in the U.S.**

In the early '80s, Bosch had a great technological advantage over its American competitors in the automotive equipment field: with regard to gasoline injection and ABS, which didn't even exist in the U.S., and with respect to diesel injection, for which there were only a few, less important, companies. However, the actual sales revenues were still very low. The U.S. share of worldwide Bosch sales was only about 3 %.

Merkle set the goal of realizing at least 10 % of the global sales of the Bosch Group in the U.S. within a foreseeable period of time. To achieve this goal, he believed that an approach was needed that differed completely from that of the organization in Europe. At the beginning of 1984, he charged one of the members of the Board of Management – Rudolf Stahl – with the sole direction of all U.S. activities, with headquarters in Chicago. It was necessary for our colleague to travel regularly, in order to be able to participate in a meeting of the Board of Management at least once a month. This activity was relatively strenuous, and for this reason a different board member was selected for this position every two to three years. I, myself, was the second in this series from 1987 to 1990.

What is noteworthy is the pragmatism Merkle applied to the selection of management principles. Because of the special nature of the U.S. market and also because of the management methods of U.S. companies, a centralized top position was the right solution for the U.S. With this arrangement, the various lines of business within the parent company exerted influence by means of a kind of a matrix organization. The resultant success was impressive: by the mid '90s we had not only by far passed the 10% we had sought, but we presently realize 18% of our worldwide sales in North America including Mexico.

In the meantime, the disadvantages of this special organization in the U.S. are becoming evident, as our customers, particularly those in the automotive sector, make their purchases on a global scale. For this reason, we will have to introduce in the foreseeable future also for North America the full business responsibility of the product divisions which are in charge of the various business segments.

7. The Participation of Hans L. Merkle in Bodies outside the Bosch Group

As we have already heard from Dr. Kissinger, Hans Merkle played an important role as a business leader in the business communities in Europe and in North America.

He participated in a very large number of bodies: supervisory boards in Germany and in other countries; in political and scientific associations as well as advisory boards.

It is worth noting that Merkle was already a member of the supervisory boards of important German companies in the early '60s – at

Allianz, Deutsche Bank, BASF and Volkswagen, among others, when Bosch was still a relatively small company. Starting in the early '70s, mandates were increasingly added in supervisory and advisory boards of foreign companies such as Chase Manhattan Bank, the New York Stock Exchange and Shell.

In addition to fulfilling his obligations as a member of the respective bodies, Merkle took particular advantage of the resultant connections in the interest of his own company. Thus extraordinarily important personal ties to the respective CEOs of our big customers in Italy, France and the U.S. were formed, particularly in the automotive field. Hans Merkle formed lasting friendships with some of these and employed his ties very actively, especially in Italy, France and the U.S., in order to expand the Bosch business. He regularly invited key figures from the automotive industry to our technical center in Schwieberdingen near Stuttgart in order to present the latest Bosch technologies. Closer ties also developed toward Japan, especially to Eiji Tojoda, the then-head of Toyota. As mentioned earlier, Merkle usually assigned me the task of organizing these events and giving presentations.

A key area of particular interest to Hans Merkle was the participation in bodies of scientific associations like the German Max-Planck-Gesellschaft. He always prepared himself thoroughly, and sometimes consulted experts from the company for this purpose. Even though he never had any technical or scientific education, Hans Merkle possessed quite astonishing knowledge in those areas. I remember how as a young member of the Board of Management I frequently had to give presentations on technical subjects during Board meetings. I always had to prepare very carefully and my statements had to be very precise to avoid running the risk of being corrected by Merkle.

8. **The Big International Acquisitions of the Bosch Group**
No big international acquisitions took place between 1963 and the end of the '80s. There was a great need for financial resources in order to expand our own production in Germany as well as outside Germany. This applied in particular to the automotive equipment field, which experienced especially strong growth thanks to our new innovative products. Large acquisitions in the U.S. or Japan did not take place until the second half of the '90s. Merkle always gave vigorous support to such request from the Board of Management submitted to the holding company Robert Bosch Industrietreuhand KG, which controls Bosch and which ultimately decided these matters, even though, formally, he no longer had a vote. His advice was always listened to.

In 1958, the year Hans Merkle joined Bosch, the foreign share of our sales were barely 20 %. In the year 2000, it was 72 %.

9. **International Bodies in the Bosch Group**
Hans Merkle was very interested in having members from the respective country participate in the administrative councils of our regional subsidiaries. This was particularly important to him in the build-up phase and as long as the companies were managed from within the country in the respective closed markets. With the increasing interdependence of the global economy and the greater internationalization of the business, our regional subsidiaries were increasingly being directed by the product divisions of the parent company. The importance of the administrative councils in the various countries decreased. In addition, participation was no longer of special interest to the members from these countries, since all major decisions were made by the parent company. For this reason Merkle established an international advisory council in 1981, composed of members from all those countries in which Bosch had a heavy presence. The advisory council meets once a year at a Bosch

location, either in Germany or in another country. Dr. Kissinger has been a member of this advisory council since its inception in 1981.

Ladies and Gentlemen, I would like to summarize.

The convergence of Hans Merkle and the Bosch Group in 1958 was a lucky coincidence – a lucky coincidence for the Bosch Group, which was thus able to gain one of the most capable and important business leaders in Germany. Hans Merkle led and guided the Bosch Group for over 40 years, and turned it into a company with the best international positioning among the big suppliers of the automotive industry.

But at the same time, the Bosch Group was the ideal platform for Hans Merkle, enabling him to demonstrate his exceptional abilities as a business leader.

At the end of the '80s, I was the head of our U.S. company. During this time I spoke repeatedly with Hans Merkle about the project of the Carnegie Bosch Institute. It is for this reason I know that one thought was of particular importance to him: with the establishment of the Institute he wanted to demonstrate above all that Bosch, as a German company, feels a strong commitment to the host country and expresses that commitment.

I am extraordinarily grateful today to Servan Schreiber, who was back then a professor at Carnegie Mellon University, and especially to Dr. Kissinger, for having encouraged Hans Merkle to establish the Carnegie Bosch Institute together with Carnegie Mellon University.

Ladies and Gentlemen, with these last remarks I have concluded a wide loop and I am finally back at our CBI conference in Berlin.

Thank you.

Hans L. Merkle

Beruf als Erfahrung

ÜBER DEN EIGENEN WEG

Ich stand eines Tages vor der nüchternen Frage, wovon ich leben sollte. Als ich Anfang 1931 aus der Schule entlassen wurde, das Reifezeugnis in der Tasche, gab es im Deutschen Reich mehr als fünf Millionen Arbeitslose. Im verräucherten Lesesaal eines schönen Weinbrennerhauses meiner Heimatstadt Pforzheim lag die Weltpresse aus, die ich verschlang. Mit den Anwesenden, die von der dumpfen Wärme angezogen wurden, verband mich, daß wir Arbeit suchten.

Ich mußte mir eine Existenz aufbauen – von Berufung war keine Rede, auch nicht von Studium. Das Familienvermögen war in der Inflation untergegangen, ein Stipendium nicht aufzutreiben. Was immer ich an akademischer Arbeit seither leisten konnte: Es waren, wie ich nie verhehlt habe, Studien und kein Studium, Studien ohne Abschluß. Ich räume ein, das hat mich lange betrübt, aber 1945 war es belanglos geworden.

Die Hörerkarte, von der Universität Tübingen ausgehändigt, und ein vergleichbares Papier der Landesuniversität Heidelberg – mein Heimatland Baden war damals noch nicht nach Württemberg eingemeindet – gaben mir die Möglichkeit, Vorlesungen zu hören und, in einigen Fällen, auch an Übungen teilzunehmen.

Ich hörte in Heidelberg Gustav Radbruch, der Reichsjustizminister der Weimarer Republik gewesen ist, einen Rechtsphilosophen, der uns auch heute noch etwas zu sagen hat. Er erhielt als Sozialdemokrat 1933 Lehrverbot, Veröffentlichungen wurden erschwert. Ich sehe es als eine bescheidene Wiedergutmachung an, daß ich für die Gesamtausgabe seiner Werke, die bisher fehlte, etwas tun konnte.

Radbruch warnte uns nicht vor dem, was kommen sollte, vielleicht mußte. Es war eher Karl Jaspers, der uns beunruhigte. In dem berühmt gewordenen Göschenband 1000 analysierte er die »Geistige Situation unserer Zeit«, charakterisierte Bolschewismus und Faschismus als »Auswege zu leichterer Möglichkeit«. Aber in seiner fast dunklen Sprache fehlte die Warnung, die uns noch nicht Zwanzigjährige aufgeschreckt hätte.

Der philosophische Weg, den er wies, was nicht ohne Wirkung; er befürchtete den Verlust der inneren Freiheit. Aber er sagte auch: »Die pazifistischen Argumente verschweigen, was es heißt, versklavt zu werden und zu leben nach dem Grundsatz, keinen Widerstand zu leisten.« In meinem Exemplar des kleinen Göschenbandes hat Karl Löwith, der es von Karl Jaspers erhalten hatte, angestrichen: »Die Möglichkeit des Krieges wird ... nicht durch den Verzicht ... auf Wehrhaftigkeit ausgeschaltet.«

In einer existentiell ungesicherten Zeit, am Rande, zeitweise in einer Besatzungszone lebend, war damit die Bereitschaft zur Wehrhaftigkeit zunächst einmal vorbereitet; das ging, aus sehr persönlichen Gründen, Hand in Hand mit der Wahl eines Brotberufs. Ich geriet in die statistische Kategorie der kaufmännischen Angestellten. Ohne Reue bin ich geblieben, was ich damals wurde; ein Ausbruchversuch in die Jurisprudenz war ohne Erfolg. Ich hatte, in der seelenlosen Sprache von heute, einen Job.

Dann stieß ich auf Theodor Heuss. Doch half auch er politisch nicht weiter. Sein 1932 erschienenes Buch »Hitlers Weg« blieb lau; kürzliches Wiederlesen bestätigt die damalige Wirkungslosigkeit. Daß er, Theodor Heuss, dann im März 1933 im Reichstag für das Ermächtigungsgesetz stimmte – nachdem er vorher im Kreis seiner Freunde vergeblich für Ablehnung plädiert hatte –, rundete die Orientierungslosigkeit des jungen Kaufmanns ab.

Schließlich fand ich einen Mann, der für meine geistige Entwicklung besonders bedeutsam werden sollte: Hans Peter. Er konnte an der Rechts- und Staatswissenschaftlichen Fakultät der Universität Tübingen nicht mehr als (aber immerhin) Oberassistent werden; man verdächtigte ihn sozialistischer Gedankengänge. Ich wurde sein Hörer, sein Seminarteilnehmer und sein Mitarbeiter; mein Arbeitgeber gewährte mir großzügig die Zeit, und Peter gewann mich für die damals junge Ökonometrie – ich übte Beruf als Erfahrung, nicht ohne Gewinn aus der methodischen Strenge dieses Wissenszweiges.

Als der Krieg begann, wurde für Hans Peter der Boden in Tübingen zu heiß; Freunde, man darf raten, brachten ihn in Berlin unter, beim Reichswirtschaftsministerium und, sicherer noch, bei der Deutschen Arbeitsfront. Er kam unversehrt nach Tübingen zurück, wurde Ordinarius. Unsere Wege trennten sich, weil er diejenigen übersah, die ihm geholfen hatten. Doch er ist tot, schon lange … de mortuis nil nisi bene. Beruf als Erfahrung.

*

Zur Erfahrung wurde jetzt, daß das Jahr 1945 *nicht* das Jahr Null war. Blanke Not, vielleicht war auch einige Weitsicht dabei, war Anlaß, das Geschäft über die Grenzen hinweg wieder aufzubauen. Man war draußen bereit, mit uns Handel zu treiben, aber nicht, uns die Hand zu reichen. Das Gefühl der Befreiung von unheimlichem Druck, der Erleichterung hielt nicht lange an.

Die Erfahrung ging um so tiefer, als längst die Selbstprüfung eingesetzt hatte – unabhängig vom Urteil der Sieger, das eine Vorverurteilung war und dennoch im Grunde gerecht. Es nützte dem kritischen Bewußtsein wenig, daß der amerikanische Anklagevertreter im Nürnberger Prozeß sagte, es sei nicht beabsichtigt, »das ganze deutsche Volk zu beschuldigen«.

Karl Jaspers rechnete mit denen ab, die nicht in den offenen Widerstand gegangen waren. Im Wintersemester 1945/46 las er in

Heidelberg über die »Schuldfrage« (so der Titel seines kleinen Buches von 1946): Schuld, Verantwortung, Haftung – politisch, moralisch, metaphysisch; doch wurde auch die Schuld der anderen erörtert. Jenseits aller philosophischen Differenzierungen blieb als Konsequenz die Erfahrung, die gerade auch aus dem Beruf des Kaufmannes kam: Das Vertrauen mußte wiederhergestellt werden – »in Demut und Maßhalten«, so beendete Jaspers seine Vorlesung. Unabhängig von jedem Schuldspruch, von jedem rechtlichen Standpunkt, allein aus dem Bewußtsein, daß Unrecht geduldet, kein wirksamer Widerstand geleistet worden war.

*

Die These von der übergreifenden Einheit der Kultur – sie stammt nicht von mir, aber ich vertrete sie – hatte sich in Jahren des Nachdenkens stärker herausgebildet. Sie verlangt von jedem Staatsbürger, daß er sich über seinen Beruf hinaus Erfahrung in den Fragen des Gemeinwesens verschaffe, sie verlangt seine Mitwirkung.

Für mich war klar, daß die Wissenschaft an dem Prozeß der Wiedergewinnung des Vertrauens mitzuwirken hatte, und ich sah dort eine Aufgabe für mich, die mich aber von meinem Beruf nicht abhalten sollte.

Man kann sich fragen, ob es gerade Martin Heidegger sein mußte, dem erste wissenschaftliche Kontakte galten. Ich hatte ihn nie für den gehalten, den manche bis heute aus ihm machen möchten – trotz seiner oft mißverstandenen Freiburger Rektoratsrede vom Mai 1933 (was später Jaspers daran rügte, war, nebenbei gesagt, zunächst die schlechte Übersetzung des Platon-Zitats am Schluß der Rede). Nun saß er in seiner Holzhütte in Todtnauberg im Schwarzwald, und es ging ihm nicht gut. Aber sein Ruf über die Grenzen hinweg galt noch immer, und ich konnte Brücken schlagen helfen.

Älter war meine Beziehung zu Gerhard Ritter, die 1940 begonnen hatte und bis zu seinem Tod 1967 dauerte. Sie war als Erfahrung wichtig, gerade weil sie meinem Brotberuf scheinbar ebenso fernlag wie die zu Heidegger. Im Jahre 1940 war Ritters Buch »Machtstaat und Utopie« erschienen. Der Untertitel »Vom Streit um die Dämonie der Macht seit Machiavelli und Morus« zeigte, deutlicher als der Titel selbst, daß Ritter seinerzeit kühn genug war, das Problem der Macht und ihrer Korrumpierung öffentlich aufzugreifen.

»Dämonie«, schrieb er, »ist Besessenheit«, und zitierte Jacob Burckhardt: »Und nun ist die Macht an sich böse, gleichviel, wer sie ausübt.« Viele verstanden damals – 1940 –, was Gerhard Ritter meinte, wenn er von »der ungeheuren, seit den Tagen der althellenischen Polis so nicht mehr erlebten Verantwortung für den Fortbestand echter Sittlichkeit und Rechtlichkeit« sprach.

Die kleingedruckte Anmerkung Ritters auf einer der letzten Seiten, daß er die geistige Vorgeschichte des modernen Nationalismus »totalitärer« Prägung absichtlich nicht behandle, mag manchem entgangen sein; fett drucken konnte man dies damals nicht. Gerhard Ritter, der nach dem 20. Juli 1944 verhaftet worden war, konnte erst nach dem Kriege die Tarnung aufhellen. Die Neuauflage seines Buchs erschien nunmehr unter dem Titel »Die Dämonie der Macht«.

Mir kam Ritters Buch während des Krieges in die Hand. Ich las es in dunklen Tagen. Ein Exzerpt überdauerte die Jahre. Aus den verblichenen Blättern konnte ich Gerhard Ritter später bestätigen, daß der aufmerksame Leser gespürt haben mußte, worauf es dem Verfasser ankam, wenn er darauf hinwies, der hemmungslose Machttrieb eines einzelnen könnte imstande sein, den Glauben an »die höchsten sittlichen Güter der Menschheit« selber sich dienstbar zu machen.

Ritter, gewiß, eine Erfahrung am Rande, von langer Wirkung, nicht nur auf einen.

*

Eine Erfahrung ganz anderer Natur: Im Juni 1947 initiiert George Marshall den nach ihm benannten Plan, in Paris entsteht die OECD für die Verwaltung des Plans, die Besatzungszonen in Deutschland werden einbezogen. Ich befinde mich bei der ersten deutschen Delegation – bedrückt davon, daß Deutsche noch als Kriegsgefangene in Frankreich zurückgehalten werden, während ich in Paris frei umhergehe. Diese unverdiente Bevorzugung eines Deutschen und das geradezu schizoide Verhalten von Europäern gegenüber Amerikanern lehrten mich, wie schwer es ist, in bestimmten Situationen den Maßstab nicht zu verlieren.

Die Bundesrepublik entstand, der Südweststaat – heute Baden-Württemberg – wurde konzipiert, die Konzeption mußte propagiert werden. Der in Baden geborene, in Württemberg lebende Kaufmann wurde dafür eingespannt; er sollte die Idee mit verkaufen. Was dieser Tätigkeit für die »öffentliche Sache« folgte, war nichts anderes als die Konsequenz aus der These, daß sich wirtschaftliche Kräfte nicht autonom entwickeln können und dürfen, sondern eingebunden werden müssen in den kulturellen Bezug, in den umfassenden Begriff der Kultur – ich wage zu sagen, der politischen Kultur.

Eine Syn-These also, die, entgegen jeder andersgearteten Befürchtung, nicht zu einer Dominanz einzelner Sphären – etwa der wirtschaftlichen – führt, sondern zu der Optimierung aller Kräfte einer Nation, die sich international behaupten will – und kann. Was folgte, hatte Folgen und machte mich an Erfahrung reicher – ich wurde in die Parteispendensache hineingezogen. Ich habe mich sowohl vor einem parlamentarischen Untersuchungsausschuß als auch vor Gericht in aller Offenheit zur Notwendigkeit der Finanzierung demokratischer politischer Parteien bekannt, denen vom Grundgesetz eine staatspolitische Aufgabe übertragen ist. Die pluralistische parlamentarische Demokratie braucht Parteien.

Ich sagte »Nation«, ich meine die deutsche. Karl Jaspers glaubte noch 1946, darunter könne man alle, die Deutsch sprechen, verstehen. Das muß man inzwischen wohl korrigieren, das heißt verengen, berechtigterweise oder nicht. Ob diese Nation dem Verhängnis hätte entrinnen können oder ob es ein unentrinnbares Schicksal war – meine Erfahrung geht nicht weit genug, dies zu beantworten. Doch bekenne ich mich zu dieser Nation, in die ich, wie viele meiner Vorfahren, hineingeboren bin, obgleich ich die Chance gehabt hätte, mich zu lösen. Oder gerade deshalb.

*

Von den mancherlei Brückenschlägen im Sinne eines umfassenden Kulturbegriffs erwähne ich nur meine Mitwirkung bei der Errichtung der Robert Bosch Stiftung in der ersten Hälfte der sechziger Jahre. Diese Stiftung geht auf die Weitsicht und den Großmut des Unternehmensgründers zurück, zu dem ich, aus der Textilindustrie kommend, inzwischen gestoßen war. Sie wäre aber ohne die Selbstbescheidung der Erben nicht zustande gekommen. Heute besitzt die Stiftung mehr als neunzig Prozent der Anteile an der Robert Bosch GmbH und verwendet denselben Hundertsatz der Dividende dieser Gesellschaft ausschließlich für gemeinnützige Zwecke – in geringem Maß karitativ, überwiegend aber im Sinn unseres Kulturbegriffs.

Was ich möglicherweise als Ausfluß meiner beruflichen Erfahrung bedacht habe, als ich lange über den Entwürfen für diese Stiftung saß, versuche ich zu vermitteln. Kann vom Unternehmer überhaupt erwartet werden, daß er Opfer bringt? Spricht man der unternehmerischen Tätigkeit von vornherein kulturelle Qualität zu, so ist es der vornehmliche Beitrag des Unternehmers zum materiellen und kulturellen Potential einer Region, daß er Waren erzeugt und Leistungen erbringt.

Diese Überlegung befriedigt freilich aus mancherlei Gründen nicht – vor allem, weil der Staat im Zweifel nicht immer die glücklichste Hand bei der Verwendung von Steuergeldern für kulturelle

Zwecke im engeren Sinn hat und deshalb private Initiative – ergänzend, ausgleichend und ermutigend – unerläßlich ist.

Wir erwarten also vom Unternehmer eigene Beiträge in vielfältiger Form, ohne daß sie Alibicharakter annehmen oder gar der Öffentlichkeitsarbeit dienstbar gemacht werden. Er kommt dennoch letzten Endes in den Genuß seiner Leistung, wenn auch transformiert, nicht meßbar und mit Zeitverzug. Denn der Bildungsstand einer Nation bestimmt ihre kulturelle Ausstrahlung und damit auch ihre wirtschaftliche Kraft. Unmittelbare kulturelle Betätigung des Unternehmers führt also tendenziell zur Rückkoppelung auf die Unternehmung.

Nachdem die Bosch-Stiftung auf den Weg gebracht war, konnte ich meine Erfahrungen in der Verknüpfung wirtschaftlicher und kultureller Zielsetzung abrunden. Ich wurde da und dort zu Rate gezogen, wenn es um die Errichtung von Stiftungen ging, ich wurde um Mitarbeit im laufenden Geschäft gebeten. Zehn Jahre Zugehörigkeit zum Kuratorium der Stiftung Volkswagenwerk haben meinen Blick geweitet, ohne daß ich meine Aufgabe in der Leitung eines Unternehmens hätte vernachlässigen müssen. Es war nur einen Schritt weiter, wenn ich auch in den Führungsgremien wissenschaftlicher Einrichtungen – wie zum Beispiel der Max-Planck-Gesellschaft zur Förderung der Wissenschaft – tätig wurde. Ich fühlte mich nirgends über die Maßen beansprucht, doch überall bereichert.

*

Ich will noch einige Erfahrungen anführen, losgelöst von bestimmten Vorgängen und Zusammenhängen. Mit dem Beruf des Kaufmanns hat das unmittelbar nichts zu tun, wohl aber mit dem Beruf des Unternehmers – sagen wir des angestellten Unternehmers –, in den man im Lauf eines langen Lebens hineingewachsen ist, ehe man sich dessen versah. Entscheiden, Führen wurde zur täglichen Pflicht.

Man fragt mich hin und wieder, was das mit dem »Führen« auf

sich habe, wie man mit dieser Bürde denn fertig werde. Ob meine Antwort allenthalben Zustimmung findet, bleibe für heute offen: Führen ist, intellektuell gesehen, nicht ganz so schwer, wie es aussieht, doch auch nicht ganz so einfach, wie man in Handbüchern über Führung liest.

Voraussetzungen erfolgreichen Führens sind frühzeitiges Erfassen der Probleme, das Erkennen der Zusammenhänge, das Einfühlen in die Spannungsfelder und letzten Endes der entschlossene Mut. Ziel ist die Entscheidung, die, einmal getroffen, von allen mitgetragen wird.

Was aber »kollektives« Entscheiden angeht, so glaube man bitte nicht das Ammenmärchen, daß anderswo, im Fernen Osten, jede Entscheidung alle Stufen eines Unternehmens, womöglich mehrmals, durchlaufe, bevor es Brief und Siegel gibt. Grundsätzliche Entscheidungen sind hier und dort das Werk weniger oder einzelner, die gerne einmal die Verantwortung teilen würden und dann doch die Bürde nicht loswerden.

Schließlich gibt es, wie die Erfahrung zeigt, kaum eine Entscheidung, die nicht einen Menschen betrifft, einem Menschen zugute kommt oder einem Menschen zum Nachteil gereichen kann. Die reine Sachentscheidung ist in der Minderzahl. Vor allem aber gibt es keine Entscheidung, also keine Aktion, die nicht eine Reaktion auslöst, was jede Planung über den Zeitpunkt Null hinaus in Frage stellt, das heißt stetiges Anpassen erfordert.

*

Die gewichtigsten Entscheidungen, ich sagte das gerade in anderen Worten, betreffen die Auswahl von Mitarbeitern. Allen Theorien entgegen ist es meine Erfahrung, daß es Begabung *gibt*, wenn auch bei jedem Menschen der Schwerpunkt anders gesetzt sein mag. Die wichtigste Begabung ist die Lernfähigkeit; charakterliche Voraussetzung ist die Bereitschaft zu lernen, immer wieder aufs neue zu lernen. Fontanes Definition vom »Genie als Fleiß« liegt mir freilich sehr fern. Genie ist und bleibt das Unerklärliche, das Unerwartete – wir nehmen Genies hin, wir bedürfen ihrer nicht; man kann die Gefahren mit Händen greifen.

Begabung als Faktum und Begabtenauslese als Methode: das bedeutet Anerkennung des Prinzips der Elite. Selektion, als Prinzip der Natur, auf die Arbeitsstrukturen angewandt, ist weder Politik der sozialen Ausgrenzung noch die Anwendung diktatorischer Gewalt, wie Außenstehende sie in Wirtschaftsunternehmen oft zu sehen glauben.

Auch der böse Vorwurf von der »Vernichtung von Arbeitsplätzen« geht an den Tatsachen vorbei, was für jeden nachvollziehbar ist. Vernichtung von geistigem Potential kommt es freilich gleich, wenn in Forschungs- und Entwicklungsabteilungen die Arbeitszeitkürzung ebenso rigoros durchgesetzt wird wie in der Fertigung – dies ist, wenn auch Erfahrung, so doch nicht mein Thema.

Daß für den Studenten die Arbeitszeitkürzung allenfalls am Horizont aufscheint, ist der Wirtschaft bekannt; sie bevorzugt zwar den Absolventen, der zügig studiert und abgeschlossen hat, zieht aber den Menschen vor, der seine Spannkraft nicht vorzeitig verbraucht hat.

Die Behauptung des Leistungsdrucks, ob auf der Hochschule oder im Betrieb, wirkt freilich etwas abgegriffen und ist kaum geeignet, Mitgefühl hervorzurufen – um so weniger, als sich das Leistungsniveau immer mehr international einspielt. Wir können wählen zwischen mithalten oder ausscheiden. Es gibt, so Hans Jonas, den »Klassenkampf der Nationen«, nicht aber, noch lange nicht, eine »global konstruktive Politik«.

*

Um nochmals auf die Entscheidung und ihre Technik zurückzukommen: Die Behauptung, jede Entscheidung sei besser als keine, ist leichtfertig und durch bittere Erfahrung längst ad absurdum geführt;

die Neigung einzelner zu rascher Entscheidung wird aber da und dort noch immer als Kriterium der Qualifikation gewertet, obwohl operative Hektik geistige Windstille nicht ersetzen kann (eine treffliche Spitze, die ich einem unbekannten Verfasser verdanke).

Daß andererseits die Verzögerung oder die Unterlassung einer Entscheidung im Einzelfall gelegentlich richtig gewesen sein mag, ist kein Beweis für eine Gesetzmäßigkeit. Jedenfalls spricht alles für ein System sorgfältiger Entscheidungsvorbereitung, das alle Kriterien erfaßt und bewertet, ohne intuitiver Entscheidung den Spielraum zu nehmen. Systematik aber verlangt, daß man sich bevorzugt dem Wesentlichen zuwendet.

Hätte ich aber zeitlebens nur das jeweils Wichtigste getan, wäre das weniger Wichtige zeitlebens liegengeblieben – und ich hätte, dessen bin ich sicher, manches versäumt, manche Erfahrung verpaßt. Das ist nicht so paradox, wie es klingt. Denn keiner ist so erfahren, daß er immer und von vornherein weiß, was das Wichtigste ist. Und Unwichtiges kann im Lauf der Zeit wichtig werden. Im Fernen Osten sagt man: Auch im Unwichtigen steckt Wichtiges und hat seine Stunde.

Wichtig ist freilich, wenn Peter F. Drucker von der Führungsschicht zunächst einmal verlangt, daß sie sich Vertrauen verschaffe, Glaubwürdigkeit, Zuverlässigkeit nicht zuletzt darin, daß der Verantwortliche auch die Verantwortung für etwaige Fehlentscheidungen seiner Mitarbeiter übernimmt. Daß er also seine Mitarbeiter eher am Erfolg als am Mißerfolg teilhaben läßt.

*

Man muß nicht »berufen« sein, um seinen Beruf auszuüben. Verantwortungsbereitschaft genügt, wie die Erfahrung zeigt, und harte Arbeit. Charisma ist keine Führungsvoraussetzung; wo wollten wir auch hinkommen, wenn alle Führungskräfte mit einem Heiligenschein herumliefen. *(1988)*

Über die Kunst der Prognose

WAS LÄSST SICH VORAUSSAGEN?

Ich muß bekennen, daß das Thema »Über die Kunst der Prognose« ein Plagiat ist. Die »Urheberrechte« dafür liegen bei Professor Dr. Carl Friedrich Freiherr von Weizsäcker, der unter diesem Titel am 24. Mai 1968 bei der Jahresversammlung des Stifterverbands für die Deutsche Wissenschaft in Wiesbaden den Festvortrag übernommen hatte. Diesen Wiesbadener Vortrag habe ich weder gehört noch gelesen, und ich war mir nicht bewußt, daß ich eine Anleihe bei Weizsäcker nahm, bis ich durch einen Freund auf das Delikt aufmerksam gemacht wurde. Ich schrieb unverzüglich an Herrn von Weizsäcker und bat ihn um Entschuldigung, die ich auch erlangte.

*

Wenn man von Prognosen spricht, so denkt man zuerst an den Wetterbericht. Man weiß, wie häufig die Vorhersage unbestimmt oder falsch ist. Die mit großem Apparat und großer Sorgfalt hergestellten langfristigen Wettervorhersagen haben – so sagt man mir – eine Prognosewahrscheinlichkeit von nur 53 Prozent, das ist 3 Prozent über Zufall. Würde man Tag für Tag – ohne weitere Umstände zu machen – vorhersagen, morgen sei das Wetter wie heute, so hätte man in 58 Prozent der Fälle recht.

Es gibt keine Statistik über die Treffsicherheit wirtschaftlicher oder politischer Vorhersagen. Jeder erinnert sich an Einzelfälle, meist an solche, bei denen die Prognose danebenging. Die so auf Erfahrung gegründete Skepsis enthebt uns weder der Pflicht, über die

Chancen und Risiken der wirtschaftlichen Vorhersage nachzudenken, noch erlaubt sie es uns, auf die zu diesem Zweck entwickelten Methoden innerhalb der erkannten »Bandbreite« der Verläßlichkeit zu verzichten.

Die Tatsache, daß es noch keine geschlossene Theorie der Prognose gibt – wohl aber eine Überfüllle wissenschaftlicher Arbeiten über Methoden –, erschwert zwar unser Urteil. Aber sie würde keine Entschuldigung dafür liefern, daß wir uns nicht ernsthaft mit der Untersuchung möglicher zukünftiger Entwicklungslinien beschäftigten. Denn in Wirklichkeit steht jeder von uns tagtäglich – ob er sich dessen bewußt wird oder nicht – vor der Notwendigkeit, Prognosen zu stellen, die nicht ohne Einfluß auf andere sind. Tagtäglich werden Prognosen von anderen gestellt, die auch auf uns einwirken. Ein Netzwerk von Vorhersagen, von Erwartungen und von Zielsetzungen erstreckt sich über uns alle.

Eine Fallgeschichte der Kunst der Prognose ist eine Geschichte der Fehlprognosen. Manche berühmte Vorhersage, die eintraf, scheint diese skeptische Auffassung zu widerlegen. Denken wir aber – analog zur Wettervorhersage – daran, daß die Hälfte aller Prognosen, sofern sie sich nur auf ausreichend große statistische Massen und Zeiträume beziehen, auch dann eingetroffen wäre, wenn man sie nicht auf das sorgfältigste entwickelt, sondern durch das Werfen einer Münze gewonnen hätte. So genügt das Aufzählen gelungener Prognosen nicht zur Ehrenrettung der dazu verwendeten Mittel.

Nur wenige Propheten haben eine so glückliche Hand wie Goethe, der 1820 die Ahnung aussprach: »Eines schönen Tages wird die Landenge von Panama durch einen Kanal durchstochen werden, und zwar wird das durch die Vereinigten Staaten geschehen.« Nur wenige können, rückblickend auf ein langes und erfolgreiches Leben, mit dem Wiener, später Züricher Bankier Felix Somary das stolze Wort sprechen: »Die großen Katastrophen meiner Zeit haben mich nicht überrascht.« Wer es aber könnte, würde mit Somary sagen müssen: »Das Gefühl der Isolierung gerade im Augenblick klarster Voraussicht ist nicht leicht zu ertragen.«

Somarys amerikanische Zeitgenossen hatten eine weniger glückliche Hand. Das berühmte Harvard-Barometer, das auf drei Zeitreihen – Effektenmarkt, Warenmarkt und Geldmarkt – beruhte, versagte 1929 total. »Der amerikanische Konjunkturdienst« – so Ernst Wagemann – »... erlitt ein Fiasko etwa so wie später die Meinungsforschung, als Truman statt Dewey gewählt wurde.« Professor Irving Fisher von Yale sagte wenige Tage vor dem großen Krach, daß nunmehr die Aktien ein neues Niveau erreicht hätten, von dem aus sie nur noch steigen könnten. Nicht nur Irving Fisher, sondern auch Gustav Cassel muß sich von Ernst Wagemann vorhalten lassen, daß sie dem so jäh zerbrochenen Glauben an die »wunderliche Theorie von der unverwelklichen Prosperität und von dem gebrochenen Zauber der Konjunkturschwankungen« anhingen.

Einen tragischen Einfluß auf den Lauf der Weltgeschichte mag es andererseits gehabt haben, daß von Mitte 1931 an nicht allgemein erkannt wurde, daß die Krise des Jahres 1929 sich dem Wendepunkt näherte. Eines der frühesten Zeugnisse für diese – freilich politisch nicht realisierte – Erkenntnis findet sich in den Memoiren Heinrich Brünings, der am 27. August 1931 zu Alfred Hugenberg sagte, mit der Erreichung des Tiefpunkts der Wirtschaftskrise sei im Sommer 1932 zu rechnen. Wenn dann in der August-Ausgabe 1932 der *Vierteljahreshefte zur Konjunkturforschung* zu lesen ist, daß die Weltwirtschaft als Ganzes sich nunmehr anschicke, »das Krisentief zu überwinden«, so war, wie eine nachträgliche Analyse der Kurven zeigt, in der Tat der Wendepunkt bereits erreicht, und es war folglich nicht die nationalsozialistische Regierung, die die wirtschaftliche Wiederbelebung hervorrief. Man glaubt gar nicht, wieviel sich rückwirkend als eigentlich voraussehbar gewesen herausstellt.

*

Meine kritische Einstellung zur Prognose gründet sich nicht so sehr auf die partielle Fragwürdigkeit ihrer Methoden als auf die Gefahr ihres Mißbrauchs zum Zweck der Beeinflussung. In seinem 1931 erschienenen berühmten Buch »Die geistige Situation der Zeit«, das eine ungewöhnlich große Auflage erlebte, schrieb Karl Jaspers: »Ich suche sie (die Prognose) ..., um den Weg der Dinge zu ändern.« Und: »Prognose ist ... nie nur Wissen, sondern als dieses Wissen schon sogleich Faktor des wirklichen Geschehens. Es gibt kein Sehen von Wirklichem, in dem nicht zugleich Wollen ist, oder das doch Wollen erwecken oder lähmen kann.«

Karl Jaspers wollte und mußte – aus innerer Überzeugung – im Jahr 1931 den Versuch machen, den Weg der Dinge zu ändern. Er tat dies nicht als Politiker, sondern als Philosoph. Die Aufrichtigkeit seines Wollens ist unbestritten, was für die politische oder wirtschaftliche Zweckprognose um so weniger gilt, je mehr sie einem programmierten Zweck dient.

Wird eine Prognose einmal geglaubt, so geht davon ein Einfluß auf die Verwirklichung aus. Insofern kommt es also nicht so sehr auf den Wahrheitsgehalt einer Vorhersage an als vielmehr auf ihre beschwörende Kraft. Prognose kann Träger einer messianischen Botschaft werden – und hierin liegt das Gebot zur Vorsicht.

Besondere Chancen, beim Adressaten gut aufgenommen zu werden, hat eine Prognose, die weniger von den Realitäten, den Begrenzungen des Heute ausgeht als vielmehr von der Illusion einer Grenzenlosigkeit des Morgen. Vielleicht kommt daher die Liebe der Politiker zur Prognose. Die Liebe ist meist nicht gegenseitig. Das heißt, von Politikern gestellte Prognosen neigen dazu, sich von ihren geistigen Vätern unabhängig zu machen. Dies führt nur in seltenen Fällen zur Entmutigung der Politiker, zumal sie oft das Talent mitbringen, aus dem Nicht-Eintreffen ihrer Vorhersagen Kapital zu schlagen, indem sie die Fehlprognose ihren politischen Gegnern in die Schuhe schieben, sofern sie es nicht vorziehen, Gras über die

Sache wachsen zu lassen, womit sich der Staatsbürger häufig genug zufriedengibt.

Effektenberater – um für einen Augenblick von der Politik etwas abzulenken – haben es in dieser Hinsicht viel schwerer. Die Ergebnisse ihrer oft mutigen Prognosen füllen die Depots oder sind zumindest zu Lastschriften auf den Konten der von ihnen beratenen Geschäftsfreunde geworden. Obwohl hierzulande der Code Napoléon nicht mehr in Kraft ist, wünscht man ihnen, daß noch immer das Verbot der Recherche de la paternité angewandt werde, was für berechtigt zu halten ist, da ja auch die guten Ratschläge als nicht der Erwähnung wert angesehen werden.

Die Liebe der Politiker zur Prognose ist nicht nur eine Erscheinung der Gegenwart. Schon in den frühesten Stunden der aufgeschriebenen menschlichen Geschichte wurde mit Vorhersagen Politik gemacht. Carl Friedrich von Weizsäcker bezeichnete Thales von Milet als den ältesten historischen Prognostiker (640–545 v. Chr.). Ich beschränke mich auf das 5. Jahrhundert vor der Zeitenwende. Hätten zum Beispiel die Athener im Jahre 480 v. Chr. ihre Stadt den persischen Eindringlingen überlassen und auf dem Meer um ihr Leben gekämpft, wenn Themistokles sich nicht auf das Delphische Orakel berufen hätte: die Athener seien hinter dem »hölzernen Schutzwall« (ihrer Flotte) unbesiegbar? So kann Georges Roux in seinem Buch »Delphi« mit Recht schreiben: »Durch sein hohes Ansehen wurde das Orakel von Delphi ein wichtiger politischer Trumpf in den Händen der Staatsmänner. Mit der Genehmigung des Orakels konnte man die widerstandslose Annahme … einer beim Volk unbeliebten oder gewagten Politik durchsetzen.«

Kein Wunder, daß Plutarch berichten kann, daß man in Delphi schon früh die Belegschaft erhöhen mußte, indem man zwei bis drei Pythien beschäftigte. Daß im Fall des spartanischen Königs Kleomenes, der sich den Beistand der Pythia erkaufte, diese später bestraft wurde, wirkte vermutlich nicht auf Dauer abschreckend.

Mathematik und Computer sind für den Prognostiker Instrument und Standessymbol zugleich. Ich würde gerne den objektiv-instrumentellen Charakter der mathematischen Methoden herauskehren, wenn nicht die Gefahr bestünde, daß weniger der Erzeuger der Vorhersage als vielmehr der Empfänger die Tatsache übersehen könnte, daß die Güte des Ergebnisses von der Güte der Eingabe abhängt, das heißt, daß das, was herauskommt, nicht verläßlicher sein kann als das, was man eingibt.

Der brauchbaren Prognose muß eine verläßliche Diagnose des aktuellen Zustandes und seiner Entstehung nach Ursache, Menge und Zeit vorausgehen. Bei dem derzeitigen Zustand unserer *Statistik* – sowohl was Anpassung als auch was Geschwindigkeit der Aufbereitung angeht – fehlt es weithin an brauchbaren Grundlagen für eine zeitgerechte und aussagekräftige Analyse der wirtschaftlichen und gesellschaftlichen Verhältnisse.

Ich brauche nur auf die desolate Rückständigkeit der Vermögens- und Einkommensstatistik hinzuweisen, die zwar genügend Stoff für Emotionen liefert, aber keine ausreichende Grundlage für objektive Entscheidungen bietet. (Solange man »Einkommen aus Unternehmertätigkeit und aus Vermögen« in *einer* Zahl ausweist – die überdies nicht primär, sondern nur als Restposten ermittelt ist –, solange man also essentiell verschiedene Elemente wie Unternehmerlohn, Verzinsung des Eigenkapitals und Risikoprämie in den gleichen Topf wirft wie das Zinseinkommen abhängig Beschäftigter aus Sparguthaben und anderen Vermögen, kann die offizielle Statistik keinen verläßlichen Beitrag zu der *notwendigen* Neuorientierung leisten.)

Von den zahlreichen *Verfahren* der Prognose erwähne ich hier nur die häufig angewandte Trend-Extrapolation, die formal elegant ist und sich der mathematischen Behandlung anbietet. Hat Joseph Schumpeter mit seinem Aperçu recht,

– es gäbe nur zwei Gruppen von Wirtschaftswissenschaftlern: solche, die eine Differentialgleichung *nicht* verstehen, und solche, die außer ihr nichts anderes verstehen,

so leiht die mathematische Behandlung beiden Kategorien seelischen Halt. Denn die einen können sich an der Schlüssigkeit des mathematischen Ansatzes freuen, die anderen aber den Differentialen und Integralen aus einem Abstand Reverenz erweisen.

Meinen Einwendungen gegen die Trend-Extrapolation – die ich nicht als wissenschaftliche Analyse zu werten bitte, sondern eher als Lockerungsübung gegen gewisse Verkrampfungserscheinungen – muß nun eine Diskussion der Kurventypen vorausgehen:

1. Der *lineare Trend* stellt im Koordinatennetz eine Gerade dar, die über der Zeit eine gleichmäßige Steigung (ein gleichmäßiges Gefälle) aufweist. Der absolute Zuwachs in der Zeiteinheit bleibt gleich, die Zuwachsrate nimmt ab ($y = a + bx$).
2. Der *exponentielle Trend* gehorcht einer Gleichung, in der die unabhängige Variable in die Potenz erhoben ist. Er stellt sich als Kurve dar, deren Steigung zunimmt, was einer gleichbleibenden Zuwachsrate und einem steigenden absoluten Zuwachs entspricht ($y = a + be^x$).
   (Drückt man eine jährliche Zunahme von p % graphisch aus, so erhält man eine exponentielle Kurve. Sie kommt den Vorstellungen unverbesserlicher Optimisten entgegen.)
3. Zwei weitere, mathematisch etwas anspruchsvollere Kurventypen werden der Realität eher gerecht:

   – die *logistische Kurve* ($y = \frac{k}{a + e^{-x}}$)

   – die *Sinuskurve* ($y = \sin x$)

Die *logistische Kurve* strebt mit anfänglich zunehmender, dann abnehmender Steigung dem Grenzwert K zu, den man als Sättigungsniveau bezeichnen kann. Biologische Prozesse, zum Beispiel Bakterienkulturen, folgen ihm. Viele Beobachtungen zeigen, daß es eine bessere Abbildung wahrscheinlicher wirtschaftlicher Verläufe gibt als etwa der exponentielle Trend, der die Bäume in den Himmel wachsen läßt.

Die *Sinuskurve* – in ihrem tatsächlichen Auftreten weniger eine symmetrische als vielmehr eine in beiden Koordinaten »schiefe« Welle – wird Prozessen gerecht, die zyklisch verlaufen. Sie ist häufig von Grundtrends überlagert.

Die Amerikaner sprechen vom Farmzyklus. Das klassische Beispiel für einen zyklischen Ablauf der agroökonomischen Prozesse steht im Alten Testament: 1. Moses (»Genesis«) Kapital 41: der Traum des Pharao von den sieben fetten und den sieben mageren Jahren.

Edward R. Dewey hat, wenn man Presseveröffentlichungen glauben darf, 1280 Zyklen nachgewiesen, von denen eine Reihe – zum Beispiel der 8-Jahres-Rhythmus der Lachse und der 4-Jahres-Rhythmus der Mäuse – zu den Biozyklen gehört. Dewey behauptet auch – und wir versagen uns die Prüfung –, daß die kanadische Eisenbahn achtundvierzigmal hintereinander alle 9,18 Monate einen Frachtenboom hatte.

Auch wenn man die Beispiele nicht an den Haaren herbeizieht, ist klar, daß die wirtschaftliche Entwicklung weitgehend in Zyklen verläuft. Das vielgelästerte, weil die Marxsche Prognose störende Krisenmanagement hat die Amplitude verringert, die Frequenz aber nur wenig beeinflußt.

Bei der Kurvenanalyse kommt dem Wendepunktproblem besondere Bedeutung zu. Nicht Maxima und Minima sind die Feuerglocke für die wirtschaftliche Vorhersage. Entscheidend ist vielmehr der Punkt, an dem die Steigung einer Kurve zu- oder abzunehmen beginnt. Zeichnet man die Änderungsraten des Auftragseingangs über der Zeitachse auf, so kündigt sich die bevorstehende Änderung des wirtschaftlichen Klimas in einer Aufschwungphase nicht etwa erst an, wenn die Kurve den Höhepunkt erreicht oder überschritten hat, sondern schon dann – und dies ist ein wichtiger

Frühindikator –, wenn die Steigung der Tangente O abzunehmen beginnt.

Die Trendgläubigkeit vieler Prognostiker gründet sich auf die Trägheit der Trendkurven, geht aber häufig genug an der Wirklichkeit vorbei. Prinzipiell halte ich die Trendextrapolation nur für zulässig, wenn die für den bisherigen Verlauf maßgebenden Parameter nach Qualität und Quantität auch in der Zukunft wirksam sein werden, das heißt, wenn mit hoher Wahrscheinlichkeit keine neuen exogenen Einflüsse auftreten.

(In dem Moment, in dem die Kugel den auf die stehende Scheibe gerichteten Büchsenlauf verläßt, sind alle Parameter für ihren Flug bekannt, so daß der Extrapolation der Flugbahn nichts im Wege steht. Mit ihrem weiteren Flug treten zunehmend exogene Momente auf, die die Prognose des Treffpunkts erschweren, aber nicht etwa unmöglich machen. Es gibt jedoch keinen analogen Fall in der Politik und in der Wirtschaft, bei dem im Zeitpunkt Null annähernd so viele Einflußgrößen mit gleich großer Genauigkeit bekannt wären wie beim Büchsenschuß. Vor allem aber hat Robert Goodell Brown recht, wenn er sagt, Prognosen »richten sich auf eine bewegliche Zielscheibe«.)

Beispiele eignen sich natürlich weder als Beweis noch als Gegenbeweis. Aber sie schärfen die Wachsamkeit. Es sei das Kürzerwerden der Damenröcke einer positiv exponentiellen Kurve gefolgt (im ersten Jahr 1 cm, im zweiten Jahr 2 cm kürzer). Die Annahme eines exponentiellen Trends, das heißt die weitere Verkürzung mit wachsender Geschwindigkeit, wäre nun eine Vernachlässigung anatomischer Endziele; den physischen Tatsachen könnte man hier allenfalls mit einer logistischen Kurve gerecht werden, die einem Grenzwert zustrebt, das heißt, nicht ins Unendliche geht. Richtiger noch wäre es, die Lebenserfahrung sprechen zu lassen, das heißt, eine Sinuskurve anzunehmen, in der das ausgleichende Spiel der Kräfte am besten zum Ausdruck kommt.

Die Anwendung mathematischer Methoden täuscht wie auch häufig das Ausschreiben von Dezimalen eine Scheingenauigkeit vor, die die richtigen Größenordnungen verhüllt: »Die Economists von Dean Witter & Company«, hieß es am 23. September 1971 im *Wall Street Journal,* »haben ihre Schätzungen für die Gewinne nach Steuern für 1972 von 12,9 auf 18,1 Prozent erhöht, die Schätzung für die Arbeitslosigkeit von 5,6 auf 5,3 Prozent verringert.« Man springt unbesorgt um 40 Prozent nach oben (weil man sich bisher getäuscht hat) und gibt sich dann mit 1/10-Prozentpunkt das Zertifikat des Könners. Der gesunde Menschenverstand des Daumens wird hier durch die autoritäre Intelligenz des Computers ersetzt.

Die Zeitdauer, für die eine Prognose ausgelegt ist, erhöht die Gefahr der Täuschung: Je langfristiger, desto größer die Chance, daß sie sich bewährt – sei es, weil sie in die Kategorie der Schwingungsvorgänge gehört (es kommt alles einmal wieder); sei es, daß mit dem Verfließen der Zeit das Gedächtnis der Prognose-Adressaten nachläßt, die Bereitschaft, veränderte Bedingungen dem Prognostiker zugute zu halten, aber wächst; sei es, daß es dem Prognostiker gelungen ist, eine solche Menge von Tatbeständen in weder quantifizierter noch zeitlich festgelegter Weise zusammenzupacken, daß man jede zukünftige Erscheinungsweise darin erkennen kann (auch hier mit dem milder werdenden Urteil über Vorgänge der Vergangenheit; Werner Sombart sagte dazu:»Darüber Aussagen zu machen, was in drei Monaten in der deutschen Wirtschaft sein wird, würde ich mich niemals entschließen können. Was aber in 30 Jahren sein wird, darüber kann man viel eher etwas aussagen«).

Gesucht wird noch immer der Idealtypus des Prognostikers, der

- etwas häufiger recht hat, als dies der Wahrscheinlichkeitsrechnung nach sowieso der Fall wäre,
- seine Prognose laut und deutlich ausspricht und die Grundlage dafür nennt,
- wenn er später recht hat: schweigt,

– wenn er aber unrecht hat: die Umstände, unter denen seine Prognose zustande gekommen ist, mitteilt, damit man den Grund des Fehlschlags analysieren kann.

(Ratgeber für Propheten: Prophezeien Sie nur Unprüfbares oder irgend etwas, was mit großer Wahrscheinlichkeit in Kürze vergessen sein wird.)

*

Der ohne Zweifel bekannteste Wirtschaftsfuturologe war Karl Marx. Die Meinungen – auch innerhalb der marxistischen Wissenschaft – darüber,

– ob seine Prognosen sich bisher erfüllt haben,
– ob sie sich in Zukunft erfüllen werden,

gehen auseinander. Joseph Schumpeter: »Marx hatte unrecht bei seiner Diagnose der Art und Weise, in der die kapitalistische Gesellschaft zusammenbrechen würde, aber er hatte nicht unrecht in der Vorhersage, daß sie letzten Endes zusammenbrechen würde.« Enthusiastisch der Linzer Nationalökonom Kurt W. Rothschild: »Die Meisterleistung von Karl Marx bleibt das … Marxsche Werk, ein grandioses Beispiel der Methoden und Möglichkeiten langfristiger Prognosen, die natürlich ebenso wie kürzerfristig stets neu durchdacht und modifiziert werden müssen.«

Man wird Marx das Epitheton »grandios« nicht verweigern dürfen, und ich – als Anti-Marxist – stehe auch nicht an zu erklären, daß sein Erscheinen im 19. Jahrhundert eine geschichtliche Notwendigkeit war.

Mit gleicher Klarheit muß aber festgestellt werden – und dies auch gegen Rothschild –, daß Marx weder Methoden der langfristigen Prognose entwickelt hat noch daß seine wirtschaftlichen Prognosen eingetreten wären.

Man liest im ersten Band des »Kapital«: »Mit der beständig abnehmenden Zahl der Kapitalmagnaten … wächst die Masse des

Elends, des Drucks, der Knechtung, der Degradation, der Ausbeutung.« In keinem der Industrieländer – und es war die industrielle Welt, auf die sich Marx bezog – hat sich die Verelendungstheorie als richtig erwiesen. In keinem der Industrieländer kam es zu jenem Pauperismus, der im Manifest der Kommunistischen Partei von 1848 als unausweichlich hingestellt wird. Und deshalb blieb für die Revolution in den Industrieländern – entgegen der Marxschen Prognose – kein Platz. Revolutionen im Marxschen Sinn haben bisher nur in Agrarländern (wenn auch mit industrieller Substruktur) stattgefunden.

Die von Marx behauptete Tendenz, der Kapitalismus versuche die Produktionskraft der Arbeit zu steigern, um die Ware zu verwohlfeilern und durch die Verwohlfeilerung der Waren den Arbeiter selbst zu verwohlfeilern, trifft nur insofern ins Schwarze, als zwar industrielle Produkte – in festem Geldwert gemessen – säkular billiger geworden sind, während aber der Preis der Arbeit ebenso säkular stieg und weiter steigt. Einfach ausgedrückt, sagte Marx: Wenn Lebensbedürfnisse billiger werden, sinkt der Lohn. Tatsache ist demgegenüber, daß der Lohn seit langen Jahren tendenziell steigt.

Im dritten Band des »Kapital« wird behauptet, der Exploitationsgrad der Arbeit werde namentlich durch Verlängerung des Arbeitstages erhöht. Was fünfzig Jahre vorher, also historisch und auf das Beobachtungsland England beschränkt, gegolten haben mag, erwies sich als grundfalsche Prognose.

Meine Kritik an Marx dient nicht der Beruhigung des Unternehmergemüts. Nicht nur ist die massenpsychologische Wirkung, die von Marx – ungeachtet seiner prognostischen Fehlschläge – ausgeht, in den letzten Jahrzehnten und Jahren eher gewachsen als gesunken. Vielmehr sind ihm seherische Fähigkeiten vor allem dann nicht abzusprechen, wenn er sich in die politische Prognose begibt.

In der *New York Daily Tribune* vom 12. April 1853 erschien ein Leitartikel, als dessen Urheber Friedrich Engels, der Marx-Herausgeber, feststeht und von dem mit gutem Recht vermutet wird, daß er im Auftrag von und in Übereinstimmung mit Karl Marx geschrieben wurde. Faszinierend zu lesen, daß es dort heißt,

- die natürliche Grenze Rußlands gehe von Danzig oder Stettin bis Triest,
- daß dort von der drohenden Annexion Ungarns, Preußens und Galiziens die Rede ist
- und daß die (russische) Großmacht selbst dann nicht auf halbem Wege stehenbleiben werde, wenn sie dies wollte.

Richtig auch die politische Prognose, die sich auf Seite 9 des Manifests der Kommunistischen Partei findet – das Studium dieses Papiers ist für den Unternehmer meines Erachtens wichtiger als das der Steuergesetze –: es werde nunmehr ein Teil der Bourgeois-Ideologen zum Proletariat übergehen!

*

Otto A. Friedrich hat am 10. November 1971 kritisch darauf aufmerksam gemacht, daß die Menschen »ihre Wünsche an den Zuwachsraten der Vergangenheit … orientieren«. Die Unternehmer orientieren, wie er sagte, »ihre Phantasie an den Wachstumsraten des Umsatzes«. Aber nicht nur Unternehmer bauen ihre Zukunft auf dem schwankenden Boden des Wachstumsbegriffs auf. In zumindest gleichem, wenn nicht noch höherem Maß beruht die expansive Lohnpolitik der Gewerkschaften auf einer Wachstumsannahme, in deren Richtigkeit Zweifel gesetzt werden müssen.

Eine der Ursachen dieses Wachstumsglaubens liegt darin, daß in der Tat die wirtschaftlichen Entwicklungslinien in unserem Land seit der ersten Hälfte der dreißiger Jahre – mit der Unterbrechung der Kriegsjahre – stetig nach oben gerichtet waren. Selbst die Beruhigungsphasen, die wir als Rückschlag oder als Rezession zu bezeichnen geneigt waren, erwiesen sich in der statistischen Auswertung nur als Perioden langsameren, allenfalls kurzfristig stagnierenden Wachstums.

Nun wird aber die Meinung, Wachstum setze sich in alle Zukunft unvermindert fort, durch Überlegungen und durch Bewegungen verschiedenen Charakters ernsthaft in Frage gestellt:

- *Rationale Kräfte* machen darauf aufmerksam, daß wir dabei sind, die natürlichen Ressourcen dieser Welt zu erschöpfen. Ohne Zweifel laufen wir Gefahr, die Substanz der Welt zu verbrauchen. Ebenso rational ist die mit der Verbrauchskurve in Korrelation stehende Kurve des Abfallaufkommens. Ich lasse beiseite, ob die Schätzungen und Berechnungen – letztere häufig genug mit einer Scheingenauigkeit arbeitend – die Mengen- und Zeitwerte richtig wiedergeben. Ein Nebel tendenzieller Behauptungen erschwert den klaren Blick auf die Tatsachen. Diese wiegen jedoch auch dann schwer genug, wenn Korrekturen berechtigt sind.
  Der Austausch von Stoff durch Energie hilft auf der Abfallseite nicht wesentlich weiter. Denn auch Energieverbrauch führt zu »Abfall« – seien es die Rückstände aus der Verbrennung fossiler Energieträger, seien es radioaktive Rückstände aus der Gewinnung von Kernenergie oder sei es »nur« die an die Atmosphäre abgegebene Wärme.
  Natürliche Grenzen, der rationalen Untersuchung zugänglich, sind gegeben; sie erschüttern den Glauben an die Richtigkeit der »exponentiellen Kurve« weiter. (Ich will mit diesem Hinweis nicht das Geschäft unterstützen, das unter der Marke »Umweltschutz« von Politik und Massenmedien ebenso entdeckt wurde wie von der Wirtschaft und aus dem man nicht nur moralisches Kapital, sondern auch materiellen Gewinn zu schlagen versucht.)
- *Irrationale Grenzen* sind dem Wachstum gesetzt durch eine teils natürliche, teils politisch gesteuerte Erschöpfung der menschlichen Leistungsbereitschaft. Ich versage mir die Analyse neuerer Erscheinungen, die unter der Tarnbezeichnung eines »Humanismus« ganz bestimmter Observanz ein gezielter Angriff auf den Leistungswillen sind. Unsere Gesellschaft baut nicht auf Raub-

bau an der menschlichen Kraft auf, sondern auf der gemeinsamen Nutzung aller gesellschaftlichen Kräfte, was freilich voraussetzt, daß jeder den ihm gemäßen Beitrag leistet. (Leichtfertig scheint es mir freilich zu sein, wenn die Behauptung aufgestellt wird, es sei technisch möglich, ohne neue Erfindungen, daß *ein Viertel* der arbeitenden Bevölkerung alle Menschen in einer Gesellschaft mit Produktionsgütern versorge. Hier könnte die Prognose sich irren, während man meines Erachtens zustimmen muß, wenn derselbe Autor darauf aufmerksam macht, daß vermutlich die »Sättigung mit Gütern nicht mehr so fern ist, wie es Volkswirtschaftler und Industrielle gerne glauben möchten«. Der Autor rechnet deshalb mit einer Abnahme des Konsums, zumindest damit, daß der weitere Anstieg des Konsums relativ zurückgeht, also mit rückläufiger Zuwachsquote.)

Wohin die Wachstumseuphorie führen würde, wenn nicht natürliche Grenzen gesetzt wären, zeigt sich an folgendem Beispiel: Herman Kahn errechnet das bisherige Wachstum des japanischen Wirtschaftsvolumens auf 8 bis 10 Prozent jährlich. Aus dem bisherigen Verlauf zieht er den Schluß, daß nach dem Jahr 1975 weitere 25 Jahre »gleichen Wachstums« zu erwarten seien. Gleichgültig, wie hoch das derzeitige Sozialprodukt Japans in absoluten Ziffern ist: Diese Vorhersage bedeutet, daß es im Jahr 2000 auf das Sieben- bis Elffache des heutigen angewachsen sein müßte – in einem Land, das schon heute auf die Flächeneinheit nutzbaren Landes das höchste Sozialprodukt aller Wirtschaftsgebiete erzeugt!

Einige ganz triviale Zahlen zu diesem Thema:

- Bei einem jährlichen Wachstum von 5 Prozent verdoppelt sich die Ausgangszahl in 14,2 Jahren,
- von 7,2 Prozent in 10 Jahren,
- von 10 Prozent in 7,2 Jahren,
- von 15 Prozent in 5 Jahren.

Daraus ergibt sich bei einem angenommenen jährlichen Wachstum von 15 Prozent in zehn Jahren eine Vervierfachung, in zwanzig Jahren eine Verachtfachung. Wenn dadurch die bisherige Denkweise nicht ad absurdum geführt werden sollte, bedürfte es qualitativer Argumente von ganz besonderer Tragkraft.

Die uns gestellte Aufgabe liegt folglich darin – und ich habe keine Zweifel, daß diese Prognose richtig ist –, mit verringerten Wachstumsraten, ja, mit einem Rückschlag fertigzuwerden. Entgegen der herrschenden Meinung, die auf der Flucht nach vorn aufbaut – das heißt, davon ausgeht, daß der Kostensteigerung nur durch Mengensteigerung beizukommen sei –, muß die Wirtschaft es lernen, mit einem langsameren Entwicklungstempo, selbst mit einem Entwicklungstempo Null, fertigzuwerden.

Ein solcher Verlauf hat den Vorteil – er kann ihn jedenfalls haben –, daß die Flucht in den Preis erschwert wird. Es wird also der Falschmünzerei, der stetigen Geldentwertung wenigstens von dieser Seite Einhalt geboten. Die Erkenntnis in der Wirtschaft wird sich durchsetzen müssen, daß die jetzige – systemwidrige – Theorie, der Preis werde von den Kosten bestimmt, falsch ist. Richtig ist vielmehr allein, daß der Preis die Kosten bestimmt. Dieser Regeleffekt gilt freilich nur in einer Unternehmerwirtschaft, während in den sozialistischen Ländern weiterhin Preise »kalkuliert« werden.

Ich wage keine quantitative Prognose des zukünftigen Wachstums, beschränke mich vielmehr darauf, neuartige Annäherungen, Lösungen und Verhaltensweisen zu fordern. Dargestellt an einem Beispiel: Wir gehen von der Erfahrung aus, daß der Energiebedarf sich jeweils in zehn Jahren verdoppelt, also von einer exponentiellen Kurve. Die Meinung, daß wir bei ihrer weiteren Fortsetzung – wenn dies vom Bedarf her gerechtfertigt wäre – auf Deckungsgrenzen stoßen, setzt sich mehr und mehr durch. Daraus ergeben sich die komplementären Fragestellungen, die mir hoffentlich die Energiewirtschaft nicht verübelt:

– Wie schafft man mehr Energie?

– Wie kommt man mit weniger Energie aus?

Ich beziehe es nicht auf das Energieproblem, wenn ich einen kleinen literarischen Exkurs mache: Schon Thomas Mann hat im »Zauberberg« von den »Drehorgelmännern des Fortschritts« gesprochen.

*

Unternehmensplanung setzt Prognosen voraus. Ich halte Prognose für eine Pflicht des Unternehmens, wobei ich kaum der Unterstützung von Felix Somary bedarf, der in »Krise und Zukunft der Demokratie« schrieb: »Der Kaufmann hat … das Eintreten von Krieg und Krisen rechtzeitig in sein Kalkül einzubeziehen.« Wir lassen offen, was »rechtzeitig« in diesem Zusammenhang bedeutet.

Als Planungselemente – rationale Entscheidungsvorbereitung – sind Vorhersagen nur brauchbar, wenn sie täglich fortgeschrieben werden. Jedoch ist Unternehmensplanung eher Zielsetzung als Vorhersage – auch sie hat also ein magisches Element, das man in Vergleich setzen mag mit den Beschwörungsformeln des Politikers, obwohl auf der nüchternen Basis der täglichen Kontrolle durch das Ergebnis. Treffsichere Prognose gerade im Unternehmensbereich verlangt, daß nicht nur das Handwerkszeug der rationalen Analyse, sondern auch alle Kräfte der Intuition eingesetzt werden; für die letztere ist ebenfalls eine Systematisierung denkbar. Es ist keine »Konjunkturastrologie«, wenn vom Unternehmer erwartet wird, daß er aufnahmefähig, aufnahmebereit ist für Wellen, die noch nicht sichtbar sind, während sich am Vogelflug bereits das Nahen neuer Fronten ablesen läßt.

*

Vor diesem Hintergrund sei ein Exkurs über das Bruttosozialprodukt, die Einkommens- und Vermögensverteilung erlaubt:

1. Ohne Zweifel wird das Bruttosozialprodukt weiter wachsen. In seiner ungeheuren statistischen Masse wohnt die Trägheit des

Trends, ist in der Vielzahl der Parameter das Gesetz der großen Zahl erfüllt. Aber täuschen wir uns nicht. In das Bruttosozialprodukt geht auch die säkulare Falschmünzerei – die Geldentwertung – ein, und wenn wir sie jährlich mit 5 Prozent ansetzen müßten, so brauchte gar keine volkswirtschaftliche Mehrleistung erbracht zu werden, um den Gesamtwert in anderthalb Jahrzehnten auf das Doppelte anwachsen zu lassen. Um die Illusion, in die uns das stetig wachsende Bruttosozialprodukt versetzen könnte, noch weiter aufzuweichen: Das Bruttosozialprodukt ist nicht nur die Summe der am Markt angebotenen Waren und Leistungen, die zu Marktpreisen in die Berechnung eingehen; vielmehr gehören auch die staatlichen Dienstleistungen zu den Elementen des Bruttosozialprodukts, gleichgültig, ob der »Markt« sie fordert oder nicht – und dies zum Kostenpreis!

Der *Anteil des Staats* am Sozialprodukt wird weiter wachsen. Auch hier erscheint strukturell die Trend-Extrapolation zulässig. Waren es zu Beginn des Jahrhunderts noch 15 Prozent des Bruttosozialprodukts, die vom Staat beansprucht – verbraucht, investiert oder umverteilt – wurden, waren es 1960: 35,5 Prozent und 1971: 38,4 Prozent. Ein Sättigungspunkt im Sinne der logistischen Kurve ist noch nicht abzusehen. Da Prozentzahlen unanschaulich sind: Mitte der sechziger Jahre leistete ein Haushalt in der Bundesrepublik Deutschland im Mittel 8100 DM jährlich an die öffentliche Hand – 1971 waren es 14500 DM, also nominal, wenn auch nicht annähernd real, 54,3 Prozent mehr.

2. Die Einkommensverteilung wird sich weiter verschieben. Trotz der Unzulänglichkeit der angewandten Begriffe wird aus der Beobachtung des Verlaufs in den sechziger Jahren klar, daß der Anteil der »abhängig Beschäftigten« – manchmal möchte ich gerne so unabhängig wie ein Abhängiger sein – fast stetig, mit Ausnahme der Zeit von Mitte 1967 bis Ende 1968, gewachsen ist. Jene Anomalie wurde durch die sprunghafte Erhöhung der

Löhne und Gehälter in den Jahren 1969 und 1970 mehr als ausgeglichen.

3. Man behauptet, die Vermögensverteilung sei skandalös. *Ich* finde, die Art, wie man eine solche Aussage auf einen Teilbegriff – das sogenannte Produktivvermögen – stützt, sei ein Skandalon. Selbst wenn man von der Kapitalisierung der Rentenansprüche absieht, ist das Produktivvermögen im engeren Sinn des Worts nur ein Bruchteil dessen, was »produktiv« in unserer Gesellschaft wirkt. Denn auch das Geldvermögen der »Abhängigen«, das Vermögen der Landwirtschaft, der Grundbesitz dienen der volkswirtschaftlichen Werterstellung, und die Verbindlichkeiten der Unternehmen gegenüber den Besitzern von Geldvermögen sind produktiv eingesetzt.

Die Formel, weniger als 2 Prozent der bundesdeutschen Haushalte verfügten über mehr als 70 Prozent des Produktivvermögens, ist irreführend, und sie wird zur Irreführung benutzt. Denn 200 Milliarden dieser Vermögensform im Jahr 1970 standen mehr als 1000 Milliarden landwirtschaftliches Vermögen, Geldvermögen und Grundvermögen gegenüber. Von 1960 auf 1970 wuchs die Summe der letzteren Vermögensformen auf das Fünffache, das Produktivvermögen im engeren Sinn nur auf das Doppelte. Im selben Zeitraum ging der Anteil des Produktivvermögens von 35 auf 16 Prozent, das heißt auf die Hälfte zurück.

Dies ist keine Argumentierung gegen den *notwendigen* Fortschritt in der Vermögensverteilung in diesem Land, für die es Pläne gibt, die unsere volle Aufmerksamkeit und in der Zielsetzung unsere Unterstützung verdienen; kritisiert wird nur die Schiefe der Betrachtungsweise.

*

Unternehmerwirtschaft ist Wettbewerbswirtschaft. In dem Maße, in dem der Wettbewerb – aus welchen Gründen auch immer – sich vermindert, wird der Unternehmerwirtschaft der Wind aus den Segeln genommen.

Die Marxsche Verelendungstheorie wird sich auch in Zukunft als falsch herausstellen. Aber wir würden die Gefahr verkennen, wenn wir negieren wollten, daß Marx in anderer Hinsicht recht bekommen könnte, wenn die Dinge so weiterlaufen wie bisher: Er hat die Konzentration der Wirtschaft vorausgesagt, und er hat diese Entwicklung bewußt in den Dienst seiner politischen Ziele gestellt. Wir sind auf dem Weg zu einer Konzentration, die nicht etwa den von den einen erwarteten, von den anderen befürchteten Nutzen höherer Preise hat: denn der technische Nutzen der Konzentration wird in einem hohen Maße durch die damit verbundene Bürokratisierung aufgehoben. Und dahinter steht der drohende Zugriff des Staates, gleichgültig, ob die jeweils herrschende Regierung unternehmerfreundliche Erklärungen abgibt oder nicht.

Die Frage, ob es in jedem Fall die Technik ist, die diese Konzentration erzwingt, lasse ich offen. Aber ich weiß, daß wir an dem Ast sägen, auf dem wir sitzen, wenn wir dazu beitragen, daß der Wettbewerb eingeschränkt wird. Mancher meint, es lebe sich gut in einer wohlbehüteten Marktzone. Diesem Wohlleben sind Grenzen gesetzt, und das Erwachen ist bitter.

Dies ist kein Plädoyer für administrative Fusionsverbote, sondern eine Aufforderung an die Unternehmer, ihre Selbständigkeit zu wahren, auf die sie im freiheitlichen Staat ein Recht haben. Aber man kann sich Rechte verscherzen. Auch Unternehmer haben das Recht des Staatsbürgers, ihren Aggressionsstau zu entladen. Ich empfehle dafür das weite Feld des freien Wettbewerbs, der Erhaltung der unternehmerischen Unabhängigkeit. Ich empfehle den Gegenangriff auf Marx und seine Behauptung, in einer bestimmten Phase der Entwicklung nehme das Kapital »zu Formen Zuflucht, die … durch Zügelung der freien Konkurrenz … die Ankündigung seiner Auflösung … sind«.

Schumpeter – kein Advokat des Sozialismus – hat schon 1949 darauf hingewiesen, der steigende Wohlstand unterhöhle die Position des Unternehmers, er schüfe unzufriedene Intellektuelle, in denen das Ressentiment gegen die Ungleichheiten zum Ausbruch komme, ohne die das kapitalistische System nicht funktionieren könne, schließlich: die Erfolge des Kapitalismus wirkten zerstörend auf die Familie. Ich zitiere dies weniger als Beispiel einer überhörten, aber sich erfüllenden Prognose, sondern als Appell.

Zumindest seit Gracián wissen wir, wie unklug es ist, wenn man sich beklagt – über die Politik, über die Regierung, über die Gewerkschaft ... Soviel Grund wir zum besorgten Blick in die Zukunft haben – nicht wegen unserer persönlichen Existenz, die wir im Rahmen des Ganzen nicht überbewerten sollten –, so schlecht steht es uns an, Unzufriedenheit zu zeigen, statt die Existenznotwendigkeit einer unternehmerischen Wirtschaft dadurch zu rechtfertigen, daß wir die Schwierigkeiten bewältigen, denen keine sozialistische Planwirtschaft gewachsen ist.

*

Man kann nicht rational und generell voraussagen – es sei denn auf Grund seherischer Begabung –, was im politischen Feld geschehen wird. Aber man kann mit relativ großer Treffsicherheit eine Aussage darüber machen, was geschieht, wenn entweder etwas Bestimmtes geschieht oder wenn etwas Bestimmtes nicht geschieht.

Ich empfahl das von Marx und Engels 1848 verfaßte Manifest der Kommunistischen Partei allgemeiner Aufmerksamkeit. Es ist in seiner Zielsetzung noch nicht überholt, und es heißt dort auf Seite 23: »Sie (die Kommunisten) erklären es offen, daß ihre Zwecke nur erreicht werden können durch den gewaltsamen Umsturz aller bisherigen Gesellschaftsordnungen.« (Spricht man heute vom »langen Haß« – wenn auch nicht von kommunistischer, sondern von sozialistischer Seite –, so liegt man auf der gleichen Frequenz.)

Weiter ist im Manifest der Kommunistischen Partei (Seite 16) zu lesen:

»4. Konfiskation des Eigentums aller Emigranten und Rebellen.

8. Gleicher Arbeitszwang für alle, die Errichtung industrieller Armeen besonders für den Ackerbau.

10. … Vereinigung der Erziehung mit der materiellen Produktion.«

(Den Jüngeren unter uns empfehle ich ergänzend die Lektüre des Früh-Kommunisten Heß: »… Diese Jugend wird, in Arbeiterarmeen organisiert, mehr schaffen als unsere jetzige Jugend …«)

Die Prognose ist berechtigt, daß solche Dinge geschehen werden, wenn bestimmte andere Dinge nicht geschehen – wenn nämlich diejenigen, die für die Erhaltung der Freiheit verantwortlich sind, und dies sind alle Staatsbürger, sich versagen.

Die Grunddaten für die Verfassung – damit auch für die wirtschaftliche Verfassung – zu setzen, steht der Politik zu. Bei fortschreitender Verameisung – Kurt Tucholsky – ist anzunehmen, daß *jede* Regierung, in diesem Land und in anderen Ländern, in der Fortbildung ihrer Verfassung und in ihrer gesetzgeberischen Arbeit neue gesellschaftspolitische Vorstellungen verwirklichen wird. *Keine* politische Partei wird – diese Prognose wage ich – in den siebziger Jahren das gleiche Gesicht haben wie in den fünfziger und sechziger Jahren – oder sie wird aufhören zu bestehen.

In dieser Situation beiseitezustehen, weiterhin auf die Karte von Parteien zu setzen, deren Wahlerfolg erst zuletzt von den Stimmen der Unternehmer abhängt, ist kurzsichtig. Wer von der Politik erwartet, daß sie auch in Zukunft für eine freiheitliche Wirtschaftsverfassung eintritt – und dies ist für mich ein Eintreten für die Freiheit schlechthin –, kann nicht von der Tribüne aus dem Spiel zusehen wollen, ohne sich daran zu beteiligen. Die Bezahlung eines wenn auch hohen Eintrittspreises genügt nicht.

Die *Österreichische Post* – eine in der Emigration in Paris erschienene Zeitung – zitierte am 1. Februar 1939 Cicero: »Während die Verwegenen und Gewalttätigen sich in einem dauernden Fieber gegen den Sinn allen menschlichen Gemeinwesens erhitzen, verhalten sich die Guten vielfach ... schlaff und untätig. Dadurch, daß sie sich ihre Ruhe, selbst um den Preis der Würde, zu erhalten suchen, geraten sie ... in Gefahr, sowohl die Ruhe als auch die Würde einzubüßen.«

»Irrtum vorbehalten« – wir schrieben es noch als Kaufmannslehrlinge auf Kontoauszüge – eignet sich nicht als Rettungsanker, wenn es um fundamentale Dinge geht. Ein Irrtum darüber, was fundamental vor uns steht, könnte tödlich sein. Ein Zeitalter nähert sich seinem Ende. Aber die Welt geht nicht zu Ende. Und die uns gestellte Aufgabe, der Versklavung vorzubeugen, die Freiheit zu erhalten, geht ebenfalls weiter. *(1972)*

Dämonie der Macht

EINE ERINNERUNG AN GERHARD RITTER

Ich möchte einige Bemerkungen zu einem Thema machen, dessen Zusammenhang mit dem Freiherrn vom Stein noch zu erläutern sein wird – Bemerkungen zu dem Begriff »Dämonie der Macht«.

Die politische Auseinandersetzung, die uns auferlegt ist, weist dem Problem der *Macht* hohe Bedeutung zu, stellt die Macht in den Mittelpunkt der Kritik – Aufmerksamkeit ist, nebenbei gesagt, dann am Platze, wenn dem Kritiker der Macht der Griff nach derselben aus den Augen schaut.

Dämonen, einst wohl auch gute Geister, sind für uns längst Inbegriff von Schicksal, Unglück, Verderben und Tod geworden. In diesem Sinn sprechen wir heute von Dämonie. Viele von uns haben eine Periode dämonischer Machtentfaltung erlebt; die Weltgeschichte ist nicht frei von Parallelen, was Ursachen und Folgen angeht, auch wenn die Erscheinungsformen verschieden sein mögen. Wir werden gefragt, ob wir gewarnt waren, und diese Frage ist Anlaß genug, über einen Vorgang zu sprechen, der mit dem Freiherrn vom Stein, genauer gesagt: mit seinem Biographen, verknüpft ist.

Der Verfasser der »Politischen Biographie« über Stein, Gerhard Ritter, starb im Sommer 1967 im 80. Lebensjahr. Percy Ernst Schramm, der uns inzwischen selbst verlassen hat, schrieb ihm einen großartigen, lesenswerten Nachruf. Neun Jahre nach Ritters »Stein« erschien im Kriegsjahr 1940 sein kleines, doch gewichtiges Buch »Machtstaat und Utopie«, zu dem ich eine persönliche Beziehung habe, die ich an dieser Stelle der Erwähnung wert halte. Denn über diese Arbeit sprach Gerhard Ritter mit mir nicht lange vor seinem Tod eben in dem Saal, in dem wir uns heute befinden.

Der Untertitel »Vom Streit um die Dämonie der Macht seit Machiavelli und Morus« zeigt, deutlicher als der Titel selbst, daß Ritter – ich wiederhole: im Jahre 1940 – kühn genug war, das Problem der Macht und ihrer Korrumpierung öffentlich aufzugreifen. »Dämonie«, schreibt er, »ist Besessenheit«, worauf er Jacob Burckhardt zitiert: »Und nun ist die Macht an sich böse, gleichviel, wer sie ausübt.« Viele verstanden damals, was Gerhard Ritter meinte, wenn er von »der ungeheuren, seit den Tagen der althellenischen Polis so nicht mehr erlebten Verantwortung für den Fortbestand echter Sittlichkeit und Rechtlichkeit« sprach. Und viele Leser verstanden den Hinweis darauf, daß die Väter der Französischen Revolution 1790 dem Krieg für alle Zeiten abschworen, um schon 1792 den »Kreuzzug für die Freiheit« zu proklamieren, der Europa für mehr als zwei Jahrzehnte, unter diesem oder jenem Vorzeichen, mit Krieg überziehen sollte. Die kleingedruckte Anmerkung Ritters auf einer der letzten Seiten, daß er die geistige Vorgeschichte des modernen Nationalismus »totalitärer« Prägung absichtlich nicht behandle und daß überhaupt seine Schrift bewußt mehr Fragen aufwerfe, als sie beantworte, mag manchem entgangen sein; fett drucken konnte man dies damals nicht. Gerhard Ritter, der nach dem 20. Juli verhaftet worden war und den Winter 1944/45 in Unfreiheit zubrachte, konnte erst nach dem Kriege die Tarnung, zu der er 1940 gezwungen war, aufhellen. Die Neuauflage seines Buchs erschien nunmehr unter dem Titel »Die Dämonie der Macht«.

Mir kam Ritters Buch durch meinen Mentor Viktor Achter während des Krieges in die Hand, und in dunklen Tagen machte ich mich daran, es zu lesen. Ein Exzerpt überdauerte die Jahre. Aus den verblichenen Blättern konnte ich Gerhard Ritter, dem später manche Mißdeutung widerfuhr, bestätigen, daß der damalige aufmerksame Leser spüren *mußte*, daß es dem Verfasser auf eine Warnung ankam, wenn er schrieb, die Staatsräson sei »nicht Werkzeug, sondern Schranke der Macht«. Oder wenn er besorgt darauf hinwies, der hemmungslose Machttrieb eines einzelnen könnte imstande sein, den Glauben an »die höchsten sittlichen Güter der Menschheit« selbst sich dienstbar zu machen als bloßes Werkzeug, Propagandamittel und Verkleidung seines persönlichen Ehrgeizes. Ritter bezog das, wortwörtlich, auf Napoleon. Aber es war klar, wen er meinte.

Unser Geschichtsbewußtsein, lange irregeführt durch ein Übermaß an gefordertem Wissen über Herrscher, Dynastien und Schlachten, bringt den Begriff der »Dämonie der Macht« allzu leicht in Verbindung mit dem Begriff eines Machthabers – das heißt, wir neigen dazu, Macht nur personifiziert zu sehen, in den Gestalten des Herrschers, des Tyrannen, des Despoten.

Aber es hat den Anschein, als ob die Träger zukünftiger Macht die persönliche Verantwortung scheuten, zu der sich die »Großen« der Geschichte immerhin noch bekannten. Es ist denkbar, und es *muß* vielleicht gedacht werden, daß Dämonie der Macht in Zukunft nicht mehr in erster Linie auf das Individuum bezogen werden kann. Macht wird vielmehr zunehmend anonym, deshalb aber nicht weniger gefährlich für die freiheitliche Entwicklung der Menschheit sein. Begriffsverfälschung könnte der Vorspann werden für die Errichtung von Machtverhältnissen, Machtgruppierungen, Machtballungen neuer Art – unpersönlich, ungreifbar, gespenstisch –, fast muß man an Kafka denken. Vorwand können so eingängige Begriffe wie Veränderung der Gesellschaft und Demokratisierung werden. Und da die Gesellschaft, heterogen, nach der gewollten Entmannung des Staats amorph, den gesellschaftlichen Prozeß nicht ohne Werkzeug regeln kann, wird sie nolens volens die ihr gestellte Aufgabe an Organismen neuer Art übertragen, und aus der Despotie des Tyrannen wird die Despotie des Apparats entstehen.

*

Wir alle stehen auf dem Boden der Demokratie, und wir sind der Meinung, daß es nicht darum geht, weniger Demokratie, sondern mehr Demokratie zu haben. Wir stehen auf dem Boden der Demokratie, auch wenn wir bezweifeln, daß dem Gesetz der Gleichheit – das höheren Rang hat als die Regeln der Mehrheitsdemokratie – bereits entsprochen sei, wenn man den Willen der 51 Prozent berücksichtigt, die das Sagen haben. Dazu sagt Friedrich August von Hayek in seiner »Constitution of Liberty« ebenso skeptisch wie unmißverständlich: »Für den doktrinären Demokraten dagegen bildet die Tatsache, daß die Mehrheit etwas will, einen ausreichenden Grund, es auch für gut zu halten; ...«

Ich möchte klarstellen: Es gibt keinen Beweis für ein Vorrecht des Stärkeren in der Demokratie. Es gibt nur *ein* Vorrecht der Mehrheit: die Rechte der Minderheit mit zu vertreten. Die Mehrheitsdemokratie kann ihre moralische Rechtfertigung nur erfahren, wenn die Mehrheit bereit ist, ihr Mandat treuhänderisch aufzufassen und zu verwalten. Dies gilt für *alle* Parteien, insbesondere aber für diejenigen, die sich so sicher fühlen, den richtigen Weg zu wissen.

Wenn man im DDR-Duden liest, Demokratie sei »eine Staatsform, deren Charakter durch die jeweils herrschende Klasse bestimmt«werde, so drängt sich uns die Assoziation zu der »Diktatur des Proletariats« auf. Daß es sich *hier* nicht mehr darum handelt, die Rechte der »jeweils unterdrückten« Klasse zu schützen, liegt auf der Hand.

Was das »ABC des Kommunismus« dazu 1920 in schöner Offenheit sagt – unter »Diktatur« habe man Entschlossenheit in der Niederdrückung der Feinde zu verstehen, und selbstverständlich könne bei dieser Sachlage keine Rede von »der Freiheit für alle Menschen« sein –, ist noch heute ebenso gültig wie der Sarkasmus Platons im »Staat«: »Eine Demokratie also entsteht, wenn die Armen den Sieg davontragen und von der Gegenpartei die einen hinrichten lassen, die anderen verbannen.«

Doch interessieren uns zunächst subtilere Methoden des Machtgebrauchs. In der Vorstellung der Kritiker unserer derzeitigen Gesellschaftsordnung bestimmt nicht der Markt, sondern die »Gesellschaft« das Produkt. So greifbar der Begriff des Marktes ist, so verwaschen ist, trotz aller Beredsamkeit seiner Verfechter, der Begriff der Gesellschaft geblieben, wenn es darum geht, diese Gesellschaft vom Objekt politischer Spekulation zum geschichtlichen Subjekt zu machen, das heißt zu einem handlungsfähigen Gebilde. Gelänge es, unserer heutigen Lebensordnung, die ohne Staatswirklichkeit nicht zu denken ist, die Grundlagen zu entziehen, so würde zunächst das Chaos, dann aber eine Phase neuer Macht administrativen Charakters folgen. Deren Freiheitsgrad wäre – alle bisherigen Erfahrungen zeigen das – um Größenordnungen kleiner als der Entfaltungsraum, der uns heute angeboten und den zu nutzen und zu erweitern demokratische Aufgabe ist.

Ich greife nochmals auf Hayek zurück. Im Jahr 1944 veröffentlichte er in England »The Road to Serfdom«, ein Buch, das in den Jahren nach dem Krieg zahlreiche Auflagen und Übersetzungen erlebte. Seine deutsche Neuauflage 1971 »Der Weg in die Knechtschaft« ruft die Konsequenzen in die Erinnerung zurück, die er aus der Analyse des Totalitarismus gewonnen hatte; er konnte, im Gegensatz zu Ritter, offen sprechen. Es gibt drei Stellen bei Hayek, die man im Gedächtnis haben sollte, wenn man der heraufziehenden Gefahr einer ganz neuen Form dämonischer Macht – einer Macht, die auf leisen Sohlen kommt – entgegenwirken will. Hayek sagt:

1. die Konfusion von Freiheit und Macht erreiche ihren Höhepunkt, wenn man unter »Kollektivfreiheit« nicht die Freiheit der Glieder der Gesellschaft, sondern nur die unbeschränkte Freiheit des Planers verstehe, mit der Gesellschaft zu beginnen, was ihm beliebt;
2. in der Marktwirtschaft gebe es niemanden, der auch nur einen Bruchteil der Macht innehabe, die eine sozialistische Planbehörde besitzen würde;

3. daß selbst milde Formen der Planung es unweigerlich mit sich brächten, daß man den Menschen, denen man zu helfen sucht, Wertmaßstäbe und Ideale aufzwingen müsse.

Die Forderung auf Planung, muß man hier nachschalten, wird nicht nur von Ideologen gestellt. Auch Unternehmer neigen dazu, den Staat zu Hilfe zu rufen, wenn sie ihr Pulver verschossen haben. Sie dürfen sich über die Folgen nicht im unklaren sein.

*

Die Weiterentwicklung der Voraussetzungen, Bedingungen, Verhältnisse, Gegebenheiten in dieser Welt wird ihren Fortgang nehmen. Das Tempo, in dem sich ein solcher Verlauf ohne Rückschläge, ohne Gefährdung des Erreichten, ohne vernichtende Umwälzung denken läßt, hängt von der Entwicklung des Bewußtseins und der Einsicht der Gesellschaft und ihrer Mitglieder ab. Und daraus ist zu folgern, daß Demokratie sich nicht in der Ausübung des Wahlrechts erschöpfen darf. Demokratie stellt Forderungen an den Staatsbürger. Sie gibt ihm weniger, als sie von ihm verlangt. Der Staatsbürger muß Demokratie nicht nur wollen, sondern auch »lernen«, und er muß einen Spürsinn für die Gefahr entwickeln, die darin liegt, daß man sie, die Demokratie, mittels Demokratie – ich will sagen: mit pseudodemokratischen Methoden – aufs Spiel setzt.

Aber Demokratie darf ebensowenig zum Selbstzweck werden wie die Freiheit, die wir mit ihrer Hilfe erhalten, gewinnen wollen. Freiheit, die sich ihrer Verpflichtung nicht bewußt ist, würde sich selbst aufheben.

Der gesellschaftliche Fortschritt – und das heißt Fortschritt für die Gesellschaft *und* für ihre Mitglieder – ist ein Auftrag an die Demokratie, den sie nicht durch Umwälzung, also nicht destruktiv, sondern nur konstruktiv denkend und handelnd, erfüllen kann. Denn Gesellschaften werden nicht durch Revolutionen geändert. Die geschichtlichen Revolutionen waren, soweit nicht einfach

Staatsstreiche, Bestätigung bereits im Gang befindlicher Prozesse, nicht aber Ereignisse, die als solche eine neue Gesellschaft zustande gebracht hätten. Die Französische Revolution hat die französische Gesellschaft nicht geändert; dazu wäre mehr erforderlich gewesen als die Exekution einer Schicht, die man für die herrschende hielt. Die Hierarchie blieb nach der Französischen wie nach der Russischen Revolution – Inhaber und Nutznießer der Macht ändern sich, im Kern bleibt sie bestehen. Die Trägheit geschichtspsychologischer Vorgänge erlaubt keine Sprünge. Eine Revolution genügt nicht, und einer Revolution bedarf es nicht, um eine gesellschaftliche Struktur zu ändern, so daß folglich der erklärte Verzicht auf gewaltsamen Umsturz eher eine Tarnung tatsächlicher Absichten als ein Verzicht auf das Ziel sein könnte. Dieses Ziel aber ist Macht; wir brauchen nicht weit zu blicken, um ihre Umrisse, und mehr als das, zu erkennen.

*

Im Sinne Oswald Spenglers, der den Optimismus in bestimmter Situation als Feigheit bezeichnet, wollte ich auf Entwicklungslinien aufmerksam machen, über die nachzudenken unbequem ist – unbequem auf Grund eines Verdrängungssyndroms, das heißt auf Grund der Neigung des Menschen, das Drohende gerade dann aus dem Bewußtsein zu entfernen, wenn es im Grunde als unvermeidlich erkannt ist.

Vor fast 25 Jahren schrieb George Orwell »1984«. Je mehr die Zeit verrinnt, desto mehr verdrängen wir seine Botschaft. In einem Vorwort zu einem anderen Buch sagt Orwell: »Wenn die Freiheit überhaupt etwas bedeutet, so bedeutet sie auch das Recht, den Menschen das zu sagen, was sie nicht hören wollen.« Von dieser Freiheit des Individuums habe ich Gebrauch gemacht, um auf Anzeichen für eine Gefährdung unserer gemeinsamen Freiheit hinzuweisen.

Vielleicht ist es tröstlich, zum guten Ende Max Planck sprechen zu lassen. Ihn beschäftigte unser heutiges Anliegen – die Verpflichtung zur persönlichen Mitwirkung in der Demokratie als ein Gegengewicht zu übergreifender Macht – in den Jahren, in denen auch Ritter von diesem Thema gefesselt war. Im November 1941 sagte er im Harnack-Haus der Kaiser-Wilhelm-Gesellschaft, deren Vorsitz er nach 1945 zum zweiten Male auf sich nahm und die heute seinen Namen führt: »Das höchste Gut, was uns keine Macht der Welt rauben kann, ist eine reine Gesinnung, die ihren Ausdruck findet in gewissenhafter Pflichterfüllung.« Mehr kann nicht von uns erwartet werden, aber auch nicht weniger. *(1973)*

Inflation und öffentliche Finanzen

DEMOKRATIEN ÜBERLEBEN NUR DURCH SELBSTBESCHRÄNKUNG

Inflation ist nicht nur gegenwärtiges Erlebnis, sondern geschichtliche Erfahrung großer Teile der Menschheit. Das Wort Inflation ist erst seit dem amerikanischen Sezessionskrieg (1861–1865) gebräuchlich. Vorher sagte man im englischen Sprachraum »excessive supply of money« und traf damit den Nagel auf den Kopf. Wir haben zahlreiche Beispiele dafür, daß es Inflation schon im Altertum gab. Wenn nicht alles trügt, so wurde mit der Erfindung des Geldes auch die Geldentwertung erfunden – ein Fluch, von dem wir uns freimachen müssen und freimachen können.

Im »Wohlstand der Nationen« äußert sich Adam Smith über die Methode der Inflation in früheren Tagen: »Gewöhnlich wurde einfach der Nennwert der Münze erhöht, um durch eine Scheinzahlung einen unvermeidlichen Staatsbankrott zu verschleiern.« Smith kommt damit unmittelbar auf eine der häufigsten Ursachen der Geldentwertung zu sprechen: unzulängliche öffentliche Finanzwirtschaft. Er fährt fort: »Von der Antike bis zur Gegenwart haben sich allerdings nahezu alle Staaten bisweilen solcher Tricks bedient, sahen sie sich in eine solche Lage gedrängt.«

Es wäre aber ein Versäumnis, wenn ich an dieser Stelle nicht auch J.K. Galbraith zitierte, dem folgende Äußerung zugeschrieben wird: »Wie das ›Kapital‹ und die ›Bibel‹ erfreut sich der ›Wohlstand der Nationen‹ der Auszeichnung, eines der drei Bücher zu sein, auf die sich die Menschen nach Belieben berufen dürfen, ohne das Gefühl zu haben, sie sollten es gelesen haben.« Ich bemerke nur, daß ich bei

Adam Smith zumindest gelesen habe, daß er Geldwertminderung auf die gleiche Ebene stellt wie Falschmünzerei.

Inflation berührt alle, nicht nur die unmittelbar im Wirtschaftsleben Stehenden. Als Madame de Staël auf der Flucht vor Napoleon nach Österreich kam, notierte sie in ihrem Tagebuch: »Endlich betrat ich dieses Österreich, das ich noch vor vier Jahren so glücklich gesehen hatte. Ich bemerkte aber sehr bald eine ungünstige Veränderung, bewirkt durch die Abwertung des Papiergeldes ...« Auch ihr wurde die Verknüpfung von Geldentwertung und Falschmünzerei bewußt, wenn sie fortfuhr: »Während meines Aufenthalts in Österreich wurde ein Mann gehängt, weil er zu dem Zeitpunkt, wo die alten Scheine außer Kurs gesetzt wurden, beim Nachdruck von Falschgeld erwischt worden war. Noch als man ihn zum Galgen führte, schrie er: ›Nicht ich habe betrogen, sondern der Staat!‹«

Daß wir in der Bundesrepublik aufmerksamer als in vielen anderen Ländern auf inflationäre Erscheinungen achten, mag damit zusammenhängen, daß viele von uns die große Inflation der frühen zwanziger Jahre noch nicht vergessen haben. Wir erinnern uns daran, daß der Dollar – dessen Parität im Jahr 1914 4,20 Mark war und der im November 1918, am Ende des Ersten Weltkriegs, bei 7,50 Mark stand – am 20. November 1923 in die atemberaubende Höhe von 4,2 Billionen Mark hinaufgeklettert war; dort stand auch der Index der Großhandelspreise. Es war ein nur marginaler Nutzen dieser Entwicklung, daß man in jungen Jahren mit Millionen, Milliarden und Billionen umzugehen lernte. In jenen Jahren kam es zu beispielloser sozialer Umschichtung und zu persönlicher Not, von der Zerrüttung des wirtschaftlichen und staatlichen Lebens abgesehen. Der damalige badische Kultusminister und spätere Staatspräsident, der Demokrat Willy Hellpach, schrieb einige Jahre später in seiner »Politischen Prognose für Deutschland«: »Die psychologische Wirkung in Millionen von Seelen: die Vernichtung des Glaubens an den Staat – war weder zu verhindern, noch ist sie anders als in Jahrzehnten zu tilgen.«

Obwohl wir sicher sein können, daß eine Geldentwertung jenes dramatischen Ausmaßes sich nicht wieder einstellen wird – man hat unterdessen Instrumente gegen einen Erdrutsch dieser Größenordnung gefunden –, sind wir doch gebrannte Kinder und folglich nicht bereit, tatenlos zuzusehen, wenn der Geldwert gefährdet wird, entweder um mit Hilfe der Inflation die Wirtschaft kurzfristig anzuheizen, oder, schlimmer noch, weil man der Entwicklung, gedankenlos und unkritisch, ihren Lauf läßt.

Wenn wir die Lage in der *Bundesrepublik heute* beurteilen, soll nicht übersehen werden,

- daß wir in der Welt mit unserer Inflationsrate an letzter Stelle stehen, also die günstigste Position aufweisen,
- daß in den letzten Monaten eine relative, wenn auch vielleicht nur temporäre Stabilisierung gelungen ist.

Der Preisindex für die Lebenshaltungskosten, der im Oktober 1974 mehr als 7 Prozent über dem entsprechenden Vorjahresmonat gelegen hatte, zeigt im Januar 1975 eine Erhöhung von nur noch etwa 6 Prozent. Aber die Indizes, die für das Kostenniveau maßgebend sind – zum Beispiel der Preisindex für industrielle Produkte und das Tariflohn- und -gehaltsniveau – sind noch immer zweistellig. Dem stelle ich die Auffassung eines Mannes gegenüber, der an der Spitze der Federal Reserve Bank steht, Arthur Burns. Als wir vor kurzem mit ihm in Hamburg sprachen, kam die Rede auch auf die amerikanische Wirtschaftspolitik, die, ähnlich wie die unsrige, vor dem Dilemma stand und noch steht, ob der Stabilität oder der Vollbeschäftigung der Vorrang zu geben sei. Auf die direkte Frage, welchen Hundertsatz der Inflation er allenfalls noch als tragbar ansehen würde, sagte er klar und deutlich: »1 Prozent ist immer noch zuviel.« Man kann diese Antwort für realistisch halten oder nicht: Das Ziel ist damit richtig angesprochen, wenn wir den Charakter des

Geldes als Wertmaßstab für den Tausch von Gütern und Leistungen voll erhalten wollen.

Diskutiert man über »zulässige« Inflationsraten, so sollte man nicht aus dem Auge lassen, daß nach der Zinseszinsrechnung, die man in diesem Zusammenhang immer wieder erwähnen muß, eine Preiserhöhung

- von 7 Prozent jährlich zu einer Verdoppelung in zehn Jahren,
- von 10 Prozent in sieben Jahren,
- von 12 Prozent in fünf Jahren führt.

Die geschichtlichen Inflationen haben ihre Wurzel im staatlichen Bereich, wie wir schon bemerkt haben. Es wäre allerdings ungerecht, sie nur auf fiskalischen Frohsinn zurückzuführen; häufig genug gab es handfeste Gründe, die meist im äußeren politischen Raum lagen.

Die derzeitige Inflation in vielen Staaten der Welt, die für einen großen Teil jener weltwirtschaftlichen Störungen verantwortlich ist, die ihrerseits zur derzeitigen Rezession beigetragen haben, läßt sich aber viel weniger als die früheren Geldentwertungen außenpolitisch erklären. Lassen wir die Ölkrise, die zwar nach Ursache und Wirkung inflationäre Elemente in sich birgt, aber doch eher als ein außenpolitisches Ereignis aufzufassen ist, beiseite, so müssen wir die Ursachen im Innern der Währungsgebiete, ihrer Staaten, Gesellschaften und Wirtschaftselemente – bis zum Individuum hin – suchen.

Dabei wäre es verfehlt, monokausal zu denken, also zum Beispiel *eine* Gruppe, *eine* Schicht, *eine* Denkweise zum Grund zu erklären. Inflation ist als geschichtlicher Vorgang dem Einfluß mannigfacher Kräfte im guten wie im bösen unterworfen. Inflation ist unmöglich, wenn sie nicht mehr oder weniger von vielen Seiten gewollt oder zumindest geduldet wird – das letztere ist kaum weniger verwerflich als das erste.

In seiner »State of the Union Message to the Congress« vom 16. Januar 1975 hat der amerikanische Präsident eine überzeugende

Formulierung für die Problematik unserer Lage gefunden, als er sagte: »Ein Teil unserer Schwierigkeiten geht darauf zurück, daß wir zu nachsichtig gegenüber uns selbst geworden sind. Jahrzehntelang haben wir dafür gestimmt, daß die Unterstützungen durch die Regierung immer wieder erhöht worden sind – und nun wird die Rechnung fällig. Wir haben zu viele neue Programme hinzugefügt, so daß Umfang und Wachstum des Bundeshaushalts ein Eigenleben angenommen haben.«

»Es ist eine einfache Rechenaufgabe: Wenn wir nicht das übermäßige Wachstum der Bundesausgaben unter Kontrolle nehmen oder wachsende Steuern uns selbst auferlegen, werden wir weiterhin in riesige inflationäre Fehlbeträge des Bundeshaushalts hineinrennen.«

»Wenn wir das ›Moment‹, das zur Zeit in die Bundesausgaben ›eingebaut‹ ist, über die nächsten fünfzehn Jahre fortsetzen, werden die öffentlichen Ausgaben leichterdings die Hälfte unseres Bruttosozialprodukts in Anspruch nehmen. Dies vergleicht sich mit weniger als einem Drittel in 1975.«

Diese Ausführungen des amerikanischen Präsidenten könnte man nur noch durch den Hinweis ergänzen, daß zu Anfang dieses Jahrhunderts die öffentlichen Ausgaben der Vereinigten Staaten nur etwa 6 Prozent des Sozialprodukts ausmachten.

Die Situation in unserem Land ist nicht wesentlich anders. Wir sind, irregeführt durch tatsächliche oder vermeintliche Früchte einer außergewöhnlich langen Wachstumsphase, in eine Anspruchsinflation hineingeraten, die – bei stagnierendem oder rückläufigem Wachstum – in einen Verteilungskampf aller gegen alle einmünden muß, falls die Stabilität nicht wieder hergestellt werden kann. Denn die öffentlichen Haushalte unserer Zeit – so sehr sie auch zunehmend einer Eigengesetzlichkeit unterliegen – sind letzten Endes doch nur der Ausdruck dessen,

– was der Staatsbürger erwartet,

- was die Interessenvertretungen der Staatsbürger sowohl zugunsten ihrer Mitglieder als auch zur Festigung ihres eigenen Ansehens fordern,
- was Regierungen und Parteien anbieten, um aus den Erwartungen und Forderungen der Staatsbürger so viel politischen Nutzen wie möglich zu ziehen.

Noch einmal: Monokausale Erklärung träfe nicht den Kern. Es gibt keinen Idealtypus der Inflation, zumal es auch nicht das Ideal der Inflation geben darf. Wir wissen, daß es importierte Inflation gibt, und wir wissen, daß es Inflationen auch durch Export geben kann, wenn die Bedingungen dafür falsch gesetzt sind.

Für unser Währungsgebiet können wir diese beiden – meist nicht grundlegenden, sondern nur zusätzlichen – Inflationsursachen ausschließen. Denn zumindest seit 1973 ist unser Währungsgebiet gegen den Import von Inflation durch freie Devisenkurse weitgehend abgeschirmt, die, was den Warenverkehr angeht, die Kaufkraftrelation der Währungen richtig wiedergeben. Andererseits erlaubt es die Lage unserer Zahlungsbilanz, unsere Güterexporte durch Importe zu kompensieren, soweit die Warenmärkte das erfordern. Zur Erschwerung unserer Ausfuhr, die noch vor kurzem im Kopf deutscher Wirtschaftspolitiker gespukt hat, besteht also nicht der geringste Grund. Export ist ein unverzichtbares strukturelles Element der deutschen Beschäftigung.

Währungsgebiete wie das der DM stehen freilich auch unter dem Einfluß der Kapitalströme. Erhöht sich der Devisenbestand der Bundesbank, so führt das zur Erhöhung des Geldumlaufs in DM, soweit nicht abgeschöpft wird; die Bundesbank tut das im Verfolg ihrer erklärten und bisher noch nicht wesentlich erschütterten Politik der Kontrolle des Geldvolumens, deren Erfolge sichtbar und spürbar geworden sind. Stabilitätspolitik in dieser Phase der Rezession ist aber nicht ohne Gefahren:

- Das Volumen des Auftragseingangs bei der Industrie geht seit September 1974 im Vergleich zum entsprechenden Vormonat stetig zurück. Für die Industrieproduktion gilt das gleiche.

- Das reale Bruttosozialprodukt je Erwerbstätigenstunde, das 1973 noch um etwa 6 Prozent zugenommen hatte, stieg in den ersten drei Quartalen 1974 nur noch um 3 bis 4 Prozent und stagnierte im vierten Quartal 1974.
- Die Lohndrift, die immer ein Charakteristikum für günstige Konjunktur war, ist schon seit dem zweiten Quartal 1974 auf Null gesunken.

Vor allem aber ist von entscheidender wirtschaftlicher, politischer und menschlicher Bedeutung, daß wir in der Bundesrepublik Ende Januar 1975 rund 1,15 Millionen Arbeitslose und rund 900000 Kurzarbeiter bei nur etwa 220000 offenen Stellen hatten. Zum ersten Mal seit Februar 1959 hat damit die Arbeitslosenzahl die Millionengrenze überschritten. Die Zahl der Kurzarbeiter ist die bisher höchste überhaupt. Diese erste ernsthafte Rezession der Nachkriegsjahre ist nicht die Folge der Stabilitätspolitik, sie hat vielmehr ihre Gründe in einem wohl einmaligen, von der Wirtschaftspolitik vielleicht erst spät erkannten Zusammentreffen zahlreicher, teils normaler, teils anomaler Ursachen:

- die zyklische Ermüdung, die jeder Hochkonjunktur folgt,
- die Labilität der weltpolitischen Systeme,
- die weltweite Inflation und die mangelnde Übereinstimmung unter den Nationen, ob, wie und inwieweit sie zu bekämpfen sei,
- die Ölkrise – Frucht einer Überschneidung politischer Motive, psychologischer Reaktionen und inflationärer Fernwirkung,
- die Weltwährungskrise, die ihrerseits mit inflationären Erscheinungen zusammenhängt.

Die Wahrscheinlichkeit des Auftretens ökonomischer Krisen ist unabhängig von der jeweiligen Wirtschaftsverfassung und von der jeweiligen Gesellschaftsform. Denn menschliche Gesellschaften, gleich welcher Struktur, sind biologische Einheiten. Ihre Existenz verlangt zwar, daß sich immer wieder ein Gleichgewicht einstellt. Aber dieses Gleichgewicht ist nicht etwa naturgesetzlich für alle Zeiten vorgegeben, es muß vielmehr im Wege der Regelung immer wieder neu gewonnen werden, wenn auch nur einer der Parameter des Umfeldes eine auch nur geringe Änderung erfährt – was innere und äußere Einflüsse zur Ursache haben kann.

Auch die klassenlose Gesellschaft, die vergesellschaftete Gesellschaft also – in der dem Produktivkapital die gleiche entscheidende Bedeutung zukommt wie in einer kapitalistischen Gesellschaft –, besteht aus Menschen, die sich nicht unbegrenzt programmieren lassen, eben weil auch sie einer biologischen, einer lebendigen Welt angehören. Sie entgeht deshalb wirtschaftlichen Krisen ebensowenig wie andere Gesellschaften, wobei nur Benennung und Begründung abweichen.

Der drängenden Frage des Zusammenhangs zwischen Stabilitätspolitik und Arbeitslosigkeit läßt sich mit einer Analyse der Konjunkturlage indessen nicht ausweichen, wenn auch der quantitative Zusammenhang zwischen Inflation und Arbeitslosigkeit noch nicht ausreichend erforscht ist und sich vielleicht überhaupt einer rechnerischen Betrachtung entzieht. Zudem ist Arbeitslosigkeit und Arbeitslosigkeit nicht in allen Fällen das gleiche, da fast immer strukturelle Momente mitspielen.

Immerhin ist durch den tatsächlichen Verlauf in unserem Land die Vermutung widerlegt worden, zwischen Inflation und Arbeitslosigkeit bestehe eine Beziehung der Art, daß man mit Hilfe eines bestimmten Maßes an Inflation ein bestimmtes Maß an Arbeitslosigkeit verhüten könne. Jedenfalls erleben wir seit 1974 in der Bundesrepublik eine Inflation, die 5 Prozent wesentlich überschreitet, und wir haben trotzdem mehr als 5 Prozent Arbeitslose.

Auch wenn sich nicht beweisen läßt, daß Stabilität in jedem Fall zu Vollbeschäftigung führt, so kann man an weiteren Beispielen zeigen, daß Instabilität, also Inflation, noch lange keine Vollbeschäftigung verbürgt. Bei hoher Inflationsrate in den Vereinigten Staaten, in Großbritannien und in Italien haben diese Länder doch hohe Arbeitslosenraten.

Die Arbeitslosenrate in der Bundesrepublik ist hoch, zu hoch. Dabei können wir noch nicht von Stabilität sprechen. Gewiß, wir haben heute ein höheres Maß an Stabilität erreicht als vor einem Jahr, und man könnte gegen uns ins Feld führen, daß bei zunehmender Stabilität die Arbeitslosigkeit zugenommen hat. Aber dies wäre eine kurzfristige Beobachtung, nicht mehr, keinesfalls ein Beweis.

Langfristig ist die Zunahme der Stabilität eine Voraussetzung für stabile Beschäftigung. Und ein Rückblick auf die Wirtschaftsgeschichte zeigt, daß Perioden stabilen Geldwerts auch Perioden sozialer Sicherheit waren. Verzichteten wir auf die Fortführung der Stabilitätspolitik, so wäre ein Rückfall in höhere Inflationsraten zu befürchten.

Obwohl niemand von uns daran glauben kann, daß die wirtschaftliche Tätigkeit in Zukunft ohne den Wellenschlag der Konjunktur verlaufen wird, haben wir doch alle ein vitales Interesse daran, daß die Wellenbewegungen gemildert werden. Je härter die Ausschläge der Konjunkturkurve, desto größer nicht nur die unmittelbaren wirtschaftlichen Folgen, desto größer vielmehr die Wirkung auf den Menschen und desto größer auch die Wahrscheinlichkeit, daß der Wellengang späterer Konjunkturphasen eine große Amplitude hat. Inflationserwartungen führen zu Aktionen und Reaktionen der am Wirtschaftsprozeß aktiv und passiv Beteiligten, die das Einschwingen in eine Mittellage erschweren. Inflationserwartungen zum Beispiel beeinflussen die Umlaufgeschwindigkeit des Geldes, und wir wissen, daß nicht die Geldmenge allein, sondern auch die Geschwindigkeit, mit der sie sich umsetzt, für den Geldwert bestimmend ist. Inflation ist eine Gefahr für Vollbeschäftigung.

1. aus der psychologischen Erfahrung, daß Geldentwertung die Leistungsbereitschaft, also die Produktion und die Produktivität be-

einträchtigt, was die reale Deckung der umlaufenden Geldmengen verringert, also die Entwertung beschleunigt,

2. weil Geldentwertung die Sparbereitschaft verringert, die Geldumlaufgeschwindigkeit erhöht, den Verbrauch steigert, die Investitionsrate – als Ausdruck des Konsumverzichts – gefährdet.

Die Sparbereitschaft in unserem Land ist mit etwa 14 Prozent des Volkseinkommens ungebrochen hoch und wesentlich höher als in den meisten anderen Staaten. Auch wenn es sich dabei in vielen Fällen um das »Ansparen« zur späteren Erfüllung von Kaufwünschen handelt, ist doch der Bodensatz der Sparerleistung eine Finanzierungsgrundlage für Investitionen. Das Vertrauen des Sparers in den Geldwert zu erhalten, ist folglich sowohl eine politisch-moralische als auch ein wirtschaftliche Notwendigkeit.

Es ist ein Gemeinplatz, aber dennoch falsch, daß der Sachwertbesitzer in der Inflation gewinne, derjenige aber, der über Sachwerte nicht verfüge, verarme. Die Wirklichkeit belehrt uns anders: Die Empfänger von Arbeits- und Sozialeinkommen haben zumindest in den letzten Jahren eine Erhöhung ihres Einkommens erfahren, welche die Geldentwertung wenigstens ausgleicht, häufig übertrifft, während längst nicht alle Sachwerte über längere Zeiträume hinweg eine entsprechende Werterhöhung erfuhren. Vor allem der Eigentümer von Produktivvermögen – ob er es unmittelbar oder in Aktien besitzt – kann in den letzten zehn Jahren eine Werterhaltung oder gar eine Wertmehrung nicht feststellen, insbesondere dann nicht, wenn man die erhöhten Wagnisse einrechnet. Wir bedauern die Besitzer von Produktivvermögen nicht – jeder muß, unter Abwägung von Risiko und Chance, seine eigene Entscheidung treffen –, sondern stellen nur klar, daß bei rasch fortschreitender Geldentwertung Unternehmungen vor der schwer lösbaren Aufgabe stehen,

– den Realwert ihres Anlagevermögens zu erhalten – also ausreichend zu investieren –, während steuerliche Abschreibungen nur auf den Anschaffungspreis, nicht aber auf den zunehmend höheren Wiederbeschaffungspreis zulässig sind.

- das inflationär zunehmende Umlaufvermögen zu finanzieren, wofür in der Regel der einbehaltene Gewinn nicht ausreicht, so daß auf Fremdkapital mit fixer Zinslast zurückgegriffen werden muß. Die Finanzierung dieses zusätzlichen Bedarfs an Umlaufmitteln wird erschwert durch die Besteuerung der Scheingewinne, der Eigenkapitalanteil in unseren Unternehmungen nimmt tendenziell stetig ab.

Besondere Aufmerksamkeit verlangt in Zeiten der Inflation die Beobachtung,

- daß im Zeichen eines anhaltenden Verkäufermarktes die unternehmerische Initiative erschlafft,
- daß statistisch gesehen zwar im Einzelfall hohe Beschäftigung herrschen mag, die aber mit verschleierter Unterbeschäftigung in übersetzten Bereichen der Wirtschaft einhergeht.

Denn es entstehen volkswirtschaftliche Kostenerhöhungen zu Lasten *jedes* Verbrauchers, wenn die marktwirtschaftlichen Kräfte nicht am Werk bleiben. Die Rezession führt in solchen Situationen zur Entspannung, zur Entzerrung. Der Preis der Rezession ist jedoch so hoch, daß wir alles daransetzen müssen, die inflationären Ausschläge kleinzuhalten; nur so können künftige Rezessionen gemildert werden.

*

Die Überzeugung, daß den öffentlichen Finanzen eine besondere Rolle bei der langfristigen Erhaltung der Stabilität zukommt, gründet sich sowohl auf quantitative als auch auf qualitative Erwägungen, die durchaus nicht unkritischer Art sind. Denn die Entwicklung, die die öffentlichen Finanzen in unserem Land – aber nicht nur in dem unsrigen – genommen haben, zeigt, daß wir die soeben unter Schmerzen errungene relative Stabilität ernsthaft gefährden, wenn nicht bald und wirksam in die Speichen des Rades gegriffen wird.

Dabei darf die Themastellung nicht zu der Annahme verführen, zwischen Geldwert und öffentlichen Haushalten bestehe ein engerer Zusammenhang als zwischen dem Verhalten der übrigen Wirtschaftsteilnehmer und der Inflation. Inflation ist vielmehr ein Phänomen, das auch dann nicht teilbar ist, wenn es auf einem Teilgebiet seinen Anfang genommen hat.

Zunächst zum Zahlenwerk, das im einzelnen verwirrend ist, dessen Quintessenz aber an den Anfang gestellt werden muß:

1. Die öffentlichen Finanzen (öffentliche Haushalte und Sozialaufwand), deren Anteil am Bruttosozialprodukt zu Beginn des Jahrhunderts auf etwa 15 Prozent geschätzt wird, nehmen heute fast 40 Prozent des Sozialprodukts in Anspruch. Der Trend ist steigend; extrapoliert man die Wachstumsrate des letzten Jahrzehnts, so wird der Anteil der öffentlichen Finanzen zu Ende des Jahrhunderts rund 50 Prozent erreichen – es sei denn, man schöbe einen Riegel vor.
2. Das Wachstum des Staatsverbrauchs beschleunigt sich seit einigen Jahren. Er stieg von 1971 vis 1974 im Jahresmittel um fast 16 Prozent, das heißt, als Anteil am Bruttosozialprodukt von 17,1 auf 19,7 Prozent. Die Jahresquote erhöhte sich also auf 0,9 Prozentpunkte, und die öffentlichen Finanzen könnten, so gerechnet, die 50-Prozent-Marke schon 1985 erreichen.
3. Gleichzeitig mit der Erhöhung des öffentlichen Anteils am Bruttosozialprodukt
   - geht der Anteil der gesamten Anlageinvestition (Staat und Wirtschaft) am Bruttosozialprodukt tendenziell zurück,
   - nimmt der Anteil der investiven Aufwendungen innerhalb des Staatsverbrauchs zu Lasten der Personalaufwendungen ab, deren Quote von 1961 bis 1973 von 26 Prozent auf 33 Prozent anstieg und weiter steigt.

Klaus-Dirk Henke verdanke ich eine andere Darstellungsweise, die die Unersättlichkeit der öffentlichen Hände und ihrer Mitarbeiter noch deutlicher ins Licht rückt: Während das Volkseinkommen in der Bundesrepublik von 1961 auf 1971 um 125,9 Prozent stieg, nahmen die öffentlichen Gesamtausgaben um 139 Prozent zu, darin die Personalausgaben um 224,8 Prozent.

A propos: öffentliche Hände. Ich erinnere mich an eine Besprechung beim damaligen Bundeskanzler Ludwig Erhard, die dem gleichen Thema galt, das uns heute bewegt. Professor Erhard betonte einleitend, wie schwierig es sei, die Finanzpolitik der öffentlichen Hände unter Kontrolle zu bringen, zumal es deren 23 000 gebe. In der Diskussion sprach ich dann von 46 000. Erhard korrigierte mich; er habe nur von 23 000 gesprochen. Meine Antwort: »Die haben alle zwei Hände, macht 46 000.« Und leider weiß oft genug die eine Hand nicht, was die andere tut.

In Wirtschaftspolitik und Wirtschaftswissenschaft besteht Konsens darüber, daß ein Wirtschaftsaufschwung nur dann Bestand hat, wenn die Impulse von den Investitionen ausgehen. Bedingung für die dauerhafte Überwindung einer Rezession ist, genauer gesagt, daß sich das richtige Verhältnis zwischen investiven und konsumtiven Ausgaben einstellt (wobei man einräumen muß, daß es keine Formel gibt, die das »richtige« Maß zu berechnen erlaubt).

Notwendig ist folglich die Investitionsbereitschaft von Unternehmern und öffentlicher Hand bei entsprechender Konsumzurückhaltung. Jedoch sind die Bruttoanlageinvestitionen in der Bundesrepublik 1974 gegenüber 1973 real um 8,5 Prozent zurückgegangen. Da auch die Jahre 1973 und 1972 nur geringe Zunahmeraten aufwiesen, war 1974 die Summe der Investitionen geringer als 1971. Mit Ausnahme von Großbritannien, das 1974 einen Rückgang von 1 Prozent hatte, und von Japan mit einem Rückgang von 6 Prozent (aber hohen Zunahmen in 1972 und 1973) stand die Bundesrepublik mit diesem Rückgang innerhalb der Industrienationen allein da. Folgen werden nicht ausbleiben.

Die besondere Note, die den Investitionen – im Gegensatz zum

Konsum – zukommt, liegt darin, daß sie – so John Maynard Keynes – eine »multiplikatorische« Wirkung ausüben. In einem sehr weitgespannten Sinn ist Investition Daseinsvorsorge.

Man muß die Frage der Investitionen auch im Lichte der Energielage sehen. Wenn wir unsere Abhängigkeit in der Energieversorgung verringern wollen – von dem ehrgeizigen Ziel einer Unabhängigkeit in der Energieversorgung gar nicht zu sprechen –, sind Investitionen erforderlich, deren Größenordnung weit über die bisher üblichen volkswirtschaftlichen Investitionsraten hinausgehen. Wollen wir der Wohlstandsminderung, die aus unserer »Ölrechnung« folgt, auf Dauer begegnen, so werden wir um Schwerpunkt-Investitionen für Energie nicht herumkommen.

Zurück zu den öffentlichen Finanzen: Hintergründe der höheren Personalkostenquote sind

– die Zunahme der Zahl der öffentlichen Bediensteten,
– die Erhöhung der gesetzlichen und tariflichen Bezüge,
– die Höherstufungen.

Es gibt für die Abgrenzung der Personalzahlen verschiedene Methoden, so daß die folgenden Zahlen keine statistische Genauigkeit beanspruchen, sondern nur einen Größenbegriff geben wollen.

Von den 21,36 Millionen abhängig Beschäftigten im Jahr 1964 waren im unmittelbaren öffentlichen Dienst 2,87 Millionen, das heißt 13,4 Prozent, tätig. 1973 war die Zahl der abhängig Beschäftigten auf 22,1 Millionen gestiegen; die Zahl der im unmittelbaren öffentlichen Dienst Tätigen aber auf 3,34 Millionen, so daß nunmehr 15,1 Prozent aller Beschäftigten im öffentlichen Dienst standen. Das bedeutet, daß die Zahl der öffentlichen Bediensteten während dieser zehn Jahre um 16,2 Prozent zugenommen hat, während die in der privaten Wirtschaft (einschließlich mittelbarer öffentlicher Dienst) Tätigen um nur 1,5 Prozent zunahm.

Hartmut Tofaute ergänzt diese Angaben wie folgt: Das gesamte Personal im staatlichen Bereich umfaßte 1972 – einschließlich der

Teilzeitbeschäftigten, der Bundeswehr und des Bundesgrenzschutzes sowie des öffentlichen Dienstes im weiteren und im erweiterten Sinn – 5 731 835 Köpfe, das heißt rund 25 Prozent aller abhängig Beschäftigten. In anderer Darstellung sagt derselbe Autor, daß von 1960 auf 1972 die Zahl der Erwerbstätigen im verarbeitenden Gewerbe (ohne Baugewerbe) um 5,8 Prozent zunahm, im Handel um 6,6 Prozent, bei den Gebietskörperschaften aber um 36,6 Prozent. Nach Aufgabenbereichen betrug die Zunahme in der Verteidigung – ohne Soldaten – 108,7 Prozent, bei den Schulen 62,5 Prozent, in den Hochschulen 238,3 Prozent, im sonstigen Kultusbereich 46,7 Prozent und in Gesundheit, Sport und Erholung 52,3 Prozent.

Es wäre unfair, nicht auf diese Schwerpunkte der Zunahme hinzuweisen – Schwerpunkte, die nicht immer vom Staat autonom gesetzt werden, sondern vielfach gesellschaftlichen Forderungen entsprechen. Dennoch sind diese Zahlen bedrückend, zumal die reine Zahl der öffentlichen Bediensteten nicht genügend Auskunft darüber gibt, wie Gesellschaft und Wirtschaft dadurch belastet werden. Denn der Aufwand, der für einen Beamten unmittelbar und mittelbar innerhalb der Behörde entsteht, besagt nichts über die Mühe und Kosten, die zusätzliche staatliche Tätigkeit außerhalb der Behörde hervorrufen kann, freilich auch nichts über den Nutzen, der langfristig der Ausbau des Bildungswesens hervorbringen könnte. Ich möchte dazu heute keinen Kommentar geben.

Um die Zahlenspiele abzurunden: Reinhold Maier pflegte zu erzählen, daß das Württembergische Ministerium für Wirtschaft und Arbeit, dem er Anfang der dreißiger Jahre vorstand, in jener Zeit vom Minister bis zur Raumpflegerin weniger als vierzig Köpfe umfaßte. Ich habe mir nicht die Mühe gemacht, und ich hätte es auch für indiskret gehalten, festzustellen, wie viele Bedienstete ein Ministerium gleicher Zuständigkeit heute umfaßt, aber es kommt wohl der Wahrheit nahe, wenn man einen Faktor 10 annimmt – in einem größeren Land, mit größeren Aufgaben sicherlich. (Man sagt mir übrigens, Faktor 16 sei richtig.)

Dabei liegen die Verhältnisse in den verschiedenen Zweigen des öffentlichen Dienstes völlig unterschiedlich. Überfluß und Mangel stehen sich gegenüber, und wenn die Finanzverwaltung geltend macht, daß sie ihren Aufgaben mit dem derzeitigen Personalbestand nicht gerecht werden kann, so trifft das wohl zu. Man fragt sich nur, ob die chronische Verstopfung der Arbeit der Finanzämter durch eine Erhöhung der Stellenzahl behoben werden kann oder ob eine *echte* Steuerreform nicht sinnvoller wäre. Es fehlt freilich der Mut, an eine weitere Steuerreform zu denken.

Was mit der bereits erwähnten Höherstufung gemeint ist, weiß man aus der Presse. Ich las dazu, daß von 1960 bis 1962 die Zahl der Beamten und Angestellten der Gebietskörperschaften

- im höheren Dienst um 119,2 Prozent zunahm,
- im gehobenen und mittleren Dienst um rund 45 Prozent,

während sie im einfachen Dienst um 9 Prozent abnahm. Weiter, daß im Jahr 1971 die Aufwendungen für Beamtenbesoldung um 17,1 Prozent stiegen, wovon 5,9 Prozentpunkte auf »strukturelle Verbesserungen« entfielen. Schließlich, daß in der öffentlichen Verwaltung mit 1972 insgesamt 2282000 Mitarbeitern 1960 9,5 Prozent im höheren Dienst waren, 1972 aber 14,5 Prozent. Die Anteile des gehobenen und mittleren Dienstes änderten sich praktisch nicht.

Man sollte dieses recht attraktive Thema des Stellenkegels und seiner Deformation nicht überbewerten; das Argument Nachholbedarf – was die Einkommen angeht, nicht so sehr die Titel – ist nicht leicht abzuweisen. Aber es sollte auch nicht zu sehr abgenutzt werden.

Von viel größerer Tragweite ist es, wenn bei der Schaffung neuer Stellen zwar die Kosten, die den nächsten Jahreshaushalt betreffen, richtig angesetzt, die Kosten für die gesamte Lebensdauer der Stelle und ihres Inhabers aber einfach negiert werden. Dies mag im übrigen auch in der Wirtschaft vorkommen, ist aber dennoch grundfalsch.

Ein Beispiel, das die Größenordnung richtig wiedergibt: Angenommen, der Posten eines Ministerialrats im Alter von vierzig Jahren werde neu geschaffen. Das Einkommen dieses Beamten einschließlich Ministerialzulage betrage etwas mehr als 50000 DM im Jahr. Bleibt dieser Beamte bis zu seiner Pensionierung ohne weitere Beförderung im Dienst und erfüllt er nach der Pensionierung die statistische Lebenserwartung, so betragen die Gesamtkosten dieser Entscheidung »zu heutigen Preisen« 1743000 DM. Viel billiger wäre die Entscheidung, wenn es nicht um eine völlig neue Position ginge, sondern wenn ein Regierungsdirektor zum Ministerialrat befördert würde. Aber auch dann kostet diese Entscheidung, auf die Lebenszeit des Betreffenden gerechnet, noch immer 175000 DM.

Natürlich kosten nicht alle neuen Stellen gleich viel. Als ich aber kürzlich in einem großen Ministerium ein bestimmtes Zimmer suchte, so war mir, als ob ich an den Türen überwiegend den Titel des Ministerialrats oder noch höherer Chargen gesehen hätte. Kann man mit leichter Ironie daraus schließen, daß in einem Ministerium ja administriert und nicht etwa regiert wird, so daß man dort zu Recht nicht etwa Regierungsräte oder Oberregierungsräte antrifft wie in früheren Tagen? (Wir haben heute bei Bosch allerdings auch viel mehr Direktoren als früher.)

Nochmals zu der Kostenlast aus der Errichtung neuer Stellen: Seit 1960 hat sich die Zahl der öffentlichen Bediensteten jährlich im Mittel um etwa 40000 erhöht. Nimmt man den Wert einer einzelnen Entscheidung nicht mit den erwähnten 1,75 Millionen DM, sondern nur mit einer halben Million an, so würde jährlich über eine zukünftige öffentliche Mehrlast in der Größenordnung von 20 Milliarden DM entschieden, obwohl in den jährlichen Haushaltsplänen nur ein kleiner Bruchteil davon erscheint.

Die kritische Betrachtung der öffentlichen Haushalte darf uns nicht blind machen gegenüber den eigenen Fehlern. Wenn wir hier die öffentlichen Haushalte abhandeln, so klingt das so, als ob in der

Wirtschaft alles in bester Ordnung sei. Das ist nicht der Fall. 25 Jahre ohne wesentlichen Rückschlag – die Rezession 1967 war zu schnell überwunden, als daß man daraus eine bleibende Lehre gezogen hätte – haben die Wirtschaft in ihrer Gesamtheit, Unternehmer und Mitarbeiter, verwöhnt. Immer wieder konnten Fehler in der Geschäftspolitik und Mängel in der Kostenpolitik gutgemacht, die Forderungen der in der Wirtschaft Tätigen, auch wenn sie über das real Mögliche hinausgingen, erfüllt werden durch die Flucht nach vorne, das heißt durch Wachstum, das nie einen wesentlichen Rückschlag erfuhr.

Und ich bin auch nicht der Meinung, daß es fair wäre, von Bürokratie nur in der staatlichen Verwaltung zu sprechen. Meiner Ansicht nach muß sich die Wirtschaft in diesem Punkt selbst an die Nase fassen. Beamtenhaftigkeit gibt es auch in der Industrie, und ich habe im Laufe meines Lebens nicht nur eine Behörde und vor allem sehr viele Beamte kennengelernt, die – berücksichtigt man ihre Bindung an gesetzliche Vorschriften – nicht weniger effizient gearbeitet haben, als dies die Wirtschaft für sich in Anspruch nimmt. Ich bin davon überzeugt, daß wir in der Bundesrepublik ein Beamtentum haben, das nach Charakter, Intelligenz, Ausbildung und Erfahrung den Vergleich mit keinem anderen Land zu scheuen braucht.

Das Stichwort »Öffentliche Verschwendung« läßt sich aber bei allem Wohlwollen nicht unterdrücken, und damit ist eine Verhaltensweise gemeint, die nur selten personifiziert werden kann, die vielmehr eine Folge des Mangels an »öffentlichem Gewissen« ist.

Es ist nicht unbedingt allgemeingültig, wenn in diesem Zusammenhang Beispiele aus dem öffentlichen Bauwesen vorgetragen werden. Immerhin fiel es nicht nur mir auf, als vor einiger Zeit ein illustrierter Zeitungsaufsatz die Überschrift trug: »Ein Schloß am Bodensee«, gefolgt von einer zweiten Schlagzeile: »Intime und ausschweifende Architektur in Konstanz« – und wenn dann dem Text zu entnehmen war, daß es sich hier um die Neubauten für die Universität Konstanz handelte. Eher bewundernd als kritisierend, schrieb der Verfasser des Artikels, daß »dieses akademische Wunderschloß vollklimatisiert« ist, und man wußte nicht genau, ob er sich mit den Vätern dieses Baus identifizierte, als er von einem »technoiden Rokoko« berichtete. Die Bilder: Ein hinreißendes Gewirr schrägwinkliger, stumpfwinkliger Kanten und unregelmäßig gekurvter Rundungen. Nicht über Schönheit wird hier gesprochen, sondern über das Geld des Staatsbürgers, der – bei aller Unwissenheit in bezug auf staatliche Baukunst – sich doch die Frage stellt, was wohl die Modellschreinerarbeit gekostet haben mag, die für die Betonschalung erforderlich war. Man soll Beispiele nicht verallgemeinern. Aber der Staatsbürger soll auch nicht in allen Fällen schweigen.

*

Wir kommen jetzt zu der fundamentalen Frage der Verknüpfung von Inflation, Stabilität und öffentlichen Finanzen. Staatlicher und gesellschaftlicher Wille kann die öffentlichen Finanzen zu einem wesentlichen Werkzeug für die wirtschaftliche Ordnung machen. So wie Handlungen des Staats die geschichtlichen Inflationen eingeleitet und – wenn auch nicht ohne Wunden – wieder in stabile Phasen übergeführt haben, kann auch in der Gegenwart und in Zukunft von den öffentlichen Haushalten mindestens jener marginale Einfluß ausgehen, der ausreicht, um den Trend zu wenden.

Das hohe Beharrungsvermögen vor allem des administrativen Teils der Staatsausgaben und der Sozialleistungen darf nicht entmutigen; es kommt in der ersten Phase nicht darauf an, die absoluten Beträge zu ändern, sondern

- die Mechanik der überproportionalen Zunahme zu unterbrechen,
- den investiven Anteil der öffentlichen Ausgaben tendenziell zu erhöhen.

Die für die öffentlichen Finanzen primär Zuständigen müssen sich dabei von einigen grundlegenden Tatsachen und Überlegungen leiten lassen:

1. Es gibt natürliche Grenzen für eine gesamtwirtschaftlich noch effiziente Besteuerung. Die Stagnation zuerst, dann der Rückschlag der Einkommen aus Unternehmertätigkeit – der entgegen den Erwartungen der Regierung in diesem Jahr nicht überwunden werden wird – sprechen eine ebenso deutliche Sprache wie die Gefahr, daß ein Anziehen der Steuerschraube den Geldwert oder die Leistungsbereitschaft herabsetzt, wenn nicht beides.
2. Der Deckung des Fehlbetrags der öffentlichen Finanzen, der für 1975 auf rund 55 Milliarden DM geschätzt wird, durch Kreditaufnahme sind ebenfalls Grenzen gesetzt, und zwar weniger durch die bisherige Schuldenhöhe als durch die inflationäre Wirkung, die vom *deficit spending* ausgeht, sobald die Produktionsfaktoren ausgeschöpft sind. Das ist in der gegenwärtigen Rezession noch nicht der Fall; aber allein die wachsenden Zinslasten verlangen weise Beschränkung.

   Eine Bemerkung von Adam Smith ist uns auch hier behilflich, will man die Dinge zurechtrücken: »Über die staatliche Verschuldung können durch Sparsamkeit und Fleiß der Bürger die Lücken wieder aufgefüllt werden, die durch öffentliche Verschwendung und Extravaganz im volkswirtschaftlichen Kapital entstanden sind.«

   Solange der Zunahme der öffentlichen Schulden ein Verzicht der Verbraucher gegenübersteht, tritt die inflatorische Wirkung nicht ein, wohl aber, auf die Dauer, wenn ein Überhandnehmen der öffentlichen Ausgaben im allgemeinen, ihrer konsumtiven Quote im besonderen die Investitionen der Wirtschaft zurückwirft.
3. Inflationskontrolle ist Kostenkontrolle. In keiner Wirtschaftsform und an keiner Stelle – also auch nicht in den öffentlichen Diensten – darf das Gesetz der Kostenminimierung verletzt werden.

So wichtig die Erhaltung einer möglichst großen Zahl von Arbeitsplätzen ist, so gleichberechtigt ist doch die Forderung des Verbrauchers – auch des »Verbrauchers« öffentlicher Leistungen –, daß mit einem Minimum an Aufwand, also mit rationellsten Mitteln und folglich zum günstigsten Preis, gearbeitet werde. Behörden produzieren Dienstleistungen. Die Meinung, der Dienstleistungssektor entziehe sich wegen des hohen Personalkostenanteils der Rationalisierung, ist schlicht falsch. *Alle* Kosten – für die Erzeugung von Waren und für die Erstellung von Leistungen – sind letzten Endes auf Personalkosten zu reduzieren.

Öffentliche Ausgaben sind meist – wenn auch nicht immer – die Folge öffentlicher Aufgaben. Man ist schnell bei der Hand, wenn es darum geht, dem Staat weitere Aufgaben zuzuweisen und Forderungen an ihn zu stellen. Dabei vergißt man: die vom Staat geforderten Leistungen müssen durch Steuern und Abgaben gedeckt werden. Die von der Wirtschaft gezahlten Steuern müssen ihre Deckung in den Preisen finden. Die Preise zahlt der Verbraucher, also wir alle. Was wir nicht bereit sind, unmittelbar zu tragen, was wir vielmehr vom Staat verlangen, drückt sich in der Differenz zwischen unserem Brutto- und Nettoeinkommen aus. Je größer der Anteil des Staates am gesamten Sozialprodukt, je stärker also seine Rolle als Umverteiler, desto undurchschaubarer wird der Prozeß.

Vielleicht haben nicht gerade *wir* nach mehr Staat, nach Verbesserungen, Neuerungen, Reformen gerufen; Gewissensprüfung ist Sache jedes einzelnen. Doch ist die Versuchung der Schlagworte groß. So fiel mir vor kurzem zum Beispiel in einer Zeitschrift für Hochschulpolitik die Mitteilung auf, der bayerische Kultusminister habe von 13000 für 1975 und 1976 neu angeforderten Stellen *nur* 7461 bewilligt bekommen. Der Kommentar lautete: »Wenn der Rotstift im kulturellen Bereich weiter blindlings oder sachfremd angesetzt wird, darf man sicher sein, daß uns ein *Chaos* nicht erspart bleiben wird.«

Eine Nation, die mit den Begriffen Chaos, Katastrophe, Zusammenbruch ... so rasch bei der Hand ist wie die unsrige, zwingt den Staat zum Handeln. Wenn dann allein der Teil I des Bundesgesetzblattes von 1100 Druckseiten im Jahr 1950 auf 3744 Druckseiten im Jahr 1974 anschwillt – Inflationsfaktor 340 –, trifft das den Staatsbürger nicht nur von einer Seite.

Vielleicht läßt sich in dieser Hinsicht etwas von den alten Griechen lernen, denen wir die Demokratie verdanken: In Lokris, so erzählt man, mußten diejenigen »Parlamentarier«, die neue Gesetze vorschlugen, mit einer Schlinge um den Hals zur Abstimmung kommen. Wenn ihr Vorschlag zurückgewiesen wurde, war die Strafe: Tod durch Erdrosseln. Es ist kein Wunder, daß dort zweihundert Jahre lag keine neuen Gesetze eingebracht wurden.

*

Die meisten Demokratien sind nicht etwa an Regierungsfehlern im engeren Sinn dieses Wortes zugrunde gegangen. Sie sind auch nicht durch äußere Feinde vernichtet worden. Vielmehr sind sie unter der Maßlosigkeit der Ansprüche der Trägergruppen demokratischer Macht zerbrochen, an einer Interessenpolitik also, der sich die Parlamente aus Mangel an Einsicht, mehr noch aus Mangel an Entschlossenheit und Mut, nicht entgegengestellt haben. Demokratien überleben nur durch Selbstbeschränkung. Und ich würde mich sehr täuschen, wenn das nicht auch für Unternehmungen gälte, denen ungezügelte Expansion noch nie gut bekommen ist.

Über die öffentlichen Finanzen entscheiden nur vordergründig die Parlamente. Sie, meine Damen und Herren, entscheiden über die Zusammensetzung der Parlamente nach Persönlichkeit und Programm und damit auch über die Prinzipien der Beschlüsse dieser Parlamente. Das heißt: *Sie* entscheiden über das Maß an Ordnung in diesem Land. *(1975)*

Bruchzonen der Gegenwart

UNSER BEITRAG ZUR POLITIK

Der Begriff »Bruchzone« stammt aus der Geologie. So verlockend es gerade heute sein könnte, über Gesteine und über ihren Aufbau, über Kristalle und ihre Struktur, über Lichtbrechung, über die geheimnisvollen Bindungskräfte zu sprechen, die unseren Erdball trotz aller zentrifugalen Momente zusammenhalten, so wären Sie doch in Ihren Erwartungen enttäuscht. Denn das Thema lautet nicht schlechthin »Bruchzonen«, sondern »Bruchzonen der Gegenwart«. Mit Recht nehmen Sie deshalb an, daß wir heute nicht über Erdgeschichtliches sprechen, sondern über Zeitgeschichtliches, über das, was wir Gegenwart nennen.

So gewagt es ist, die Zukunft erkennen zu wollen: Die Gegenwart ist ein dimensionsloser Punkt im Zeitablauf. Wir können den Augenblick nicht zurückhalten. Wir werden von einer Sekunde zur anderen in die Zukunft gestellt. Von der Gegenwart sprechen heißt folglich: in die Zukunft blicken. Alles, was wir heute erleben, alles, was das Heute ausmacht, zeichnet das Morgen vor.

Wenn ich von Bruchzonen in unserer politischen Welt – und damit auch in unserer geistigen Welt, die letzten Endes nicht apolitisch gedacht werden kann – spreche, geht es um Politik im weitesten Sinn des Wortes: nicht um Innenpolitik oder Außenpolitik oder Wirtschaftspolitik oder Parteipolitik. Es geht um Politik als Ordnung des menschlichen Zusammenlebens – um die Ordnung als Prinzip, um die Regeln für die Verwirklichung des Prinzips und nicht zuletzt um die moralischen Maßstäbe.

Von Bruchzonen der Gegenwart zu sprechen, heißt nicht, der falschen Meinung nachzuhängen, gerade heute lebe es sich gefährlich – früher sei alles gut gewesen. Die heile Welt gibt es nicht und hat es nie gegeben. Manches aber läßt vermuten, unser Sinn für das Erfassen, das frühzeitige Erkennen von Gefahren habe nachgelassen.

Spannungsfelder, zu Bruchzonen sich entwickelnd, vergehen nicht, ohne daß Narben zurückbleiben. Wie am Schnittbild der Erdrinde ihre tektonische Geschichte abgelesen werden kann, so hat sich die geschichtliche Entwicklung der Menschheit in die heutige menschliche Substanz eingeprägt. Zu Analyse und Synthese, zu erfolgversprechendem politischen Handeln ist deshalb Geschichtsbewußtsein erforderlich.

Negation der Geschichte ist Zeichen schlechten Gewissens. Vergangenheit kann nicht durch Vergessen bewältigt werden. Die Geschichtslosigkeit, zu der unsere Zeit neigt, sei es, um die Mitverantwortung für Vergangenes, aber Nachwirkendes zu leugnen, sei es, um die Erinnerung an Schlimmes auszulöschen, sei es nur, weil wir Generationen lang versäumt haben, Geschichte so darzubieten, wie sie junge Menschen fesseln und überzeugen kann – diese Geschichtslosigkeit also, die von den Grabenbrüchen der Vergangenheit, von ihren Spuren keine Kenntnis nimmt, mag dazu beitragen, daß aus Mangel an geschichtlichem Wissen, geschichtlicher Erfahrung neue Verwerfungen entstehen. Übrigens kann man auch Staatswesen und Gesellschaft sturmreif machen, indem man sie von ihrer Überlieferung abschneidet.

Mag die menschliche Existenz im letzten Grund auch unabhängig von der politischen Existenz gedacht werden können, so wäre es doch wirklichkeitsfremd, wollte man den Menschen – das *zoon politikón* des Aristoteles – unabhängig von der Politik sehen. Wir haben folglich davon auszugehen, daß die menschliche Existenz als solche untrennbar verknüpft ist mit der politischen Existenz, und wir übergehen den Fall des Weisen, der ungeachtet seines politischen Umfeldes zu leben wüßte.

Dieses politische Wesen, das sich gegenwärtig von Bruchzonen umgeben sieht, muß sich Klarheit darüber verschaffen, wo die Gefahren liegen und wie ihnen zu begegnen ist. Denn wir beobachten eine Aufladung des politischen Spannungsfeldes – im Inneren wie im Äußeren. Ich klammere dabei die weltwirtschaftliche Lage aus – obwohl diese nach Ursache und Wirkung nicht unabhängig von der Politik gesehen werden kann –, weil es in der Geschichte Momente und Konstellationen gibt, in denen das Materielle zurückgestellt werden muß hinter dem Ideellen – Momente und Konstellationen, in denen es nur noch um den Fortbestand des Menschenbildes geht, wie es in langer Geistesgeschichte ausgeprägt wurde.

Nichts wäre befriedigender für den Redner, als wenn er sich in der Meinung irrte, daß die unmittelbar vor uns liegenden Jahre über Freiheit oder Knechtschaft für eine weitere geschichtliche Epoche entscheiden.

*

Nicht die Alltagspolitik interessiert uns heute, soweit wir nicht in ihr Zeichen der Verwitterung, der Auswaschung, der Erosion entdecken, die über den Tag hinausgreifen – Bruchzonen in Theorie und Praxis unserer Staatsform. Frucht des abendländischen Nachdenkens über die beste, die dem Menschen am besten gerecht werdende Staatsform – zweieinhalb Jahrtausende des Nachdenkens, des Verwirklichens, des Innehaltens, des Vergessens und des Rückbesinnens – ist die Idee der Demokratie: in persönlicher Freiheit wurzelnd, offen, durchsichtig, lauter, gerecht.

Wir werden diese notwendigen Eigenschaften der Demokratie nach Gedanke und Wirklichkeit im einzelnen betrachten. Die Erscheinungsformen dürfen uns dabei weniger beschäftigen als vielmehr die Ursachen: Wie sind die Spannungen entstanden, wie wurden sie ausgelöst? Sind die Grenzflächen dergestalt, daß eine Zusammenführung denkbar ist? Ist ein Brückenschlag möglich? Vorab stellt sich dann die Frage: Hat es einen Sinn – oder ist es nur eine besondere Form geistiger Inzucht –, wenn wir unter uns Nachrichten tauschen, die längst bekannt sind, wenn wir Erkenntnisse aussprechen, an denen niemand von uns zweifelt, wenn wir uns gegenseitig bestätigen, daß Staat und Gesellschaft in noch größerer Gefahr sind, als sie es schon immer waren? Es *hat* einen Sinn, *falls* es gelingt, die Lauen unter uns aufzurütteln, diejenigen, die dabei sind zu resignieren – und wie oft gerät jeder von uns in Anfechtung!

Unternehmer neigen dazu, ihre wirtschaftlichen Probleme, die Sorgen, wie es weitergeht, die Frage, ob man morgen noch von einer Unternehmerwirtschaft sprechen kann, unter sich zu behandeln. Übereinstimmung, daß es so nicht weitergehen kann, ist dann meist schnell erreicht. Ich wende mich aber heute nicht etwa an Unternehmer, um ihre politischen und wirtschaftlichen Befürchtungen zu bestätigen. Ich spreche auch nicht als Unternehmer, sondern als Bürger dieses Staats, und ich versuche zu Menschen zu sprechen, ungeachtet ihrer Zugehörigkeit zu dieser oder jener Schicht der Nation, nicht um zu klagen, nicht um Forderungen zu stellen, vielmehr um die Bruchzonen zu markieren und einzugrenzen.

Wenn gerade in der Politik die Spannungen schärfer hervortreten als in anderen Lebensbereichen, so ist das Bestimmen des eigenen Standortes um so notwendiger, freilich auch folgenschwerer und nicht ohne Wagnis möglich. Damit ist nicht die positive oder negative Fixierung auf bestimmte politische Weltanschauungen gemeint. Wer für Liberalität eintritt, muß ein besonders hohes Maß an Duldsamkeit gegenüber den Denk- und Handlungsweisen anderer aufbringen, solange nicht jene Grenze erreicht ist, an der sich die Geister scheiden. Man blicke im übrigen nicht bloß in *eine* Himmelsrichtung, wenn man die Feinde der Freiheit sucht. Sie sind weder ganz noch überwiegend nur in bestimmten Quadranten zu finden.

Was versucht werden soll, ist die Bestätigung eines Prinzips, das ich einmal als »politische Moral« bezeichnen möchte, die eine Voraussetzung für eine Gesellschaft darstellt, die vor eben diesem moralischen Gesetz bestehen will. Zumindest in einem Punkt müßte die Gesellschaft sich einig sein oder werden: daß nämlich die einmal von der Gesellschaft angenommenen Grundregeln der politischen Moral so lange gültig sind, als sie nicht einverständlich geändert werden.

*

Dies vorausgeschickt, müssen wir uns darüber klar werden, daß die Art und Weise, in der wir über unsere Verhältnisse gelebt haben und noch leben, politisch unmoralisch ist, weil zu Ungerechtigkeit führend und die Tragfähigkeit der Demokratie erschütternd. Wir sind auf diese Art der Bruchzone nahegekommen. Mitgespielt hat dabei die Verbreiterung des Fächers: War für Jahrhunderte und Jahrtausende der Staat der allein Fordernde, so tritt nunmehr neben ihm die Gesellschaft auf, die nicht zögert, eigene Forderungen zu stellen und zur Forderung führende Erwartungen bei ihren Mitgliedern hervorzurufen.

Jedoch kann »die Gesellschaft« nicht für sich in Anspruch nehmen, ihr als dem größeren Ganzen komme größere Bedeutung zu als ihren Mitgliedern. Denn daß das Ganze mehr sei als die Summe seiner Teile, ist nicht generell erweislich. Die Gesellschaft ist keine Sublimierung des Menschen. Sie ist nicht die ideale Fortsetzung des Individuums. Sie ist Werkzeug – und dies versteht sich, wie man in großem Ernst einsehen muß, in doppeltem Sinn: Werkzeug ihrer Mitglieder zur Erfüllung von Bedürfnissen, die das Individuum nicht außerhalb der Gemeinschaft befriedigen kann, aber auch mißbrauchtes Werkzeug weniger zur Verwirklichung politischer Ziele. Nicht die Gesellschaft ist fähig zu denken; die großen Gedanken sind von Menschen gedacht worden; der Zeitgeist, fälschlich der Gesellschaft zugeschrieben, wird nicht vom Kollektiv erzeugt.

Der Apotheose der Gesellschaft wird die Ernüchterung folgen. Nirgends ist der Personenkult größer als dort, wo man den Vorrang der Gesellschaft fordert. Eine Gesellschaft aber, die das Individuum vernachlässigt, wird allenfalls die Perfektion eines Ameisenstaates erreichen. Von Selbstverwirklichung kann in ihr keine Rede sein.

Was wir heute brauchen, ist folglich nicht etwa mehr Gesellschaft, sondern – im Schoß der Gesellschaft – mehr Individualität. Nach der Erforschung der Gesellschaft kommt es jetzt darauf an, den Menschen zu entdecken. Ziel darf nicht der austauschbare Mensch, der genormte Mensch sein. Die von freiheitsliebenden Völkern bevorzugte Staatsform der Demokratie setzt unabhängige, denkfähige, individuell geprägte Staatsbürger voraus.

Die Theorie der Gesellschaft scheint bei allem weiter entwickelt zu sein als die Theorie der Demokratie. Eine schlüssige Rechtfertigung der Mehrheitsentscheidung steht noch immer aus. Wir sind bereit, in Kauf zu nehmen, daß Mehrheitsentscheidungen sachlich nicht immer die klügsten, die besten, die weitsichtigsten sind – dem Ideal der Demokratie zuliebe. Aber dürften wir auch hinnehmen, daß die Rechte der Minderheit durch die Mehrheit in Frage gestellt oder beseitigt werden? Daß 51 von 100 die übrigen 49 unterdrücken? Würden wir das anerkennen, so wäre Demokratie reduziert, degradiert auf das Recht des Stärkeren. Demokratie verlangt, wenn man der Bruchzone fernbleiben will, Konsensus darüber, daß es keiner Mehrheit zusteht, die Grundrechte der Minderheit zu verletzen. Selbst dann aber, wenn es in der Demokratie dazu kommen sollte, daß Rechte der Minderheit beeinträchtigt werden, gäbe es noch immer *eine* unabdingbare moralische Forderung an die jeweils herrschende Partei oder Parteienkoalition: daß sie ihre Absichten offenzulegen hat. Jede andere Regierungsform mag aus taktischen oder aus strategischen Gründen – vielleicht aus Gründen der Selbsterhaltung – ihre wahren Absichten im dunkeln lassen. Demokratie aber verlangt Offenlegung politischer Vorhaben.

Unaufrichtigkeit wäre das Ende der Demokratie, noch bevor sie ihre Reife überhaupt erreicht hat. Sie kann ihre Aufgabe nur in der Wahrheit erfüllen; denn die Unwahrheit ist der Gegner der Gerechtigkeit. Wie steht es mit dieser Aufrichtigkeit, wenn innerhalb einer Regierungspartei von der Analyse der Notwendigkeit »demokratischer Massenmobilisierung gegen die Struktur des bestehenden Staats« gesprochen wird? Prominente Mitglieder dieser Partei haben sich von diesem Widerspruch zum Grundgesetz losgesagt; die Bruchzone ist damit aber doch kaum verdeckt.

Wie steht es mit der Aufrichtigkeit jener Bewegungen, von denen wir vermuten müssen, daß ihnen Humanität – sie führen das Wort oft genug im Munde – etwas anderes bedeutet als uns: wenn sie sowohl die »Diktatur des Proletariats« als auch die »Abschaffung jeglicher Herrschaft von Menschen über Menschen« fordern? Natürlich kennen wir die dialektischen Bemühungen, die Diktatur des Proletariats als eine unvermeidliche und sogar bedauerliche Übergangserscheinung darzustellen. Problematisch wird diese Dialektik jedoch dann, wenn die Diktatur die Liquidation der Klassenfeinde weit überdauert und wenn dies alles im Zeichen der Demokratie geschieht. Verräterisch wird es gar, wenn die *Volks*-Demokratie bemüht wird.

Demokratie, richtig verstanden, ist kein Lehrsatz, sondern ein Werkzeug. Sie ist das beste aller denkbaren politischen Werkzeuge, wenn auch kein vollkommenes. Sie ist nicht von Natur aus, nicht ohne Bemühungen gerechter als andere Regierungsformen, aber sie birgt in sich eine größere Chance zur Gerechtigkeit als jede andere. Man darf jedoch in der aktuellen Demokratisierungsdiskussion nicht übersehen: sie würde sich selbst in die Arme fallen, wenn man sie auf Räume und Gebilde ausdehnte, die ihrer Natur nach unpolitisch sein müssen; Kampf der »Demokratien« gegeneinander würde dann unvermeidlich.

*

Viele sehen Demokratie und Egalität als gegenseitig bedingt an. Die Naturgeschichte des Menschen zeigt aber, daß Egalität nie war und daß sie auch nicht in uns vorgeprägt ist. Jedenfalls kann Egalität – die Gleichheit wiederum nur für die Gleichen bedeuten würde – nicht durch naturwidrigen Mehrheitsbeschluß herbeigeführt werden. In diesem Zusammenhang fällt mir eine kürzlich gefallene Bemerkung Carl Friedrich von Weizsäckers ein: »Gleichbehandlung kann eine Benachteiligung sein.«

Demokratie ist nur in einer freien Gesellschaft möglich. Kann es eine freie Gesellschaft geben, in der die Freiheit des Individuums nicht gewährt ist?

Freiheit und Eigentum sind nicht unabhängig voneinander zu denken. An einer Theorie des Eigentums, die wesentlich hinausgeht über die bloße Rechtfertigung des urgeschichtlichen Triebs, die Beute zu behalten, fehlt es noch.

Das Grundgesetz formuliert den Eigentumsgedanken pragmatisch; Gegner des Eigentums versuchen es zu mißbrauchen. Anhänger und Verteidiger können einräumen: so wie es keine Freiheit an sich gibt, keine Freiheit auf dem Rücken der Unfreiheit anderer, so kann es in der menschlichen Gesellschaft auch kein Eigentum ohne Verpflichtung geben.

Wir alle sind Wanderer in dieser Welt, Glieder in der Generationsfolge – damit sind die Grenzen unserer Verfügungsmacht zumindest zeitlich gesetzt. »Rechtmäßig erworben« bedeutet, daß wir beim Erwerb keine Rechte anderer verletzt haben, aber es bedeutet nicht, daß wir bei der Nutzung Rechte anderer verletzen dürften. Will man jetzt aber einen Wesensunterschied machen zwischen »Nutzungsrecht« und »Verfügungsrecht« am Eigentum, so ist das eine Verharmlosung, ja, ein Täuschungsversuch: verdecktes Ziel ist die Beseitigung des persönlichen Eigentums und damit die Beseitigung eines entscheidenden Bestandteils der persönlichen Freiheit, welche die Chance materieller Unabhängigkeit voraussetzt.

Wenn die Freiheit bis zu ihrer Negation geht, das heißt bis zur Aufgabe der Freiheit, wird der Begriff »Freiheit« seines Inhalts beraubt. Es ist nicht ausgeschlossen, daß wir uns diesem Punkt nähern, daß wir dabei sind, unsere Freiheit zu verspielen, indem wir die Auslegung des Begriffs auf die Spitze treiben.

Unbedingte Freiheit zu verlangen stünde dem Staatsbürger nicht gut an; eine solche Forderung wäre ein weiterer Beitrag zu der in Gang befindlichen Entmannung des Staats. Es ist folglich notwendig, den Begriff Freiheit zu relativieren, das heißt, an die Umstände von Ort und Zeit anzupassen, aber zugleich gefährlich, den absoluten Anspruch aufzugeben: Für den Leninisten ist Freiheit nicht mehr als ein bürgerliches Vorurteil (ein Hinweis, den ich Viktor Achter verdanke).

Politische Freiheit bedeutet: sein eigenes Leben, seinem Gewissen folgend, ohne Beeinflussung leben zu können, innerhalb und außerhalb einer bestimmten Gesellschaft, ohne daß man Nachteile auf sich nehmen muß, wenn man sich innerlich frei fühlt von dieser Gesellschaft, eine Freiheit also, die in ihrer Grundlegung nicht materieller Natur ist.

In ihrer Vollendung führt diese Freiheit zum Verzicht auf Freiheiten aus eigenem Entschluß. Unverzichtbar ist jedoch das Verlangen des Staatsbürgers nach offener und wahrer Unterrichtung über Tatsachen und Absichten. Freiheit und Desinformation schließen sich gegenseitig aus.

Zur vollständigen und richtigen Information, aber auch zum politischen Ethos gehört es, daß der Staatsbürger gefordert wird, daß ihm klargemacht wird, welcher Beitrag von ihm verlangt werden muß, wenn das Staatswesen bestehen und gedeihen soll, daß ihm verdeutlicht wird, daß die politischen Pflichten vor den politischen Rechten kommen. Wird dieses versäumt, so sind wir der Manipulation nahe.

Prognostische Fehlleistungen, gewollt oder ungewollt, sind eine politische Gefahr – nicht in erster Linie, weil sie das Parteienverhältnis verschieben können, sondern weil sie die Urteilsfreiheit des Wählers beschneiden. Hätte das Methode, so müßte man es im Keim ersticken.

Mängel, Lücken in der politischen Information (zu der auch die wirtschaftliche gehört) – die Medien sind daran nicht unbeteiligt. Aber es fällt schwer, die Medien allein verantwortlich zu machen für die Vertiefung der Grabenbrüche. Die Medien werden von uns freiwillig gelesen, freiwillig gehört und freiwillig gesehen. Das ist ein Quasi-Konsensus. In anderen Worten: Die Medien sind wir. Ich weiß, daß dies eine überspitzte Formulierung ist. Aber Medien leben von ihren Lesern, Hörern, Zuschauern, Auftraggebern. Kein Land hat bessere Medien, als es verdient.

*

Die Denaturierung des Unternehmers – ich mache diese Bemerkung nun doch als solcher – stünde bevor, wenn man in dem gegenwärtigen Streit über Investitionslenkung auch nur das kleinste Zugeständnis machte. Wenn ich dieses Stichwort anschneide, so nicht wegen seiner wirtschaftlichen Bedeutung – darüber sprachen andere, besser Legitimierte –, sondern nur wegen der politischen Implikationen. Was nützt es zu beteuern, »die letzte Entscheidung liege beim Unternehmer«, wenn die Weichen, die zuvor liegen, so gestellt werden, daß gar kein Entscheidungsspielraum mehr übrigbleibt? Dann bleibt dem Unternehmer nichts als die Verantwortung für eine Entscheidung, die von anderen Kräften vorgezeichnet ist.

Abwertend bezeichnete man kürzlich die Marktwirtschaft als Ideologie. Während aber Sozialisierung – und Investitionslenkung führt unvermeidlich dorthin – unbestritten zu den Ideologien gehört, handelt es sich bei der Marktwirtschaft nicht um ein Glaubensbekenntnis. Sie ist Instrument, nicht Idol. Ihr steht diametral gegenüber die ideologisch geprägte, das heißt nicht rational fundierte, zentrale Planung, die Raum geben soll für »gesellschaftspolitisch erwünschte Bedarfsdeckung« und für »emanzipativ orientierte Ausgaben«. Aus Erfahrung wissen wir, wie rasch Planung des Bedarfs in Planung des Mangels umschlägt.

Sicher, es gibt Befürworter der Investitionsdeckung, die keine Enteignungsabsichten haben. Sie wollen lenken, weil sie glauben, alles besser zu können. Die Arroganz der Besserwisser könnte man vernachlässigen, wenn sie nicht in den Chor des doktrinären Hochmuts einstimmten.

Die Beseitigung des auf Kapitalbildung beruhenden Systems der Marktwirtschaft wäre ein tiefer Rückfall in dunkle Zeiten – nicht allein wegen der unvermeidlichen wirtschaftlichen Nachteile, sondern in erster Linie wegen der Beschneidung der politischen Rechte des Verbrauchers, wegen seiner Entmündigung.

*

Konservative sind nicht fortschrittsfeindlich. Sie bauen Fundamente für den Fortschritt. Der nur Progressive zaubert den Fortschritt aus dem Ärmel: Seifenblasen, Luftschlösser, leere Versprechungen. Konservativ heißt, das Bestehende zu erhalten, soweit es tragfähig ist für den Fortschritt. In einer Zeit gedankenloser Vernachlässigung und gewollter Zerstörung des Gebauten ist schon die Erhaltung des Erhaltenswerten ein Fortschritt.

Der hohle Glaube an den Fortschritt, an das Gute des Fortschritts, ist ein Erbe, das uns aus dem 18. und 19. Jahrhundert überkommen ist, kein gutes Erbe. Wer Veränderung will, muß beweisen, daß sie Sinn hat. Der Schritt nach vorne darf nicht in die Tiefe führen. Fort-Schritte: ja. Aber wir brauchen Gegenwart und Vergangenheit als Trittplatten. Der unreflektierte Glaube an Fortschritt, Wachstum, Größe korrumpiert. Es gibt viele Arten der Korruption – in dem weiteren Sinn dieses Wortes: Sittenverderbnis.

Lange, zu lange Perioden ungedämpften Wachstums verwöhnen Unternehmer und Arbeitnehmer, verzerren Proportionen, verwischen Konturen und verstellen den Blick auf das Wesentliche, das Notwendige, das Mögliche. Sie verbergen die Gefahr, die jeder Gesellschaftsform, jeder Wirtschaftsform droht, die zu lange vorherrscht, ohne daß sie sich dauernd bewähren muß. Schlägt der Wind um, kommt rauhes Wetter auf, naht die Stunde der Bewährung, stellt sich heraus, wer die Wetterkarte lesen konnte und wer gegen den Wind aufkreuzen kann.

Verwöhnt sind wir alle. Verwöhnt ist der Staat, der seinerseits die Wahlbürger verwöhnt. Hier wird es zulässig, von einer Korrumpierung zu sprechen, die mehr als ein Staatswesen in den Bankrott führte, was in vielerlei Gestalt vor sich gehen kann. Die Gegenwart bietet Beispiele.

Freilich fällt nicht jede öffentliche Finanzmisere in die Bruchzone. Es gibt Konstellationen, in denen es legitim ist, Defizite zu machen, um größeren Schaden vom Gemeinwesen abzuwenden. Bedenklich wird es, wenn der Fehlbetrag auf Wahlversprechen zurückgeht – soweit man solche überhaupt einhält – oder dem Kampf um den Wähler dient, noch bedenklicher, wenn die finanziellen Schwierigkeiten auf der Forderung von Gruppen beruhen, von denen der Staat sich abhängig gemacht hat.

Steuererhöhung kann in gewissen finanziellen Situationen nicht nur notwendig, sondern auch zweckmäßig sein. Ihre Beurteilung hängt nicht so sehr vom Hundertsatz ab als vielmehr von der Verwendung des Aufkommens und von der Wirkung auf die künftige wirtschaftliche Leistungskraft. Steuern können die Vermögensverteilung im tragbaren Maß verbessern, können aber auch insgeheim – und hier sind wir wieder an einer Bruchstelle – auf Konfiskation, Liquidation der Freiheit hinauslaufen. Es gibt hier einen *point of no return*.

Chancen zu versprechen, ohne Leistung zu verlangen, verwöhnt, verdirbt, korrumpiert. Die Bildungspropaganda hat dies getan, hat uns in eine Bruchzone geführt. Gewiß hat Bildung einen menschlichen Eigenwert. Niemand ist unter uns, der auch nur *einem* Menschen nicht die Chance der Bildung im Sinne der Selbstverwirklichung vergönnte – vorausgesetzt, daß ein aktiver Prozeß in Gang gebracht wird, daß die Bildungsinhalte verarbeitet, nicht nur rezipiert werden, vorausgesetzt also, daß ein eigener Beitrag, eine eigene Leistung erbracht wird. Wird das Bildungsangebot nicht verbunden mit der Leistungsforderung, so ist es unlauter.

Die Stimmen, die sich rechtzeitig vor der Verkündung des bildungspolitischen Programms in der Bundesrepublik erhoben haben, um auf die Irrealität der Vorstellungen hinzuweisen, wurden überhört. Wirtschaftliche Restriktionen sprachen und sprechen ebenso gegen dieses ehrgeizige Programm wie die Sorge, daß Berufs- und Lebenserwartungen geweckt würden, die in der beruflichen Struktur des Landes kein Spiegelbild finden. Wer warnte, wurde als Gegner der Chancengleichheit markiert. Die Ernüchterung mußte kommen. Flucht aus der Wirklichkeit, Lebensangst, Berufsnot – induziert durch Versprechungen, Illusionen, Traumvorstellungen von Politikern – haben die Chancen nicht gleicher, sondern eher ungleicher gemacht.

Das Motiv der Bildungsphilister des 19. Jahrhunderts, »Bildung macht frei«, genügt nicht, um die Bildungspolitik des letzten Jahrzehnts zu rechtfertigen: Bildung genügt nicht zur Erhaltung der Freiheit, wenn der Wille zur Freiheit fehlt.

Leistung im Bildungswesen, in der Wirtschaft, im Leben ... Der Bundeswirtschaftsminister hat dazu letzter Tage in Wiesbaden gesagt: »Wer sich was leisten will, muß vorher was leisten.« Eine Woche früher hatte ich zu dem gleichen Thema vor der Deutsch-Brasilianischen Handelskammer in São Paulo erklärt: »Einer der grundlegenden ökonomischen Irrtümer unserer Zeit ist, man könne sich leisten, was man sich leistet, auch wenn man sich mehr leistet, als man selbst leistet.«

Als Individuum mag man den Sinn seines Lebens, seine Lebensaufgabe in einer Tätigkeit zum Beispiel in der Verwaltung, in der Wissenschaft, im Kulturleben oder in der Wirtschaft sehen – mit Recht *so lange*, als ein politisches System vorausgesetzt werden kann, das alle Kräfte einer pluralistischen Gesellschaft duldet und fördert. An eine Bruchzone würden wir gelangen, stünde eine Periode bevor, in der eine verschwindend kleine Schicht das Ruder der Politik in die Hände bekäme, eine Schicht, die Politik als Lebensaufgabe betrachtet, und zwar eine Politik, in der Toleranz nicht geduldet werden will und nicht geduldet werden kann.

Es bleibe dahingestellt, welchen Bekenntnisses diese neue politische Schicht sein könnte. Zu ihrer Charakterisierung genügt, daß Politik ihr Schicksal ist und daß sie – sofern keine Gegenkräfte auftreten – Politik auch zum Schicksal aller Zeitgenossen machen wird. Kein Lebensbereich wird dann noch seiner Eigengesetzlichkeit folgen können. Der Primat der Politik wird sich vielmehr in extremer Weise durchsetzen.

Wir haben heute in den westlichen Demokratien eine vergleichsweise ideale Kräfte- und Machtverteilung. Allenfalls kann jene Schicht, die den unbedingten Vorrang der Politik nicht nur theoretisch, sondern faktisch beansprucht, geltend machen, die Machtgier des derzeitigen Systems zeige sich darin, daß es die Usurpation durch demokratisch nicht legitimierte Kräfte verhindere. Ironie ändert aber nichts an der Unerbittlichkeit der gegen die Freiheit stehenden Kräfte, jener Utopisten, die sich frei nach Gracián von der Leidenschaftlichkeit der Sehnsucht (nach Macht) mehr versprechen als von der Lauheit des Besitzes (an Freiheit). Ob sie die Revolution wollen oder nur die Systemveränderung – wie groß wäre der Unterschied? Beides heißt und meint Umwälzung.

In unsere Lebenszeit fallen blutigste Revolutionen in allen Kontinenten. Unblutige sind nicht unbedingt humaner als blutige. Fehlt es uns an dem Einfühlungsvermögen für das Leiden, das mit jenen unblutigen Revolutionen verbunden ist: vertrieben, enteignet, ohne

Verfahren unterdrückt, zum Schweigen gebracht, verhaftet ... Vielleicht läßt man an dieser Stelle Leszek Kolakowski sprechen – an Stelle eines Deutschen. Dieser polnische Marxist und Philosoph, der sein Land 1968 verließ, nachdem er aus der Kommunistischen Partei ausgeschlossen worden war, schrieb, wie man in der Juni-Ausgabe des *Encounter* lesen konnte: »We must not be fervent moralists in some cases and *Realpolitikers* or philosophers of world history in others, depending on political circumstances ...«

Kann man – die Frage drängt sich auf – aus der kürzlichen Reaktion gegen ein westliches Land die Hoffnung schöpfen, daß in Zukunft gleiches Recht für alle gilt, auch wenn es sich, um mit der *Neuen Zürcher Zeitung* zu sprechen, zum Beispiel *nur* um die Einweisung Oppositioneller in eine psychiatrische Klinik handelt?

*

Spannungen in der Erdrinde führen zum Bruch. Ob es gelingt, in der menschlichen Geschichte mit dem vor uns stehenden Dunkel fertig zu werden, wird letztlich davon abhängen, ob es gelingt, die bestehenden Spannungen zu beseitigen oder zu überbrücken.

Spannungen sind freilich auch Quellen der Kraft. Gefälle legen Kräfte frei. In der Vergangenheit konnte manche Spannung durch technische Innovation überwunden werden. Beobachtungen zeigen aber, daß sich der große technische Fortschritt nicht kontinuierlich vollzieht, sondern in Stufen. In der Spannungslage, in der wir uns heute befinden, kann folglich nicht auf Innovation gewartet werden. Wir sind auf andere Wege angewiesen.

Die Versöhnung der Gegensätze zwischen den Schichten, aber auch zwischen Gesellschaft und Individuum, ist ein Idealziel. So notwendig der Kompromiß ist, so gibt es doch eine Grenze der Verständigungsmöglichkeit – keine scharf gezogene Linie, vielmehr eine »Pufferzone«. Jenseits dieser Bandbreite bedeutet Verständigung Selbstaufgabe. Toleranz ist nur so lange ein Zeichen der Stärke, als sie sich selbst eine Grenze dafür setzt, wo sie aufhören muß, um sich nicht selbst zu gefährden. Liberalität, die so weit geht, dem Gegner die Zerstörung der Freiheit zu erlauben, ist nichts als Schwäche. Die Gegner der Freiheit sind, aus Dogma, aus Strategie, aus Taktik, erfolgreich intolerant. Sie sprechen endgültige, unwiderrufliche Urteile – über Gedanken, Dinge, Menschen – im Zeichen der Humanität.

Was die geschichtlich ebenfalls intoleranten christlichen Religionen immerhin kennen: die gute Tat, die Bekehrung, die Erlösung durch Gnade, geht der totalitären Religion des 20. Jahrhunderts ab, die nur die lebenslange Strafe kennt, allenfalls mit der Begnadigung zum Tode.

Unsere Gegner sind Kämpfer. Sie aktivieren Gefühle auf Grund kühler, plausibler, einleuchtender psychologischer Erkenntnisse. Sie sind nicht nur Strategen und Taktiker, sie sind Techniker der Macht. Sie sind wenn nicht klug, so doch intelligent. Vor allem sind sie systematisch. Sie denken und handeln folgerichtig, von einer klaren Zielsetzung aus. Es hieße aber ihre Intelligenz überschätzen, wenn man ihnen auch unsere mangelnde Wachsamkeit zurechnete – im Sinne Churchills, der einmal gesagt haben soll, man überschätze die Klugheit des Fuchses, wenn man ihm auch die Dummheit der Hühner zugute halte.

Überleben ist nicht nur Schicksal, sondern – sofern und solange wir an Willensfreiheit glauben – Selbstbestimmung. Gemeint ist nicht ein Leben als Trauma des geschichtlich Erlittenen, nicht ein Leben des eschatologisch zu Erleidenden, vielmehr ein bewußtes, auf die Bewältigung der Gefahren eingestelltes und eingerichtetes Leben.

*

Bruchzonen kennzeichnen heißt: Nachdenken hervorrufen, aus der Überzeugung heraus, daß die politische Willensbildung zunächst der Erkenntnis bedarf, vielleicht sogar von dem Glauben geleitet, daß denkendes Wollen zum wollenden Handeln werden kann.

Wenn die Politik und ihre Moral auf dem Spiel stehen, sind wir alle angesprochen, und wenn es uns um Aufrichtigkeit zu tun ist, müssen wir uns fragen: Haben wir selbst, als Individuen, unsere Pflicht getan, unseren Beitrag zur Politik geleistet?

Die Einrichtung des Ablasses ist seit Luther überholt. Es wäre ein Rückfall, wenn man glaubte, man könne sich seiner politischen Pflicht durch einen Ablaßkauf entziehen. Gefordert ist persönliche Mitwirkung, *Mitbestimmung!*

Politische Aktivität heißt nicht: Sprung in die große Politik. Teilnahme an der Politik heißt (wir sollten es endlich lernen), an der Basis mitzuwirken: dort, wo Meinungen gebildet werden, dort, wo die Personen ausgewählt werden. Teilnahme an der Politik heißt, in den Parteien, in den Gemeinden, Kreisen und Bezirken, in allen öffentlichen Einrichtungen mitzuwirken, überall dort, wo Information gefragt ist, wo Auffassungen entstehen, wo es um Gesinnungen geht, gleichgültig, ob es sich um unmittelbar oder mittelbar Politisches handelt.

Nichts spricht für einen Weltuntergang, der sich im Zeitlichen abspielen könnte. Alles spricht dafür, daß wir den Mut aufbringen, den Erscheinungen des Verfalls, wie sie in allen geschichtlichen Epochen zu beobachten waren, entgegenzutreten, nicht mit dem Mut der Verzweiflung, sondern mit dem Mut der Hoffnung.

Was wir auf alle Fälle lernen müssen, wenn wir überleben wollen: unsere Neigung zu unterdrücken, das Drohende gerade dann aus dem Bewußtsein zu entfernen, wenn es im Grunde als unvermeidlich erkannt ist.

*

Unsere Gedanken kreisten heute abend um Gesellschaft und Mensch, um Freiheit und Gerechtigkeit, Gerechtigkeit ist ein leicht verletzliches Gut. Jakob Wassermann – in seinem schönen Beitrag zum 50. Geburtstag von Hugo von Hofmannsthal – empfindet sie als

»bindende Kraft im kristallenen Element«. Wolle man sie greifen, so müsse man »still werden wie ein Wasser in der Ebene, in dem sich nichts als der Himmel spiegelt«.

Der außergewöhnliche Mann, dem wir den heutigen Abend verdanken und dem wir mit diesem Abend danken wollen für das, was er der *res publica* war und beispielgebend noch ist, ohne dabei seine Identität, seine Individualität einzubüßen: Sie, sehr verehrter Herr Schneider, sind kein Geologe, kein Kristallforscher – ein Mann aber, für den die kristalline Transparenz des Porzellans, aus Erde geformt und im Feuer gereift, eine symbolhafte Bedeutung gewonnen hat.

Dies erinnert mich daran, daß man mir – dem Unkundigen – einmal gesagt hat, die wichtigste Regel des Sammlers sei: Porzellan nimmt man in beide Hände. Freiheit ist so transparent, so aus sich selbst leuchtend und so zerbrechlich wie Porzellan. Wir müssen sie in beide Hände nehmen, wenn wir sie bewahren wollen. *(1975)*

Die Ordnung des Wettbewerbs

GEDANKEN EINES KAUFMANNS ZUM RECHTS- UND WIRTSCHAFTSSYSTEM

Im Mittelhochdeutschen war »reht«, von dem sich unser Wort Recht ableitet, noch das, was man zu leisten *und* zu fordern hatte, also Recht und Pflicht. Es ist deshalb nicht nur etymologisch, sondern auch sinngemäß dem lateinischen »regere« näher als dem »ius«, bei dessen Übersetzung die Deutschen auf die indogermanische Wurzel »reg-« zurückgegriffen haben. Vielleicht stand dabei der Gedanke Pate, daß regeln, gestalten besser, vernünftiger ist als verbieten. Jedenfalls darf ein Staat, der eine bestimmte Wirtschaftsordnung will – in unserem Fall die durch Wettbewerb gekennzeichnete Marktwirtschaft –, sich nicht darauf beschränken, ganz oder überwiegend durch Verbote charakterisierte, auf die Vermutung straffälligen Verhaltens abgestellte Gesetze zu erlassen (die in der Form von Geboten mehr zur Motivation der Rechtssubjekte beitragen würden, ohne darum die Sphäre der Passivität zu verlassen). Vielmehr sollte er in erster Linie gestalten, indem er durch seine Politik Voraussetzungen schafft und Impulse gibt, ohne selbst zu wirtschaften.

Vor mir liegt das gegen Reichsmark erworbene, im April 1948 auf bräunlichem Zeitungspapier gedruckte Buch »ORDO I«, in dem es heißt, daß nur die »Veranstaltung von Wettbewerb ... eine volle Lösung des Problems der Wirtschafts- und Sozialordnung zu erbringen« vermöge. Damit »auch eine volle Lösung der wichtigsten sozialen Fragen«. Walter Eucken läßt in diesem Band die Frage des »Wie« noch offen: »Nun also ist es nötig, von Grund auf die Lenkungsfrage, wie sie sich in der modernen Welt in concreto stellt, zu erfassen.

Und diese Fragestellung führt zu den Lenkungsformen und zu dem Denken und Handeln in Ordnungen.« Daß es Eucken dabei um weit mehr als um Gesetzgebung ging, wurde ein Jahr später deutlich, als der Weg zwischen »ORDO I« und »ORDO II« zurückgelegt war: »Der Staat hat die Formen, das institutionelle Rahmenwerk, die Ordnung, in der gewirtschaftet wird, zu beeinflussen, und er hat Bedingungen zu setzen, unter denen sich eine funktionsfähige und menschenwürdige Wirtschaftsordnung entwickelt. Aber er hat nicht den Wirtschaftsprozeß selbst zu führen.«

Die Bedingungen, von denen Eucken spricht, kann der Staat ohne große Mühe herstellen, soweit es sich um Akte der Gesetzgebung handelt. Aber damit ist es nicht getan, solange und sofern nicht die Voraussetzungen dafür gegeben sind, daß die Ziele der damit angestrebten Ordnung von allen, die der betreffenden Rechtssphäre angehören, wenigstens im Prinzip erreicht werden können. Zu den Voraussetzungen für die Erreichung des Ziels wirtschaftlicher Gesetze gehört ein dem Gesetzeszweck adäquates Wirtschaftssystem. Nach einem Zusammenbruch der Lebensmittelversorgung in Krisenzeiten zum Beispiel hat der Staat das Recht verwirkt, den Kartoffeldieb zu bestrafen. Ein Gesetz ist also überall dort, wo es auf die *Gestaltung* einer Ordnung ankommt – und das gilt insbesondere für alle wirtschaftlichen Komplexe –, nicht mehr als ein Entwurf, eine Ideenskizze, ein Pflichtenheft, ein Auftrag – weit entfernt von der Verwirklichung.

*

Auch in der Bundesrepublik sind wir vom Idealzustand der von uns vertretenen, weil wirksamen und gerechten Marktwirtschaftsordnung weit entfernt. Dafür gibt es mehrere Gründe; von zweien soll kurz die Rede sein:

1. Der Staat betreibt eigene Geschäfte. Unternehmen in Staatshand haben, als Kategorie in der Zeit des Merkantilismus geboren, den Laisser-faire-Liberalismus den 19. Jahrhunderts überlebt – ge-

nauer gesagt: Sie feierten schon im Laufe des 19. Jahrhunderts fröhliche Urständ, wodurch der Spielraum privater Unternehmen erheblich eingeengt wurde. Man denke dabei an die administrierten Preise, die die kostenpolitische Freiheit des Unternehmers um so mehr begrenzen, als er im Regelfall dem Angebot der öffentlichen Hand an Leistungen auf den Gebieten des Verkehrs, der Nachrichtenübermittlung oder der Versorgung mit Elektrizität, Gas und Wasser ausgeliefert ist – Monopolen gemeinhin, deren Preise sich in den letzten Jahren rascher erhöht haben als das Niveau der Preise industrieller Produkte, weil einem Angebot in einer Hand oder, bestenfalls, in verhältnismäßig wenigen Händen eine nicht oder kaum organisierbare Nachfrage gegenübersteht. (Die Lage auf den Weltrohstoffmärkten wird bei dieser Betrachtung unberücksichtigt gelassen.)
An dieser Stelle muß angemerkt werden, daß die Versicherung, das Verhalten der Unternehmen am Markt sei unabhängig von der Zusammensetzung ihres Gesellschafterkreises, unbegründet, ja schlicht falsch ist. Denn nicht nur dort, wo Staatsunternehmen ein Monopol besitzen oder monopolähnliche Vorteile genießen, stellt nicht-marktgerechtes Verhalten die weithin zu beobachtende Regel dar – wobei dahingestellt bleibe, ob auf Grund politischer Weisung oder mangelnder Führungseignung der Verantwortlichen oder einfach, weil Defizite unternehmensfremd gedeckt zu werden pflegen (also auf Kosten der Allgemeinheit statt zu Lasten der Leistungsempfänger). Auch solche Unternehmen in öffentlicher Hand, die sich durchaus im Wettbewerb befinden, legen oft ein Verhalten an den Tag, das weder dem Grundsatz höchster Wirtschaftlichkeit entspricht, noch dem Erreichen einer Marktbalance aus gleicher Startlage heraus gerecht wird.

2. Die Belastung der Wirtschaft durch den Staat ist beunruhigend gewachsen. Der sogenannte Staatsanteil – roh definiert als derjenige Teil des Bruttosozialprodukts, der zunächst Bund, Ländern und

Gemeinden zufließt und von ihnen investiert, konsumiert oder umverteilt wird: Steuern, öffentliche Abgaben, Sozialbeiträge – hat sich inzwischen auf mehr als 47 Prozent erhöht und geht in berechenbarer Zeit auf die Hälfte des Bruttosozialprodukts zu, wenn diesem Trend nicht begegnet wird. Der Staatsanteil verengt den Entscheidungsfreiraum der Unternehmen nicht nur graduell, sondern auch essentiell; es ist nicht ausgeschlossen, daß sein weiteres Anwachsen zu Ausweichbewegungen, zu Reaktionen führt, die nicht notwendigerweise das Gesetz brechen, aber doch die angestrebte Ordnung gefährden können.

Hier wird nicht die dem sozialstaatlichen Gedanken adäquate Höhe des Staatsanteils kritisch erörtert – es geht zunächst lediglich um die Tatsache, daß eine Marktwirtschaftsordnung nur funktioniert, wenn sie über eine finanzielle Manövriermasse verfügen kann, die ausreichend groß ist im Verhältnis zu dem Teil, der ihr nicht unterliegt. Die Funktionsfähigkeit hängt aber auch von der Zahl der Marktteilnehmer ab, weshalb die Zusammensetzung des Staatsanteils fast noch wichtiger ist als seine Höhe, weil sie, vor allem was die Steuern angeht, die Existenz der kleinen und mittleren Unternehmen beeinflußt. Die derzeitige Steuergesetzgebung wird diesem Gesichtspunkt nicht gerecht; diese kritische Bemerkung bezieht sich unter anderem auf die zunehmende Last ertragsunabhängiger Steuern.

Die Finanzwissenschaft kennt den Begriff der Kostensteuer. Sie meint damit, vereinfacht ausgedrückt, diejenigen Steuerarten, die in die Kostenrechnung des Unternehmens eingehen und von denen der Gesetzgeber vermutet, daß sie auf den Abnehmer abgewälzt werden. Daß die Unterbringung eines Kostenelements in der Kalkulation im Falle von Verlustpreisen keine faktische Abwälzung bedeutet, wird in der Erörterung der Frage meist übersehen, was den Unternehmer insofern ehrt, als man offensichtlich annimmt, er sei tüchtig genug, um zumindest Kostendeckung zu erreichen. Mit der Wirklichkeit stimmt das nicht immer überein, und das ist für die Sicherheit der Chancengleichheit im Wettbewerb von Bedeutung – sowohl im Binnen- als auch insbesondere im Außenhandel. Die Erhöhung von Kostensteuern ohne Rücksicht auf die De-facto-Abwälzbarkeit beschränkt den Handlungsraum des Unternehmers.

Ungeachtet der Problematik der Abwälzbarkeit ist im Zusammenhang mit der Steuerlastquote – oder mit dem Staatsanteil – ein viel weitergehender Begriff der Abwälzung zugrunde zu legen: Strenggenommen muß der Unternehmer insofern jede Steuerart als Kalkulationselement verwenden. Denn bei der Bemessung der angestrebten Gewinnspanne, die für die Substanzerhaltung des Unternehmens und damit für sein Überleben entscheidend ist, hat der Unternehmer auch die Höhe der Steuern zu berücksichtigen, die auf Ertrag und Vermögen erhoben werden. Eine Steuerpolitik, die die Wettbewerbsordnung nicht im Auge hat, gefährdet sie.

*

Ordnungspolitische Gefahr droht indessen auch von einer anderen Seite – von der Zahl der Gesetze. Winston S. Churchill hat sich dazu drastisch geäußert: »Wenn man zehntausend Vorschriften erläßt, vernichtet man jede Achtung für das Gesetz.« Davon sind wir in der Bundesrepublik nicht mehr so weit entfernt, wie wir gerne glauben möchten; auf jeden Fall stiftet der Umfang der gesetzlichen Vorschriften bereits Verwirrung und Unsicherheit, was sich an der überall in der Wirtschaft zu beobachtenden Vergrößerung der Rechts- und Steuerabteilungen gut ablesen läßt. Tatsächlich war das Bundesgesetzblatt im Jahre 1975 etwa fünfmal so stark wie 1950, ohne daß es dem Bürger auch nur annähernd um so viel besser ging (Umfang des Bundesgesetzblattes 1950: 1100 Seiten: 1975: 5601 Seiten). Allein zwischen 1969 und 1973 wurden beinahe 500 Steuergesetze, -verordnungen und -richtlinien erlassen sowie unzählige Urteile des Bundesfinanzhofes verkündet, die mehr als 4000 Druckseiten füllen.

Dabei sind die Vorschriften der Europäischen Gemeinschaft – jährlich immerhin über 3000 (in Worten: dreitausend!) – nicht einmal berücksichtigt. Vor diesem Hintergrund verheißt die altrömische Sentenz »Pessima tempora plurima leges», wenn man sie frei übersetzt: »Je schlechter die Zeiten, desto mehr Gesetze«, für die Gegenwart nichts Gutes.

Die Welt durch Gesetze zu verbessern, ist ein uralter Traum der Philosophen. Ihnen mag das verziehen werden; bei unseren Politikern sollte, kann man weniger Nachsicht walten lassen. Liest man, daß wir ein Verbandsgesetz brauchen, ein Insidergesetz, eine Novellierung des Fusionsrechts, so ist das bestürzend, weil dadurch die Illusion der »Machbarkeit« genährt, das Vertrauen in die Kräfte der Selbstheilung gefährdet wird – vor allem aber, weil Parlament und Regierung sich selbst in dem Glauben wiegen, mit dem Erscheinen eines Gesetzes im Bundesgesetzblatt ihre Pflicht im wesentlichen getan zu haben, während gerade legislative Akte wirtschaftlicher Natur nur dann Leben gewinnen, wenn die Politik in allen ihren Facetten sich darauf einstellt.

Der Hang zur Gesetzgebung – den man als »Beruf unserer Zeit« bezeichnen könnte – geht auf eine Reihe von Ursachen zurück. Sieht man von der Betriebsamkeit ab, die nicht selten vordergründige politische Ziele verfolgt, so wird einerseits Mangel an Selbstvertrauen der Politik, andererseits Mangel an Vertrauen in die Mündigkeit und Bildungsfähigkeit des Staatsbürgers erkennbar. Nur am Rande sei auf die Fälle verwiesen, die einen Mangel an Um- und Weitsicht beim Entwurf der bestehenden Gesetze offenbaren. (Jene Mängel können ihrerseits wiederum Folgen von Betriebsamkeit sein.) Die dadurch allzu häufig notwendig werdenden »Reparaturen«, die auf Ungeduld des Gesetzgebers, der Verwaltung und der Interessengruppen beruhende, fast ununterbrochene Neigung zu Änderungen und Erweiterungen, die Bemühungen um (vermeintliche) Vervollkommnungen, die Ergänzung der Gesetze durch Regierungsverordnungen und Verwaltungsanordnungen, durch Richtlinien, Anweisungen und Rundschreiben erlauben die Vermutung, daß Legislative und Exekutive über die einzuschlagenden Wege unsicher sind, wenn nicht sogar befürchtet werden muß, daß dabei Zielkonflikte ausgetragen werden.

Die Unsicherheit des Gesetzgebers erzeugt Unsicherheit beim Staatsbürger; sie verleitet ihn unter Umständen auch dazu, den Mangel an fester Haltung auszunutzen. Rechtssicherheit ist ein Anspruch des Staatsbürgers, der sich der Staatsgewalt vor allem deshalb unterwirft, weil er weiß, daß gleiches Recht für alle anstelle des Rechts des Stärkeren nur in einem staatlichen Gefüge durchsetzbar ist. Aber diese »Unterwerfung« ist ethisch und faktisch eben nur zu begründen, wenn Rechtssicherheit verbürgt wird.

Rechtssicherheit hängt nicht zuletzt von den ordnungspolitischen Vorstellungen ab, die mit Hilfe von gesetzlichen Vorschriften verwirklicht werden sollen. Deshalb kann beispielsweise die Pflicht des Unternehmers, sich der Wettbewerbsordnung zu fügen, nicht einseitig gedacht werden. Es steht ihr eine Pflicht des Staates gegenüber, die Voraussetzungen für die Wirtschaftsordnung zu schaffen. Der Staat, stark genug mit Hilfe der Parlamentsmehrheit, kann, das wissen wir, Gesetze auch dann erlassen, wenn die Bedingungen für ihre gerechte – das heißt allgemeine, den Grundsatz der Gleichheit wahrende – Anwendung nicht erfüllt sind. Die Verfassung verbietet ihm den Erlaß unrealistischer Gesetze nicht, und es wird immer wieder versucht werden, das Unmögliche zu erreichen, nämlich Gesetze zu schaffen, die ihrer Substanz, ihrem Wesen, ihrer Verfahrensweise nach den Realitäten nicht entsprechen.

Droht der Gesetzgeber dem Einbrecher Strafe an, so erwartet man nicht, daß jeder Einbruch aufgeklärt, jeder Einbrecher bestraft wird. Aber erwartet wird, daß er Vorkehrungen der öffentlichen Sicherheit trifft, die Einbrüche nach Möglichkeit verhindern, zumindest erschweren, potenzielle Rechtsbrecher entmutigen und zum Rechtsbrecher Gewordene ihrer Strafe zuführen. Gelingt das nicht in einem

Maß, daß die Öffentlichkeit davon überzeugt, daß hinter dem Gesetz der Wille steht, seine grundsätzliche Anwendung zu erzwingen, so schwindet das Gefühl der Rechtssicherheit.

Wir sprechen über Wettbewerbsordnung und stellen die Frage, ob es genügt, wenn der Gesetzgeber tätig wird, indem er ein Gesetz erläßt und die für seine Anwendung erforderliche Behörde einrichtet. Vom Standpunkt eines Kaufmanns aus ist das Gesetz zwar eine notwendige, aber keine zureichende Bedingung dafür, daß das Ziel der Wettbewerbsordnung erreicht wird.

Wenn der Staat im Gesamtgefüge seiner Rechts-, Finanz-, Wirtschafts- und seiner Sozialpolitik, seiner Handels-, ja seiner Außenpolitik das von ihm gesetzte Ziel eines geordneten Wettbewerbs nicht zur Maxime seines Handelns macht, reduziert sich der Gedanke der Wettbewerbsordnung auf Maßnahmen der Verwaltung und der Rechtsprechung.

Darüber hinaus verlangt, nein: bedingt Rechtssicherheit Verständlichkeit des Gesetzes für alle Staatsbürger. Es gehört zu den vornehmsten, wenn auch oft vernachlässigten Pflichten des Gesetzgebers, sich so auszudrücken, daß selbst der Nicht-Jurist Gebote und Verbote sowohl in ihrer Einbindung in die Rechtsgrundlagen als auch in ihrer Verknüpfung mit den jeweiligen anderen Rechtssphären verstehen kann. Die Meinungen darüber, ob in dieser Hinsicht das Erreichbare erreicht ist, können nicht auseinandergehen. Wer als juristischer Laie die legislative Arbeit seines Lebenskreises und seiner Lebensspanne beobachtet und dabei auch einen Blick in die Geschichte und über die Grenzen wirft – vor allem auf das Ende des vergangenen Jahrhunderts so klar formulierte BGB und hinüber in den romanischen Rechtsraum, aus dem, wie ein Leuchtturm, der Code Napoléon herausragt –, findet, daß die Flut der Gesetze ihrer Sprache nicht gut bekommen ist.

Die Frage drängt sich auf, wo die »haarscharfe Genauigkeit« geblieben ist, die ihr noch Gustav Radbruch in seiner 1914 erschienenen »Rechtsphilosophie« bescheinigen konnte. Die »Kälte« und »Armut«, die er ihr bezeugte, würde der Staatsbürger gern in Kauf nehmen, wenn Begreiflichkeit, Unmißverständlichkeit, wegweisende Klarheit, Substanz an die Stelle der Abstraktion träte. Fordert man Rückkehr zum Grundsatz sprachlicher Genauigkeit – was nicht einmal im Widerspruch zu einem gewissen Maß an Bildhaftigkeit stünde –, so resultiert das aus der Beobachtung, daß Denkvorgang und sprachlicher Ausdruck untrennbar sind. Unklarer Ausdruck ist Zeichen unklaren Denkens.

Wer mit dem Wettbewerbsgesetz zu tun hat, weiß freilich – daran ändert der vorangegangene Exkurs in das Rechtsdenken und in die Rechtssprache nichts –, was gewollt wird. Es gibt keine sprachphilosophischen Ausflüchte, und der Sinn des Gesagten ist nur, dem Gesetzgeber und seinen Beratern nahezulegen, bei der Fortgestaltung des Wettbewerbsrechts auf Vervollkommnung zu verzichten, dagegen aber das Gewollte klar auszudrücken und der Rück- und Querverweisung zu entraten.

Denn je mehr es dem Gesetzgeber gelingt, seinen Willen klar auszudrücken, desto größer ist die Aussicht, daß ein Gesetz vom Staatsbürger »angenommen« wird. So wie es rechtsgeschichtlich eine Rezeption gibt, so wäre es ein rechtspsychologischer Fehler, zu verkennen, daß die Verständlichkeit eines Gesetzes seine Wirkung befördert und umgekehrt – unabhängig davon, ob die wirklichen oder scheinbaren Interessen der Betroffenen beeinträchtigt werden.

*

Hier wird nicht auf philologischem Umweg einer Ordnung das Wort geredet, in der die Wirtschaft ihre Interessen erst dem Gemeinwohl opfert, um dann selbst zum Almosenempfänger zu werden. Auch im Wohlfahrtsstaat – oder gerade in ihm! – gibt es Grenzen der Staatswohlfahrt, deren Überschreitung gefährlich, destruktiv, widersinnig, systemwidrig wäre. Unternehmen dürfen sich nicht auf die Hilfe des

Staates verlassen; es wäre eine *contradictio in adiecto,* wenn sie auf den Staat bauten.

In Johann Gottlieb Fichtes »geschloßnem Handelsstaat« findet sich ein Hinweis, der nicht nur dem Unternehmer, sondern jedem Staatsbürger sagt, an wem es liegt, wenn es ihm nicht gutgeht – nämlich an ihm selbst. Fichte sieht das im Rahmen seiner Utopie, der er wohl nicht lange anhing, das heißt, er sieht das im Rahmen einer Wirtschaftsordnung, die Chancengleichheit verbürgt, auch wenn zu seiner Zeit der letztere Begriff noch nicht bekannt war.

In seinem Handexemplar hat Arthur Schopenhauer die Stelle angestrichen, wo Fichte sagt, es sollten zwar alle »ohngefähr gleich angenehm leben können«, aber »keineswegs müssen«. Und: »Es muß nur an ihm selbst liegen, wenn einer unangenehmer lebt, keineswegs an irgend einem andern.« Unter der Voraussetzung, daß der Staat nicht nur die Grenzen des Spielfeldes zieht, sondern auch die Regeln setzt und auf ihre Einhaltung achtet, sie nötigenfalls weiterentwickelt, wenigstens aber geänderten Verhältnissen anpaßt, überhaupt für die Ordnung in einem allgemeinen Sinn eintritt, sorgt der Unternehmer für sich selbst.

Zu den Voraussetzungen, die der Staat zu schaffen hat, gehört auch die Notwendigkeit, europäische Maßstäbe an das Wettbewerbsrecht anzulegen. Es ist widersinnig, wenn nicht, in moralischer Betrachtung, widerrechtlich, in einem Lande wie der Bundesrepublik, die sich der freien Einfuhr aus allen Teilen der Welt weiter geöffnet hat als alle anderen Wirtschaftsgebiete und in die sich, rechtlich und tatsächlich ungehemmt, beliebig große Warenströme aus anderen Ländern ergießen, Marktanteile nach wie vor so zu berechnen, als lebten wir in dem »geschlossenen Handelsstaate« Fichtes, als herrsche Importbeschränkung, Währungsbewirtschaftung und Hochzoll. Eine der Wirklichkeit entsprechende Anwendung und Auslegung des Gesetzes würde nicht so sehr europäischen Geist als vielmehr gesunden Menschenverstand beweisen.

Es rührt jedenfalls an die moralische und faktische Existenz, wenn das Recht der Europäischen Gemeinschaft, soweit es auf die Angehörigen der Mitgliedsländer anwendbar ist, ohne Rücksicht auf die besonderen Umstände praktiziert wird, die sich aus der verbleibenden Souveränität der Mitgliedsländer und aus ihrer historischen Struktur ergeben. Unzumutbar wäre folglich die Anwendung des Wettbewerbsrechts der Europäischen Gemeinschaft auf Unternehmen, die in Mitgliedsländern ihren Sitz haben, ohne Ansehung ihrer komparativen Wettbewerbsfähigkeit, die eine Funktion ist sowohl des Standes, den die Wettbewerbsordnung juristisch und faktisch in den einzelnen Ländern erreicht hat, als auch der übrigen wirtschaftspolitischen und wirtschaftsrechtlichen Tatsachen.

Dieser Überlegung liegt kein »Fall« zugrunde, sondern die deduktiv gewonnene Überzeugung, daß das Recht der Europäischen Gemeinschaft wirksam nur angewendet werden kann nach Maßgabe des jeweils »europäisch Erreichten« und des »europäisch Erreichbaren«. Andererseits ist die Zielrichtung der Europäischen Gemeinschaft und die Aufnahme wettbewerbsrechtlicher Vorschriften schon in die ihr zugrunde liegenden Verträge eine nachdrückliche Aufforderung an alle Beteiligten, in Fragen der Wettbewerbsordnung nicht mehr partikularistisch, sondern europäisch zu denken.

Solche Überlegungen münden nicht selten in die Forderung, das europäische Wettbewerbsrecht dem amerikanischen anzupassen – Forderungen, die vor allem in der Bundesrepublik laut werden. Denn die »Gebildeten unter den Deutschen sind von wenigem so überzeugt wie von der Überlegenheit des angelsächsischen Rechtssystems über das deutsche« (Johannes Gross). Aber das amerikanische Wettbewerbsrecht hat andere Wurzeln und Ursachen als seine europäischen Nachahmer. Zu begreifen ist es nur aus der Zeit seiner Entstehung, der zweiten Hälfte des 19. Jahrhunderts, in der ein grenzenloser Kontinent, während eines vom »Frontgeist« geprägten Jahrhunderts des Vordringens in neue Wirtschaftsräume, der individuellen wirtschaftlichen Entfaltung freies Spiel gelassen hatte – weit entfernt von staatlicher Aufsicht oder auch nur systematischer Beobachtung.

Eine Unternehmerwirtschaft, noch nicht durch Reflexion ihrer gesellschaftlichen Stellung und der politischen Folgen ihres Handelns bewußt, hatte wichtige Märkte in wenige Hände gebracht und mußte sich nun Mißbrauch wirtschaftlicher Macht vorhalten lassen; es gab keine gesetzliche Handhabe. Die Unbedingtheit des amerikanischen Wettbewerbsrechts, seine Bemühungen um Lückenlosigkeit und die Härte, mit der es angewandt und durchgesetzt wird, erklären sich aus der Situation, die mit der unsrigen nicht vergleichbar ist. Die Übertragung seiner Strenge auf das kleinräumige Europa wäre um so weniger konsequent, als es aus einem Rechtskreis stammt, dessen Grundsätze und dessen Verfahrensweise von den kontinental-europäischen essentiell verschieden sind.

Nur in einem Punkt läßt sich die amerikanische mit der europäischen Entwicklung vergleichen: Es waren hier wie da Unternehmer, die die Grenzen eines Kontinents ausloteten, in ihm einen einheitlichen Wirtschaftsraum sahen, den es zu erobern galt – auch wenn der amerikanische Unternehmer zunächst eher als Produzent, der europäische dagegen als Händler auftrat. Es sei, um das zu beleuchten, eine Abschweifung in die Antike erlaubt. Dem Altmeister ihrer Wirtschaftsgeschichte, dem aus Kiew stammenden Michael Rostóvtzeff, verdanken wir die Erkenntnis, daß es nicht griechische Krieger oder Priester waren, die zuerst über das Schwarze Meer kamen und deren Spuren in Südrußland zu finden sind, sondern griechische Kaufleute, die – im Sinne Platons – »die Aus- und Einfuhr zu besorgen« hatten.

Wir gehen nicht fehl in der Annahme, daß Platon im »Staat« nicht etwa einen Idealzustand, sondern eine Tatsache beschrieb, die bereits geschichtlich geworden war: Der Unternehmer jener Zeit, der Kaufmann, hatte die Aufgabe, für den Ausgleich von Überschüssen und Fehlmengen lebenswichtiger Bedürfnisse zu sorgen. Man kann bei Rostóvtzeff nachlesen, daß dieser sich »mit wenigen Ausnahmen durch das Gesetz von Angebot und Nachfrage« vollzog.

Bedarf und Nachfrage auszugleichen, ist auch heute die Kernaufgabe des Unternehmers; das gilt gleichermaßen für Industrie, Handel und Bankgewerbe. Dieser Ausgleich funktioniert – so die Erfahrung der Praxis, wenn auch in der Theorie nicht unangefochten –, sofern er sich im Markt abspielt, sofern die Gesetze des Marktes beachtet werden und sofern dieser Markt seinerseits unter dem Gesetz einer Wettbewerbsordnung steht.

Man kann sich nur schwer einen Kaufmann vorstellen, der die Entartungsformen des Wettbewerbs im Sinne von Wilhelm Röpke als für die Gesamtwirtschaft brauchbare Mechanismen ansähe. Das bedeutet nicht zwingend, daß er in seinem eigenen Handeln nicht immer wieder versucht wäre, die Bandbreite zu testen, die die Wirtschaftsordnung vorgibt. Aber er weiß, daß die Zukunft der Marktwirtschaft und damit seine Zukunft davon abhängt, daß »Wettbewerb veranstaltet« wird. Deshalb ist er an der Ordnung des Wettbewerbs vital interessiert – an einer Ordnung freilich, die seinen, durch von ihm nicht beeinflußbare Umstände begrenzten Handlungsraum beachtet, ihn nach Möglichkeit wieder ausweitet und die der höheren Umlaufbahn einer politisch ganzheitlichen Lösung zustrebt, sich also nicht auf der engen Bahn positivistischer und damit partieller Betrachtung bewegt. *(1976)*

Die Kräfte der unbelebten Natur

ZUM GEDÄCHTNIS VON ROBERT MAYER

Als ich vorschlug, die 109. Versammlung der Gesellschaft Deutscher Naturforscher und Ärzte unter das Zeichen des Heilbronner Arztes und Naturforschers Robert Mayer zu stellen, war ich mir wohl seiner schwäbischen Herkunft und wissenschaftlichen Leistung, nicht aber seiner tiefen, für ihn teilweise schmerzlichen Beziehungen zu unserer Gesellschaft bewußt. Heute wissen wir, daß Mayer mit ihr viel mehr verbindet, als es zunächst den Anschein hatte. Denn er besuchte von 1858 bis 1869 nicht nur sechs ihrer Versammlungen, sondern betrachtete die Einladung zum Vortrag auf der Innsbrucker Tagung als den Höhepunkt seines Lebens.

Damals, am 18. September 1869, waren 27 lange Jahre vergangen, seit seine »Bemerkungen über die Kräfte der unbelebten Natur« in den von Justus von Liebig herausgegebenen *Annalen der Chemie und Pharmacie* erschienen waren. Obwohl Mayer in diesem Aufsatz als erster das Gesetz von der Erhaltung der Energie, und damit eines der Prinzipien der modernen Physik, formuliert hatte, blieb ihm die Anerkennung zunächst versagt. Das mag man darauf zurückführen, daß er für die Veröffentlichung auf Liebigs Annalen angewiesen war, die nicht zur Pflichtlektüre der Physiker gehörten. Bei dem Redakteur von Poggendorfs Annalen, die von den Physikern gelesen wurden, hatte der physikalische Autodidakt keinen Anklang gefunden. Auseinandersetzungen mit Helmholtz (auch dieser hatte bekanntlich als Arzt begonnen) und mit Joule traten hinzu. Erst als der Widersacher Helmholtz, der Mayers Anspruch anfangs hartnäckig bestritt, einräumte, dem Arzt aus Heilbronn gebühre die Priorität, häuften sich die Ehrungen, unter denen sich schließlich zwei Ehrendoktorhüte und der königlich-württembergische Adelsbrief befanden.

1863 wurde Mayer zum ersten Dr. rer. nat. der Welt promoviert – von derselben Universität Tübingen, die ihn ein Vierteljahrhundert zuvor relegiert hatte, weil neben seiner »unschicklichen Kleidung« seine Zugehörigkeit zu einer allzu fortschrittlichen Studentenverbindung unliebsam aufgefallen war. Man sieht, das gab es schon in früheren Zeiten. Ich füge an, daß der renitente Student von einst in den revolutionären Wirren von 1848/49 als Anhänger der Monarchie galt und in Sinsheim, während des badischen Aufstandes, als royalistischer Spion denunziert, nur knapp einem Standgericht der Freischärler entging. Alles in allem war es aber eine unpolitische Natur, die in erster Linie ihren wissenschaftlichen Neigungen nachging.

Die Gesellschaft Deutscher Naturforscher und Ärzte – das kann und darf in diesem Zusammenhang nicht verschwiegen werden – ehrt mit Robert Mayer freilich nicht etwa nur den bedeutenden Wissenschaftler, der aus dem Lande stammt, dessen Hauptstadt 1976 Gastgeberin ihrer 109. Versammlung ist. Sie schmückt sich auch nicht bloß mit dem Bilde eines Mannes, den sie,weil er ihre Tagungen besuchte und an ihrer Arbeit Anteil nahm, für sich in Anspruch nehmen möchte. Sie bekennt mit dieser Ehrung auch, daß sie ihm Wiedergutmachung schuldet – nicht nur in einem ganz allgemeinen Sinn, stellvertretend für die vielen, die ihn zu Lebzeiten unterschätzten und mißachteten, sondern auch, weil die Physikalische Sektion der 59. Versammlung Deutscher Naturforscher und Ärzte Helmholtz – als habe Robert Mayer überhaupt nie existiert – 1886 in einem Telegramm als Vater des Energieerhaltungsgesetzes feierte.

Mayer ist 1878 im Alter von 63 Jahren gestorben, nachdem er schon zuvor mehrmals totgesagt worden war. An seinem Grabe sagte der Geistliche: »Es ist die Weise der geheimnisvollen Ratschlüsse Gottes über des Menschen Leben, daß die glänzendsten Gaben und Kräfte oftmals in zerbrochene Gefäße gelegt werden« – womit angedeutet war, was dieses Leben verdunkelt hatte. Theodor Heuss, der ihn in seinen »Deutschen Gestalten« porträtiert hat, schrieb: »Man blickt mit Schmerz auf die tragischen Jahre, da sich … ein weltweiter Geist in der Kleinstadtenge wundstößt …« – »Er erfuhr« – so Heuss weiter – »jenes Schicksal des Außenseiters, der, von der Fernwirkung seines Gedankens gepackt, vergeblich auf Echo wartet, und dann, als doch die Frage die Menschen zu bewegen beginnt, nicht seinen, sondern andere Namen hört.«

Robert Mayer teilt das Schicksal, verkannt zu werden, mit anderen Forschern. Denn es entstehen in manchen Phasen der wissenschaftlichen Entwicklung neue Gedanken und Entdeckungen in vielen Köpfen zugleich, als ob es einen Zeit- und Weltengeist gebe, der die Durchbrüche heranreifen läßt. Häufig genug fällt es dann den Zeitgenossen schwer, die Prioritäten richtig zu erkennen, den Lorbeer gerecht zu verteilen, und Auseinandersetzungen in der Öffentlichkeit waren und sind nicht selten. Nachdem Leibniz in den Acta Eruditorum des Jahres 1684 erstmals den Calculus, die Differentialrechnung, beschrieben hatte, kam es zwischen ihm und Newton zu jahrelangem Streit, der von Rechtsanwälten geführt wurde; Newton machte geltend, er habe Leibniz im vorangegangenen Briefwechsel auf die Spur gebracht.

Die Geschichte unserer Gesellschaft liefert ein Beispiel dafür, was aufbauende Zusammenarbeit vermag, um Erkenntnisse zu sichern. Man kann bei Max Born nachlesen, daß »die Relativitätstheorie um 1900 sozusagen in der Luft lag«. Im Jahr 1905 publizierte Albert Einstein seine grundlegende Arbeit. Aber es blieb Hermann Minkowski vorbehalten, ihr die endgültige mathematische und logische Darstellung zu geben – und dies geschah in einem Vortrag auf der 80. Naturforscherversammlung 1908 in Köln.

Im Auftreten des Empirikers und Arztes Mayer und des Theoretikers und Physikers Minkowski in den Versammlungen unserer Gesellschaft drückt sich die Spannweite aus, die eine Gesellschaft von Naturforschern *und* Ärzten auszeichnet, also eine Gesellschaft, die sich der übergreifenden wissenschaftlichen Arbeit schon vor anderthalb Jahrhunderten angenommen hat, längst bevor der Begriff der interdisziplinären Forschung geprägt worden war.

So steht auch die 109. Versammlung der Gesellschaft unter einem die Grenzen sprengenden Thema: *Der Mensch und sein Lebensraum – Eingriff und Wandel.* Sprechen wir von Wandel, so könnte noch immer ein Stück Fortschrittsglaube mitschwingen, der doch in vieler Hinsicht kritischer Betrachtung bedarf, seitdem wir nach mancher Enttäuschung gelernt haben – oder gelernt haben sollten –, daß nicht jeder Wandel ein Fortschritt ist – und vielleicht auch, daß nicht jeder Fortschritt Umwälzung bedingt.

Auf das »finstere Mittelalter« blickten wir mit der Überlegenheit der Fortschrittsgläubigen zurück oder herab, ohne uns bewußt zu sein, wie nah wir ihm noch sind. Es ist nicht viel mehr als hundert Jahre her – unsere Großväter waren Zeitgenossen –, daß man Robert Mayer in die Zwangsjacke steckte, um seinen »Größenwahn« zu brechen, den man darin sah, daß er für sich beanspruchte, das Gesetz von der Erhaltung der Energie als erster entdeckt zu haben. Mir scheint die Finsternis zeitlich und räumlich noch nicht so weit von uns entfernt zu sein, als daß wir uns völlig von Mitverantwortung freisprechen könnten, und es gibt Hinweise auf die Anwendung der Zwangsjacke auch in unserer Zeit – ich meine das nicht nur in übertragenem Sinn. *(1976)*

Der staatsfreie Raum des Unternehmens

WIRTSCHAFTLICHE UND PERSÖNLICHE FREIHEIT

Der Staat engt den Spielraum der Wirtschaft immer mehr ein, er interveniert immer mehr, er wirtschaftet immer mehr selbst, erwartet aber die Kooperation der Wirtschaft bei der Lösung seiner Probleme. Die Frage ist, ob dieser Bodengewinn des Staates – und der mit ihm verbündeten Organisationen – ein Gewinn für das Ganze ist. In anderen Worten: Wer ist der Verlierer?

Ich stelle die Antwort, als Provokation, an den Anfang: In dem Maß, in dem der Staat wirtschaftet, verliert der Staatsbürger an Freiheit, und ich versuche, dies darzutun, indem ich mich bemühe, Mißverständnisse auszuräumen.

Die Politikfremdheit eines großes Teils der Unternehmer ist für das zwischen Wirtschaft und Politik entstandene Mißverständnis mitverantwortlich – das Mißverständnis darüber, was in der pluralistischen Demokratie angesichts der darin aufgebauten Machtstellungen politisch realisierbar ist, ohne daß die demokratische Position aufgegeben wird, und auch darüber, welcher Beitrag der Wirtschaft zur Lösung politischer Fragestellungen erwartet werden kann und muß, ohne daß dadurch die Grundvoraussetzung marktwirtschaftlichen Denkens und Handelns in Frage gestellt wird.

*

Objektiv meßbar ist das Vordringen des Staates in allen Lebensbereichen an der stetigen Erhöhung des Staatsanteils am Sozialprodukt in den meisten westlichen Ländern. In der Bundesrepublik Deutschland sind die Staatsausgaben von 1965 bis 1975 auf das Dreifache gestiegen. Die Staatsausgabenquote am Bruttosozialprodukt stieg von 36,2 Prozent auf 48,2 Prozent – den geschichtlichen Höchstwert. Gleichzeitig fiel der investive Anteil an den Staatsausgaben um ein Viertel, und der Anteil des Personals im öffentlichen Dienst an der Gesamtzahl der Beschäftigten stieg um ein Fünftel. Jeder sechste Beschäftigte steht jetzt im öffentlichen Dienst.

Setzen wir die Steuereinnahmen im gleichen Land zu der Entwicklung des Sozialprodukts in Beziehung, so erhalten wir für die neueste Zeit folgendes Bild: Im Jahr 1977 nahm das Bruttosozialprodukt um 69,5 Milliarden DM zu, das heißt um 6,2 Prozent. Im gleichen Zeitraum stiegen die Steuereinnahmen um 11,7 Prozent, das heißt um 44 Milliarden DM, und die öffentliche Verschuldung nahm um 31,5 Milliarden DM zu. Die öffentliche Hand verfügte folglich im Jahr 1977 über 75,5 Milliarden DM mehr als 1976 – diese Zahl übertrifft die Zunahme des Bruttosozialprodukts in dieser Zeit um 6 Milliarden DM.

Auch wenn man Staatseinnahmen und Staatsverschuldung auf der einen Seite, die Entwicklung des Sozialprodukts auf der anderen Seite nicht in einen unmittelbaren kausalen Zusammenhang bringen darf, ist doch die Gegenüberstellung der beiden Zahlenblöcke bezeichnend dafür, wie wenig produktiv es ist, wenn dem Staat die Disposition über Geldmittel in einer Größenordnung überlassen wird, für deren erfolgreichen Einsatz ihm Instrumente und Instinkt offenbar abgehen. Jede sinnvoll gezielte, nicht etwa gestreute Steuersenkung an der richtigen Stelle und zum richtigen Zeitpunkt hätte zu einem Mehrfachen an nachhaltiger Zunahme der Produktion geführt, und in einer Phase, in der den Regierungen bestimmter Länder vorgehalten wird, sie unternähmen zu wenig, um die Weltwirtschaft anzustoßen, scheint mir die Beobachtung wichtig zu sein, daß es keine positive Korrelation zwischen Staatsquote und Wirtschaftswachstum gibt, wahrscheinlich aber eine negative.

Weit gefehlt wäre es nun anzunehmen, der geschilderte Trend sei inzwischen gestoppt oder auch nur gemildert worden. Wurde noch am 20. April 1978 bekanntgegeben, die Steuereinnahmen würden im Jahre 1978 nur um 4 Prozent steigen – gegenüber den erwähnten 11,7 Prozent im Vorjahr – und die Steuerquote werde zurückgehen, mußte man schon neun Tage später erklären, daß im ersten Vierteljahr die Steuereinnahmen um 10,1 Prozent zugenommen hätten – dies bei einer Inflationsrate von nur etwa 3 Prozent.

War bisher nur von der Bundesrepublik Deutschland die Rede – weil mir deren Zahlen leichter zugänglich sind als diejenigen der anderen Länder –, so nenne ich jetzt einige Ziffern aus der Steuerstatistik der Europäischen Gemeinschaft in Brüssel. Der Anteil, den der Staat durch Steuern und Sozialbeiträge am Brutto-Inlandsprodukt der neun Länder der Europäischen Gemeinschaft beansprucht, stieg in der Zeit von 1970 bis 1976 beständig von 35,0 auf 38,7 Prozent. Dieser Anteil streut von Italien – Zunahme von 30 auf 33,6 Prozent – bis zum Spitzenreiter, den Niederlanden, die 46,1 Prozent erreicht haben.

Soeben hatte ich für die Bundesrepublik Deutschland von einem Staatsanteil von 48,2 Prozent gesprochen, während Brüssel für dieses Land nur 38,5 Prozent nennt. Die Methoden für die interne Berechnung und für die Berechnung durch Brüssel stimmen nicht überein; der aufwärtsweisende Trend bleibt so oder so der gleiche: Der Staat scheint unersättlich. Wie schwierig es im übrigen ist, Europa zu bauen, sieht man an dem Mangel einer gemeinsamen Zahlensprache, der hier zutage tritt, an dem Mangel einer *lingua franca statistica*.

Gleichzeitig mit dieser Nachricht kam das *Wallstreet Journal* vom 26. April 1978 auf meinen Tisch; ich las dort, großgedruckt, aber natürlich nicht auf die Bundesrepublik Deutschland bezogen: »Lord help us to resist fiscal sin, but not just yet.«

Der französische Finanzminister im letzten Jahrzehnt des alten Regimes in Frankreich, Jacques Necker, schrieb 1791 in seinem

Buch über die »Administration des Finances«, eine Nation sei nur frei, wenn sie das Recht und die Macht habe, Steuern zu billigen oder zu verweigern. Er ging von der für das Jahr 1978 illusionären Vorstellung aus, das Parlament bestehe aus den Steuerzahlern. Das ist, zumindest in der Bundesrepublik Deutschland, längst nicht mehr die Regel. Mehr als die Hälfte der Mitglieder des Deutschen Bundestages gehört dem öffentlichen Dienst an, und alle sind mit ihren Einkünften aus der parlamentarischen Tätigkeit zu einem großen Teil steuerfrei.

Bis jetzt sprachen wir nur von dem Kriterium des Staatsanteils, um handgreiflich zu machen, was »mehr Staat« bedeutet. Außer acht blieb die unmittelbare Betätigung des Staates in der Wirtschaft. Die Beispiele, denen wir in unseren Ländern tagtäglich begegnen, sind anschaulich genug. Wir stoßen auf Regiebetriebe, auf verstaatlichte Unternehmungen oder auf solche, die »nur« nationalisiert sind; wir treffen Unternehmungen an, die scheinbar der freien Wirtschaft zugehören, während die Mehrheit der Anteile oder die Mehrheit der Stimmen de jure oder de facto dem Staat gehören. Viele dieser staatlichen Aktivitäten sind sachbedingt, andere historisch geprägt, und man findet sich mit ihnen ab, seitdem unser kritisches Bewußtsein abgestumpft ist. Der Schatten, der von diesen staatlichen Operationen auf die Idee der Unternehmerwirtschaft fällt, ist um so dunkler, je mehr der Staat sich gezwungen sah, wirtschaftlich tätig zu werden, weil die gestellte Aufgabe von unternehmerischen Kräften nicht oder nicht mehr bewältigt werden konnte.

Wohin immer wir blicken: Tabakregie, Staatseisenbahn, nationalisierte Banken, die Staatshand auf der Kohle, auf dem Öl, auf dem Stahl, in der Chemie, im Schiffsbau, in der Luftfahrtindustrie ... Was am meisten wiegt: die anscheinend unaufhaltsame Bewegung aus Unternehmerhand in Gemeineigentum. Was am meisten bedrückt: daß eine Phase staatlicher Initiative zu eigenem Wirtschaften abgelöst zu werden scheint durch den Ruf nach dem Staat, der nicht etwa nur von den bekannten Anhängern der Sozialisierung, sondern auch von zermürbten Unternehmern kommt.

Dehnt der Staat seine wirtschaftliche Tätigkeit aus, so verliert der Staatsbürger an Boden, an Aktionsraum, und mehr als nur das. Wilhelm von Humboldt drückte das in seinem Aufsatz »Ideen zu einem Versuch, die Gränzen der Wirksamkeit des Staats zu bestimmen« so aus: »durch eine zu ausgedehnte Sorgfalt des Staats« leide »Energie des Handelns überhaupt und der moralische Charakter«. Und weiter: »Daher« nehme »in den meisten Staaten von Jahrzehnt zu Jahrzehnt das Personale der Staatsdiener und der Umfang der Registraturen zu und die Freiheit des Untertanen ab«.

Der Staat als Gesetzgeber, der den Grundsatz verlernt hat: Wenn es nicht notwendig ist, eine Vorschrift zu machen, so ist es notwendig, keine Vorschrift zu machen – der Staat also, der in konfuser Kreativität Gesetze, Verordnungen, Richtlinien, Leitsätze ... produziert, ist gerade in letzter Zeit von allen Seiten so scharf unter die Lupe genommen worden, daß ich mich darauf beschränken kann, den administrativen Wildwuchs eben zu erwähnen, ohne ihn zu analysieren.

Als Reaktion auf die Einengung des unternehmerischen Spielraums muß man es beurteilen, daß der Anteil der Selbständigen im Wirtschaftsleben der Bundesrepublik Deutschland stetig zurückgeht. Da zu den »Selbständigen« auch die Landwirte, die Einzelhändler, die Handwerker, also nicht nur die industriellen Unternehmen, rechnen und in den zuerst genannten Kategorien die Zahl der selbständigen Betriebe zurückgehen *muß*, weil größere Wirtschaftsräume und raschere Verbindungen größere Betriebseinheiten verlangen, kann man nicht den Schluß ziehen, der Rückzug aus unternehmerischer Betätigung sei ausschließlich eine Folge staatlicher Bevormundung, staatlicher Eingriffe und staatlicher Überforderung. Dennoch trifft die Beobachtung zu, daß vielerorts die Wirkungsmöglichkeiten unternehmerisch begabter und befähigter Menschen beschnitten werden, womit man sie aus dem Feld des »Wägen und Wagens« in die Arme einer »sozialen« Sicherheit treibt, die doch auf Dauer eine nur scheinbare ist.

Eine pluralistische Gesellschaft, die nicht nur auf Toleranz aller gesellschaftlichen Schichten eingerichtet ist, die vielmehr aktive Strukturpolitik in einem weitgefaßten Sinn treibt, kann auf das nährende Element – es ist mehr als ein Spurenelement – nicht verzichten, das in der gesellschaftlichen Schicht jener liegt, die bereit sind, ihre Haut zu Markte zu tragen, denen aber durch das Übergewicht des Staates die Flügel beschnitten werden. Dabei hielte ich es für eine gute Finanzpolitik des Unternehmens Staat, die Unternehmerwirtschaft zu erhalten. Wären alle Unternehmungen Staatseigentum, so würden sie auch nicht annähernd die gleiche Pachtsumme zahlen können, wie das der Steuerlast der Unternehmungen in der Marktwirtschaft entspricht.

Die Einengung des Spielraums des Unternehmers zeigt sich auch am Verlauf der Lohnquote und des Verhältnisses zwischen den Einkommen aus unselbständiger Arbeit einerseits, aus Unternehmertätigkeit und Vermögen andererseits. Das »Gegengutachten« zu dem von der deutschen Bundesregierung angeforderten Sachverständigengutachten 1978, das von einigen linksstehenden Wirtschaftswissenschaftlern in der Bundesrepublik Deutschland veröffentlicht wurde und das eine »alternative Wirtschaftspolitik« empfiehlt – eine Wirtschaftspolitik der Intervention, des Dirigismus hin bis zur Vergesellschaftung –, behauptet freiweg, die »Profite« der Unternehmen seien in den letzten Jahren »drastisch gesteigert« worden. Das Gegenteil ist der Fall. Aus dem Monatsbericht der Deutschen Bundesbank für April 1978 ergibt sich, daß die Bruttoeinkommen aus unselbständiger Arbeit von 1970 bis 1977 um 85 Prozent zugenommen haben, das Bruttoeinkommen aus Unternehmertätigkeit und Vermögen aber nur um 60 Prozent. Mit Ausnahme *eines* Jahres – 1976 – lag die jährliche Zunahme der Unternehmereinkommen *unter* der Zunahme der Löhne und Gehälter. Deren Steigerung ging in jedem Jahr über die Produktivitätszunahme weit hinaus – und je größer die Diskrepanz war, desto stärker ist der wirtschaftliche Rückschlag in der darauffolgenden Phase gewesen.

Diese Entwicklungslinie darf zwar nur mit Vorsicht verallgemeinert werden, aber auch wenn man die Zahlen unterschiedlich interpretiert, sind sie kein Ansporn für den Unternehmernachwuchs, der durchaus bereit ist, Freiheit als Wagnis zu nehmen, nicht aber Freiheit als Gefahr.

*

Der Zusammenhang zwischen Lohnerhöhungen und Arbeitslosigkeit ist der Mehrheit der Staatsbürger, bewußt oder unbewußt, klar. Der Wirtschaftsverlauf in der Bundesrepublik Deutschland zeigt über die letzten zwanzig Jahre, daß auf Hochlohnphasen im Abstand von im Mittel zwei Jahren ein Beschäftigungsrückschlag gefolgt ist – Folge verringerter Wettbewerbsfähigkeit im Auslandsgeschäft, nachgebenden Absatzes im Inland und eingeschränkter Investitionsspielräume.

Man kann extrem sagen: Betrachtet man nur den Geldbeutel der Beschäftigten, so ist jede Lohnerhöhung möglich, falls die Allgemeinheit – samt den Lohnempfängern – früher oder später dafür zu zahlen bereit ist. Die Arbeitslosen werden freilich dabei vergessen; das Bündnis derer, die in Arbeit sind, nimmt auf sie in der Lohnpolitik keine Rücksicht.

Wir gehen einmal davon aus, jeder als arbeitslos Gemeldete sei arbeitswillig – wozu natürlich gehört, daß er bereit ist, andere Arbeit, an anderem Ort, zu anderen Bedingungen anzunehmen. Dann haben wir in den meisten europäischen Ländern in der Tat ein Maß an Arbeitslosigkeit, das weniger aus wirtschaftlichen als vielmehr aus politischen und aus menschlichen Gründen nicht hingenommen werden kann; dabei darf nicht übersehen werden, daß die statistische Vergleichbarkeit nicht zureicht.

In der Bundesrepublik Deutschland betrug die Arbeitslosenquote im Mittel des Jahres 1977 4,5 Prozent – das waren immerhin 1030000 Menschen. Welche strukturellen Probleme sich hinter diesem Mittelwert verbergen, ergibt sich einmal aus der Streuung unter den Bundesländern: 5,5 Prozent in Niedersachsen, aber nur 2,9 Prozent in Baden-Württemberg. Noch aussagefähiger aber ist die Gliederung nach den Problemgruppen:

- 11,6 Prozent der Jugendlichen unter 20 Jahren,
- 11,8 Prozent der Arbeitnehmer ab 55 Jahren,
- 16,6 Prozent der Arbeitsuchenden mit gesundheitlichen Einschränkungen,
- 17,1 Prozent der Frauen, die nur Teilarbeit suchten,

waren arbeitslos.

Nichts würde mehr in die Irre führen, als wenn man bei der Bekämpfung der Arbeitslosigkeit von dem trivialen Mittelwert ausgehen würde. Nun hält man uns vor, die sozialistischen Staaten kannten keine Arbeitslosigkeit – darin sei, von allen Zukunftserwartungen einmal abgesehen, ein Vorsprung des sozialistischen vor dem kapitalistischen System zu sehen. Aber hier verwechselt man Quantität mit Qualität. Man verwechselt Recht auf Arbeit, Recht auf Berufswahl und, im Extrem, Recht auf Arbeitsverweigerung mit der nackten Arbeitspflicht.

Die Rezepte für die Überwindung der Arbeitslosigkeit, die man uns aus dem Lager der Planwirtschaft offeriert, sind in ihren Langzeitfolgen nicht zu Ende gedacht. Erhöhung der Zahl der Beschäftigten im öffentlichen Dienst schafft nicht Arbeit, sondern streckt sie bloß – und dies auf dem Rücken der Steuerzahler, die dafür keine Gegenleistung erhalten. Kürzung der Arbeitszeit unter Lohnausgleich erfordert ein außerordentliches Maß zusätzlicher Investitionen in Arbeitsplätze, schafft aber nicht mehr Produktion und verringert folglich den Realanteil aller.

Das schlechteste Rezept von allen wäre der Verzicht auf die Rationalisierung – oder auch nur ihre Verlangsamung. Es wäre weltfremd anzunehmen, darauf könne man sich international einigen. Wer resigniert, verliert also Markt, *er* »vernichtet« Arbeitsplätze (um einmal diese schlimme Formel von der »Vernichtung von Arbeitsplätzen« zu benützen). Das Gegenteil des Gewollten wird erreicht. Binnenwirtschaftliches Denken und protektionistisches Handeln wären die Folgen. Es widerspräche aller geschichtlichen Erfahrung, die Erleichterung, die Vereinfachung der menschlichen Arbeit – und darum geht es bei Rationalisierung – ließen sich weltweit eindämmen. Nur ein Durchbruch des Irrationalen – für den es aber keine Anzeichen gibt – könnte den Sturm des letzten Jahrhunderts auf die Maschine nochmals hervorrufen.

Was haben die Vertreter der Marktwirtschaft dagegen anzubieten?

- Die tatsächliche Lage auf dem Arbeitsmarkt zusammen mit Regierung und Gewerkschaft unvoreingenommen zu analysieren; das Resultat, dessen bin ich sicher, wird uns einerseits enttäuschen, andererseits Hoffnung machen.
- Die Bereitschaft, mit den Gewerkschaften über eine Art von Lohnfindung zu sprechen, die langfristig und antizyklisch, nicht aber kurzfristig und prozyklisch angelegt ist.
- Die Bereitschaft, auf jede Art von Protektionismus zu verzichten, falls die Regierungen für gleiche Startbedingungen und freien Warenverkehr sorgen, Verzerrungen aber beseitigen.
- Die Bereitschaft, weitsichtig zu investieren und damit Arbeitsplätze zu schaffen, falls die Regierungen die Bildung von Risikokapital durch langfristig gedachte Steuervernunft ermöglichen und zum Risiko ermutigen, indem sie die Prinzipien der Marktwirtschaft anerkennen und von Interventionen in die Entscheidungsprozesse der Unternehmungen absehen.

Hier muß ich klarstellen, daß ich von niemandem legitimiert bin, eine solche Bereitschaftserklärung abzugeben. Ich spreche zu beiden Seiten, ich mache Vorschläge, ich setze mich für einen Brückenschlag der Vernunft ein – gegen Interventionismus, gegen Dirigismus, gegen die Allmacht der Anonymität.

*

Dem verstärkten Zugriff des Staates auf die Wirtschaft ist, wie man sieht, bisher der strategische Erfolg versagt. Dennoch verstummt der Ruf nach noch »mehr Staat« nicht. So sagte Heinz Oskar Vetter, er »höre die Gralshüter von Marktwirtschaft und Privatinitiative bereits pflichtgemäß aufschreien: Gewerkschaften wollen noch mehr Staat«. Vetter fuhr fort, er »entgegne in aller Ruhe: So ist es«. Weiter sagte er, die Gewerkschaften huldigten nicht der simplen neo-liberalen Formel: So wenig Staat wie nötig, so viel Privatinitiative wie möglich. Diese Formel sei »sicher im persönlichen Bereich akzeptabel« – ich wiederhole: »akzeptabel«, nicht etwa richtig, zweckmäßig, notwendig, sondern nur eben akzeptabel –, aber schädlich sei diese Formel im Bereich der Wirtschaftspolitik.

Vetter hat recht, wenn er diese Formel als eine Simplifikation bezeichnet. Ich halte es aber für eine Über-Vereinfachung, wenn man schlechthin »mehr Staat« verlangt, solange man weder definiert, was man unter Staat in dieser Hinsicht versteht, welches Staatsverständnis man hat, welche staatliche Wirtschaftsordnung bisher bewiesen hat, daß sie die Bedürfnisse des Staatsbürgers besser, schneller, billiger, kurzum: effizienter decken kann als der Markt. Was wir brauchen, ist nicht »mehr Staat«, sondern allenfalls einen besseren Staat – einen Staat, der seine Aufgaben und seine Grenzen genau kennt, in dem regiert und nicht administriert wird.

Staatlicher Eingriff in die Wirtschaft bedeutet Verminderung des Freiheitsraums nicht nur der Unternehmungen, sondern vor allem der Staatsbürger. Könnte man das erste – unter Verzicht auf das wirtschaftliche Optimum – hinnehmen, so ist doch die Entscheidungsfreiheit des Verbrauchers, des Staatsbürgers, unverzichtbar. Wir sprechen von der Würde des Menschen, von der Humanisierung der

Arbeitswelt – ein Begriffs*inhalt*, den wir uns durchaus zu eigen gemacht haben. Aber es wäre eine Entwürdigung des Menschen, wenn staatliche Bürokratie dem Bürger vorschreiben wollte, was er verbrauchen darf, was zu verbrauchen verboten ist und was er verbrauchen muß. Und – was für den Begriff persönlicher Freiheit schlechthin vernichtend wäre – wenn sie ihm vorschreiben wollte, was er zu lernen (und was er nicht zu lernen), was er zu arbeiten (und was er nicht zu arbeiten) hat, wie lange er arbeiten muß (und wie lange er höchstens arbeiten darf).

Mehr Staat, die schwere Hand eines dirigistischen Staates ist also nicht in erster Linie Zugriff auf die Wirtschaft, sondern Zugriff auf die Person. Der Staat, der Investitionen regelt, regelt auch den Verbraucher. Man kann dann allenfalls sagen, der Staat wisse besser, was dem Verbraucher fromme als dieser selbst. Der Verbraucher jedoch, den man soeben zum mündigen Bürger befördern wollte, fühlt sich entmündigt.

Die Deckung des kollektiven Bedarfs mag durch Dirigismus – und »mehr Staat« *ist* Dirigismus – mit unendlicher Anstrengung möglich sein, die Deckung des individuellen, des eigentlich menschlichen Bedarfs nicht. Die Planung bleibt im Unverbindlichen; der Planer kann in der Regel nicht zur Verantwortung gezogen werden, wenn die Planung nicht stimmt. Sie stimmt nie, solange wir den planungsgerechten Menschen nicht, noch nicht haben.

Die Unfähigkeit der staatlichen Organisation, ihrer Verantwortung gerecht zu werden, tritt überall dort zutage, wo vorprogrammierte Strukturen bestehen, die sich niederschlagen

- in der Unerbittlichkeit und Unnachgiebigkeit ihrer Formalisierung,
- in der Unbeweglichkeit und Lebensfremdheit ihrer Bürokratie,
- in der Illusion, Lebensvorgänge könnten durch menschliche Gesetze abgelöst oder geregelt werden,
- schlechthin in der Vernachlässigung der naturgesetzlichen Er-

kenntnis, daß das Zusammenspiel der Kräfte dieser Welt auf Rückkopplung beruht.

Es gibt keine Planwirtschaft, in der nicht früher oder später Organisation als Eigenwert auftritt – Organisation, die auf sich selbst zielt, und man unterschätze nicht das ungeheure Maß an Herrschaft, das jede organisatorische Struktur aus ihrem Wesen heraus ausüben muß. Überhören wir Karl Popper nicht – er ist kein Anhänger der von uns vertretenen Wirtschaftsform –, wenn er Interventionismus als »äußerst gefährlich« bezeichnet, weil »jede Art der ökonomischen Intervention die Gewalt des Staates tendenziell« vergrößere.

Wenn auch Globalsteuerung ein noch nicht ausgereiftes Werkzeug ist, so ist sie doch das einzige Mittel, das eine gesamthafte Wirtschaftspolitik erlaubt, und das in einer Demokratie, die sich zur Marktwirtschaft bekennt – oder, wenn sie den Mut zu diesem Bekenntnis nicht hat, sie doch praktiziert, weil es nichts Besseres gibt –, erlaubt ist.

Im Gegensatz dazu ist die staatliche Intervention – soweit sie sich überhaupt mit unserer Verfassung vereinbaren läßt – entweder ohne Wirkung, also nutzlos, oder aber, wenn sie Wirkung erzeugt, gefährlich und schädlich. Die Geschichte der Konjunkturpolitik, der Eingriffe in den Konjunkturverlauf zeigt, daß man damit allenfalls symptomatisch, nicht aber kausal wirken kann.

*

Die Kritik am staatlichen Interventionismus hilft nicht weiter, wenn sie zur Negation des Staates als Idee und als Wirklichkeit führt. Wirtschaftsordnung – darauf ist auch eine liberale Wirtschaftsauffassung angewiesen – setzt staatliche Ordnung voraus.

Man muß, wenn man vom Staat spricht, mit der Frage beginnen: Welcher Staat? Was für ein Staat? Staaten in ihrer Machtfülle, in ihrer Allmacht sind für uns eine ebenso bittere Erfahrung wie Staaten in ihrer Ohnmacht. Der Staat kann Hoffnung und Verzweiflung in einem sein.

Meinen wir Platons Staat, Hegels Staat – oder die Staatsmaschine, die uns heute umgibt und die in unser Leben eindringt, es zu erleichtern vorgibt, aber in Wirklichkeit erschwert? Den Staat als eine an sich entstandene Tatsache, die ein Eigenleben angenommen hat, weitab vom Bedürfnis des Staatsbürgers – oder den Staat als ein Instrument, das nach Maßgabe der Verfassung vom Staatsbürger in Anspruch genommen werden kann?

Wie wäre es anders möglich, als daß auch unser Staat, in welchem freien Land wir ihn uns immer vorstellen, einer jener Kompromisse ist, auf denen die Tragfähigkeit unserer Welt überhaupt beruht – Kompromiß insofern, als das Notwendige und das Mögliche in Übereinstimmung gebracht und gegen die Illusion, das Wünschbare, aber Unwirkliche abgegrenzt werden.

Der Staat, von dessen Wirkungsgrenzen wir heute sprechen, ist eine Zweckgemeinschaft, die sich sowohl von dem Gedanken einer bloßen Erwerbsgenossenschaft als auch von dem Ziel rein politischer, möglicherweise usurpierter Macht klar abhebt. Der politische Auftrag, das muß man hier sagen, ist dem Staat und den Parteien, nicht aber anderen Verbänden erteilt. Wenn Gewerkschaften, Studentenschaften, möglicherweise auch Zusammenschlüsse der Unternehmer von einem »politischen Auftrag« sprechen, so befinden sie sich nicht auf dem Boden einer strukturierten Demokratie, sie gefährden vielmehr deren Aufrechterhaltung, weil sie ihrer Natur gemäß, ihrer Zwecksetzung und ihrer Arbeitsweise nach nicht die Gesamtinteressen einer Gesellschaft vertreten können, sondern immer nur partielle Interessen.

Hält man eine Erweiterung des Freiraums der Wirtschaft für notwendig, so ergibt sich spiegelbildlich die Frage nach dem Freiraum des Staates – aus theoretischen, wenn man will philosophischen, aber auch aus durchaus praktischen Beweggründen. Die Wirtschaft ist an der Funktionsfähigkeit des Staates, an seiner Regierbarkeit, an seiner Konzentration auf die politischen Kernprobleme vital interessiert.

Der Politiker in der Demokratie ist abhängig, wir müssen das einräumen, von seinem Wähler; er ist in einem weiteren Sinn des Wortes erpreßbar. Er ist außerstande, rationale Entscheidungen zu treffen, rationale Politik zu machen, solange der Wähler irrational, politikfern entscheidet. Andererseits ist das Geschäft mit der Unzufriedenheit der Massen zwar nicht neu, aber noch immer wirkungsvoll. So ist der Politiker an seinem Los nicht ganz unschuldig.

Ob es möglich sein wird, den Wähler zu »rationalisieren«, bleibt offen. Wer Fortschritt will, muß es versuchen. Ein Durchbruch ist unwahrscheinlich, eine Annäherung aber denkbar, wenn die Parteien das ernstlich wollen. Solange dieser Wille nicht besteht oder nicht wirksam wird, liegt es am Mut, an der Entschlossenheit, kurzum am Charakter der *regierenden* Politiker, ob und inwieweit sie aus ihrer Gesamtsicht heraus unter Respektierung der Demokratie als politischer Grundform bereit sind, rationale Politik gegen emotionalen Wählerwillen durchzusetzen.

So emotional der Wählerwille ist, so irrational ist oft genug der Wille parteilicher Minderheiten, der den agierenden Politiker zu Zugeständnissen zwingt und seinen Freiraum verengt. Eine Regierung nun, die ihre Entscheidungen nicht auf das Mandat stützt, das sie hat, sondern auf das Mandat, das sie sich erhalten, das sie wiedergewinnen will, gefährdet den Gedanken des Staates, dessen Kompetenz über den tatsächlichen oder vermeintlichen Willen der Majorität schon deshalb hinausgeht, weil nichts die gewählte Regierung von der Verpflichtung befreit, die Interessen der Minorität zu beachten. Es ist das hohe Privileg einer demokratisch gewählten Regierung – und hierin liegt ihr Freiraum –, einen Ausgleich zwischen dem objektiv Richtigen und Möglichem und dem subjektiv Gewollten zu schaffen. Das Überleben der Demokratie hängt davon ab, ob die amtierenden Politiker die darin liegende Mutprobe bestehen. Und es hängt davon ab, ob sie einem Staat voll natürlichen Selbstbewußtseins vorstehen, der weder Drohgebärden gegenüber einzelnen Schichten nötig hat, noch sich selbst dadurch in Frage stellt, daß er in mißverstandener Toleranz die Handhabe zu seiner Überrollung liefert.

Wenn er andererseits meint, sich im Massenzeitalter am besten als Wohlfahrtsstaat behaupten zu können, so könnte es sein, daß er die wahren Bedürfnisse des Individuums falsch einschätzt – des Individuums, dem aus Tätigkeit und eigener Vorsorge mehr an Selbstgefühl zuwächst als durch Fürsorge. Ist es freilich in einem auf die Spitze getriebenen Wohlfahrtsstaat ertragreicher, sich von der Arbeit fernzuhalten, als Arbeit zu leisten, so sind die politischen Folgen leicht vorstellbar – Stabilität ist jedenfalls nicht zu erwarten. In den Besorgnissen gegenüber einem Wohlfahrtsstaat liegt kein Widerspruch zu der von allen getragenen Überzeugung, daß der Staat aus materiellen und ideellen Gründen sozial sein muß; er muß, soweit die Kraft zureicht, ausgleichen, wo Gerechtigkeit das verlangt.

*

Diese Tatsachen schränken sämtliche Ansprüche ein. Auch die Wirtschaft muß sich darüber klar sein, daß ihre Anmeldung eines Freiraums nur insoweit und insolange in der Demokratie überhaupt realisierbar ist, als der spätere Nutzen von Vorleistungen – Element jeder »kapitalistischen« Wirtschaftsform, die auf Konsumverzicht als Voraussetzung der Investition beruht – für alle Staatsbürger einsichtig gemacht werden kann. Die Forderung eines Freiraums ist folglich komplex:

- Freiräume für einzelne Elemente der Gesellschaft begrenzen notwendigerweise die Freiheit anderer, sind also nicht ohne Konsensus möglich. Freiraum für sich selbst fordern, bedeutet gleichzeitig, anderen Freiraum zu gewähren.
- Strukturlose Freiheit ist eine Illusion, aber Strukturierung bedeutet die Anerkennung von Hierarchien, die im übrigen eine biolo-

gische Tatsache sind, die sich durch spekulatives Denken vielleicht negieren, nicht aber aus der Welt schaffen läßt.

- Die Verwirklichung von Freiräumen ist an die Bedingung geknüpft, daß sie nicht der Befriedung partieller Bedürfnisse dienen dürfen, keine Reservate an sich sind, sondern Werkzeuge zur Förderung des Gemeinwohls sein müssen.
- Die bloße historische Effizienz einer freiheitlich organisierten und strukturierten Wirtschaft genügt nicht zur Rechtfertigung zukünftiger Freiräume; vielmehr ist die Nützlichkeit marktorientierten Wirtschaftens sowohl theoretisch als auch praktisch jeweils aufs neue nachzuweisen.

Es gibt deshalb keinen Freibrief für eine wirtschaftliche Betätigung, die mit dem Staatsziel nicht im Einklang steht. Wirtschaftliche Freiheit ist nur insoweit möglich, als die Wirtschaft bereit und in der Lage ist, ihre Ziele in die gemeinsamen Aufgaben einzuordnen, die sich der Staat gestellt hat.

Mögen wir auch Zweifel an dem absoluten Staatsbegriff Hegels haben – »die höchste Form des objektiven Geistes ist der Staat« –, so sehen wir doch, daß er die Freiheit treffend charakterisierte, wenn er sie als die »erkannte Notwendigkeit« bezeichnete, wobei ich die Erkenntnis und die daraus folgende Freiwilligkeit des *notwendigen* Tuns betonen möchte.

Der Staat, als von seinen Bürgern getragen, ist nur denkbar, wenn hinter ihm eine gesellschaftliche *Vielfalt* steht – eine Vielfalt der Schichten, der Strukturen, der Bestrebungen, aber auch der Unternehmensformen und der Unternehmensgrößen. Wenn Unternehmer und Unternehmungen einsehen würden, daß Größe kein Wert an sich ist, ließe sich die Notwendigkeit und eine Möglichkeit des *freiwilligen Verzichts auf Freiheiten* demonstrieren. Freilich ist Größe relativ. Das Unternehmen des Jahres 1980 muß absolut eine andere Größenordnung haben als sein Vorgänger 1880. Der Weltmarkt war, solange es ihn gibt, noch nie eine Idylle. Romantik ist nicht am Platz. Aber die *raison d'être* einer marktverpflichteten Wirtschaft ist nicht in erster Linie die Erhaltung der Wirtschaft als solcher, sondern die Erhaltung des Marktes, seiner Funktionsfähigkeit – des Marktes, der nicht etwa eine Schimäre ist, wie manche uns glauben machen wollen, sondern die Realform der Warenversorgung in *allen* Wirtschaftsformen. Wer davon überzeugt ist, oder diese Überzeugung bekundet, daß das Prinzip des *freien Marktes* die beste Wirtschaftsform darstellt, der muß in ihr *operieren*, auch wenn sie ihm eines Tages *unbequem* wird. Anderenfalls würde der Markt, und damit die Unternehmerwirtschaft, in Frage gestellt.

*

Freisetzen von Naturkräften ist eine grundlegende technische Aufgabe. Gleich wichtig, wenn nicht wichtiger ist es, menschliche Kräfte freizusetzen, indem man Freiraum schafft. Illusion wäre es, Schöpferisches zu erwarten, wenn das Eigentum daran untergeht – in der weltfremden Vermutung, die menschliche Natur sei altruistisch.

»Die Enteignung rechtmäßig erworbenen Besitzes durch Anwendung politischer Gewalt ohne Entschädigung ist ungesetzlich.« Die progressivste Verfassung der Geschichte, diejenige der Französischen Revolution, sagt das wörtlich, und Hegel bezieht sich darauf in seiner Philosophie der Geschichte; dort setzt er Freiheit des Eigentums und Freiheit der Person auf die gleiche Stufe. Wir kennen Steuern, die Enteignungscharakter haben, und es gibt Verwaltungsakte, die der Enteignung gleichkommen, ohne daß sie eine Entschädigung vorsehen. Eben jene Verfassung versteht unter »Sicherheit« den gesetzlich verbürgten Schutz des Staatsbürgers – Schutz nicht nur seiner Person, sondern auch Schutz seines Eigentums.

Da es keinen grenzenlosen Anspruch auf Freiheit gibt, gibt es auch keinen grenzenlosen Anspruch auf Eigentum. Aber diese Grenzen liegen nicht im Quantitativen, sondern nur darin, daß Eigentum vernünftig verwendet wird. Es überschreitet die Weisheit des Staates, dem Staatsbürger zu sagen, was er unter Vernunft zu verstehen hat. Dieser muß in eigener Verantwortung entscheiden, und er muß für seine Entscheidung einstehen.

Wilhelm von Humboldt, ein Diener des Staates und der Wissenschaft, beileibe kein Unternehmer, schrieb in dem bereits erwähnten Aufsatz zu einer unternehmerischen Kernfrage: »Jedes Geschäft – welcher Art es auch sei – wird besser betrieben, wenn man es um seinen selbst willen als den Folgen zuliebe treibt … weil dem Menschen Tätigkeit lieber ist als Besitz, allein Tätigkeit nur, insofern sie *Selbsttätigkeit* ist.« Damit ist jene Spontaneität gemeint, vor deren Unterdrückung Ortega y Gasset im »Aufstand der Massen« gewarnt hat.

Es sind Schicksalsfragen, ob es uns gelingt,
- den Freiraum zu erhalten, wo er besteht,
- den notwendigen Freiraum zu schaffen, wo er fehlt,
- den Freiraum weise zu nützen.

Tragisch wäre es, dem Kampf um diese Werte in der irrigen Meinung auszuweichen, es löse sich alles von selbst, auch dort, wo es auf den Charakter ankommt.

*

Gegen die Übergriffe, gegen die Hypertrophie des Staates kommt man mit klugen Reden und gelehrten Deduktionen nicht an. Man braucht vielmehr Männer, die Geschichte machen – in unserem Sinn Männer, die die wirtschaftlichen Probleme fest in die Hand nehmen und sie, trotz aller Widrigkeiten, im Sinne der marktgesteuerten Unternehmenswirtschaft lösen. *(1978)*

Rechte und Pflichten in der Republik

ZUM 30. GEBURTSTAG DER ZWEITEN DEUTSCHEN DEMOKRATIE

Wenn auch die Republik, über die wir sprechen, erst seit dreißig Jahren besteht, so reicht doch die Geschichte dieser Staatsform in unserem Land weiter zurück. Vor sechzig Jahren beschloß die Nationalversammlung in Weimar die »Verfassung des Deutschen Reiches« – eine republikanisch-demokratische Verfassung. Diese erste deutsche Republik war schon 1933 an ihrem Ende angelangt, und während mehr als der Hälfte ihrer vierzehnjährigen Existenz mußte sie mit Hilfe von Notgesetzen und -verordnungen regiert werden.

Ihre Anfangsjahre waren nicht nur gezeichnet von Freiheit, Gleichheit, Brüderlichkeit. Es trat nicht nur Liberalität an die Stelle der Bevormundung des Staatsvolkes, die man in der konstitutionellen Monarchie bis dahin empfunden hatte. Im Gegenteil: eine Zeit der Auseinandersetzung zwischen Freiheit und Zwang, zwischen bürgerlicher Entfaltung und dem Versuch zur Gewalt. Kein überzeugendes Bild einer Republik, die, politisch im Innern nicht gesichert, von außen aber unter Druck stehend, weder das wirtschaftliche noch das geistige Gleichgewicht wiederfinden konnte. Außenpolitische Erfolge, Schritte in der Richtung auf Europa waren kurzfristiger Natur.

Ich halte es für einen Irrtum, ihre Schwäche und die daraus resultierende folgenschwere Bevorzugung der Präsidialgewalt allein der Struktur der Weimarer Verfassung anzulasten; dies wäre eine Überschätzung der Form. Viel näher liegt die Vermutung, die Weimarer Republik sei daran gescheitert, daß ihre Bürger auf diese Staatsform nicht ausreichend vorbereitet waren, daß ihnen die Reife mitdenkender und mithandelnder Republikaner fehlte.

Dies sage ich in dem Bewußtsein, daß man die Geschichte der deutschen Republiken noch länger zurückverfolgen kann. Im Laufe der ersten Hälfte des 19. Jahrhunderts hatten sich die geistigen Voraussetzungen herausgebildet, die zu den Erhebungen von 1848/49 führten. Der Versuch, eine freiheitliche deutsche Verfassung, eine auf das Gemeinwesen gerichtete Verfassung zu schaffen, blieb damals ohne sichtbaren Erfolg. Der Gedanke einer demokratischen Republik war zurückgeworfen. Obwohl dann die Periode von der Gründung des Deutschen Reichs bis zum Umbruch im Jahre 1918 demokratischer und liberaler Züge nicht entbehrte, hat sie als Lehrzeit für Republikaner nicht ausgereicht.

Wir haben also zwei vergebliche Anläufe zur Republik in vier, fünf Generationen hinter uns. Das zeigt, daß man erst lernen muß, Republikaner, Mitglied einer Republik zu sein, die ihren Bürgern nicht als Fremdkörper gegenübersteht, von ihnen vielmehr verkörpert wird.

*

Es gibt ohnehin nur wenige alte, in Kämpfen erprobte, aber viele junge Republiken. Doch kann man die Republik nicht schlechthin als kurzlebig bezeichnen; den Formen des Staates scheint ganz allgemein kein langes Leben beschieden zu sein. Sie sind vom Fortschritt ebenso bedroht wie vom Rückschritt, weil die Tagespolitik der Erhaltung und der Förderung des Bewährten nicht immer das notwendige Gewicht beimißt. Dabei kann, wie die Geschichte zeigt, ein Staat nicht überleben, wenn er nicht, in ganz präziser Wortbedeutung, konservativ ist, das heißt, wenn er nicht das Gemeinwesen als solches erhält. Konservativ ist in diesem Sinn Gegenpol zu einer anarchistisch-destruktiven Einstellung, aber keineswegs ein Gegensatz zu konstruktivem Denken und Handeln.

Dreißig Jahre der gegenwärtigen Republik – das ist gerade eine Generation. Ob die Kluft zwischen den Generationen breiter ist als früher, braucht man gar nicht zu untersuchen – der Bruch *ist* tiefer. Noch wissen wir nicht genau, ob die Nachkriegsgeneration – die weder die schwere Verantwortung für den moralischen und den materiellen Zerfall des alten Staates tragen muß noch mit dem Aufbau der weltgeschichtlich so jungen Republik zu tun hatte – das Erbe antreten will. Deshalb stehen wir vor der schweren Aufgabe, die Fundamente zu erhalten, ohne den Nachfolgern die Hände für den Weiterbau zu binden. Wir müssen versuchen, Erfahrungen zu übertragen – unabhängig davon, ob sie angenommen werden. Der Schluß ist erlaubt, daß es eine Synthese geben muß zwischen der Bewahrung des Bewährten und der nie endenden Aufgabe, das Bewährte der Feuerprobe zu unterwerfen, die Änderung der Bedingungen zu erkennen und zur Weiterentwicklung des Überlieferten beizutragen.

Erkenntnisse der letzten Jahre haben uns davon überzeugt, daß der Begriff des Fortschritts, so hinreißend er lange gewirkt haben mag, nur wenig aussagt. Oft schreiten wir weiter, aber im Dunkel der Begriffe, in der mangelnden Auflösung der immer größer werdenden Zahl von Erkenntnissen haben wir die Richtung verloren; der Schritt geht nicht immer nach vorn, sondern häufig genug auch zurück, und erst später wird die Fragwürdigkeit des Fortschritts, an den wir glaubten, klar. Dies spricht nicht gegen Reformen, solange und soweit sie nicht Schlagworte sind.

Zunächst war das Schicksal der ersten Hälfte *unseres* Jahrhunderts zu bewältigen, bevor 1949 – hundert Jahre nach der Nationalversammlung in der Frankfurter Paulskirche – ein Neubeginn möglich wurde. An uns liegt es jetzt, was wir aus dem Grundgesetz machen, das sowohl in seinen konkreten Bestimmungen als auch in seinen Optionen zeigt, daß seine Autoren Lehren aus der Vergangenheit gezogen haben.

In der letzten Zeit ist die Erörterung über Grundrechte und Grundwerte unserer Verfassung wieder in Gang gekommen. Man könnte als Bürger der Bundesrepublik befriedigt sein, wenn es sich um eine Auseinandersetzung mit dem Gefüge und mit dem Inhalt unseres Staatswesens handelte. Es hat aber den Anschein, als solle hier auch parteipolitisches Profil erlangt werden. Da wir, der Demokratie anhängend, die Einrichtung der Parteien bejahen, wäre dem nicht unbedingt zu widersprechen. Doch fällt auf, daß der Begriff der Grund*pflichten* nicht erscheint. Keine Staatsform, auch nicht die Republik, kann aber aus dem vollen schöpfen. Keine kann, in anderen Worten, mehr Grundrechte gewähren, als sie dem Staatsbürger Grundpflichten auferlegt.

Es ist kein unerlaubter Gedankensprung, von eher immateriellen Werten auf das ganz konkrete Bild des Güterverzehrs überzugehen. Wir haben, seit der Antike und bis auf den heutigen Tag, immer wieder sehen müssen, wie eine Regierung nach der anderen – ungeachtet der Staatsform – abtreten mußte, sobald sie die von ihrer Vorgängerin ererbten Güter zur Erfüllung von Wahlversprechen unter die Leute gebracht hatte, ohne dafür zu sorgen, daß die Vorräte durch Beiträge der Staatsbürger wieder aufgefüllt wurden.

Grundrechte lassen sich eben genauso »verbrauchen« wie die Rücklagen der Rentenversicherung, um ein Beispiel zu nennen, wenn nicht ein System von Pflichten, so abgestuft es sein mag, dafür sorgt, daß der Vorrat an Grundrechten und Grundwerten immer wieder erneuert wird.

Republikaner zu sein, bedeutet also nicht in erster Linie einen Anspruch, sondern eine Pflicht. Eine Republik bietet keine Gratisleistung, keinen Kundendienst für den Staatsbürger; sie ist eine verpflichtende Gemeinschaft, die nicht existieren kann ohne den stetigen, tätigen Beitrag der Staatsbürger. Die Staatsverdrossenheit, von der wir hören, kommt nicht davon, daß die Republik zu wenig leistet, sondern daß sie zu wenig fordert.

Das Recht des Staates, den Bürger zu fordern, ist – in einem Land wie dem unsrigen, das den Staatsanteil am Sozialprodukt im Vergleich mit den anderen Industrieländern auf eine fast einsame Spitze getrieben hat – zunächst nicht materiell gemeint. Jedoch wird es für den Bürger von Tag zu Tag spürbarer und einschneidender, daß er die Wohltaten, die er vom Staat empfängt, letzten Endes selbst – und teuer – zahlen muß. Also nicht der materielle Beitrag in Form von Steuern und anderen Abgaben macht die vom Bürger geforderte Mitwirkung an der Republik in erster Linie aus. Gemeint ist vielmehr der höchstpersönliche Einsatz, für den es kein Rezept gibt. Hier wird nicht nur die Bereitschaft, sondern auch die Phantasie des Republikaners angesprochen.

*

Die Republik, unsere Bundesrepublik Deutschland, ist keine Selbstverständlichkeit. Sie wurde weder ihren geistigen Vätern noch uns geschenkt. Sie ist in harter Arbeit geschaffen worden, und ihr Fortbestand hängt von dem Maß an Entschlossenheit ab, den vor dreißig Jahren begonnenen Bau durch eigene Beiträge weiterzuführen. Sie ist uns anvertraut. Eine Republik gehört in eine völlig andere Wertvorstellung als jede andere Staatsform. Sie verlangt Leistung, Gegenleistung.

Man kann bei Montesquieu – in seinem berühmten Buch »Vom Geist der Gesetze« – nachlesen, in einem Staate, der vom Volke regiert werde, sei als Triebfeder die »Tugend« erforderlich. Diese Tugend, sagt der französische Philosoph, sei eine sehr einfach Sache: die Liebe zu den Gesetzen, zum Vaterland, zur Republik. Tätige Liebe meinen Plato und Cicero, wenn der eine die Weigerung, Ämter anzunehmen, unter die Merkmale des Verderbens einer Republik rechnet, der andere fordert, jeder solle und müsse für die Gemeinschaft tätig sein – schon um seine Gedanken zu klären.

Es ist ein weiter Weg von Plato – der Bürger, die ein Gewerbe ausüben, bestrafen will, weil er fürchtet, daß diese dadurch von ihrer eigentlichen Aufgabe: dem Gemeinwesen zu dienen, abgehalten werden – bis zu der Auffassung unseres Jahrhunderts, man mache sich in der Politik die Hände schmutzig. Würden wir uns diese Auffassung zu eigen machen, so wäre nicht auszuschließen, daß uns eines Tages die Rechnung präsentiert wird, nicht nur für das, was wir, unter Mißachtung der Gegebenheiten, zuviel gefordert haben, sondern auch für das, was wir dem Gemeinwesen schuldig geblieben sind.

Heute setzen wir Republik und Demokratie gleich. Wir können uns – anders als frühere Epochen – eine aristokratisch regierte Republik nicht mehr vorstellen. In jeder Demokratie muß aber immer aufs neue die Frage gestellt werden, wo denn die Begründung dafür liegt, daß die Meinung von 51 Wählern nicht nur ein größeres Entscheidungsgewicht hat als die Meinung der 49, sondern auch eine mehr als nur numerische Rechtfertigung in sich trägt. Schärfer formuliert: Die Legitimation der größeren Zahl steht noch aus, und nur dann, wenn die Mehrheit es nicht als ihr Recht ansieht, die Minderheit zu überwältigen, sondern es als ihre Pflicht betrachtet, der Meinung der Minderheit gerecht zu werden, ist sie gerechtfertigt.

*

Demokratie ist ein Werkzeug und kein Lehrsatz. Sie ist das beste aller denkbaren politischen Werkzeuge, wenn auch kein vollkommenes. Sie ist nicht von Natur aus, nicht ohne Bemühungen gerechter als andere Regierungsformen, aber sie birgt in sich eine größere Hoffnung auf Gerechtigkeit als jede andere.

Minimalbedingung der Demokratie ist die Toleranz. Eine Demokratie ohne Duldsamkeit, ohne Verständnis für die Mängel, die man beim politischen Nachbarn sehen mag, ohne Bereitschaft, ja Entschlossenheit, das menschliche Grundgefühl des Neides zurückzustellen, entbehrt der entscheidenden Vorteile, die sie, in der Vollendung ihrer Form, bieten könnte.

Demokratie – das kann in der Wortgeschichte nicht nur Herrschaft des Volkes heißen, sondern auch Herrschaft über das Volk. Die Sorge ist nicht unbegründet, daß die Diskussion über die Regierungs*form* am Kern der Sache vorübergeht. Jedenfalls zeigt die Geschichte – ich trete dafür ein, daß wir sie, richtig verstanden, weiterhin als Lehrmeisterin betrachten –, daß in *jeder* Regierungsform die Gefahr der Tyrannis »lauert« – so Karl Büchner in seiner Einleitung zu Ciceros »De re publica«.

Wer für die Demokratie eintritt, sagten wir, muß ein besonders hohes Maß an Duldsamkeit gegenüber den Denk- und Handlungsweisen anderer aufbringen, solange nicht jene Grenze erreicht ist, an der sich die Geister scheiden. Es hat nichts mehr mit Toleranz zu tun, wenn extreme Gruppen geltend machen, die Machtgier des derzeitigen Systems zeige sich darin, daß es die Usurpation durch demokratisch *nicht* legitimierte Kräfte verhindere.

Toleranz muß sich also Grenzen setzen. Grenzenlose Toleranz wäre Selbstaufgabe, und es wäre das republikanische, das demokratische Mißverständnis an sich, wenn der Staat und seine Bürger glaubten, sie müßten dem Angriff auf ihre Integrität Vorschub leisten. Toleranz, man könnte auch sagen: Liberalität, die so weit geht, dem Gegner die Zerstörung der Freiheit zu erlauben, ist nichts als Schwäche.

Eine Republik, die auf sich hält – und sie geht unter, wenn sie das nicht tut –, muß nicht nur sich selbst schützen, sondern auch ihre Staatsbürger. Übersieht sie, wo das Recht der Öffentlichkeit an der Person endet und das Recht des Individuums auf sich selbst beginnt, kann es geschehen, daß sie die Grenze übersieht, bis zu der Liberalität Vorrang haben muß, während jenseits davon – und Grenzen sind schmale Striche – die Selbstentäußerung beginnt.

Als er von der Tugend in der Republik und der Liebe zur Republik schrieb, sagte der schon einmal zitierte Montesquieu, die Liebe zur Demokratie sei auch noch die Liebe zur Sparsamkeit. Das klingt, vor mehr als zweihundert Jahren gesagt, ebenso zeitgemäß wie die nochmals zwei Jahrhunderte früher getroffene Feststellung von Jean Bodin – in seinen »Sechs Büchern von der Republik« –, »die Finanzen seien die Nerven der Republik«.

Jeder weiß, daß *unsere* Republik, die so lange haushälterisch gewirtschaftet hat, in den letzten Jahren einen Stand und vor allem ein Tempo der Staatsverschuldung erreicht hat, die zwar ihren Bestand noch nicht gefährden, aber doch an ihren Nerven zehren. Wir ziehen Tag für Tag weitere Wechsel, die von der nachfolgenden – voraussichtlich der Zahl nach verringerten – Generation eingelöst werden müssen. So sehr es die Aufgabe der Regierenden ist, die Maßlosigkeit zu bekämpfen, so ist doch jeder Staatsbürger mit verantwortlich, der den Staat überfordert.

Unsere Republik hat wirtschaftliche Erfolge erzielt – größere, als man sie nach dem Zusammenbruch von 1945 je erwarten konnte. Es war nicht nur unsere eigene Leistung; jeder von uns kennt die Beiträge unserer politischen und wirtschaftlichen Partner, deren Gegner wir einmal waren. Daraus ergeben sich Verbindlichkeiten; je unauffälliger, je anspruchsloser wir sie erfüllen, desto größer ist die Aussicht, das Ansehen unserer Republik in der Welt zu festigen, desto größer die Aussicht, die Zurückhaltung, die wir da und dort uns gegenüber noch immer spüren, zu überwinden. Wir haben gerade in dieser Hinsicht zunächst einmal nicht an Grundrechte zu denken, sondern Grundpflichten zu erfüllen – der Republik, der Nation zuliebe.

Wir hatten noch nicht die Zeit, die Republik zu Ende zu denken. Eine Republik bleibt die ewig Unvollendete. Dies gibt die Chance, daß Generation nach Generation an ihr weiterbaut. So betrachtet ist die Phrase von der Sinnentleerung unserer Zeit hohl. Die Republik zu erhalten, ist eine Aufgabe, die sich jeden Tag neu stellt, eine sinnvolle Aufgabe.

Mit der Addition der Kräfte ist es freilich nicht getan. Man muß sie integrieren. Ich weiß nicht, wem wir das Wort verdanken – es mag von einem unserer großen Männer stammen oder als Denkergebnis vieler im Laufe der Jahrhunderte sich herausgebildet haben –: Menschen werden durch Meinungen getrennt, durch Gesinnung vereinigt. Eine von allen getragene Republik bietet das ideale Feld für eine Vielfalt von Meinungen, aus denen sich, getragen von übergreifender Gesinnung, ein gemeinsamer Handlungsspielraum ergibt.

(1979)

Dienen und Führen

ANMERKUNGEN ZUR ABWERTUNG VON BEGRIFFEN

Der Versuch, Dienen und Führen als Begriffspaar, als nicht nur voneinander abhängig, sondern ineinander übergehend, nicht als Gegensatz, sondern als Sequenz zu behandeln, stürzt beide Seiten, den Referenten und das Auditorium, in Probleme. Der Vortragende gerät in Beweisnot. Er konnte in der Literatur wohl viel über Führen, sehr viel weniger über Dienen und kaum ein Wort über den inneren Zusammenhang der beiden Begriffe finden. Die Zuhörer sehen sich in dem Dilemma, entweder ihrer Überzeugung Ausdruck zu geben, daß Dienen und Führen sich diametral gegenüberstehen, oder aber höflich zu schweigen. Wir werden sehen.

*

Ich bin ein Wort zur Wahl meines Themas schuldig. Der tertiäre Sektor, sagen Wirtschaftspolitiker und Wirtschaftswissenschaftler, aber insbesondere auch die darin Tätigen, wird im Verhältnis zu den anderen Sektoren weiter zunehmen. Der tertiäre Sektor, also die Dienstleistung, das Dienstleistungsgeschäft.

Ein unhandliches Wort: Dienst-Leistungs-Geschäft – vor allem aber ein Wort, genauer gesagt, ein Wortungetüm, dessen Bedeutungsinhalt zu den Schwundformen unserer Zeit zählt: Dienen – Leisten – Schaffen – das letztere in dem Sinn verstanden, den Schaffen in meiner schwäbischen Wahlheimat hat: Arbeiten. Die moralische Abwertung, die diese Begriffe in unserer Zeit bereits erfahren haben und weiter erfahren werden, wenn nicht Widerstand geleistet wird – diese Aushöhlung also war für mich der Anstoß, das Thema zu wählen, das auf den ersten Blick – und besonders in seinem ersten Teil: Dienen – fast wirklichkeitsfremd zu sein scheint.

Dienstleistungsangebote stehen und fallen mit der Bereitschaft zu dienen und zu leisten. Herbert Marcuse spricht im Zusammenhang mit dem Leistungsbegriff von der »großen Weigerung«, die wir in der Tat beobachten, wenn wir bestimmte Ausschnitte unserer Wirklichkeit betrachten.

Was hier Ursache, was Wirkung ist, kann an dieser Stelle nicht beweiskräftig untersucht werden; ich bezweifle, daß es sich um eine spontane Bewegung, eine Bewegung aus heiterem Himmel handelt. Denn wenn man uns klarmachen will, das Ende der Expansion der wirtschaftlichen Kontrolle der Natur werde einen Großteil der heute selbstverständlichen Werte der Gesellschaft wie Leistung, energisches Zupacken und Tatkraft obsolet machen, so tritt Absicht zutage, und unser Widerspruch wird herausgefordert. Das Gegenteil ist der Fall: Je schwieriger es wird, die existentiellen Grundmengen an Energie, an Rohstoffen, an Nahrungsmitteln für eine noch immer wachsende Menschheit zu gewinnen, desto mehr müssen wir denken, vermitteln, ausgleichen, überbrücken, erfinden. Die Zeit der rohen und bitteren Muskelarbeit liegt hinter uns. Aber gerade Denken setzt Leistungsbereitschaft voraus. Genaues Denken – und ich füge hinzu: redliches Denken – ist sowohl ein Element des Leistens als auch des Dienens, letzteres im Sinne der Bereitschaft zur Anerkennung zwingender Gedankengänge.

Die Geschichte jener Befreiung der Menschen von körperlicher Fron ist auch eine Wirkungsgeschichte der Unternehmerwirtschaft. Unternehmerische Disposition hat – nicht ohne die schmerzlichen Lehrjahre des frühindustriellen Zeitalters – die Faktoren menschliche Arbeit, maschinelle Arbeit, energetische Arbeit optimiert, was unerläßlich für die Minimierung der physischen Arbeitslast war, die inzwischen erreicht wurde.

Man kann es als einen der Pendelschläge der Menschheitsgeschichte empfinden, daß auf diesem Weg zunächst nicht etwa das Bedürfnis auftritt, den eingeprägten menschlichen Betätigungsdrang durch Arbeit höherer Art zu befriedigen – daß vielmehr zunächst die Reaktion der Arbeits- und Leistungsverweigerung zu beobachten ist.

Ich bin mir der Gefahr dieser Vereinfachung bewußt – der Gefahr, den Arbeits- und Leistungswilligen, die noch immer in der Überzahl sind, unrecht zu tun. Die Zeiterscheinung als solche aber, die uns in dieser Form in der Sozialgeschichte des Abendlandes seit der Auflösung des Römischen Reichs nicht mehr begegnete, ruft nach sorgfältiger Analyse, wenn man sie überwinden will – und daß sie überwunden werden muß, wenn es nicht zu einer globalen Kräfteverschiebung kommen soll, wird von Tag zu Tag deutlicher.

Zur Analyse gehört die Feststellung, die hier ganz kühl getroffen werden soll, daß die Weltverbesserer der letzten zwei Jahrhunderte ein gerüttelt Maß an Schuld daran haben, daß sich die Illusion von der Möglichkeit des mühelosen Lebens breitmachte. Der utopische Sozialismus wird sich früher oder später gezwungen sehen, die Erfüllung seiner Versprechen ins Jenseits zu verlegen, worin (nicht unbedingt: wohin) ihm kluge Religionsstifter schon lange vorausgegangen sind.

Das alles mag ironisch klingen, ist aber als Betrachtung der Zusammenhänge zwischen Arbeit und Ertrag, zwischen Leisten und Gewinn, schließlich, etwas abgewandelt, auch zwischen Dienen und Führen von erregender Realität.

Ich sagte schon: Die hier geäußerte Skepsis gilt nicht dem Kern unserer Mitarbeiter, der nach wie vor nicht nur leistungsbereit ist, sondern auch von der Notwendigkeit der Leistung überzeugt. Sie betrifft vielmehr jene, die meist außerhalb der Arbeitswelt stehend, Verwirrung stiften und bei denen wir humanitäre Ziele nicht in jedem Fall vermuten dürfen, wohl aber fast immer eine nicht zu übersehende Neigung, an den Wohltaten einer leistungsbewußten Industriegesellschaft auf diese oder jene Art teilzunehmen.

Die Weltgeschichte, in ihrer unerbittlichen Konsequenz, wird über die Anhänger der Leistungsverweigerung hinweggehen; die Revolution frißt ihre Kinder. Lenin war es bitterernst, als er von der »Disziplinierung der Arbeiter« sprach. Wir, in einer der diszipliniertesten Arbeitswelten lebend, haben es nicht nötig, die »strengste Kontrolle … seitens des Staates über das Maß der Arbeit und das Maß der Konsumtion« zu fordern – so nochmals Lenin. Was wir fordern müssen, ist, daß jene »freischwebende Intelligenz«, von der bei Karl Mannheim die Rede ist, auf den Boden der Tatsachen zurückgeholt wird.

*

Das im Begriff »Dienstleistung« steckende Element »Leistung« hat mich nun für eine Wegstrecke von meiner Absicht abgelenkt, einige Anmerkungen zu dem Thema des Dienens zu machen – vor allem aber, Dienen und Führen als Aspekte *einer* Grundtatsache, als Erscheinungsformen *eines* Phänomens darzustellen. Meine These ist, daß Dienen und Führen keine Gegensätze sind – weder historisch noch zukunftsbezogen –, daß vielmehr die Führungseignung aus der Bereitschaft zum Dienen hervorgeht, daß Führen eine besondere Kategorie des Dienens ist – eine These, die der Differenzierung bedarf.

Lassen Sie uns zunächst vom Dienen sprechen. Ob man Dienen als Last oder als Tugend betrachtet, mag vom Standort des Betrachters abhängen. Wir sind geneigt, Dienen als moralische Kategorie zu betrachten, ohne Urteil darüber, ob und inwieweit sie noch eine Realität ist.

Die sprachliche und damit auch begriffliche Spannweite ist größer, als man bei einem so einfach klingenden Wort, wie es »Dienen« ist, vermuten könnte; die Vorstellung der Sklaverei fällt ebenso darunter wie der Dienst an der Wahrheit, der Dienst an der Freiheit – soweit man letztere nicht nach Lenin nur als ein »Vorurteil der Bourgeoisie« betrachtet. Die Spannweite des Wortes reicht bis zum

»Staatsdiener«, einer Ausprägung, die Freiheit der Pflichterfüllung und Unterwerfung unter der Staatsraison in sich vereinigt.

Zu Riemer äußerte Goethe am 13. August 1809 (der Zeitpunkt ist nicht ohne Bedeutung): »Das jetzige Unglück der Welt rühre doch meist davon her, daß sich alles zu Herren gebildet habe. Der Adel sei von jeher dienstpflichtig, und der erste Staatsdiener, wie von Joseph II. schon gesagt, sei der Fürst.« Hier irrt Goethe. Denn nicht Joseph II., sondern spätestens Friedrich II. ist der Urheber dieses Wortes. Im »Antimachiavel« heißt es 1739: »Le Roi est le premier Magistrat des peuples.« Daß »Magistrat« weithin mit »Diener« übersetzt wird, geht übrigens auf die fast fünfzig Jahre später erschienene Ausgabe letzter Hand zurück – nunmehr unter dem Namen Friedrichs erschienen, während seinerzeit Voltaire als Herausgeber auftreten mußte. Und dort – ein halbes Jahrhundert später – tritt nicht mehr der »Magistrat«, der Beamte, auf, sondern der »Domestique«, der Diener. Wird hier sichtbar, wie sehr die Pflichterfüllung den Rücken des Königs gebeugt hat? Daß aber Dienen und Führen gleichen Stammes sind, zeichnet sich in Friedrichs Leben ab.

Die Assoziation Goethes – er denkt nicht an Friedrich II., sondern an Joseph II. – verrät den alten Reichsstädter, für den das Zentrum der deutschen Nation, wenn er überhaupt an eine solche dachte, nicht in Berlin, sondern, ganz natürlich, in Wien lag. Im Jahr 1764 hatte der fünfzehnjährige Goethe die Krönung Josephs in Frankfurt am Main miterlebt.

Es ist in diesem Zusammenhang nicht ohne Reiz, von Erich Marcks, dem deutschen Historiker, der sich viel mit Bismarck beschäftigt hat, zu wissen, daß er versuchte, eine innere Beziehung zwischen Goethe und Bismarck herzustellen, wobei ihm Frankfurt als der Ort vorschwebte, an dem Bismarck – dort als preußischer Gesandter beim seinerzeitigen Bundestag tätig – die Formung zum Staatsmann erlebte, die »Hinleitung zur staatsmännischen Wirksamkeit«.

Wir sind noch beim Staatsdiener. In der »Geschichte eines Staates – Preußen –« von Hans-Joachim Schoeps lesen wir: »Staatsdiener in Preußen war immer auch ein Stück Selbstverleugnung, aber das gehörte zur ›Idee‹ und wurde als sittliche Leistung angesehen. Derlei ist heute vollkommen unzeitgemäß – aber gefordert.«

Es gibt viele Gründe, warum gerade Schoeps ein unverfänglicher Zeuge ist. Ein Verfechter einer Auffassung, die nicht so sehr einem bestimmten Topos verhaftet ist, sondern einer Geisteshaltung, von der wir gar nicht bestreiten wollen, daß sie sich nicht im Dienen erschöpfte, sondern daß die Willensbildung, die auf der Dienstbereitschaft fußte, zu politischem Machtstreben und zu politischen Fehlern führte. Aber auch zu einem Gemeinwesen, das lange nach dem Ende der Monarchie noch immer, nicht nur politisch, weiterlebte. Die zwanziger Jahre haben das erwiesen.

Die Beseitigung dieses Staates, die vielleicht weniger seiner faktischen Existenz als vielmehr eben seiner ideellen Kraft galt, war das Ergebnis einer dunklen Zeit, die wir Deutsche zu verantworten haben. Es gibt Anzeichen dafür, daß diejenigen, denen daran lag, Preußen auszulöschen, zu verstehen beginnen, welche Werte getroffen wurden. Dabei geht es hier nicht um eine »konservative Revolution« – auch wenn sich in »conservare« (erhalten, retten) nicht nur zufällig der alte Sprachstamm »serv« erhalten hat, mit dem auch »servire« (dienen) zusammenhängt. Wir wollen nicht den Geist einer vergangenen Zeit heraufbeschwören – immerhin, wir sprechen von einer geistigen Kraft –, sondern einfach Verschüttetes freilegen.

An dieser Stelle kann ich der Versuchung nicht widerstehen, bei Goethe nachzulesen, ob er sich wohl zu unserem Thema an anderer Stelle, bei anderer Gelegenheit, zu anderer Zeit nochmals geäußert habe – und im Zweifel hat er das getan, weil ihm nicht nur ein langes, tätiges Leben beschieden war, sondern weil er bewußt gelebt und ebenso bewußt seine Mitwelt an seinen Gedanken und Gefühlen beteiligt hat. Ob Sie das nun als ein Plädoyer für Goethe nehmen oder als eine Exkulpation für den Mißbrauch des Zitierens ... lassen Sie mich auf alle Fälle einmal meinen Fund vortragen. In dem Gedicht »Ilmenau« sagt Goethe:

»Der kann sich manchen Wunsch gewähren,
Der kalt sich selbst und seinem Willen lebt;
Allein, wer andre wohl zu leiten strebt,
Muß fähig sein, viel zu entbehren.«

So wäre also Entbehren – die Bereitschaft zum Verzicht auf Annehmlichkeiten – als eine weitere Voraussetzung für das Privileg des Führens anzusehen: ein Privileg, das eben nicht nur ein Recht, sondern vielmehr eine Pflicht, vielleicht eine schwere Last ist.

Mitunter fragt sich der eine oder andere, ob die Zeit, in der wir gedient und entbehrt haben, für unsere menschliche Entwicklung so schlecht war – ich nehme in Kauf, hier mißverstanden zu werden.

»Zu leiten strebt ...« klingt bei uns noch nach.

Als der Ausgang des Ersten Weltkriegs sich abzeichnete, untersuchte Alfred Weber das Problem der »geistigen Führer in Deutschland«. Weber bezeichnete es als einen Irrtum, das Wesen der Demokratie in ihren Mechanismen zu erblicken. Er sah dieses Wesen »vielmehr in einer neuen Stellung zur Grundtatsache der Führung, letztlich und hauptsächlich aber in einer neuen Art der Auslese der Führer und einer neuen Dezendenz derselben zu den Massen ...«. Damit ist viel, fast alles vorweggenommen, was nicht nur zu dem Problem der Führung im Staat, sondern auch, und gerade, zu dem Problem der Führung im Unternehmen zu sagen ist.

Was die Auswahl angeht, so kritisiert Weber, daß es sowohl im geistigen als auch im politischen Leben »an dem Aufstieg der kräftigeren Talente, die von unten kommen«, fehlte, und er erwähnte die Beobachtung, daß sogar im *Ancien régime* die Führungsauslese demokratischer gewesen sei als in unserem Jahrhundert. Er machte aber auch klar, und damit nähern wir uns einem Kernpunkt, daß, wenn einmal die Führungsauslese getroffen, die Entscheidung gefallen ist, wer führt, geführt werden muß.

Wenn auch aus Webers Überlegung der Begriff des Dienens nicht unmittelbar herzuleiten ist, so ist es doch nicht abwegig, wenn man aus dem »Aufstieg der kräftigeren Talente«, von dem er spricht, die zwingende Stufung herausliest: vom Dienen zum Führen.

Dieser Aufstieg setzt sowohl gleiche Startbedingungen und Durchlässigkeit als auch die Anerkennung der Notwendigkeit von Eliten voraus – Forderungen, die nur für kleine Geister einen Widerspruch zu enthalten scheinen, die aber der biologischen Realität ebenso gemäß sind, wie wir sie gerade deshalb für gerecht halten müssen.

Gelänge es, über die Freiheit des Bildungswegs – aber dennoch unter eindeutiger Bevorzugung von Qualität vor Quantität, von Ebenmaß vor Übermaß – die Kluft zwischen den Schichten zu überbrükken, wären endgültig die Prämissen des Klassenkampfs beseitigt.

Möglich ist das nur durch eine Politik der weitschauenden Konstanz der Zielsetzung, nicht aber durch eine solche der kurzsichtigen Opportunität. Führungsnachwuchs – darauf machte kürzlich jemand aufmerksam – bekommt man nicht in neun Monaten.

*

Die Wirtschaft bezieht einen wachsenden Teil ihres Führungsnachwuchses von den Hohen Schulen. Sie nimmt auf die Bildungsinhalte keinen Einfluß. Das ist im Prinzip gut so. Sie hängt aber von den Leistungsmaßstäben ab, die der Staat setzt, von den Lehrmethoden und von den Ausbildungsergebnissen, also von der Effizienz des Bildungsbetriebs. Die Bildungsreform, die in den sechziger Jahren einsetzte, ist mit ihrer zunächst ideal orientierten, dann aber politisch festgelegten, wenn nicht politisch festgefahrenen Zielsetzung methodisch und zum Teil auch personell in die Irre gegangen. Der Verlust für die Volkswirtschaft liegt auf der Hand, der Nutzen für den einzelnen ist weithin ungewiß.

Wir müssen, wenn wir von Führen sprechen, erkennen, daß Führung nicht durch Demokratie ersetzt werden kann. Mit anderen Worten: Entscheidungen, die der Führungsverantwortliche zu treffen hat, können nicht durch anonyme Mehrheitsbeschlüsse ersetzt werden. Dies gilt gleichermaßen für den Staat wie für die Wirtschaft; für den Staat um so mehr in einer Zeit, in der interessengebundene Minderheiten die Mehrheit zu tyrannisieren versuchen.

Mit klarer Trennung zwischen Legislative und Exekutive wird das demokratische Grundrecht weder im Staat noch in der Wirtschaft in Frage gestellt, im Gegenteil. Denn Führen ist nicht gleichzusetzen mit »Schalten und Walten« – jeder von uns weiß das, und doch stößt man immer wieder auf das wirklichkeitsfremde, aber wirkungsvolle Bild von jenen Wirtschaftsführern, die »an den Schalthebeln der Macht« sitzen, die »alle Fäden in der Hand« halten. Ich sage das nicht, um die Medien zu bevormunden, sondern um uns ins Bewußtsein zu rufen, daß es in der Unternehmensführung nicht darum geht, einen Willen durchzusetzen, sondern eine gemeinsame Willensanstrengung hervorzurufen. Es handelt sich um Akte der Willensbildung, die freilich nicht ungesteuert denkbar sind, die aber zur Verwirklichung nur führen, wenn jeder Beteiligte davon überzeugt ist, daß er selbst, an seiner Stelle einen Teil dieses Willens verkörpert.

So blaß sich die Formel des kooperativen Führungsstils ausnimmt: Wir werden unserer Aufgabe, unserer Führungsaufgabe in einer Welt, in der das Bewußtsein des Individuums sich entfaltet hat, nur gerecht werden, wenn wir das Führen eines Unternehmens als eine gemeinsam und freiwillig erbrachte Leistung ansehen – eine Vorstellung, die gestaltlos bliebe, stünde nicht dahinter eine stilbildende Idee.

Es mag schwerfallen, die Außenwelt davon zu überzeugen, daß der von den Unternehmen angestrebte Führungsstil nicht autoritär ist, sondern auf Zusammenarbeit bei der Vorbereitung, beim Treffen und beim Verwirklichen von Entscheidungen beruht. Gerade dann, wenn die Übereinstimmung der Auffassungen, die Gemeinsamkeit der Willensbildung erreicht wird, kann, vielleicht: muß für den Außenstehenden der Eindruck diktatorischer Führung entstehen. Aber Selbstzucht und Fingerspitzengefühl können der Außenwelt, der Öffentlichkeit beweisen, daß Unternehmungen Schrittmacher einer jeder Mechanik abholden Gestaltungsfreiheit sind, und daß wir es heute nicht mehr mit Anspruch auf Führung, sondern mit Ansprüchen an die Führung zu tun haben.

An dieser Stelle ist die Frage am Platz: Welcher Handlungsspielraum der Unternehmensführung in einer Wirtschafts- und Sozialstruktur bleibt, die noch das Siegel ihrer Herkunft aus liberalem Ordnungsdenken trägt, deren Realität aber von den Prinzipien zunehmend abweicht? Während politische Gegner den Grund für die Abschwächung marktwirtschaftlicher Kräfte, die wir hin und wieder beobachten, in grundlegenden Mängeln des Systems sehen wollen, gibt es Tatsachen genug, welche die Vermutung nähren, daß fehlender Realitätssinn der Gegner die Ursache ist.

Zweifel bestehen aber auch daran, ob die Reformanhänger, für die Veränderung häufig weniger ein pragmatisches Ziel als vielmehr ein Zauberwort ist, ein Schlüssel zum Paradies ..., ob also die Reformatoren sich mit dem Erreichten zufriedengeben. Es gibt Andeutungen, Äußerungen, Belege genug, daß das Ziel viel weiter gesteckt ist, was die Reglementierung der Wirtschaft angeht – und gemeint sind damit nicht nur Maßnahmen kurzfristiger Natur, die Engpässe überbrücken sollen, gemeint ist vielmehr eine grundlegende Umstrukturierung, deren potentielle Sprengkraft nicht dadurch gemildert wird, daß man sie als hypothetisch bezeichnet.

Ich bin noch einmal auf ein Zitat angewiesen: In der »Wirtschaftsdemokratie« von Fritz Naphtali, 1928 erschienen (der Autor war in den zwanziger Jahren Wirtschaftsredakteur der *Frankfurter Zeitung,* später Regierungsmitglied im Staat Israel), lesen wir:

»Wenn die deutschen Gewerkschaften die Forderung der Wirtschaftsdemokratie aufstellen, so bedeutet das für sie keinen Verzicht auf das sozialistische Ziel und keinen Ersatz für den Sozialismus, sondern es bedeutet eine Ergänzung der sozialistischen Idee in der Richtung der Klärung des Weges zur Verwirklichung.« Das sind zwar sehr viele Substantive, aber die Absicht ist klar. »Sozialismus und Wirtschaftsdemokratie sind« – ich zitiere weiter – »als Endziel untrennbar miteinander verknüpft.«

Naphtali, der möglicherweise der Vater des Begriffs »Mitbestimmung« war – während Wirtschaftsdemokratie, das Wort, das er als Titel seines Buches verwendete, oder genauer »Industrial Democracy« viel älteren Ursprungs ist –, Naphtali also schreibt gegen Ende seines Buches in schöner Offenheit: »Erst die organisierte und von den Gewerkschaften kontrollierte Wirtschaft, die auch den einzelnen Unternehmer zum beauftragten und gebundenen Führer eines Betriebes macht, wird die wirksame Kontrolle dieser Betriebsführung ... möglich machen.«

Wir wollen dieses Zitat nicht überstrapazieren; den deutschen Gewerkschaften, die Naphtalis Buch heute noch lesen und verbreiten, ist die Zeitbedingtheit seiner Darlegungen bewußt. Wir dürfen aber auch nicht Äußerungen aus neuester Zeit überhören, die sehr wohl an Naphtali anklingen. Wir wissen, daß viele jener wirtschaftsfremden, wirtschaftsfeindlichen Ideologien nicht etwa endgültig als falsch erkannt, nicht etwa überwunden, sondern nur zurückgestaut sind. Dies muß uns veranlassen, den Handlungsspielraum des Führens – und damit finde ich wieder zum engeren Thema zurück – zu definieren und zu sichern, nicht zum Nutzen der Führenden, sondern des Ganzen.

*

Methoden und Philosophie der Führung haben in meinen Augen grundverschiedene Struktur. Was die Methoden angeht, so zieht der

Entwurf von Führungslehren viele an und ist offenbar einträglich, deren Anwendung den Unternehmungen aber nicht in allen Fällen zuträglich. Das liegt wohl nicht an den Autoren, sondern an der Materie, die in der Generalisierung nichts hergibt, im Detail aber den Teufel hervorkehrt.

Ich bitte, richtig verstanden zu werden: Die wissenschaftliche Durchdringung dieses Stoffes ist notwendig. Sie schafft aber weder die intellektuellen noch die charakterlichen Voraussetzungen für Führung; sie liefert Handwerkszeug, Instrumente.

Wenn wir als Geschäftserfolg den Saldo aus geglückten und mißglückten Entscheidungen ansehen, wobei wesentlich der Überschuß, das positive Vorzeichen ist, so nimmt diese simple Erkenntnis sorgfältiger Entscheidungsvorbereitung nichts an Bedeutung. Aber sie beseitigt den Nimbus, es gäbe wissenschaftliche Entscheidungsmethoden, die Erfolg verbürgen. Das ist schon prinzipiell unmöglich. Das deterministische Weltbild hat auch in der Wirtschaft ausgedient. Nur die Daten der Vergangenheit, allenfalls diejenigen der Gegenwart, niemals aber die Daten der Zukunft können in die Formeln eingehen, deren Bündigkeit an sich hier nicht in Frage gestellt wird.

Was wir von diesen Methoden erwarten dürfen und freilich auch erwarten müssen, ist die Eingrenzung der Wagnisse, also die Angabe der Bandbreite, innerhalb derer wir uns bewegen.

Wer an den Vorrang der Organisation im Rahmen des Führungskomplexes glaubt – ich habe begonnen, daran zu zweifeln –, kennt auch die vielfältigen Vorstellungen und Systeme, die vor allem aus den Business Schools von jenseits des Ozeans zu uns gedrungen sind. Von den zahlreichen Varianten des »Management«, die man uns anbietet, greife ich die Variante des »Management by delegation« heraus, weil damit häufig die bedenkliche Vorstellung verbunden ist, man könne primäre Verantwortung delegieren – ein Irrtum, der darauf zurückzuführen ist, daß bei der Delegation von Aufgaben ganz natürlich auch die damit verknüpfte Verantwortung gegenüber dem unmittelbaren Auftraggeber übergeht, nicht aber die Verantwortung des Auftraggebers für die Auswahl des Mitarbeiters, für die Kontrolle und letztendlich für den Erfolg. Delegation bedeutet im Grenzfall geradezu, den Erfolg wegzugeben, den Mißerfolg aber selbst zu tragen.

Wenn Sie an dieser Stelle einen kleinen linguistischen Umweg erlauben, so wäre der Hinweis im »Oxford English Dictionary« zu erwähnen, daß »Manager« von dem italienischen Wort »maneggiare« kommt, das insbesondere »Pferde zureiten« bedeutet, und das französische »manège« ist nicht nur klang-, sondern auch stammverwandt. Ob dies ein Grund sein könnte, weniger von Management zu sprechen? Ich lasse das offen.

Delegation einer Aufgabe setzt voraus, daß man sie selbst genau kennt. Man kann also nichts mit Aussicht auf Erfolg – und im Blick auf die letztendliche eigene Verantwortung, von der wir sprachen – delegieren, was man selbst nicht überblickt.

*

Führungsphilosophie läßt sich nicht in gleicher Weise konkretisieren wie die methodischen Fragen. Wer führt, muß mitreißen, dies verlangt tiefe Überzeugung, ja Passion des Führenden, zu dessen Pflichten es gehört, die *unité d'action* seines Unternehmens herzustellen, zu verkörpern. Dies verlangt eine innere Haltung, die den Führenden im Erfolg zügelt und vor Übermut bewahrt, im Mißerfolg zum Durchhalten befähigt, vor allem aber befähigt, der unteilbaren Verantwortung gerecht zu werden, die mit der Führung verbunden ist – eine Verantwortung, die häufig genug über das einzelne Unternehmen hinausgeht und die hin und wieder dazu zwingt, Farbe zu bekennen.

Für mich war, wenn es ans Entscheiden ging, immer ein Gedanke wichtig, den Moritz Heimann so formuliert hat: Die Wahrheit liegt nicht in der Mitte. Er meinte das wohl nicht wirtschaftlich. Aber gerade in wirtschaftlichen Fragen ist es gefährlich, immer in der Mitte bleiben zu wollen, um die Risiken zu minimieren; man minimiert damit auch die Chancen. Und man müßte ja zuerst einmal wissen, wo die Mitte liegt, jetzt und später.

Der Erfolg liegt im Mut zum Extrem und in der Beharrlichkeit zur Mitte. Ohne Vorstöße in neue, in höhere Quantenbahnen ist der Rückschlag wahrscheinlich, und die »sichere« Mitte verbürgt allenfalls Mittelmäßigkeit.

Erwarten wir folglich letzten Endes intuitive, wenn auch auf das sorgfältigste vorbereitete Führungsentscheidungen, so muß bei der Führungswahl – wenn die faßbaren Bedingungen der Qualifikation erfüllt sind – der Charakter, genauer gesagt: die Charakterhaftigkeit vor der professionellen Perfektion den Vorzug genießen. Ich schlage an dieser Stelle den Bogen zu meiner Auslegung des Begriffs »Dienen«: die Bereitschaft zur Unterstellung unter eine Idee – anstelle des Willens, diese Idee zu beherrschen.

Hier breche ich mein Thema ab. Man soll nie alles sagen, was sich sagen ließe, keinesfalls mehr als man gewißlich weiß. Und unser Wissen ist allemal begrenzt. Es kommt mir hier ein Bild aus der Elektronik unserer Tage in den Sinn: Die Fehlstellen in bestimmten Kristallstrukturen sind für den Elektronentransport verantwortlich. Die Fehlstellen in meinem Vortrag mögen Ausgangspunkt von Überlegungen sein. Ich möchte dazu noch ein Wort von Thomas Mann beisteuern: »Niemand kann andere Menschen gut führen, wenn er sich nicht ehrlich an deren Erfolgen zu freuen vermag.«

*

Von diesen »Variationen eines Themas« zu dem Anlaß zurückzukehren, der uns zusammengeführt hat, erlaubt und fordert zugleich ein persönliches Wort an den Jubilar, der die sechs Jahrzehnte seines Lebens in beispielhafter Weise gestaltet hat, auch wenn ihm das Schicksal Jahre raubte, die er zunächst vielleicht als verloren betrachtete, die aber, rückblickend, in einem höheren Sinn dennoch nicht gänzlich verloren sind.

Leben spielt sich in jener dem Nichtphysiker, trotz Einstein, noch immer rätselhaften Dimension ab – der Zeit. Die Alten haben darüber viel nachgedacht; möglicherweise hatten sie mehr Zeit – oder sie nahmen sich mehr Zeit.

Nun ist freilich nichts so sehr für die gute alte Zeit verantwortlich wie das schlechte Gedächtnis. Eines wird uns jedoch zuverlässig berichtet: daß es Zeiten gegeben hat, in denen man nicht etwa weniger arbeitete, aber ruhiger, bewußter und damit vielleicht auch konzentrierter. Geschichte wiederholt sich nicht – was nicht ausschließt, daß man aus ihr lernt –, verflossene Zeit läßt sich nicht zurückholen. Wir sollten uns aber wenigstens bewußtmachen, sowohl daß Zeit ein im strengen Sinn des Wortes einmaliges Geschenk an uns ist, als auch, daß man nur führen kann, wenn man Herr seiner Zeit ist.

In »De Brevitate Vitae« sagt Seneca: »Vivere tota vitae discendum est« – Leben müsse man ein Leben lang lernen; und er fährt fort, nur ein großer und über menschliche Irrtümer erhabener Geist bringe es fertig, sich von seiner Zeit nichts nehmen zu lassen.

Wenn Sie mir in diesem großen Kreis eine sehr persönliche Bemerkung gestatten, so will ich nicht unterdrücken, was meine Frau fragte, als ich ihr diese Stelle aus Seneca vorlas: »Anderen gibst du Ratschläge – und wie hältst *du* es mit deiner Zeit?«

Ich antwortete mit einer kleinen Geschichte, die man sich von einem Kölner Moralphilosophen der zwanziger Jahre erzählt – er ist längst tot. Einer seiner Schüler traf ihn zu vorgerückter Stunde an einem Ort, an dem man seinesgleichen nicht erwartete. Auf die erstaunte Frage: »Herr Professor, Sie hier?« antwortete der Philosoph: »Ein Wegweiser *geht* nicht dorthin, wo er hinweist.«

Manchmal ist es nützlich, einen Wegweiser zu haben – einen Wegweiser in die Zeit, einen Zeitenweiser. *(1979)*

Führung im multinationalen Unternehmen

ÜBER DAS INTERNATIONALE GESCHÄFT DER BOSCH-GRUPPE

Wenn es in Europa eine Stadt gibt, in der man in der Führung multinationaler Unternehmen seit Generationen Erfahrung hat, so ist das Basel. Ich betrachte es als einen Vorzug, daß ich aufgefordert worden bin, über ein Thema zu sprechen, worüber man gerade in dieser Stadt keiner Belehrung bedarf.

Nun hängt das Bild, das man von einem mehrdimensionalen Körper gewinnt, vom Standort ab; daß Führung viele Dimensionen hat, ist ebenso unbestritten wie die Tatsache, daß Struktur und Methoden der Führung standortbedingt sind. Ob man Führung als System oder als Organisation oder als einen Begriff der Philosophie ansieht: In der Grundlage handelt es sich immer um die gleichen Probleme, in der Ausführung aber gibt es Alternativen und Varianten. Ich beschränke mich deshalb im wesentlichen auf die Erfahrungen, die in der Führung des internationalen Geschäfts der Bosch-Gruppe gemacht wurden, ohne den Versuch einer Verallgemeinerung zu machen.

*

Bosch ist ein international konzipiertes Unternehmen, ohne daß ich damit das Prädikat »multinational« schlechthin für unser Haus anerkennen würde. Zumindest fehlen in unserem Fall jene Kennzeichen, mit denen die Kritiker operieren – Kennzeichen, mit denen man Multis zu charakterisieren (um nicht zu sagen: zu brandmarken) pflegt:

– die Herrschaft über internationale Warenströme und
– die Herrschaft über internationale Geld- und Kapitalströme.

Ich möchte nicht falsch verstanden werden: Wenn ich sage, daß diese beiden Kriterien meiner Firma abgehen, so wollte ich damit nicht jenen recht geben, die das Wesen, ja das Übel der »Multis« darin erkennen wollen, daß sie über Geld, Kapital, Energie, Rohstoffe, Nahrungsmittel verfügen und sich über den politischen Willen der Regierungen hinwegsetzen – eigensüchtiger Vorteile wegen. Behauptungen dieser Art treffen nicht den Kern des Problems.

Die internationale Orientierung der Bosch-Gruppe geht, wenn man es genau nimmt, auf die Zeit vor ihrer Gründung zurück. Robert Bosch der Ältere, 1861 geboren, war in den frühen achtziger Jahren des vorigen Jahrhunderts bei Edison und Bergmann in den Vereinigten Staaten tätig. Er brachte starke Eindrücke zurück, die nicht nur technischer, sondern auch ökonomischer und politischer Natur waren. In jungen Jahren wurde er zum Kosmopoliten – und er blieb dies zeitlebens (er starb 1942), nicht nur als Unternehmer, sondern auch als Staatsbürger. Als solcher gründete er während des Ersten Weltkriegs zusammen mit anderen deutschen Industriellen den Rhein-Verlag in Basel, der sich vor allem die deutsch-französische Verständigung zur Aufgabe machte. Heute ist die Robert Bosch Stiftung, die 90 Prozent der Anteile der Robert Bosch GmbH hält, intensiv auf dem Gebiet der Völkerverständigung tätig.

Nach dieser Einblendung zurück zum Unternehmen, das 1886 in Stuttgart begonnen wurde, noch vor der Jahrhundertwende die ersten Ableger nach Frankreich und England trug, zu Anfang unseres Jahrhunderts die erste Fertigungsstätte in den Vereinigten Staaten und 1911 die erste Niederlassung in Japan (Yokohama) errichtete. Schon 1914 war der Umsatz der amerikanischen Bosch-Gesellschaft größer als der des Stammhauses.

Die Verluste, die durch die beiden Weltkriege eintraten, sind wettgemacht. Mit Ausnahme der ursprünglichen US-Gesellschaft, die in andere Hände gelegt werden mußte, sind alle Auslandspositionen wieder in unserer Hand. In den Vereinigten Staaten wurde eine neue Fertigungs- und Vertriebsgesellschaft errichtet; das Recht auf den Namen konnte vor kurzem zurückerworben werden.

Neue Fertigungspositionen wurden aufgebaut in den Niederlanden, in Spanien, in Südafrika, in der Türkei, im Iran, in Indien, in Malaysia, in Australien, in Taiwan, in Japan, in Mexiko, in Venezuela, Brasilien und Argentinien. In fünf weiteren Ländern wurden neue Vertriebsaktivitäten aufgenommen. Nach dem Stand vom 1. März 1981 sind etwas mehr als 40500 – etwa 37 Prozent der rund 110000 Bosch-Mitarbeiter außerhalb der Bundesrepublik Deutschland tätig.

Die Bosch-Gruppe ist nach ihrer Geschichte, ihrer Gegenwart und – ich bin sicher – auch nach ihrer Zukunft ein international tätiges Unternehmen. Sie hat also mit Führungsproblemen zu tun – und muß diese lösen –, die sich einem nur national orientierten Unternehmen in gleicher Form und mit gleichem Gewicht nicht stellen.

*

Multinationale Unternehmen zeichnen sich in der Regel, von anderen Charakteristiken abgesehen, durch *Größe* aus. Da *Größe an sich kein Unternehmensziel* ist, bietet sie kein Argument für die Entwicklung zum multinationalen Unternehmen. David schlug Goliath, und wenn die Dinosaurier längst ausgestorben sind, so vermutlich, weil sie, unbeholfen und träge, von behenden und sprungbereiten jüngeren Gattungen in die Enge getrieben wurden. Auslandsinvestitionen, die die Manövrierfähigkeit groß, übergroß werdender Wirtschaftsgebilde verringern, bestehen den Ausleseprozeß nicht.

Die Rechtfertigung des *großen* Unternehmens sehe ich nur in zwei Grundzügen:

- den Synergien, die man sich in vieler Hinsicht und in vielen Ebenen vorstellen kann und ohne deren Nutzung internationale

Wettbewerbsfähigkeit in einer Reihe von Wirtschaftszweigen gar nicht erwartet werden darf,
- der Wirtschaftlichkeit der großen Stückzahl (economy of scale), für die das gleiche gilt: Vorbedingung dafür, daß man im Wettbewerb seinen Mann stehen kann.

Während economy of scale meist eine Rechengröße ist, ein kalkulierbarer Wert, sind wir bei der Bewertung der Synergien weit mehr auf qualitative Merkmale angewiesen, was uns nicht daran hindern darf, Maßstäbe anzulegen und abzulesen.

Die Nutzung weltweiter Erfahrung zum *weltweit* optimalen Einsatz aller Ressourcen (Personal, Kapital, Material, Potential an Wissen und Erfahrung ...) ist es, was die *multinationale Unternehmung* vor jeder anderen auszeichnet, die sich provinzielle Schranken auferlegt. Die Schweiz ist *in sich* multinational und mit ihrem starken Selbstbehauptungswillen ein Beweisstück dafür, daß Grenzüberschreitung die gestaltenden Kräfte nicht mindert, sondern stärkt.

Das Unternehmen, das sich multinational entwickelt, entgeht, mehr oder weniger, einer Reihe von Zwängen, beispielsweise
- der Enge des Marktes,
- dem Mangel an Rohstoffen,
- dem Fehlen einer Infrastruktur,
- der Knappheit an Energie.

Es überwindet, wiederum nur beispielhaft gesagt,
- Transportprobleme,
- den wachsenden Protektionismus der Importländer.

Es entspricht dem Charakter der Unternehmung als marktwirtschaftlicher Kategorie, daß sie früher oder später die Grenzen sprengt, die ihr zunächst gesetzt waren. Das gilt auch für die politischen Grenzen. Ihre Leitung muß sich dann über die Richtung, in der sie sich ausdehnt, über die Kräfte, die sie verwendet, über das Ziel, das sie sich vornimmt, klarwerden – ein Entscheidungs- und

Führungsprozeß setzt ein, zu dessen Aufgaben es insbesondere gehört, einmal erkannte und definierte Synergien zu nutzen.

*

Hier muß ich einen kleinen geschichtlichen Exkurs einschalten: Unternehmen über die staatlichen Grenzen hinweg sind keine Errungenschaft unserer Zeit. Die Geschichte der Zivilisation des Mittelmeerraums im ersten Jahrtausend vor der Zeitenwende kann auch als eine Geschichte der Auslandsinvestition aufgefaßt werden. Der Fernhandel des späten Mittelalters und der frühen Neuzeit, wiederum mit Produktionsinitiativen verbunden, dann das Kolonialzeitalter waren Phasen einer relativen Blüte des multinationalen Unternehmens.

Werden hier geschichtliche Parallelen gezogen, so um der Irrlehre zu begegnen, das multinationale Unternehmen sei eine Fehlentwicklung der kapitalistischen Wirtschaftsweise. Befreit von Zeiterscheinungen ist die Auslandsinvestition über alle Perioden hinweg Ausdruck der Notwendigkeit weltweiter Kommunikation, weltweiten Austausches auf wirtschaftlichem Gebiet, unabhängig von der jeweils geltenden Wirtschaftsordnung. Das multinationale Unternehmen ist weder Wildwuchs noch gezielter Übergriff, sondern natürliches und notwendiges Element der Weltwirtschaft.

*

Eine der wesentlichen Führungsaufgaben im multinationalen Unternehmen ist Koordination. Im *New Yorker* erschien kürzlich ein Cartoon, der einen verzweifelten Vorsitzer des Stammhauses eines Multis zeigt, als er seinen Kollegen sagen muß: »It doesn't look good. Some of our nationals are at war with some of our other nationals.«

Damit sind wir bei der Problematik des Führens. *Führungswerkzeuge* sind nützlich, in einem gewissen Maß notwendig. Aber Führung ist nicht notwendigerweise eine Funktion eines Instrumentariums. Im Einzelfall ist sie ohne »philosophy«. Wäre der Ausdruck nicht abgenutzt, könnte man von der Notwendigkeit einer weltanschaulichen Grundlegung sprechen, ohne die man sich die von den Führungsgruppen geforderten Eigenschaften und Fähigkeiten nur schwer, wenn überhaupt, vorstellen kann: selbstkritische, bis zum Selbstzweifel gehende Analyse des Erreichten – Festigkeit, aber nicht Starrheit in der Bewältigung des Gegenwärtigen, aufgeschlossener Weitblick in der Beurteilung des Kommenden.

Alles dies sind weltanschauliche und zugleich, oder eben deshalb, menschliche Dimensionen, menschliche Probleme. Ich sage bewußt: Probleme, um auszudrücken, daß es nicht nur eine menschliche Kategorie ist, sondern ein im Kern widersprüchlicher Kreis von Fragen, deren Interdependenz auf der Hand liegt. Die Geschichte unserer Gesellschaft hat Perioden gekannt, in denen Führerschaft eher eine logische als eine psychologische Grundlage hatte, in dem Sinn, daß es jedem einleuchtete, daß Führerschaft, die Bereitschaft einzelner, die letzte Verantwortung ebenso zu übernehmen wie die Wegleitung, Notwendigkeiten des Überlebens sind.

Hier stoßen wir übrigens – ich wage diese scheinbare Abweichung vom Thema – auf den Grundirrtum der Demokratie am Ende des 20. Jahrhunderts: nämlich den Irrglauben

- nicht nur an die höhere Klugheit einer noch so dünnen Mehrheit,
- nicht nur daran, jede beliebige Mehrheit dürfe geradezu naturrechtlich über die Andersgläubigen, die Minderheit verfügen,
- nicht nur daran, in der Demokratie bedürfe es keiner Toleranz,
- bestehe keine Fürsorgepflicht gegenüber der Minderheit,

sondern vor allem den Irrglauben, der Mehrheitsdemokratie sei im Prinzip die Entscheidung über jede Sachfrage übertragen. Gerade letzteres ist eben nicht der Fall: Demokratie ist Entscheidung über Personalfragen, über Vertrauen oder Mißtrauen gegenüber bestimmten Führungsgruppen.

Zurück zum Unternehmen. Weder die Gesetze noch die Statuten, noch die Organigramme sind geeignet, Führung zu generieren, Autorität zu schaffen. Sie, die Gesetze, sind eher passiv als aktiv zu interpretieren; denn sie setzen eher Schranken, als daß sie Inhalte zu schaffen vermögen. Auch das zeigte die Geschichte: Gesetze sind Ausdruck eines Nachvollzugs. Wirksame Gesetze sind Abbilder des Zeitgeistes, sie bilden ab, was in den Köpfen schon existiert.

Ich laufe Gefahr, wenn ich diesen fast anarchistischen Gedanken weiter verfolge, daß ich an Grundfesten des Gedankens der Organisation rüttle, die Wissenschaft von der Organisation in Frage stelle. Das will ich nicht; Organisation als Ausdruck betrieblicher Ordnung ist unerläßlich. Worauf ich hinaus will, ist nur das: Autorität wird nicht durch organisatorische Schritte geboren. Vielmehr zeugt erst die Autorität, die menschliche Qualifikation, ich sage vielleicht besser: die menschliche Qualität, die Grundmauern, auf denen wir dann das Gebäude der Organisation errichten.

Autorität heute ist aber etwas anderes als Autorität gestern. Aus dem Consilium des römischen Senats, also aus dem guten Rat, dem man auctoritas damals zusprach, ist in unserer Zeit eher der Charakter des Ausschlaggebenden getreten, um nicht Entscheidungsgewalt zu sagen.

Autorität und autoritär haben nur die Wortwurzel, nicht aber den Sinngehalt gemeinsam. Wer für Autorität eintritt, als Element unserer abendländischen Geschichte, ist kein Vertreter autoritärer Führungsmethoden oder gar Staatsformen. Dafür, daß gewachsene, auf Überzeugen, nicht auf Macht beruhende Autorität möglich ist, haben wir in Karl Jaspers – dem Basel nach dem Kriege eine Wirkungsstätte geboten hat – einen unverfänglichen Zeugen, wenn er in seinem Werk »Von der Wahrheit« sagt, Autorität sei »die Fülle des Tragenden, das Bergende und das Beruhigende«. An gleicher Stelle spricht sich Jaspers für Führung und Disziplin aus, wenn er schreibt:

»Wer nicht unter dem Zwang einer unentrinnbaren Führung arbeiten muß, wird … undiszipliniert, weich gegen sich selbst und billigt sich immer mehr zu.«

In der Politik unterscheiden wir, in extremer Vereinfachung, *autokratische* und *demokratische* Führungsstile – beide sind ungeeignet, wenn ein Unternehmen nachhaltig Erfolg erzielen will. Während Autokratie im Unternehmen letzten Endes versagen *muß*, weil sie den Informationsfluß beeinträchtigt und den Kräftefluß mindert, ist Demokratie im Unternehmen zu verwerfen, weil sie die Stetigkeit des Unternehmensziels ebenso in Frage stellt wie die Beständigkeit des einzuschlagenden Weges.

Parallelen zum militärischen Führungsstil zu zeigen, halte ich teils für sinnvoll, teils für unzulässig. Militärische Führung ist notwendigerweise autoritär, wenn auch, innerhalb demokratisch vertretener Ziele, weder diktatorisch noch autokratisch. Insoweit sie klar zwischen Auftrag und Befehl differenziert, ist sie sogar partizipativ – und, darauf will ich hinaus: anzustreben ist – und von uns angestrengt wird – ein kooperativer und folglich partizipativer Führungsstil, der den freien Informationsfluß in alle Richtungen verbürgt und der die Kräfte aller Ebenen in den Dienst des Unternehmens stellt.

Führen, auch wenn es mit Befehlen verbunden sein kann, ist eben nicht identisch mit Befehlen, es bedeutet hinführen zu einem Ziel, worüber durch Überzeugen Konsensus erreicht worden ist. Führen – ob im nationalen oder im multinationalen Rahmen – setzt Kommunikation voraus, die in beiden Richtungen vor sich gehen muß: von der Führung zur Ausführung und zurück.

Wissenschaft und Technik der Kommunikation haben in den letzten Jahren – nach stetiger Entwicklung seit Mitte des letzten Jahrhunderts – rasche und bedeutende, vermutlich einschneidende Fortschritte gemacht. Deren praktische Anordnung in der Führungstechnik ist im Gang oder steht noch in den achtziger Jahren bevor.

Übergang von der analogen zur digitalen Nachrichtentechnik, Erhöhung der Übertragungsgeschwindigkeiten und Einführung größerer Bandbreiten setzen zwar erhebliche Investitionen – zum Beispiel die Einrichtung digital konzipierter Vermittlungsstellen und hochleistungsfähiger Kabelnetze (Glasfaserkabel, optische Signalübertragung) – voraus. Die nationalen Fernmelde-Monopole sind aber entschlossen, diese Investitionen zu verwirklichen und eine Vielzahl wesentlich verbesserter, vielfach gänzlich neuer Dienste anzubieten.

Kein Zweifel also: Das Ausmaß und Tempo der Kommunikation, die Fülle der Informationen, der Grad der Verläßlichkeit des Nachrichtenverkehrs – alle diese einerseits notwendigen Führungswerkzeuge werden essentielle Fortschritte machen. Andererseits wird dann aber, und das ist einer meiner Kernpunkte, die Gefahr entstehen – und es gibt schon durchaus alarmierende Anzeichen –, daß große (aber nicht nur große) Unternehmen mit weitgespanntem Radius von der strategischen Führung zur operativen Führung übergehen, und von da aus ist der Weg zur taktischen Führung von der Zentrale aus nicht mehr weit – ein Gefahrenherd für die Dezentralisierung, die für mich Leitsatz und Erfahrung ist.

Führen setzt Delegieren voraus, besteht aber beileibe nicht daraus. Ich kenne kaum eine größere Platitüde der Lehre von der Unternehmensführung als den Begriff »Management by Delegation« – eine gängige Münze, aber ein Begriff, der nicht zu Ende gedacht ist, weil man nicht führen kann, indem man die Führung, sozusagen unreflektiert, aus der Hand gibt. Es war kein Spaßvogel, sondern ein ernstzunehmender Praktiker, der vorgeschlagen hat zu sagen »Management by Managers«.

Ich bin, wie eben gesagt, für Dezentralisierung; wir führen die Bosch-Gruppe seit Ende der sechziger Jahre weitgehend dezentral, wobei wir aber säuberlich, wenn auch nicht ausdrücklich, die Ebenen der politischen, der strategischen, der operativen und der taktischen Führung unterscheiden.

Die Unternehmenspolitik wird auf Vorschlag der Geschäftsführer vom Gesellschafterkreis umrissen, damit ist das Ziel festgelegt. Die Geschäftsführung erarbeitet die Unternehmensstrategie und trägt die Verantwortung für das Erreichen des Ziels. Sie überträgt die von ihr zu definierenden operativen Aufgaben den Geschäftsbereichen im In- und Ausland, sie koordiniert deren Tätigkeit und überwacht sie; die Verantwortung für das Erreichen der operativen Teilziele liegt bei den Leitern der Geschäftsbereiche, die ihrerseits taktische Aufträge an ihre Einheiten weitergeben.

Die *Zentralabteilungen*, in der Schweiz häufig als Stäbe bezeichnet, haben keine operativen, sondern Dienstleistungsaufgaben. Sie sind ausdrücklich keine Zwischeninstanz auf den Befehlswegen, sondern beratend tätig; zu ihren wichtigen Pflichten gehört Herstellen und Aufrechterhalten des Informationsflusses in beiden Richtungen, ohne den kein Unternehmen gedeihen kann, und, wichtiger noch, ohne den keine Motivation denkbar ist.

Den Zentralabteilungen ist insbesondere die *Nutzung der Synergien* auferlegt, die in unserem Fall vor allem folgende Gebiete betreffen:

- Finanzierung,
- Sachanlageinvestitionen,
- Akquisitionen,
- Personalpolitik,
- Fertigungs- und Vertriebsprogramme und deren Verbund.

Zwei dieser Gebiete sind besonders zu erläutern: Finanzieren wird, bei allem Bekenntnis zur Dezentralisierung, immer zentraler Steuerung, häufig auch zentraler Ausführung bedürfen; denken wir an weltweites Cash- and Currency-Management, das unverzichtbar in *einer* Hand liegen muß, was weder den örtlichen Bankenverkehr innerhalb der gesetzten Schranken ausschließt noch die Bemühung der regionalen Einheiten um tragfähige eigene Kapitalausstattung. Dem Werben der Landesgesellschaften um Eigenkapitalzuweisung seitens der Zentrale ist nur die Grenze der Rentabilität gesetzt; wer ansprechende Dividenden versprechen und zahlen kann, verschafft sich Zutritt zur »Hauptkasse«, die natürlich an übergeordnete Kriterien gebunden bleibt. Die »globale Finanzmobilität« ist freilich ein Idealziel, das bei dem Zustand vieler Währungsgebiete nur teilweise erreicht werden kann.

Zentrale Personalpolitik, um ein zweites Beispiel zu behandeln, beschäftigt sich sowohl mit der Auswahl, der Ausbildung und der weltweiten Rotation der leitenden Mitarbeiter als auch mit den Grundfragen der Nachwuchsgewinnung und der Beziehungen zu den Mitarbeitervertretungen und Gewerkschaften; letztere orientieren sich zunehmend weltweit, was eine Antwort verlangt.

Daß die *Zentralabteilungen* bei der Entwicklung und bei der Fortschreibung der Unternehmensstrategie eine wichtige Rolle spielen, daß sie die Ressourcen-Zuteilung durch die Geschäftsführung vorbereiten, daß sie die Daten für Planung und Kontrolle aufbereiten, gibt ihnen keine originären Führungsrechte, macht sie vielmehr zu Führungsgehilfen.

Man könnte ein Wortspiel anwenden, wenn man die Polarität zwischen Zentrale und regionaler Organisation beschreibt: Beschäftigt sich die erste mit Welt und Umwelt, so sind Feld und Umfeld der letzteren vorbehalten. Daß gerade die regionalen politischen Beziehungen, die rechtlichen Verhältnisse sowie die religiösen und sozialethischen Gegebenheiten in die »Kampfzone« der Regionalgesellschaften fallen, erklärt sich aus der Aufstellung der operativen Einheiten an der (Verkaufs-)Front.

Das alles klingt etwas theoretisch und nimmt sich allenfalls auf dem Papier gut aus. Unternehmen zeichnen sich von Behörden vor allem dadurch aus, daß ihre Führungs- und Ablaufregeln ebenso durchlässig wie anpassungsfähig sind – oder zumindest sein können. So wird sich nicht nur jedes Unternehmen anders darstellen als seine Wettbewerber, sondern auch morgen anders aussehen als heute. Immer aber muß es nach dem Grundgesetz leben, das für den Aufbau der belebten Natur gilt: daß das Ganze mehr sein muß als (nur) die Summe seiner Teile, daß es sich also – ich sage das in der Stadt der Bernoullis und Leonhard Eulers – beim Unternehmen um eine Integration teilweise infinitesimaler Elemente handelt und nicht um eine bloße Addition definierter Teile. Das ist nicht ohne tieferen Sinn.

Führen ist ein perennierender Prozeß, eine kontinuierliche Aufgabe, so daß es auf den ersten Blick merkwürdig anmutet, wenn man im Zusammenhang damit von Phasen spricht – ein Ausdruck, der nur gerechtfertigt ist, wenn man damit die Schritte meint, in denen Führungs*entscheidungen* zustande kommen:

1. die Problemphase,
2. die Datenphase,
3. die Entscheidungsphase,
4. die Phase der Durchsetzung,
5. die Kontrollphase.

Wenn ich einmal beiseite lasse, daß *Führung* in der *Durchsetzung* des *einmal festgelegten Führungswillens* gipfelt, so kommt den Entscheidungsphasen 1 und 5 besonderes Gewicht zu: der Schärfe und der Prägnanz der Formulierung des Problems einerseits, der Rückmeldung, der Rückkopplung im Sinne der Regeltechnik andererseits. In der Kontrollphase handelt es sich also weniger darum festzustellen, ob sich die Führung durchgesetzt hat, als vielmehr darum, daß sich das, was erreicht worden ist, in neuen Plänen niederschlägt.

Natürlich halte ich, schon pflichtgemäß, viel von Planung, solange sie in einem *Mikro*organismus vorgeht, der ja, innerhalb der National- und der Weltwirtschaft, auch der größte Multi noch immer ist und bleibt. Was ich verwerfe, ist der in der bisherigen Geschichte stets mißglückte Versuch der Globalplanung oder -steuerung, der mißglücken muß, weil in ihm jene nach dem Gesetz der großen Zahl – und aufgrund individueller Interessenanlage ohne Verzug – verlaufende Rückkopplung fehlt, die allein den zeitgerechten Ausgleich unvermeidlicher, aber nur partieller Fehlentwicklungen herbeiführt. Um mit Herbert Giersch zu sprechen: Die Marktwirtschaft ist die Wirtschaft der vielen Köpfe, Sinne, Meinungen, Erfahrungen, Energien.

Bei aller Bereitschaft aber, der Planung im Unternehmen Raum zu geben, kann ich das Bedürfnis nicht unterdrücken, hier ein kleines Gedicht von Erich Kästner herzusagen: »Je üppiger die Pläne blühen, um so verzwickter wird die Tat. Man nimmt sich vor, sich zu bemühen, und schließlich hat man den Salat!« Wir sollten aber dennoch unverdrossen im multinationalen Unternehmen weiter planen; denn Planen macht ja nicht nur Freude, sondern zwingt auch zum Nachdenken, vor allem über Alternativen.

*

Führungsprobleme lassen sich mit *organisatorischen Mitteln* allein nicht lösen; ich gehe soweit zu sagen, sie lassen sich auch ohne organisatorische Mittel lösen – wenn überhaupt. *Organigramme* pflegen zweidimensional zu sein. Stellen wir uns das Unternehmen zumindest räumlich vor, fehlt die dritte Dimension. Doch ist die Wirklichkeit verwickelter. So schwer es uns, soweit wir Nicht-Mathematiker sind, fällt, den Weg vom Einmaleins zur n-ten Dimension nachzuvollziehen, so leicht fällt es uns doch, ein Unternehmen – und insbesondere ein multinationales – als multi*dimensional* zu begreifen. Dessen Lebens- und Wirkungsbedingungen kommt man mit den zwei Koordinaten des klassischen Organigramms nicht bei.

Ich erinnere mich in diesem Zusammenhang an die Frage eines klugen Besuchers, dem ich, auf seine Bitte, das *Organigramm* erläutert hatte, das zu jener Zeit bei uns gültig war – die Frage: Und wie läuft das Geschäft in Wirklichkeit ab? Ich konnte darauf zunächst nur sagen, das übliche Organigramm beschränke sich auf die Darstellung des Sollzustands der hierarchischen Beziehungen. Und wenn man in die Tiefe geht, dann muß man einräumen, daß häufig genug nicht einmal die personellen Beziehungen, geschweige denn die persönlichen im Organigramm deutlich werden, das eben üblicherweise statischer Natur ist.

Unternehmen aber, die überleben wollen, brauchen Dynamik. Bei ihnen geht es um Menschen, um Ideen, um Ziele, um Wege, um Kräfte, um Kraftfelder – nicht um Papier. Immer wieder, wenn es um die Ordnung oder die Neuordnung eines Bereichs geht, macht man mich auf Überschneidungen oder auf die Gefahr, daß solche entstehen, aufmerksam. Ich bekenne, daß ich zwar Überschneidungen nicht schätze, sie meistens auch nicht anstrebe, sie aber doch auch nicht annähernd so sehr fürchte wie Lücken. Es ist zwar kostspielig und führt oft zu menschlichen Reibungen, wenn zwei sich gleichzeitig um dieselbe Aufgabe kümmern. Aber unerträglich wäre es, wenn keiner sich darum kümmerte, vielmehr auf den anderen wartete. So lassen wir in unseren Arbeitsbeschreibungen eher Überlappungen zu als zu scharfe und zu hohe Grenzzäune. Und wir helfen durch gezielte Job-Rotation nach, daß möglichst viele unserer Mitarbeiter möglichst bald die Dinge auch von der anderen Seite des Zaunes kennenlernen.

*

Betrachten wir jetzt einmal die Organisations*formen*, stoßen wir auf eine große Mannigfaltigkeit, die sich nicht leicht in eine Organisationstypologie einfügen läßt, aber doch eine Reihe charakteristischer Strukturformen erkennen läßt:

1. Die »*zentrale*« Führung des gesamten nationalen und internationalen Geschäfts durch das Stammhaus (wobei je nach dessen Grundgliederung funktionale oder aber produktorientierte Führung vorliegen kann).
2. Die für das Gesamtgeschäft außerhalb der Stammländer zuständige »*International* Division« – mit der Sonderform regionaler

Kopfstellen, die jeweils eine Gruppe von Landesgesellschaften führen.

3. »*Ländergesellschaften*«, die regional gewinngesteuert sind, zwar in den Grundzügen zentraler Führung unterstehen, nicht aber den Produktbereichen des Stammhauses zugeordnet sind.
4. »*Ländergesellschaften*«, die zwar aus rechtlichen und finanziellen Gründen ergebnisbezogen sind, aber verlängerte Arme der Produktbereiche des Stammhauses darstellen, so daß der Weltertrag der Produktbereiche zumindest statistisch zu ermitteln ist.

Es ist trivial zu sagen, daß in einer multinationalen Unternehmung kaum eine dieser Formen rein vorkommt; strenggenommen stehen sie auf dem Papier. Der Begriff der Typologie, den ich angewandt habe, bedeutet ja Unterdrückung der Individualität, die im internationalen Geschäft nach unserer Erfahrung eine entscheidende Rolle spielt. Immerhin ist es nützlich, wenn man sich immer wieder aufs neue mit den denkbaren organisatorischen Varianten beschäftigt, damit man seine Pflicht als Unternehmensleiter erfüllt, die ich unter anderem darin sehe, daß man die Gegenwart im Blick auf die Zukunft immer wieder in Frage stellt.

Eine kritische Diskussion der Organisationsformen zeigt in jedem Fall Vor- und Nachteile, die man sehr kategorisch so sehen kann: *Je zentraler* geführt wird – und das gilt auch für den Fall der International Division –, desto stärker wird das Denken in internationalen Dimensionen gefördert.

Ist das Stammhaus produktorientiert gegliedert, führt zentrale Führung zu klarer Erfassung der Leistungsfaktoren, von Aufwand und Ertrag. Zentrale (oder pseudo-zentrale) Führung durch eine International Division oder durch Regional Headquarters führt, wie man sagen muß, zu gebrochenen Wegen, zu Informations- und Zeitverlust und erregt Konfliktpotentiale.

Je dezentraler geführt wird, desto flexibler, anpassungsfähiger erweist sich eine Struktur. Denn sie erlaubt von Kontinent zu Kontinent, von Land zu Land individuelle Lösungen, wenn auch Überschneidungen und Mehrgleisigkeiten nicht ausgeschlossen sind.

Die Bosch-Gruppe hat eine Matrixstruktur gewählt, die Relais in Form einer International Division oder von Regional Headquarters ausschließt, so daß die Ländergesellschaften dezentral am langen Zügel geführt werden. Dies verhindert die Fernwirkung von Zentralabteilungen und den Durchgriff der Produktabteilungen des Stammhauses – deshalb spreche ich eher von einem Gittergefüge, das Rückhalt gibt, aber dem Durchschlüpfen immer wieder Raum bietet, wie wir überhaupt Starrheit für einen größeren Schaden halten als Bewegungsfreiheit innerhalb einer gegebenen Bandbreite. Ob das Spektrum eingehalten wird, zeigt der Erfolg.

An dieser Stelle muß ich die Position des Controlers erwähnen, der in der Bosch-Gruppe in jedem Geschäftsbereich und in jeder Ländergesellschaft vorhanden ist – in einer nicht ganz leichten, aber notwendigen Doppelrolle: Er »reportiert« sowohl dem Leiter seines Bereichs als auch der zuständigen Zentralabteilung, nach Spielregeln, deren Darstellung hier zu weit führen würde.

Die große Gefahr organisatorischer Strukturen liegt darin, daß sie häufig dem Tempo der Entwicklung, oft aber auch der Richtung der Entwicklung nicht folgen können – sie würden sich ja aufgeben in ihrer Selbstüberschätzung. So sehr die Stabilität des Unternehmens eines gewissen organisatorischen Gerüstes bedarf, so sehr wird doch seine Flexibilität durch verkarstete organisatorische Gebilde eingeschränkt, wenn nicht verhindert. Ist einmal eine Organisation nicht mehr durchlässig genug, so mag sie selbst die zeitgerechte Information hemmen, auf alle Fälle die Aktion stören, die der Information folgen muß. Womit ich nicht sagen will, *jede* neue Nachricht verlange unverzügliches Handeln – im Gegenteil, zu den essentiellen Führungsqualitäten gehört die Fähigkeit und die Nervenkraft, zwischen echtem und falschem Alarm zu unterscheiden.

*

Bevor ich, abschließend, über den für den Erfolg der multinationalen Unternehmung *letztlich entscheidenden* Komplex der Personalführung einige Worte sage, sollten wir uns einen Augenblick lang einem politischen Fragenkreis zuwenden.

Es *gibt* eine Multi-Problematik, und es ist im Prinzip zu begrüßen, daß sich internationale Stellen damit beschäftigt haben. Die Wirtschaft der Länder, in denen Multis ansässig sind, hat mit den internationalen Organisationen bei der Analyse des Begriffs und beim Entwurf von Richtlinien zusammengearbeitet, die dazu beitragen, Spannungen zu mildern und Gegensätze zu überbrücken, die mit der Aktivität solcher Unternehmungen zusammenhängen.

Die OECD hat unter dem 21. Juni 1976 Leitsätze für multinationale Unternehmen herausgegeben, die Regeln für eine nutzbringende Zusammenarbeit von Investoren und Gastländern enthalten. Die Bosch-Gruppe hat wie eine ganze Reihe anderer Unternehmen die Leitsätze längst anerkannt und ihr Verhalten darauf eingestellt, soweit es sich nicht schon bisher von selbst verstand, daß im Sinne dieser Regeln vorgegangen wurde. Wir erwarten also von unseren Regionalgesellschaften, daß sie sich in das Gebiet, in den Staat, in die Nation *einfügen*, in denen sie tätig sind.

Das Prinzip, nicht als Fremdkörper in ein Gastland einzudringen, sondern dort ein »guter industrieller Bürger« zu werden, verlangt die Beteiligung nationaler Kräfte an führender, zumindest an leitender Stelle; es wäre ein Rückfall in koloniale Sitten, wenn den einheimischen Mitarbeitern nur die untergeordnete Arbeit überlassen würde. Viele multinationale Unternehmen haben bewiesen, daß sie in der Lage sind, eine Symbiose der Nationen zu erreichen; man wird vorteilhaft Schritt für Schritt handeln, nicht aber, ohne im Grundkonzept die Etappen vorzuzeichnen. Die Ausbildung und Einweisung ausländischer Arbeitskräfte im Stammhaus gehört zu den erforderlichen Schritten.

*

Die internationale Tätigkeit eines Unternehmens steht und fällt mit den richtigen *Personalentscheidungen.* Die personellen Probleme sind bei internationaler Tätigkeit aus verschiedenen Gründen noch größer als im Inland:

1. Die Tätigkeit im fremden Land verlangt eine größere Vielseitigkeit und eine größere Anpassungsfähigkeit.
2. Gleichzeitig wird eine größere Selbständigkeit, größere innere Unabhängigkeit und größere Bereitschaft zum Tragen unternehmerischer Wagnisse verlangt – wobei Entscheidungen häufig auf eigene Faust und ohne Rückfrage beim Stammhaus getroffen werden müssen.
3. Loyalität gegenüber dem Unternehmen und Legalität gegenüber dem Staat sind bei einer Auslandstätigkeit stärker gefordert als im Inland.
4. Was im Inland unter tagtäglicher Kontrolle steht, vollzieht sich im Ausland auf weite Strecken ohne direkten Einblick des Stammhauses. Notwendig ist also Vertrauenswürdigkeit – oder in anderen Worten: ein Vertrauensvorschuß.
5. Mehrsprachigkeit ist in Gebieten, in denen nicht die Muttersprache herrscht, eine unbedingte Voraussetzung für den Erfolg. Neben der Beherrschung der englischen Sprache als Weltsprache muß die Landessprache in Wort und Schrift geläufig beherrscht werden.
6. Wo im Inland Spezialisten zur Verfügung stehen, ist draußen der Rückgriff auf den Fachmann nicht immer möglich. Wer ins Ausland entsandt wird, muß folglich eine breitere Wissens- und Erfahrungsgrundlage haben als für die Inlandstätigkeit verlangt. Er muß lernfähig sein.

Der Typus der Führungskraft für internationale Tätigkeit wird von der Natur nur selten angeboten. Unerläßlich ist folglich die Heranbildung begabter geeigneter Kräfte. Dies ist eine Aufgabe, die von langer Hand vorbereitet und mit System angefaßt werden muß.

Statt eine globale Statistik vorzutragen, nenne ich einige Beispiele für *unser* Bestreben, die Nationen, in deren Land wir tätig sind, an der Führung der Gesellschaften zu beteiligen. In der *Schweiz* sind Präsident und Direktor der Fertigungsgesellschaft – an der übrigens Hunderte von Schweizer Aktionären beteiligt sind, wenn auch minoritär – Schweizer. Die Vertriebsgesellschaft hat zwar als Präsidenten einen Deutschen, aber der Direktor ist Schweizer. In unserer großen *indischen Fertigungs- und Vertriebsgesellschaft*, deren Majorität bei uns liegt, gilt seit Jahrzehnten in der Spitze Parität: Ein Inder hat seit eh und je die kaufmännische Leitung, während die technische Spitze von Deutschland gestellt wird; mehr als 9700 Mitarbeiter sind durchweg Inder, denen nur 5 deutsche Berater zur Seite stehen. Mehr als 250 der Inder sind durch eine Ausbildung in Deutschland gegangen: eine sehr wirksame Form von Technologietransfer. Seit einer Reihe von Jahren fällt, nebenbei gesagt, in dem von der indischen Regierung ausgeschriebenen Wettbewerb der erste Preis für die Lehrlingsausbildung an unser indisches Unternehmen. In den *Vereinigten Staaten* ist die Führungsmannschaft gemischt. Um nach Europa zurückzukehren: *französisches Übergewicht* in der dortigen Gesellschaft; die Unternehmen in *Nordeuropa* sind fest in skandinavischer Hand.

Um dem Nachwuchs das Risiko, das mit der Annahme eines *Auslandspostens* verbunden ist, schmackhaft zu machen, müssen bestimmte *Voraussetzungen* geschaffen werden:

1. Das Einkommen muß einen Wagniszuschlag enthalten.
2. Die örtlichen Lebensverhältnisse müssen bei der Bemessung des Einkommens berücksichtigt werden.
3. Die Ersparnisbildung in Hartwährung muß gesichert bleiben, ohne daß dadurch das Gesetz verletzt wird.
4. Die Rückkehr muß gesichert werden.

Der letztere Punkt ist der wichtigste und der schwierigste. Die »Rückfahrkarte« allein genügt nicht. Befürchtet wird, daß die Inlandsposition verlorengeht, solange man draußen ist, und daß man von anderen, die sich der Auslandstätigkeit entziehen, überholt wird. Es muß folglich dafür gesorgt werden, daß der Rückkehrer nicht das Gefühl bekommt, während seiner Auslandstätigkeit Boden verloren zu haben.

Wir haben bei Bosch ein Prinzip – dessen praktische Anwendung wie immer, wenn es sich um Prinzipien handelt, nicht ganz leicht ist–: Die Annahme einer Auslandstätigkeit ist Beförderungsvoraussetzung. Wer einen angebotenen Auslandsposten ohne triftige Begründung ablehnt, läuft Gefahr, bei einer Inlandsbeförderung übergangen zu werden. Weiter bemühen wir uns, den Rückkehrer nicht nur auf gleicher Ebene wieder aufzunehmen, sondern nach Möglichkeit bei dieser Gelegenheit zu befördern.

Unerläßlich bei allem sind Lob und Anerkennung. Jeder muß wissen, daß es ohne ihn nicht geht, daß es aber allein mit ihm auch nicht geht, daß der Fortschritt, auch wenn auf der Intuition, der Eingebung einzelner beruhend, eine Gemeinschaftsleistung und häufig genug in den Zeitläufen vorgezeichnet ist.

*

Im Weltmaßstab bewährt sich letzten Endes die unternehmerische Leistung, weil sie dort dem Wettbewerb aller potentiellen Gegenkräfte ausgesetzt ist. Dies ist keine Abwertung der Leistung aller jener Unternehmungen, die je nach Branche, nach Struktur, nach Volumen auf kleinere Wirkungsradien begrenzt bleiben, innerhalb oder außerhalb einer nationalen Begrenzung – aus objektiven und subjektiven Gründen. Denn für die meisten Unternehmen gibt es gute Gründe dafür, auf die Entwicklung zum multinationalen Unternehmen zu verzichten. Wenn ich sage, die Welt des Unternehmers sei die Welt, so wird dies für die weitaus größte Zahl der Unternehmen nichts anderes bedeuten können, als daß man sich den Auslandsbeziehungen, dem Export zuwendet.

Unternehmen, auf die bestimmte Voraussetzungen zutreffen, werden multinational weniger aufgrund eigenen Entschlusses als vielmehr aus einer innewohnenden Gesetzlichkeit. Wie man mit der »Explosion« in den Weltmaßstab fertig wird, ist eine Führungsaufgabe. Darüber wollte ich einiges sagen. *(1983)*

Die Seele der Wirtschaft

UNTERNEHMER IM WANDEL DER ZEITEN

Wenn die Baden-Badener Unternehmergespräche auf ihr 30jähriges Bestehen zurückblicken, liegt es nahe, über den Unternehmer im Wandel der Zeiten zu sprechen. Manchmal glauben wir, der Beruf des Unternehmers sei erst in unserer Zeit entdeckt worden. Ein kurzer Rückblick in die Geschichte wird zeigen, daß dem nicht so ist.

Bevor ich darangehe, dem Ursprung des Unternehmertums nachzuspüren, einige wenige Worte zu dem Thema des Wandels. Ich warne sowohl vor der Überschätzung des Tiefgangs dieses Wandels als auch vor einer Überschätzung des Tempos, mit dem er sich vollzieht. Vor einer *Unter*schätzung zu warnen ist unnötig; wir lesen und hören heute über dieses Phänomen tagtäglich. Man will uns glauben machen, daß morgen oder übermorgen kein Stein unseres wirtschaftlichen, unseres industriellen Gebäudes noch auf dem anderen stehen werde.

»Im Wandel der Zeiten« – das klingt nach 19. Jahrhundert, romantisch, sentimental ... und paßt insofern schlecht in unsere nüchterne Betrachtung. Was damit gesagt werden soll, ist ein Doppeltes, nämlich einmal die mehr als säkulare Beobachtung, daß die Welt nicht stillsteht, dann aber, daß der Wandel sich offenbar seit geraumer Zeit schneller vollzieht, als das viele Jahrtausende lang der Fall gewesen sein dürfte. Dennoch bleibe ich bei dem Begriff der Evolution.

Der Philosoph Hermann Lübbe spricht von der »Geschichtlichen Akzeleration«, und er zieht daraus den Schluß, »die Zukunft gleiche immer weniger der Gegenwart und der Vergangenheit, so daß sie aus der bloßen Lebenserfahrung der einzelnen Individuen immer weniger vorhergesagt werden könne«.

Alfred Weber, der Bruder Max Webers, hat diesen rascher werdenden Ablauf 1946 in »Abschied von der bisherigen Geschichte« dargestellt. Während schon in vorgeschichtlicher Zeit in der Entwicklung der menschlichen Gesellschaft und ihrer Fähigkeiten eine Beschleunigung eingetreten sein dürfte, stellt Weber seit Mitte des 16. Jahrhunderts eine Dynamisierung fest, die das Tempo des historischen Prozesses erhöhte. Das Verhältnis von Mensch und Erde, so Alfred Weber, änderte sich, und »eine gänzlich neue Art des Gesamtablaufs« sei eingetreten; die politschen Vorgänge entwickelten sich rascher.

Daß die Geschwindigkeit, mit der die Geschichte in allen ihren Aspekten weiterschreitet, größer geworden ist, beobachten wir zumindest seit dem Beginn der Industrialisierung am Ende des 18. Jahrhunderts. Beunruhigt ist der Zeitgenosse aber erst, seitdem man ihn mit dem »technologischen Wandel« beschäftigt, der die Nachkriegsjahrzehnte ergriffen hat. Wir können den Beginn mit der Erfindung des Transistors, der ersten miniaturisierten Halbleiter-Bauelemente gleichsetzen – das war 1949. Doch blieb dieser technologische Wandel zunächst unbeobachtet von der Politik. Diese wurde erst in den letzten Jahren aufmerksam, wenn nicht nervös. Aber die Arbeitslosigkeit in der Bundesrepublik Deutschland, die man der heutigen Bonner Koalition in die Schuhe schiebt, ist ganz eindeutig keine technisch-technologische, sondern eine politische, nämlich eine Folge der verfehlten Sozial-, Finanz- und Wirtschaftspolitik der vergangenen Bonner Koalition der siebziger Jahre. Das heutige Bonn hat diese Arbeitslosigkeit als Hypothek übernehmen müssen, geerbt. Immerhin: Der technologische Wandel könnte eine Zukunftsfolge haben, weil seinetwegen ein wesentlicher Abbau der derzeitigen Arbeitslosigkeit bis zum nächsten Wahlgang sehr schwierig sein wird.

*

Das Unternehmerbild, der Unternehmertypus ändert sich im Laufe der Jahrhunderte, der gesellschaftlichen und technischen Entwicklung folgend zeitweise – und ich halte das für sehr wichtig – auch ihr vorangehend.

Ich sagte bereits, der »Unternehmer« sei keine Errungenschaft der Neuzeit, er existierte bereits in der Antike. Aus der wechselvollen Geschichte dieses Stands, einer Kategorie sui generis, ergibt sich seine wechselvolle soziale Stellung.

Man kann sich den Fernhandel der Antike nicht ohne Unternehmer denken. Hier haben wir wohl den frühesten Realtypus des Unternehmers, über den man bei Rostóvtzeff Wissenswertes erfahren kann – auch in der Erweiterung seines Bildes auf Industrielle, Bankiers und Steuerpächter. Die Industriellen waren zum Beispiel in der Metallgewinnung und in der Waffenherstellung tätig (letzteres offenbar ein historischer Geschäftszweig). Massenproduktion war ihnen fremd; aber sie waren Eigentümer von Produktionsmitteln; Rostóvtzeff spricht von Bourgeoisie, von Kapitalisten; im Sachverzeichnis seiner Gesellschafts- und Wirtschaftsgeschichte der hellenistischen Welt kommt das Wort Unternehmer mehr als dreißigmal vor.

Sie waren Individualisten, jene antiken Unternehmer – Handelsgesellschaften kamen erst im Mittelalter auf. Wir müssen aus Zeitgründen die spannenden Phasen der frühkapitalistischen Unternehmungen Italiens, Oberdeutschlands und im Nord- und Ostseegebiet (Hanse) überspringen und haben auch keine Zeit für die etwas spätere Entwicklung in Rußland, bei der es um die Erschließung Sibiriens ging – Unternehmer wie die Stroganoffs waren dafür nötig. Unternehmer gab es dann auch schon im Merkantilismus; der Staats-Kapitalismus der Zeit der Manufaktur kam nicht ohne sie aus.

*

Aber die Kernfrage, die uns heute beschäftigt, ist keine historische mehr: Was ist das eigentlich für ein Mensch – dieser Unternehmer?

Toynbee, bekannt für die große Sorgfalt, die er der Differenzierung des Aufstiegs und des Verfalls der Kulturkreise zuwendete – im Widerspruch zu seinem großen Gegenspieler Spengler –, sagt ganz einfach, die Unternehmer seien die »creative minority«. Wir empfinden das als ehrenvoll, wenn wir auch nicht ganz sicher sind, ob die »majority«, deren »creativity« hiermit in Frage gestellt ist, das ebenso empfindet. Es ist bekanntlich in der Demokratie mit dem Respekt vor der Minderheit nicht weit her, solange man diese nicht zur Mehrheitsbildung dringend benötigt und solange sie sich so gut beträgt, wie die Unternehmer-Minorität das zu tun pflegt.

In der starken Verkürzung, die uns auferlegt ist, sage ich zur Typologie des Unternehmers, daß es vor allem in der wissenschaftlichen Diskussion der letzten fünfzig Jahre immer wieder darum gegangen ist, ob nur der als Unternehmer gilt, der sein eigenes Kapital einsetzt (Eigentümer-Unternehmer) *oder* ob auch der »nur« mit der Führung Beauftragte, der keine Anteile am Unternehmen besitzt, als Unternehmer gilt und sich als solcher fühlen und bezeichnen darf.

Ich habe den Streit, ob Unternehmer ist, wer sein Kapital oder wer nur seine Position und seinen guten Ruf riskiert, für um so müßiger, je anonymer das Kapital wird, für um so müßiger, je mehr man Kapitalrisiken auf diese oder jene Weise absichert. Beide Typen von Unternehmern riskieren »Kopf und Kragen«, wenn sie Mißerfolge aufhäufen.

Vielleicht ist es wissenswert, daß das Unternehmen, für das ich noch immer arbeite, von einer Kommanditgesellschaft gelenkt wird (sie besitzt 90 Prozent der Stimmrechte, wenn auch nur geringe Vermögensrechte), deren Komplementär nicht etwa eine Gesellschaft mit beschränkter Haftung ist, sondern leibhaftig vor Ihnen steht – fast ein Relikt in seiner vollen persönlichen Haftung.

So antiquiert folglich heute ein Streit um den Unternehmertypus ist, so halte ich es doch für historisch relevant, daß ein Adam Smith in dem Unternehmer, der nicht sein eigenes Kapital einsetzte, nur einen »Stellvertreter« sah und daß ihm Ricardo darin im Grundsatz zustimmte – was es Marx erleichterte, aus ihm den »Ausbeuter« zu machen, den Unterdrücker, den er als Propagandafigur brauchte. Dabei kannte Marx nachweislich den funktionellen Unternehmer durchaus – der paßte ihm aber nicht in den Kram. Thorstein Veblen, in seinem Buch über die »Leisure Class«, sprach dann später vom »Schmarotzer«, und es blieb schließlich Paul Tillich vorbehalten, den Unternehmer als »dämonische« Figur zu bezeichnen, was theologischem Sprachschatz nahezuliegen scheint.

Blenden wir zurück zu einer wissenschaftlichen Betrachtungsweise, so kommt der nicht nur bis zu seinem Tod (1950) häufig zitierte Schumpeter unserer Vorstellung am nächsten. Er läßt die Frage des Kapitalrisikos beiseite und verlangt vom Unternehmer, wie Toynbee, schöpferische Kraft, er verlangt von ihm die Fähigkeit des Gestaltens, er will, daß der Unternehmer Führer auf neuen Wegen sei. Man legt ihm heute den Zielbegriff »Innovation« in den Mund, obwohl er das Wort wohl nie benützt hat; es existierte mit diesem Inhalt noch nicht.

Schumpeter hatte schon 1928 geschrieben, bei der Unternehmerfunktion handele es sich um »die Durchsetzung einer anderen als der bisherigen Verwendung von Produktionskräften«, wobei er »Innovation« im Sinn hatte, letztere aber weniger als Ergebnis intellektueller Bemühung ansah als vielmehr als das Resultat von Willenseigenschaften, und ich glaube, daß gerade das wichtig ist für die Definition dessen, was wir von einem Unternehmer erwarten.

Wir sind damit gar nicht weit entfernt von Sombart, der wesentliche Beiträge zu unserem Thema geleistet hat. Er sagt, »trotz aller Objektivierung, Mechanisierung, Standardisierung der Betriebsvorgänge ist es (noch immer) der Mensch, der in einer nicht vorhersehbaren Welt Entscheidungen zu treffen hat, die er nicht delegieren kann«. Er, der Mensch, bestimme den Geist, die Politik und das

Schicksal des Unternehmens. Ich halte das für eine der besten Beschreibungen dessen, was vom Unternehmer verlangt wird. Von den Grenzen des Delegierens wird noch zu sprechen sein.

Wir sind also beim menschlichen Zusammenspiel, auf das es im Unternehmen maßgebend ankommt – und an dieser Stelle eine fast nebensächlich erscheinende und recht subjektive Bemerkung: In dem Entscheidungszentrum Unternehmen fallen die Entscheidungen nicht immer dort, wo das Organigramm das vorsieht oder vermuten läßt.

Wenn wir den Unternehmer charakterisieren, sind wir nicht weit entfernt von dem lange verpönten, plötzlich aber wieder ins Gespräch gekommenen Begriff der Elite. Ich greife hier zustimmend den Vorschlag des Präsidenten der Stuttgarter Industrie- und Handelskammer, Roland Klett, auf, der riet, statt »Elite« einfach »Qualität« zu sagen. Wer von Qualität spricht, meint nicht Mittelmaß, und er verneint damit auch jene »verdammte Nivellierung nach unten«, die aus der Förderung einer falsch verstandenen Chancengleichheit folgte.

Zur Qualität gehört neben der erwähnten Willenskraft ein angemessener Betrag an Verstand, was ich nur deshalb erwähne, um ein französisches Sprichwort zitieren zu können: nichts sei gerechter verteilt als der Verstand; denn jeder glaube, davon genügend zu besitzen. Ich sage das nicht ohne den Hintersinn, daß es der Unternehmer in der Öffentlichkeit schwer hat, weil man seine materielle Lage nicht ohne Neid betrachtet – stimmt das Sprichwort, so wird man ihn wenigstens nicht wegen seines Verstandes beneiden.

Wir wissen aber – und die Öffentlichkeit weiß es auch, unterdrückt aber ihr Wissen allzuoft –, daß der Unternehmergewinn nicht verbürgt ist und nicht dauerhaft, er ist »keine laufende Einkommensgröße«. Der Grund dafür liegt auf der Hand. Schumpeter sagte dazu 1928: das »Lebensinteresse des Unternehmers steht unter dem Druck gegebener Verhältnisse einerseits und jeweils engbegrenzter

Handlungsmöglichkeiten andererseits«, die wir vor allem in den harten Tatsachen des Marktes zu sehen haben.

*

Vom Idealtyp des Unternehmers zum Manager, zu den Methoden des Management ist ein kurzer Weg. Ich fürchte, es brächte uns in unseren Überlegungen über den Unternehmer nicht viel weiter, wenn wir heute die vielen Arbeitsweisen diskutierten, die dem Unternehmer und seinem engsten Mitarbeiter bei der Führung der Unternehmung zur Auswahl, zur Verfügung stehen. Es sollte genügen zu sagen, daß Witz und Ironie mehr Möglichkeiten zutage gefördert haben, als sie im Tageslauf der Unternehmer ausgeschöpft werden könnten. Aber vielleicht lohnt es sich zu unterstreichen, daß Geschäft und Geschäftigkeit unüberbrückbare Gegensätze sind. Der italienische Humanist des Cinquecento, Leon Battista Alberti, hat gesagt, noch nie habe er einen fleißigen Menschen anders als langsam gehen sehen.

Wer das Zeug zum Unternehmer hat, weiß auch, wie man die Aufgabe löst, ein Unternehmen zu managen – wobei mir noch immer am besten die Formel gefallen hat: Management by managers. Keine Formel aber sollte größere Skepsis hervorrufen als: Management by Exception. Daß Delegation ein nicht ersetzbares Führungswerkzeug ist, hat jeder von uns erfahren. Jeder von uns weiß aber auch, daß sich das dem Unternehmer gemäße Führungsverfahren iterativ entwickelt, durch »trial and error«. Man könnte sich vorstellen, daß auf diese Weise jene Geschmeidigkeit, jene Flexibilität der Führung erreicht wird, die den deutschen Unternehmern abgeht, wenn man dem *Wall Street Journal* vom 25. September 1984 glauben darf. Lehrbücher helfen hier nicht viel weiter – im Gegensatz zum lebendigen Erfahrungsaustausch.

Um nicht zu lange zu ernsthaft zu sein, will ich aus der amüsanten Zusammenstellung von »Gesetzen« des Amerikaners Augústine nur *einen* Satz vorlesen, der zu denken geben sollte: »Wenn man eine genügende Zahl von Management-Ebenen übereinanderlegt, kann man sicher sein, daß das Unglück nicht zufällig eintritt.« Augústine ist übrigens der Mann, der gesagt hat, das optimale Komitee habe keine Mitglieder – womit auch die Vorstellung eines »management by committees« verworfen ist.

Dabei fällt mir noch eine boshafte Lesefrucht ein: Die Arbeit einer Administration pflege so verteilt zu sein, daß sich ein großer Teil der Mitarbeiter damit beschäftige, Fehler zu machen, eine noch größere Zahl von Mitarbeitern bemühe sich, diese Fehler zu beseitigen. Nur einige wenige dächten darüber nach, wie man jene Fehler von vornherein vermeiden könne.

*

Ob Früh-, Hoch- oder Spätkapitalismus – die Grenzen sind schwankend, und wesentlich ist nur, daß Kapitalbildung eine Conditio humana sine qua non ist. Kapitalbildung drückt sich aus in jenen »produktiven Umwegen«, die durch die Herstellung von Werkzeugen gekennzeichnet sind: Wer ein Werkzeug herstellt, verbraucht nicht, sondern spart, konsumiert nicht, sondern investiert.

Unternehmer aller Zeiten haben sich durch Mut zu Investition ausgezeichnet, erfolgreich aber nur dann, wenn es sich nicht um »Investition an sich« handelte – wenn vielmehr vorher die Frage »Investition wozu« ausgelotet war. Investieren aus Begeisterung, aus Überfluß, aus steuerlichen Gründen, wegen verlockender staatlicher Förderung oder weil ein Vergleich mit »der Branche« zeigt, daß man relativ weniger investiert als der Wettbewerber, war immer gefährlich für das Unternehmen, aber auch für die Gesamtwirtschaft.

Sinnvolle Investitionsvorhaben scheitern auf mittlere oder längere Sicht nie an der Finanzierung. Dabei kann man eine Antwort auf die Frage beiseite lassen, ob der unternehmerische Elan dadurch induziert wird, daß Kapital Anlage sucht, oder ob der unternehmerische Elan das für eine Investition benötigte Kapital aufspürt oder sogar schafft. Wichtig ist nur, daß es im Grunde keiner »Venture Capital Funds« bedarf, um Innovation erst möglich zu machen, sondern daß man Unternehmer braucht, die realistische, realisierbare, früher oder später gewinnträchtige Investitionsideen haben.

*

Die Beziehungen des Unternehmers zum Staat sind eines Exkurses wert. Man sagt vom frühkapitalistischen Unternehmer, er habe staatliche Eingriffe *jeder* Art in seine wirtschaftliche Tätigkeit verurteilt, und ich bemerke dazu nur, daß es seinerzeit weder eine Einkommens- noch eine Körperschaftssteuer gab. Vom Staat von heute genügt es zu sagen, daß 39,6 Prozent aller Mitglieder unseres Bundestags Beamte und andere Behördenangehörige sind, während 61,6 Prozent aller Bonner Parlamentarier einer Gewerkschaft angehören. Unternehmer und freie Berufe verschwinden im Verhältnis dazu, während die Neigung einer überdimensionierten Administration zur Reglementierung durch eine solche Zusammensetzung des Bundestages tatkräftig unterstützt wird. Bonn hat Abhilfe gelobt; wir werden sehen.

Dennoch ist der Unternehmer eine Stütze nicht nur des Staatsgedankens, sondern auch des konkreten Staates. Der Unternehmer braucht die Institution Staat als Garanten der freiheitlichen Gesellschaft. Wir glauben nicht an Lenins Wort: »Solange es einen Staat gibt, gibt es keine Freiheit. Wenn es Freiheit geben wird, wird es keinen Staat mehr geben.«

Daß es in der Sowjetunion keine Freiheit gibt, wissen wir, aber auch, daß sich eine Gesellschaft ohne Staat im luftleeren Raum befindet. Der Staat ist Grundmauer und Überbau jeder modernen Gesellschaft. Die lange Geschichte der Menschheit ist eine Geschichte der Staaten, aber nicht der Gesellschaft. Ein sinnentleerter Begriff, wenn man Gesellschaft als amorphes Gebilde beschreibt, das der Organisation nicht bedürfe; jeder Kristall, jede Zelle ist organisiert.

Dabei befinden wir uns in einer merkwürdigen Spannungslage zwischen den Polen Individuum – Gesellschaft – Staat. Was das Individuum fordert – den individuellen Nutzen –, wird rücksichtslos beim Staat eingetrieben, dem man die Identität mit der Gesellschaft verweigert und dem die Gesellschaft den Gehorsam verweigert. Und die Gesellschaft treibt rücksichtslos ihre Forderung beim Individuum ein, indem sie dieses zu knechten trachtet.

Ich weiß nicht, ob jeder meine Meinung teilt, daß dies mit dem Thema »Unternehmer und Staat« sehr wohl etwas zu tun hat – doch sagte ich dazu früher, die Staatsverdrossenheit, von der wir hören, komme nicht davon, daß die Republik zu wenig leiste, sondern daß sie zu wenig fordere.

Der Unternehmer wäre überfordert, wenn man von ihm erwartete, daß er sich kritiklos den Forderungen des Staates beuge. Aber er bejaht ihn als eine unabdingbare Voraussetzung nicht nur vernünftigen Wirtschaftens, sondern auch menschlichen Zusammenlebens. Das sage ich nicht ohne eine Äußerung wiederzugeben, die man einem Abgeordneten der Regierungsparteien zuschreibt: Eine schlechte Regierung könne einem Land noch mehr Schaden zufügen als eine gute.

Wie dem auch sei: Gerrit Wagner, der Vorsitzende des Aufsichtsrats von Royal Dutch Petroleum, stellte kürzlich öffentlich fest: »Business has to do it in spite of government«.

*

Die dem Typus des verantwortlichen Unternehmers adäquate Wirtschaftsform ist die der Marktwirtschaft. Ihrer bedienen sich in der Praxis auch politische Systeme, die Planwirtschaft auf das Banner ihrer Theorie geschrieben haben. Angebot und Nachfrage werden über den Preis ausgeglichen. Der Gewinn ist der Überschuß des Preises über die Kosten; er entsteht im uneingeschränkten Wettbewerb und unter bestimmten Bedingungen. Der sowjetrussische Professor E. G. Libermann meinte dazu in seinen »Methoden der Wirtschaftslenkung im Sozialismus«:

- Der Preis spielt »die Rolle eines Maßstabs der Übereinstimmung von Produktion und Konsumtion«. Er dient »als Methode zur Bestimmung und Erhaltung der Optimalität«.
- Der »Gewinn (ist der) entscheidende Wertmesser der Tätigkeit der Unternehmen«, ein »Stimulans« der Produktion.

Man fühlt sich fast zu Hause, wenn man diese »kapitalistischen« Formeln hört, hätte man nicht auch Worte von Marcuse im Ohr wie zum Beispiel: »Selbstbestimmung bei der Produktion und Verteilung lebenswichtiger Güter und Leistungen« wäre »verschwenderisch«, sie müsse durch »wirksame Kontrolle« ersetzt werden.

Warum, wozu diese Auseinandersetzung mit einem Gegner, der doch nicht zuhört? Es geht mir nicht in erster Linie darum, den Gegensatz zwischen wirtschaftsnahem Handeln und wirtschaftsfremder Propaganda im Sozialismus polemisch darzustellen – obwohl das nicht ohne Reiz wäre. Auch nicht darum, unser Bewußtsein gegen die im Gang befindliche Unterwanderung zu schärfen. Vielmehr will ich dem Unternehmer, der einer freiheitlichen Wirtschaftsverfassung angehört, sagen, daß es nicht zuletzt an ihm, an seinem Handeln liegt, ob Marktwirtschaft erhalten bleibt oder in Planwirtschaft umschlägt. Wie halten wir es mit dem Wettbewerb? Geraten wir ins Stottern, wenn man uns fragt, was wir zum Beispiel vom Kartellrecht, der Fusionskontrolle, dem Verbot gebundener Preise halten? Sind wir uns im übrigen immer darüber klar, daß jeder Unternehmer nicht nur Verkäufer, sondern auch Einkäufer ist? Ich räume ein, daß auch mir diese Fragen schon unbequem waren.

*

Wir nähern uns damit der Frage, ob der Unternehmer zur Politik berufen ist. Einem unserer Unternehmerkollegen wird die Aussage in den Mund gelegt, das Unternehmen sei eine gesellschaftliche Veranstaltung. Ich zögere, das zu unterschreiben. Denn ich werde zu Unrecht einer Richtung zugerechnet, die unternehmenspolitische Entscheidungen den politischen, wirtschaftspolitischen, sozialpolitischen Gegebenheiten, Notwendigkeiten und Bestrebungen unterordnen will.

Ich stelle klar, daß der Unternehmer zunächst einmal Unternehmenspolitik zu machen hat. Man kann auch sagen: zunächst einmal gute Waren und Leistungen zu international wettbewerbsfähigen Kosten und Preisen zu produzieren hat. Nochmals in anderen Worten: zunächst einmal sein Unternehmen erfolgreich führen muß. Dies alles unter Wahrung der moralischen und der staatlichen Gesetze.

So wenig vom Lohn- und Gehaltsempfänger de facto erwartet werden kann, daß er seine Forderungen an den volkswirtschaftlichen Daten mißt – die von der früheren Bonner Koalition gestützte Lohnpolitik der siebziger Jahre mit ihrer verheerenden Wirkung auf den Arbeitsmarkt von heute zeigt das –, so wenig kann vom Unternehmer verlangt werden, daß er Marktchancen ausläßt, daß er seine Ware verschenkt.

Doch hat der Unternehmer, ich sagte das soeben, das gewollte und das gesetzte Recht zu respektieren und sich in die Wirtschaftsordnung einzufügen. Mehr noch: Er hat diese marktwirtschaftliche Ordnung anzustreben und mitzutragen, auch wenn sie sich im Einzelfall gegen ihn wendet.

Sozialromantik ist aber nicht Aufgabe des Unternehmers, von dem die Volkswirtschaft nicht mehr und nicht weniger verlangen kann, als daß er sein Unternehmen gesund, leistungsfähig erhält. Betriebliche Sozialpolitik auf dem Rücken des Verbrauchers ist markt- und ordnungswidrig; sie muß produktiven Sinn haben, wenn sie in das System passen soll, dessen Erhaltung für uns mehr ist als eine wirtschaftliche Kategorie.

Mit dieser harten und scharfen Abgrenzung mögen Illusionen zerstört, politische Hoffnungen in Frage gestellt werden. Aber der Unternehmer ist als solcher weder ein Altruist noch ein Wohltäter. Vielmehr hat er, in erster Linie, seine Produktion nach dem Grundsatz höchster Wirtschaftlichkeit zu organisieren.

Sind nun nicht Männer wie Ernst Abbé und Robert Bosch Beispiele dafür, daß eine mitarbeiterorientierte Personal- und Sozialpolitik eines Unternehmens in der Marktwirtschaft möglich ist? Ich will mich nicht damit herausreden, daß die Ausnahme die Regel bestätigt – Ausnahmen sind diese Beispiele, aber man darf sie gerade nicht als Bestätigung einer Regel ansehen. Ich kann versichern: Robert Bosch hat zeitlebens jede seiner – gelegentlich durchaus bahnbrechenden – Sozialmaßnahmen als Produktivitätssteigerung konzipiert und auch realisiert; das gilt gerade auch für den von ihm 1906 eingeführten Achtstundentag.

Ganz anders – und jenseits der Unternehmung – ist es mit dem Instrument der Stiftung, bei der es nicht darum geht, den Mitarbeitern laufende zusätzliche Zuwendungen zu Lasten des Betriebsertrags zu machen, sondern um die Entäußerung eines Unternehmers, der die Früchte einer Lebensarbeit gemeinnützigen Zwecken überweist – eine sinnvolle Entscheidung, die in manchem Falle nicht nur der Allgemeinheit zugute kommt, sondern auch der Erhaltung des Unternehmens über Generationen hinweg dient. Mit der Typisierung des Unternehmers hat das Stiftungsunternehmen nichts zu tun, sehen wir davon ab, daß gerade dann Unternehmenserfolg Bedingung ist, wenn eine Vermögensmasse zustande kommen soll, die eine Stiftung rechtfertigt.

Erhaltung und Ausbau unserer freien und erwiesenermaßen leistungsfähigen Gesellschafts- und Wirtschaftsordnung gehören freilich zu den Aufgaben des Unternehmers – aber eher in seiner Eigenschaft als Staatsbürger. Bei der Wechselwirkung zwischen dem Ganzen und den Unternehmern können wir ihn – bei aller Bevorzugung und Betonung der ursprünglichen Unternehmeraufgabe – von seiner staatsbürgerlichen Pflicht nicht freisprechen. Aber es ist eben gerade nicht seine ursprüngliche Aufgabe, Politik zu machen, so sehr wir es als Defizit ansehen müssen, daß in unserem Land – anders als in der Schweiz oder in den Vereinigten Staaten – der Unternehmer die Teilnahme am politischen Leben geringschätzt. Der Sachverstand des Unternehmers wird benötigt; gerade die von mir angestrebte Trennung der Sphären erlaubt es, ihn in den Parteien geltend zu machen, nicht zum Zweck der Beeinflussung, sondern der Information – um den Dialog zwischen mündigen Bürgern an die Stelle des Monologs der Administration zu setzen.

*

Der Unternehmer steht im Rampenlicht der öffentlichen Meinung. Zur Beeinflussung der öffentlichen Meinung durch die Medien sagte Professor Schmidtchen vor nicht allzu langer Zeit öffentlich, die Gesellschaft werde von der *negativen* Meldung her weiterentwickelt, und in ihrer Nachrichtenselektion wirkten die Medien auf einen großen Teil der Bevölkerung desorientierend.

Es ist kein Selbstmitleid – so sehr wir Deutschen seit geraumer Zeit dazu neigen, diesen Charaktermangel zu pflegen –, wenn man beobachtet, daß eine solche Desinformation häufig genug die Berichterstattung über Unternehmen und Unternehmer betrifft.

Salopp gesagt: Der Unternehmer hat eine schlechte Presse, und es ist nicht damit getan, daß man sagt, jede Nation, jede Schicht habe die Presse, die sie verdient. Aber ist die »schlechte Presse« in der Tat nur eine Erscheinung der neuesten Zeit? War nicht schon vor drei Jahrzehnten im Handwörterbuch der Staatswissenschaften zu lesen, an der Spitze der sozialen Pyramide habe der deutsche Unternehmer nie gestanden? Sein Minderwertigkeitskomplex tendiere dazu, in Großspurigkeit umzuschlagen?

Lassen wir die historische Wahrheit offen – blicken wir in die neueste Ausgabe der überwiegend von uns selbst finanzierten Magazine. Wir finden dann rasch, daß es unternehmerische Mißerfolge sind, die den Stoff liefern für eine kritische, skeptische, boshafte, schadenfrohe Berichterstattung, von der ich aber umgekehrt sage, daß sie ihre Wurzel auch in dem *Erfolg* unseres unternehmerischen Systems haben könnte – ein Erfolg, der in der Regel nicht nur auf dem Fehlen widriger Umstände beruht – hin und wieder ist das die Ursache –, sondern erarbeitet, erkämpft, durch Wagnisbereitschaft erreicht ist.

Ich sehe ein, daß ich mit einer Spekulation dieser Art aufs Glatteis gerate. Aber hier geht es um ein Phänomen, das an die Wurzel unternehmerischen Selbstverständnisses rührt: ob der deutsche Unternehmer seiner gesellschaftlichen Rolle gegenüber der Öffentlichkeit gerecht wird – und was zu tun ist, wenn die Antwort nein lautet.

Ich überlasse Antwort und Lösung einer jüngeren Generation. Obwohl ich persönlich nie darunter gelitten habe, daß das Unternehmerbild fast leidenschaftlich verzerrt ist, wünschte ich jüngeren Freunden doch, daß ihre Bestrebungen und Bemühungen in Zukunft mit einem objektiveren Maßstab gemessen würden, als ihn viele Medien heute anlegen. Wenn ich den Erfolg als denkbaren Ursprung mancher hämischen Bemerkung genannt habe, so bin ich doch sein erklärter und entschlossener Anhänger. Man soll von uns, die wir etwaigen Verlust auf der linken Seite unserer Bilanzen zu verbuchen haben, nicht sagen können, er sei unser größtes Aktivum!

*

Man bringt den Unternehmer immer wieder mit dem recht komplexen Fragenkreis der Kultur in Verbindung, man erwartet sein Eingreifen. Doch glaube ich nicht, daß ein Vollblut-Unternehmer mit seinen Unternehmungen von vornherein kulturelle Ziele verfolgt, verfolgen darf, und dabei lassen wir einmal offen, was wir unter Kultur verstehen wollen. Der junge Hofmannsthal verengte den Kulturbegriff, wenn er schrieb: »Was ist Kultur? Zu wissen, was einen angeht, und zu wissen, was einen zu wissen angeht.«

Wir meinen mit Kultur, über Hofmannsthal hinausgehend, das unbewußt-bewußt durch den planenden und bildenden Menschen und unter seiner pflegenden Hand jenseits der unmittelbar materiellen Bedürfnisse Entstandene und Entstehende. Wir sprechen von politischer Kultur, von der Kultur eines Unternehmens, und damit sind wir zurück beim Unternehmer und bei der Frage, ob und inwieweit von ihm erwartet werden darf und kann, daß er seine Unternehmungen kulturellen Zwecken dienstbar macht.

Es mag mein persönliches Ansehen schmälern, wenn ich den Standpunkt einnehme, das Verfolgen kultureller Ziele könne und dürfe nicht Kernpunkt unternehmerischer Überlegung und Handlung sein. Unternehmerische Entscheidungen sind primär und prinzipiell wirtschaftlicher Natur oder aber sie entfernen sich von der Grundpflicht der Unternehmer, über die wir an anderer Stelle gesprochen haben. Aber wir begegnen dem Unternehmer, dem Geschmack, Stil, Kultur zur zweiten Natur geworden sind, der aufgeschlossen ist für alle menschlichen Möglichkeiten und Entfaltungen jenseits meßbarer Leistung mit allem Respekt. Wir wissen ihm Dank, wenn er, die Grenzen seines Betriebs überschreitend, die Künste liebt und fördert.

Wir gehen einen Schritt weiter und sagen, von ihm sei zu erwarten, daß er sich höchstpersönlich dem kulturellen Leben tätig öffne – doch Grundelement seines Trachtens und Handelns ist und bleibt, von meinem Standpunkt aus gesehen, die Unternehmung.

*

Ich habe nun so wichtige Problemfelder wie Umwelt, Bildung, ja selbst Forschung, Entwicklung, Technik, Technologie … ausgelassen. Das scheint mir gerechtfertigt zu sein; denn nichts ist langweiliger als Vollständigkeit.

Jeder dieser Komplexe fordert den Unternehmer in anderer Weise; sein Interesse ist teils unmittelbar, teils mittelbar gegeben. Doch gilt fast durchweg, daß auch diese Felder primär vom Unternehmenszweck her gesehen werden müssen; die Lösung politischer Probleme – ich denke zum Beispiel hier an Umweltfragen – ist nicht die Sache des Unternehmers, sondern der Politik.

Zu unserer Philosophie als Unternehmer aber gehört es, zu akzeptieren, daß der Wandel das einzig Beständige ist. Doch bleiben Umfang und Tempo des Wandels unvorhersehbar. Das unternehmerische Risiko *jeder* Entscheidung bleibt. Es gibt keine rückwirkenden Entscheidungen. So trivial das klingt: Jede unternehmerische Entscheidung betrifft die Zukunft. Ihre Verwirklichung entfernt sich exponentiell von den Daten, die ihr zugrunde gelegen haben. Dies enthebt uns nicht äußerster Sorgfalt der Entscheidungsvorbereitung – im Gegenteil.

Wandel ist ein Element der unternehmerischen Welt. Aber es *muß* eine Synthese geben zwischen der Bewahrung des Bewährten und der nie endenden Aufgabe, das Bewährte der Feuerprobe zu unterwerfen, die Änderung der Bedingungen zu erkennen und zur Weiterentwicklung des Überlieferten beizutragen.

Zu dem Wandel, von dem wir sprechen, gehört der Wachwechsel in unserer Zeit. Die Vorkriegsgeneration hat ihre Posten verlassen; die Kriegsgeneration ist nicht mehr weit davon entfernt; die Nachkriegsgeneration ist dabei, die Führung zu übernehmen. Den Baden-Badener Unternehmensgesprächen kommt angesichts dieses Generationswechsels eine Verantwortung zu, die wir nicht unterschätzen dürfen. Es geht hier um eine Bemühung, von der wir wissen, daß sie historisch nicht oder nur selten erfolgreich war: um den Versuch, Erfahrung zu übertragen. Die Notwendigkeit, die Erfahrung vieler Jahrzehnte zu erhalten, ist ebenso evident wie die Erkenntnis, daß jeder Versuch, Erfahrung zur Regel zu machen, notwendigerweise bewußten oder unbewußten Widerstand hervorrufen muß. Dabei müssen wir den Informationsverlust bei jeder Weitergabe von Erfahrung in unsere Überlegung einbeziehen.

Was nun den Wert dieser Erfahrung angeht, so ist das folgende nicht ironisch gemeint: Erfahrung sei häufiger nur die Summe der Fehler, die einer in den letzten Jahrzehnten gemacht habe. Aber genauso ist es: Man lernt – wenn man lernbereit ist – am besten an seinen Fehlern, und Erfolg ist letztlich doch nur der positive Saldo aus richtigen und falschen Entscheidungen.

Unternehmer gelten häufig gemeinhin als ungeduldige Menschen, und eine Art schöpferischer Ungeduld gehört in der Tat zu ihren notwendigen Eigenschaften. Doch müssen sie beurteilen können, wann und wo es sich um Unvermögen und Trödelei oder um die natürliche Wachstumsperiode handelt, um verschenkte oder um gewonnene Zeit. Geduld hat sich oft ausgezahlt, vor allem, wenn es um Fort-Schritte ging, die sich im Innern des Menschen abspielen.

Der Unternehmer ist in meinen Augen letzten Endes nicht zur Rechenhaftigkeit berufen. Gewiß, Erfolg setzt voraus, daß er Werte, Größen beurteilen und verarbeiten kann – ich spreche lieber von Größenordnungen als von Zahlen. In seinem intuitiven Denken spielt ganz unbewußt die Mengenlehre eine größere Rolle als die Arithmetik, was ihn nicht daran hindern darf, von seinen Mitarbeitern die Kenntnis des Einmaleins zu erwarten, so sehr das heutzutage manche Schule überfordert.

Der auf der Breite und in der Tiefe seines Arbeitsfeldes erfolgreiche Unternehmer leidet nie Mangel an guten Mitarbeitern, er sucht sie, er findet sie, er bildet sie aus; er weiß, die Zukunft seiner Mitarbeiter ist die Zukunft seines Unternehmens.

Wenn ich hier die menschlichen Eigenschaften beschreibe, durch die der Unternehmer sich auszuzeichnen hat, spreche ich über einen Ideal-, nicht über einen Realtypus. Es liegt mir fern, den Unternehmer idealisieren zu wollen, wenn ich sage, er sei nicht nur in persona die Kraftquelle seines Unternehmens; vielmehr kenne er die Kräfte, die über seine eigene Initiative, seine Vitalität, seine Dynamik hinaus jene Anstrengung zuwege bringen, von welcher der Erfolg mehr abhängt als vom Kapitaleinsatz.

Spricht Ludwig von Mises von der »Beseelung« wirtschaftlicher Vorgänge durch das Handeln der Unternehmer, so klingt das in einer technisierten Welt romantisch und mag mit dem Augenschein, mit dem greifbaren Vorgehen der Unternehmer in Widerspruch stehen. Und doch liegt darin eine jener Kraftquellen, von denen ich eben sprach.

*

Mehr als ein Vierteljahrhundert Mitarbeit an den Baden-Badener Unternehmergesprächen liegt hinter mir. Ich erinnere mich noch an jenen Besuch des älteren Freundes Karl Guth Anfang der fünfziger Jahre, bei dem er mir klarmachte, man dürfe sich nicht versagen – Wiederaufbau sei zuvor Arbeit am und für den Menschen. Seither sind Tausende durch Baden-Baden gegangen, dankbar für jene Tat der Männer wie von Witzleben, Vaubel und, nochmals, Guth.

Wir hatten damals, zu Beginn der fünfziger Jahre, vor allem Glauben und Hoffnung. Durch Wunder werden zwar keine Realitäten erzeugt. Aber man kann Realitäten häufig nur erreichen, wenn man an Wunder glaubt. Andererseits wird das »Prinzip Hoffnung«, insoweit es die Auflösung aller Spannungen vorhersagt, nicht aufgehen ohne unser eigenes Zutun. Das ist die Quintessenz eines langen, nicht mehr behüteten, immer ausgesetzten Lebens, das dennoch bestanden werden konnte.

Ganz zum Schluß nehme ich noch Zuflucht zu einem Wort von Leo Tolstoi. Er sah das Scheitern der kommunistischen Heilslehre voraus, die mit dem Ideal von Gleichheit und Gerechtigkeit das Gefühl überwinden wollte, andere hätten es besser, andere seien glücklicher, weil ihre Wünsche in Erfüllung gingen. Tolstoi schrieb: »Einen ewigen Fehler machen alle jene Menschen, die sich unter Glückseligkeit die Erfüllung ihrer Wünsche vorstellen.« *(1984)*

Über die deutsch-französischen Beziehungen

EINE BILANZ DER BEIDERSEITIGEN INVESTITIONEN

Frankreich ist Deutschlands größter Handelspartner. Die Frage drängt sich auf: Wie steht es mit den gegenseitigen Investitionen? Die auf die Zeit von 1952 an zurückgehenden deutschen Direktinvestitionen im Ausland wiesen Ende 1984 einen Gesamtbestand von rund 111 Milliarden DM auf. Davon lagen 8,6 Milliarden DM in Frankreich, was einem Anteil von fast 8 Prozent entspricht.

Der Gesamtbestand hat sich im Laufe der letzten 25 Jahre ziemlich gleichförmig, wenn auch mit wachsender Geschwindigkeit, aufgebaut:

1961 bis 1966 + 140 Prozent
1966 bis 1971 + 140 Prozent
1971 bis 1976 + 100 Prozent
1976 bis 1981 + 80 Prozent
1981 bis 1984 + 30 Prozent

Der Hundertsatz von 30 Prozent bezieht sich auf nur drei Jahre; extrapoliert auf fünf Jahre kommt man auf fast 55 Prozent. In Hundertsätzen gerechnet stellen wir seit den siebziger Jahren eine Verlangsamung fest; die absoluten Zuwächse steigen nach wir vor.

Beim französischen Anteil, der im Jahr 1961 mit 207 Millionen DM ziemlich genau 5 Prozent ausgemacht hatte, Ende 1984 aber mit – wie gesagt – 8,6 Milliarden DM auf 7,8 Prozent anwuchs, haben wir eine bemerkenswerte Kurve vor uns: Jener Anteil von 5 Prozent im Anfangsjahr der Betrachtung 1961 stieg bis zur ersten Hälfte der sechziger Jahre fast stetig an, bis zu einem Spitzenwert von 10,9 Prozent im Jahre 1976. Seither nimmt der Anteil, den die Investitionen in Frankreich an den deutschen Gesamtinvestitionen einnehmen, von Jahr zu Jahr ab – eben auf den genannten Endwert von 7,8 Prozent, und in gleichem Maß nahmen die deutschen Direktinvestitionen in den Vereinigten Staaten zu.

Die französischen Investitionen in Deutschland – das ist nicht *mein* primäres Thema – erweisen sich, in Kurvenform, als viel stetiger. Der geringe Anfangsbestand 1961 von etwa einem Prozent wuchs von Jahr zu Jahr auf 6,7 Prozent aller ausländischen Investitionen – absolut auf etwas mehr als 4,8 Milliarden DM.

Die Bezugsgröße – ausländische Gesamtinvestitionen in Deutschland – von rund 72 Milliarden DM ist mit dem Bestand deutscher Investitionen im Ausland von mehr als 110 Milliarden DM nicht vergleichbar. Denn die Statistik der deutschen Sachanlagen beginnt in den fünfziger Jahren nach den Verlusten durch Krieg und Kriegsfolgen mit Null, während die ausländischen Investitionen in Deutschland durch Krieg und Kriegsfolgen zumindest rechtlich nicht beeinträchtigt waren.

Vergleicht man die Investitionsstatistik mit der Statistik des Waren(spezial)handels, so fällt auf, daß letzterer viel stärker auf Frankreich gerichtet ist als die Sachanlagen. Anders gesagt: *Der Warenverkehr über die Grenze zwischen unseren beiden Ländern ist lebhafter, als das die Investitionsströme sind.* Denn von 1981 bis 1984 gingen 12,6 bis 14,1 Prozent des deutschen Warenexports nach Frankreich – zuletzt (1984) waren es 12,6 Prozent –, während die deutschen Importe zu 10,6 bis 11,4 Prozent aus Frankreich stammten – der neueste Wert für 1984 ist 10,6 Prozent.

Ich nenne diese Zahlen, ohne sie zu werten. Denn Kapitalverkehr und Warenverkehr gehorchen unterschiedlichen Gesetzen, was aber den Vergleich nicht weniger reizvoll macht.

Was uns für eine sorgfältige Analyse fehlt, ist eine Gliederung der Direktinvestitionen nach den wichtigsten Kriterien wie

- Industriegruppen,
- Wirtschaftskategorien (Handel, Banken, Versicherungen, Industrie),
- Regionen,

während wir für den Warenverkehr eine sehr viel weitergehende Aufteilung haben. Man kann hier nur Vermutungen anstellen. Das gilt auch für die Vergangenheit. Wirtschaftlich waren vermutlich zu allen Zeiten bis zum Beginn der Neuzeit die Nord-Süd-Verbindungen lebhafter als der Ost-West-Verkehr. In anderen Worten: Deutschland lag im Mittelalter und in der beginnenden Neuzeit auf der Achse Italien-Skandinavien mit Abzweigung nach dem Nordwesten über Rhein und Maas und den Niederlanden, nach dem Nordosten und Osten über die Hanse. Mit dem in Frankreich entstehenden Merkantilismus nahm das West-Ost-Geschäft zu (das Manufakturwesen, das Bank- und Börsenwesen waren in Frankreich früher entwickelt). Es gab französische Investitionen in Deutschland, aber kaum umgekehrt; vermutlich war auch die relative Kapitalbildung in Deutschland geringer als in Frankreich. (Nur als Aperçu erwähne ich hier eine französische Investition in Deutschland, die nicht als solche gemeint war: Im Jahre 1700 befanden sich zwei Drittel aller gewerblichen Betriebe Berlins in der Hand hugenottischer Refugiés.)

Ich konnte keine Zahlen über gegenseitige Investitionen in der Vorkriegszeit beschaffen. Zu vermuten ist, daß früher sowohl die Interessenlage eine andere war als auch die Größenordnung der Kapitalbildung. Die Interessen Frankreichs waren eher auf mediterrane, frankophone, koloniale und osteuropäische Gebiete gerichtet. Die Züge in meiner Schulzeit, denen wir mit Fernweh nachsahen, kamen aus Paris und gingen nach Wien, Budapest, Bukarest, Prag, Warschau – nicht nach Berlin. Immerhin gab es französische Textilinteressen im Süden, Handels- und Bankinteressen im Westen – und natürlich den Einfluß auf die Montanindustrie.

*

Das Unternehmen, dem ich angehöre, hat schon in den letzten Jahren des vergangenen Jahrhunderts in Frankreich investiert. Der Gründer unseres Hauses, Robert Bosch, war ein Kosmopolit. Vor gerade hundert Jahren aus den Vereinigten Staaten zurückgekommen, errichtete er 1886 die Firma, die heute in Frankreich fast 5000 Mitarbeiter beschäftigt, hierzu legte er den Grundstein 1899, obgleich die industrielle Betätigung erst 1928 begann, als sich Bosch an der Fabrikgründung des Grafen Lavalette beteiligte.

Ich will nicht die Rückschläge aufzählen, die in einem Jahrhundert wie dem unsrigen nicht ausbleiben konnten. Vielmehr will ich mich darauf beschränken, die sehr vielseitigen – und teilweise widersprüchlichen – Motive herauszuarbeiten, die zu den Investitionen unseres Hauses hinführten. Daraus können dann generelle Schlüsse gezogen werden auf grenzüberschreitende Investitionspolitik der Wirtschaft und auf ihre Argumentation.

Bevor ich aber die Motive untersuche, einige wenige Zahlen: Seit der deutschen Währungsreform von 1948 hat die Bosch-Gruppe in Frankreich *finanziell* investiert, das heißt als Kapitalerstausstattung, als Kapitalerhöhung oder zum Beteiligungserwerb den Gegenwert von 440 Millionen DM transferiert.

Seit 1961 – weiter lassen sich die Zahlen nicht zurückverfolgen, weil wir erst Anfang der sechziger Jahre schrittweise wieder Einfluß auf unsere früheren französischen Beteiligungen nehmen konnten beziehungsweise in die Lage kamen, Beteiligungen zu erwerben –, seit 1961 also machen die Sachanlageinvestitionen der Bosch-Gruppe in Frankreich den Gegenwert von rund 415 Millionen DM aus, das sind rund 13 bis 14 Prozent aller Bosch-Auslandsinvestitionen.

Bezogen auf die Gesamtheit der Direktinvestitionen der deutschen Wirtschaft in Frankreich ist das ein hoher Anteil *eines* Unternehmens. Dabei ist die Vergleichbarkeit wegen der Änderungen des Wechselkurses, vielleicht auch wegen zwischenzeitlicher Abschreibungen, eingeschränkt.

Um nun endlich auf die Kernfrage zu kommen: Warum investierte der junge Bosch in Frankreich, warum ließ er sich durch den Verlust seiner Position im Ersten Weltkrieg nicht entmutigen? Warum war und ist Frankreich für seine Nachfolger erneut zum bevorzugten Investitionsland geworden – nachdem man nochmals politisch auf den Nullpunkt zurückgeworfen war?

*

Zunächst einmal möchte ich die Aufgeschlossenheit Frankreichs für Mathematik und Naturwissenschaften und damit für die technischen Wissenschaften erwähnen. Dies prägt sowohl das französische Bildungswesen (darunter insbesondere die Grandes Ecoles) als solches, dann aber, und nicht zuletzt, auch deren Absolventen. Viele von ihnen haben durch technische Großtaten brilliert, während alle sich durch Exaktheit des Denkens auszeichnen. Auf dem Gebiet des Automobils hat das dazu geführt, daß Frankreich sich diesem heute unverzichtbaren Verkehrsmittel in der wirtschaftlichen Breite und in der wissenschaftlichen Tiefe früher zugewandt hat als Deutschland. Bei dem verständlichen Interesse, das meine Firma dem Automobil entgegenbringt, *ein* Grund zur Investition.

Dies alles – ich meine die technische Offenheit, die Rationalität – gilt bis heute, obwohl die Automobilindustrie der Bundesrepublik längst aufgeholt und auf bestimmten Gebieten die Führung übernommen hat. Und es gilt eben nicht für *eine* Industrie, sondern für Naturwissenschaft und Technik schlechthin. Ich brauche nur auf die Zusammenarbeit in der Luft- und Raumfahrt hinzuweisen, wo Spitzentechnologien ohne nationale Vorurteile und Vorbehalte gemeinsam entwickelt und angewandt werden.

*

Hier muß ich ein Wort zu *Eureka* einschalten: Ohne Zweifel ist es notwendig – im Wortsinn: um eine Not zu wenden –, daß wir zu einer europäischen Forschungspolitik, einer europäischen Technologiepolitik kommen. Die Zahlen über die Aufwendungen für Forschung und Entwicklung weisen darauf hin: In den Vereinigten Staaten wird in diesem Jahr dreimal soviel für Forschung und Entwicklung ausgegeben werden wie in Japan – und in Japan wird man soviel ausgeben wie in den Ländern der Europäischen Gemeinschaft insgesamt, aber eben (noch nicht) zusammen. Dabei hat Japan eine Bevölkerung, die nicht vielmehr als 40 Prozent der EG-Bevölkerung ausmacht, und letztere ist 10 Prozent größer als die US-amerikanische.

Ich glaube nicht, daß man durch staatliche Initiative, geschweige denn durch staatliche Intervention, Wesentliches erreichen kann. Papier ist, wie man bei uns sagt, geduldig. Man kann vielleicht Steine aus dem Weg räumen, die heute die technische Zusammenarbeit schwermachen. Aber die Gefahr, daß neue bürokratische Schwellen geschaffen werden, ist viel größer als die Hoffnung, daß praktische Erfolge erreicht werden, zumal bereits von »politischer Kontrolle« und von der Errichtung einer neuen »Agentur« die Rede gewesen ist.

Meine Bedenken gelten zumindest solange wir keine gemeinsame Philosophie haben – der Begriff ist etwas schillernd, aber an dieser Stelle berechtigt, wie ein Beispiel zeigt: Aus Frankreich kommt die Anregung, die technischen Kräfte unserer Länder zusammenzufassen; aber gerade Frankreich hat einen großen Teil seiner relevanten Industrie nationalisiert; soweit man reprivatisiert, geschieht das nur unlustig und ohne daß man die Staatsmajorität aufgibt – eine Kluft des wirtschaftspolitischen Denkens innerhalb Europas.

Zusammenarbeit zwischen Unternehmen, im Interesse Europas notwendig, kann durch staatlichen Eingriff allenfalls angeregt, keinesfalls erzwungen werden. Sie wird erschwert, solange die grundsätzliche Denkweise nicht übereinstimmt, das heißt insbesondere, solange autark und protektionistisch gedacht und gehandelt wird.

Wenn es in der Tat Element der französischen Wirtschaftspolitik wäre, den »heimischen Markt zurückzuerobern«, so verspreche ich mir von der Allianz der Regierungen nichts Gutes.

*

Die politische Motivierung für Investitionen in Frankreich liegt nicht in dem protektionistischen Aspekt, sondern in der Stabilität sowohl der französischen Gesellschaft als auch der französischen Bürokratie. Diese Formulierung beruht auf jahrzehntelanger, wenn man will: lebenslanger Beobachtung und Erfahrung – und sie gilt hoffentlich noch lange weiter, wofür freilich radikale personelle Maßnahmen nicht immer ein gutes Vorzeichen sind. Doch hat diese Republik, bei aller politischen Wandlungsfähigkeit, im Wählerwillen letzten Endes immer Stabilität gezeigt.

Und die französische Bürokratie, bei aller Treue zu ihrer immanenten Logik, hat ihre rationale Geschmeidigkeit bewahrt und ermangelte nie der Pragmatik. Ein Land, das diese Qualitäten hat, zieht um so mehr auswärtige Investitionen an sich, je mehr es zu erkennen gibt, daß es nicht gewillt ist, sich die eigene Zukunft durch ideologische Aspirationen zu verbauen, je unvoreingenommener es anderen Nationen gebenübersteht.

Dies auch, wenn der eigene Unternehmergeist eher lateinischer Ratio zuneigt, das heißt Klarheit, Transparenz bis zu einem Anflug von Dirigismus mehr schätzt als unternehmerische Phantasie. Dabei hat gerade ein französischer Philosoph – Henri Bergson – die Begriffe »Evolution créatrice« und »Elan vital« geprägt, auch wenn er damit nicht primär an den Unternehmer und das Unternehmertum dachte.

*

Als Robert Bosch während des Ersten Weltkrieges den »Rhein-Verlag« gründete, wollte er zum besseren Verständnis zwischen Deutschland und seinen Nachbarn beitragen. Er dachte vor allem an die Beziehungen zu dem nahen Frankreich, und er hielt Basel, in der Dreiländerecke, für einen Standort, der sich selbst rechtfertigte. Der gewählte Weg erwies sich nicht als gangbar. Aber ein Ziel war gesetzt, und die Politiker der zwanziger Jahre – nennen wir Aristide Briand und Gustav Stresemann – waren ebenso davon überzeugt wie Robert Bosch, daß man Brücken über den Rhein schlagen müsse, die in beiden Richtungen begehbar sein sollten.

Ich weigere mich übrigens, in diesem Zusammenhang eine Äußerung von Friedrich Sieburg von 1929 anzuerkennen, der damals den wahren Einigungswillen Frankreichs in Zweifel zog, als er in seinem berühmten Buch »Gott in Frankreich?«, schrieb: »Was hat man von einer europäischen Föderation zu erwarten, die Frankreich nur darum angeregt zu haben scheint, um sich die Wirkungen einer solchen Idee durch rechtzeitige Kontrolle und Verflachung zu ersparen!« Selbst wenn das 1929 richtig gewesen sein sollte – inzwischen haben sich doch Zeiten, Erkenntnisse und Überzeugungen geändert.

Heute gehört die Verständigung zwischen unseren beiden Nationen zu den zentralen Zielrichtungen der *Robert Bosch Stiftung*, der rund 90 Prozent des Unternehmens gehören; ihre Arbeit ist nicht wirtschaftlich, sondern politisch-kulturell orientiert. Aber gerade hier, am Politischen, muß man ansetzen, wenn man zu einer wirtschaftlichen Integration Europas kommen will. Es wird keine wirkliche Europäische Gemeinschaft geben, solange nicht übereinstimmender politischer Wille entsteht. Wille – damit meine ich mehr als Worte.

Gemeinsame Willensbemühungen setzen gegenseitiges Vertrauen voraus. Investitionen hängen ja langfristig auch davon ab, ob der Investor damit rechnen kann, daß er im Lande der Investition willkommen ist. Franzosen können in Deutschland damit rechnen, daß sie in die Industrial Community aufgenommen werden – wir können nur hoffen, daß das auch vice versa der Fall ist. Faire l'Europe pour survivre – Europa herstellen, wiederherstellen, damit dieser

Kontinent im Kampf der Kontinente nicht untergeht, setzt übereinstimmende Wirtschaftsgesinnung und Öffnung, Offenheit gegenüber den Partnerländern voraus.

*

Ich erwähnte Aristide Briand, dem Annette Kolb 1929 Aufrichtigkeit bezeugte. Er sagte in seiner großen Rede im Völkerbund am 26. Februar 1926: »Und Frankreich ist der Meinung, daß Deutschland eine Rolle zu spielen hat – in Europa und in der Welt.« Aber er sagte damals auch, daß »die Nachbarn« – er meinte die Deutschen – »manchmal den wünschenswerten Takt in ihren Reden vermissen lassen«. Ich hoffe, ich muß *mir* einen solchen Vorwurf nicht machen. *(1985)*

Die Chancen Europas

UNSER KONTINENT MUSS MEHR BIETEN ALS NUR WIRTSCHAFTLICHE LEISTUNG

An den Anfang seines Beitrags über Friedrich List, den Theodor Heuss für »Die großen Deutschen« geschrieben hat, stellte er den Satz: »Wenn der Name von Friedrich List genannt wird, bekommen die Deutschen ein schlechtes Gewissen.«

Wenige Jahre vorher – 1931 – war die List-Biographie von Walter von Molo »Ein Deutscher ohne Deutschland« erschienen. Was mir von Friedrich List zutiefst bewußt ist, stammt von Molo. Ich war achtzehn Jahre alt, als ich das Buch zum ersten Male las; Molo hat List freilich ebenso überzeichnet wie teilweise auch Heuss.

Mit Recht stellt Heuss jedoch klar, daß man in Friedrich List nicht einfach »den Begründer und Verteidiger des Schutzzolls« sehen dürfe. Denn dessen Kampf, insbesondere im Jahre 1819, das für ihn schicksalhaft werden sollte, »galt nicht der Errichtung, sondern der Niederlegung von Zollgrenzen«. Der »Lehre von den Werten« eines Adam Smith steht – ich zitiere noch immer Heuss – die »Lehre von den produktiven Kräften« gegenüber. Ging es Smith um die regelnde Kraft des Marktes, so ging es List darum, »Werte zu schaffen«. Und »Zoll war für ihn nicht Schutz der Rente, sondern Verpflichtung zur Arbeitsintensivierung«.

Über das Verhältnis Friedrich Lists zu Europa sagt Theodor Heuss, es sei vielleicht »das Größte an ihm, daß er in der Zeit der deutschen Ohnmacht … in unbefangener Klarheit und Nüchternheit von der deutschen Lage in *Europa* sprach«.

Wenn Theodor Schieder sich mit List etwas schwertat – als »zeitbedingt«, als »rationalitätsfremd« bezeichnete er ihn –, so übersah er vielleicht, daß List nicht gegen Europa war, aber zunächst eine Zelle: Deutschland schaffen und daher die »Verkrustung« innerhalb des Deutschen Bundes lösen wollte.

Wenn wir heute von Europa sprechen, welches Europa meinen wir dann? In Jalta – so berichtete damals der BBC-Sender – einigten sich die Staatsmänner der westlichen Welt mit Stalin über eine Demarkationslinie, die durch Lübeck und Innsbruck gehen sollte. Man muß bezweifeln, ob Roosevelt und Churchill sich darüber klar waren, daß sie damit nicht nur Deutschland, sondern Europa teilten. Wenige Jahre später wurde das evident. Der Abbé de Pradt schrieb 1827, »jenseits der Weichsel« falle »ein Vorhang herab«; er nahm das Wort Churchills vom »Eisernen Vorhang« vorweg. Aber dieser fiel nicht jenseits, sondern diesseits der Weichsel.

Sprechen wir heute nur noch von Europa westlich des Vorhangs? Ich bin sicher, daß wir damit die Kritik, ja den Zorn aller jener hervorrufen würden, die sich östlich des Vorhangs nach wie vor als Europäer betrachten und fühlen. Polen ist nicht Asien, Polen ist Europa. Das gilt nicht minder für die Tschechoslowakei. Im ungarischen Parlament wurde noch Mitte des letzten Jahrhunderts eine zentrale europäische Sprache gesprochen: Latein. Wir sind in Baden-Württemberg stolz darauf, daß wir 1977 das 500jährige Bestehen der Universität Tübingen begehen konnten. 1986 ist das Jubeljahr der Universität Heidelberg, die 1386 gegründet wurde. Aber damals bestanden längst Universitäten in Prag (1348), in Krakau (1364) und in Pécs (Fünfkirchen, 1367).

Wir sind uns dessen bewußt, daß es nicht in unserer Hand läge, die Grenzen Europas in ihrer heutigen politischen Wirklichkeit nach Osten zu verschieben, und ich möchte mit meinen Reminiszenzen das Rad für heute nicht zurückdrehen. Ich will nur erreichen, daß sich unser Blick nicht immer bloß auf das Europa westlich jener

Linie Lübeck–Innsbruck richte, und daran erinnern, daß Osteuropa nicht nur ein geographischer, sondern auch ein geopolitischer Begriff ist, und daß man unseren Kontinent eben nicht etwa als den »kleinen Vorbau Asiens« ansehen darf, wie das Paul Valéry in den zwanziger Jahren schrieb – als eine Reaktion auf die Vorstellung, die sich vor dem Ersten Weltkrieg mit dem Namen Europas verband: die eines mächtigen Brennpunktes, der auf alle anderen Kontinente ausstrahlte. Mehr und mehr erkennt man, daß in der deutlichen und in einer schicksalsträchtigen Zeit auch verständlichen Prägung Valérys ein Aufruf an die Europäer liegt, die Schwächephase zu überwinden, in die wir durch eigene Fehler hineingeraten sind.

Der amerikanische Historiker Oskar Halecki, der in Polen zu Hause war, schrieb vor einem Vierteljahrhundert, wenn das historische Europa weiterleben wolle, könne es sich nicht auf den Grenzen des karolingischen Reiches zurückziehen. Europa dürfe sich nicht »damit abfinden, im zwanzigsten Jahrhundert auf mehr oder weniger alles zu verzichten, was sich im zehnten, eben deswegen so entscheidenden Jahrhundert an Alteuropa angeschlossen und das Gesamteuropa des folgenden Jahrtausends gebildet hat«. Wenn er in seinem Streben, Europa richtig zu sehen, vor allem auf die Ostseeländer blickt: »Heute müßte es klar sein, daß alle Ostseeländer, einschließlich der an der Ostküste gelegenen, ein wesentlicher Bestandteil jeder echten atlantischen Gemeinschaft sind«, hören wir die Stimme Osteuropas.

Ich gehe nicht so weit, die Sowjetunion in das Europa meiner Betrachtungsweise einzubeziehen. Wir haben zwar gelernt, daß, geographisch, Europa bis zum Ural gehe. Aber die Sowjetunion hat, wie auch schon das Zarenreich, diese Gebirgsgrenze längst nach Osten übersprungen und eine geopolitische Einheit aufgebaut, die man euro-asiatisch nennen könnte, nicht aber europäisch. Dabei haben wir viele Zeugnisse eines russischen Europa-Denkens vor allem aus dem letzten Jahrhundert, die mir aber dennoch nicht veraltet zu sein scheinen, weil sie in die Gegenwart fortwirken. Nehmen wir Dostojewski, der in seinen Tagebüchern der siebziger Jahre geschrieben hat, die Zukunft Europas gehöre Rußland. Aber das war wohl eher Ausdruck eines russischen Ziels als etwa eine Identifikation mit Europa.

Es spricht nicht Ideologie, sondern Pragmatik dafür, daß wir uns ein Europa vorstellen, das im wesentlichen diesseits des Eisernen Vorhangs liegt, aber nie vergißt, daß »gestern« Europa größer war als heute und «morgen« wieder größer sein könnte – nicht als Ergebnis gegenwärtigen politischen Wollens, eher aufgrund geistiger Kräfte, die sich an geographischen Grenzen nicht aufhalten lassen.

*

Eine starke Währung ist Ausdruck nachhaltiger Wirtschaftskraft, fundierten Gleichgewichts einer Region. Daß die Wechselkurse von kurzfristigen Kapitalbewegungen – man darf sagen: spekulativer Natur – beeinflußt werden, daß objektive Tatbestände und subjektive Erwartungen – letztere ihrerseits nicht ohne Einfluß auf das, was real geschieht – sich überlagern, berechtigt die Verantwortlichen nicht, die Herstellung und die Erhaltung des Gleichgewichts zu vernachlässigen. Eine verläßliche und gegenüber allen gerechte Währung läßt sich deshalb nur innerhalb eines fest umrissenen Gebiets denken, das stabil »regiert« wird.

Bretton Woods war nach dem Zweiten Weltkrieg sowohl notwendig als auch möglich – für eine begrenzte Zeit. Die Märkte sind darüber hinweggegangen. Internationale Währungsabkommen verlangen den *Glauben* an feste Maßstäbe, seitdem es nicht mehr möglich ist, echte Goldwährungen zu schaffen und zu erhalten.

Das Vertrauen in eine Währung hängt also – national und international – von der Stabilität der ihr zugrundeliegenden wirtschaftlichen Strukturen und Ordnungen ab. Die Geldordnung eines Wirtschaftsgebiets ist ein notwendiges, aber kein hinreichendes Element einer wirtschaftlichen Gesamtordnung.

Es bleibt – auch nach allem, was deutsche offizielle und offiziöse Stellen in der letzten Zeit geäußert haben – dabei, daß gemeinsamer Währungspolitik gemeinsame Wirtschaftspolitik vorausgehen muß. Da wir uns auf die letztere noch nicht geeinigt haben, ist die erste wirklichkeitsfremd. Es sei denn, der Realismus europäischer Nachbarländer (ich klammere einmal amerikanische Überlegungen aus) liege darin, daß man die Bundesrepublik über eine Härtung des europäischen Währungssystems zur Kasse bitten will.

*

Wie stark ist nun das Europa, von dem wir heute sprechen können? Stellt man die Zahlen der großen Wirtschaftsgebiete nebeneinander, kommt man auf die folgenden Größenordnungen und Beziehungen: Die Bevölkerung Westeuropas übertraf im Jahr 1985 (wie auch in den Vorjahren) die addierten Einwohnerzahlen der Vereinigten Staaten und Japans:

– Westeuropa	403 Millionen Einwohner
– USA	239 Millionen Einwohner
– Japan	121 Millionen Einwohner
– USA + Japan	360 Millionen Einwohner

Nun wird die Wirtschaftskraft eines Gebietes nicht in erster Linie durch die Einwohnerzahl oder durch die Fläche verkörpert. Würde man nur in Größe denken, so stünden die Blöcke China und Indien weit an der Spitze; auch nach der Fläche schlagen sie Westeuropa und, erst recht, Japan: nur die Supermächte weisen noch größere Flächenzahlen auf. Kennzeichnender ist das Bruttosozialprodukt, das 1985 in

– den USA	3990 Millionen Dollar
– Japan	1330 Millionen Dollar (1400)
– Westeuropa	2830 Millionen Dollar (5450)

betrug. Bei dem »überhöhten« Dollar-Kurs des Jahres 1985 erscheinen hier Japan und Westeuropa zu niedrig; zu Wechselkursen von 1980 gelten die in Klammern stehenden Zahlen. War der Dollarkurs 1985 überhöht, so war er aber 1980 mit 1 US-Dollar = 1,82 DM eher unterbewertet. Doch ist es in der Größenordnung nicht falsch, davon auszugehen, daß Westeuropa den Vereinigten Staaten im Bruttosozialprodukt nicht nachsteht, Japan gegenüber aber sehr viel stärker ist.

Im Pro-Kopf-Einkommen 1985 laufen die USA Westeuropa davon:

- USA 16700 Dollar
- Japan 11000 Dollar (11550)
- Westeuropa 7000 Dollar (13500)

(Auch hier in Klammern zu Wechselkursen 1980)

Welchen Wechselkurs man immer annimmt: Im Pro-Kopf-Einkommen stehen die Vereinigten Staaten an der Spitze, Japan in der Mitte, und erst dann folgt Westeuropa. Dabei sind die Zahlen für Westeuropa Mittelwerte mit großer Bandbreite – von der Schweiz bis Portugal.

Auch bei der Gegenüberstellung des realen Wirtschaftswachstums 1980 bis 1985 fällt Westeuropa vergleichsweise zurück:

- USA 2,6 Prozent jährlich (3,4)
- Japan 4,0 Prozent jährlich (5,0)
- Westeuropa 1,3 Prozent jährlich (2,9)

(In Klammern die Ziffern für 1975 bis 1980)

Das Tempo des Wachstums in Japan ist evident, und es sieht so aus, als ob es den Japanern trotz externer und interner Probleme gelänge, schneller zu wachsen als die Amerikaner und Europäer.

Bei allen Zahlenangaben sprach ich von Westeuropa, nicht etwa von jenem erweiterten Europa-Begriff. Sowohl statistische Gründe als auch der Wunsch, keinesfalls einer Annexionslust bezichtigt zu werden, sprechen dafür, daß wir bei konkreten Überlegungen den Eisernen Vorhang beachten.

Die Arbeitsmärkte der betrachteten Gebiete klaffen weit auseinander. Ob in den unausgeschöpften Arbeitspotentialen Europas mehr Chance als Risiken liegen, ist schwer zu beantworten. Wirtschaftlich sind Chancen nicht auszuschließen, während ich die politischen Risiken nicht überblicke, keinesfalls aber aus dem Bewußtsein verdrängt sehen möchte.

In Europa steigt in diesem Jahrzehnt die Arbeitslosenquote weiter an; die Schmerzgrenze ist, bei unterschiedlicher Wellenhöhe, in einzelnen Ländern erreicht; das hat sich in hinter uns liegenden Wahlen offenbar ausgewirkt, und man kann nicht ausschließen, daß es sich auf kommende Wahlen auswirken könnte.

Die Vereinigten Staaten und Japan stehen, was den Arbeitsmarkt angeht, weitaus besser da als Westeuropa, wenn auch aus Gründen und mit Konsequenzen, die strukturell unterschiedlich sind. Japan hat eine in den letzten drei Jahren gleichbleibende Arbeitslosenquote von nur 2,6 bis 2,7 Prozent. Man spricht freilich bei Regierung und Wirtschaft in Japan von latenter oder zurückgestauter Arbeitslosigkeit, was nicht etwa statistisch bedingt ist (»standardized unemployment rates«), sondern sozioökonomisch begründet.

Die Vereinigten Staaten können über eine zurückgehende Arbeitslosenquote berichten: 1983 bis 1985 von 9,5 auf 7,4 auf 7,1 Prozent fallend. Vor allem aber ist es in USA und in Japan in den letzten Jahren gelungen, das Beschäftigungsniveau wesentlich zu erhöhen. Es gibt Zahlen aus USA, die für die letzten 15 bis 20 Jahre von einer Erhöhung der Beschäftigtenzahl von rund 20 Millionen sprechen. Von 1980 bis 1985 hat sich die Zahl der Beschäftigten, in einem Zeitraum von nur fünf Jahren, von 99,3 auf 107,2 Millionen erhöht. In der gleichen Zeit meldet Japan eine Steigerung der Beschäftigung von 55,4 auf 58,3 Millionen. In Westeuropa ist es allenfalls gelungen, das Wachstum der Arbeitslosenquoten einzudämmen; Beschäftigungserfolge werden im wesentlichen nur in der Bundesrepublik in kleinen Schritten sichtbar.

Immerhin gibt es *ein* Segment, in dem Prognose sich aufdrängt: die Bevölkerungsentwicklung (etwas anspruchsvoller: die demographische Entwicklung). Das politisch aufgeheizte Lamento über die angeblich zu geringe Zahl von Ausbildungsplätzen wird, wie wir wissen, in wenigen Jahren in der Bundesrepublik keinen Boden mehr haben. Denn seit Anfang der siebziger Jahre hat sich die Geburtenzahl in der Bundesrepublik fast halbiert (mit den Geburten von Kindern ausländischer Eltern beträgt sie noch 60 Prozent früher erreichter Zahlen). Schon Ende der achtziger Jahre wird die Nachfrage nach Ausbildungsplätzen zurückgehen, und bereits in der ersten Hälfte der neunziger Jahre wird es an Facharbeitern, in der zweiten Hälfte der neunziger Jahre an qualifizierten, in den richtigen Fächern ausgebildeten Akademikern fehlen.

*

An dieser Stelle mag ein Exkurs über die Lage in den USA angebracht sein: Während der letzten Monate war man sich weithin uneinig über die weitere wirtschaftliche Entwicklung in den Vereinigten Staaten. Der hohe Fehlbetrag im Haushalt, die daraus entstandene, fast unerträglich hohe öffentliche Verschuldung, der Fehlbetrag der Handelsbilanz, die, unter anderem, auch daraus folgende Schwäche des Dollars, die zunehmende Konsumneigung – insoweit positiv – mit der Folge hoher privater Verschuldung und geringer Sparneigung, die im Vergleich zu Japan und zur Bundesrepublik unzureichende Bereitschaft der amerikanischen Unternehmer zu Sachanlageinvestitionen (etwa im Gegensatz zu Take-overs auf Basis von Junk Bonds) – alles Kennzeichen einer Region voller wirtschaftlicher Probleme.

Aber: Die Leading Indicators weisen nach oben. Der Chief Economist der New York Stock Exchange sagte im April in Amsterdam eine Wachstumsrate von 3 bis 4 Prozent voraus – ein Gradient, den man vernünftig nennen muß, wenn man, nicht nur einmal, erlebt hat, wie schwer sich die Wirtschaft tut, wenn sie mit Wachstumsraten von 6, 8 und 10 Prozent fertig werden muß. Inflation und Arbeitslosenquote in den USA gehen gleichermaßen zurück; die Zahl der Beschäftigten steigt weiterhin. Sinkende Zinsen auch für Hypotheken, so daß die Housing Starts wieder zunehmen. Die »Dollar-Schwäche« ist auch eine Stärke: Früher oder später werden die Exporte zunehmen, die Importe gedämpft und der Fehlbetrag der Handelsbilanz zurückgegangen sein. Zumindest *ein* Schatten wird bleiben: Die Entwicklung in den verschiedenen Sektoren fällt nach Maß und Tendenz immer stärker auseinander.

Was das für Europa an Chancen zu bedeuten hat, ist schwer abzuschätzen. Es ist 1986 wesentlich schwerer, an Exporten nach USA zu verdienen; der »warme Regen« wiederholt sich 1986 nicht. Aber das Wirtschaftsbild wird, von beiden Seiten gesehen, an Realismus gewinnen. Und schon darin sehe ich eine Chance.

*

Viele Sachkenner haben in den letzten Jahren nachgewiesen, daß es für die Moral (das heißt für die unternehmerische Initiative) bedenklich und im übrigen sachlich falsch ist, von einer technologischen Lücke auf der ganzen Breite zu sprechen; auch ich habe mich bemüht, in diese Kerbe zu hauen. Ich lasse einmal das Moralische ganz beiseite, um zu konstatieren, daß es *die* technologische Lücke, *das* Technological Gap, *nicht* gibt. Diese Feststellung soll nicht der Beruhigung oder gar der Selbstzufriedenheit dienen; sie geht auf einige generelle – und außerdem natürlich auf eine Reihe ganz spezieller – Erkenntnisse zurück.

Es versteht sich von selbst, daß wir in der Bundesrepublik, in Europa unsere Lücken und unsere Schwächen erkennen müssen. Aber wir dürfen nicht gebannt, wie das Kaninchen auf die Schlange, auf den einen oder anderen Vorsprung starren, der sich möglicherweise als nicht dauerhaft erweist. Dabei wissen wir, daß die technische Entwicklung im internationalen Zusammenspiel auf

»Geben und Nehmen« beruht und daß jeder technische (wirtschaftliche, politische) Erfolg früher oder später einen Rückschlag nach sich zieht.

Wenn die amerikanische Industrie einen großen Teil des Computer-Marktes an sich gerissen hat, wenn die japanische Industrie Marktführer in der Herstellung mikroelektronischer Bauelemente geworden ist und den Vorsprung auf diesem Sektor weiter erhöht, so sind es eher politische, auch verteidigungspolitische (USA) oder sozioökonomische (Japan) Gründe, nicht aber ein wissenschaftlich-technisch-technologischer Vorsprung, der Europa auf die Dauer aus High-Tech ausschließen würde.

Mit der Technologieeinschätzung und mit der »Aussonderung des Hochtechnologie-Sektors aus dem allgemeinen Wirtschaftsgeschehen« hat es seine besondere Bewandtnis. Die methodologischen Schwierigkeiten sind vermutlich unüberwindbar. Es ist unlogisch, eine elektronische Schreibmaschine unbesehen in High-Tech einzureihen, während eine Werkzeugmaschine (mit numerischer Steuerung!) ebenso unbesehen bei der Mittleren Technik (Med-Tech) erscheint.

Nach allem ist die Aufzählung positiver und negativer Teilausschnitte nicht aussagefähig. Europa hat die Chance im internationalen Zusammenhang, der Entwicklung zumindest zu folgen und ihr in bestimmten Feldern sogar zuvorzukommen – wenn es den unternehmerischen Mut nicht verliert und wenn es bereit ist, in dem notwendigen Maß in Forschung und Entwicklung zu »investieren«. Und Europa ist auf einigen Gebieten noch immer oder schon wieder voraus. Dabei kann man technische Stärken und Schwächen – die wirtschaftliche Stärken und Schwächen zur Folge haben – nicht anhand von Zahlen über den Aufwand für Forschung und Entwicklung der großen Wirtschaftsregionen belegen.

Zunächst einmal ist der Begriff »Forschung und Entwicklung« (Research and Development) nicht eindeutig abgegrenzt. Je größer die Neigung ist, sich mit dem Aufwand für Forschung und Entwicklung zu brüsten, desto größer ist die Gefahr, daß man Kosten in dieses immer größer werdende Paket mit einschnürt, die früher in einer viel bescheideneren Spalte der Wirtschaftsrechnung geführt wurden. Nicht jede Arbeit einer Konstruktionsabteilung, um ein Beispiel zu nennen, ist Forschung und Entwicklung im strengen Wortsinn. Vom Problem der Definition abgesehen, wird der Vergleich zwischen den Regionen problematisch, wenn man die Aufwendungen, die ja in Landeswährung erbracht werden, zum Devisenkurs in eine Einheitswährung umrechnet.

»Weltklasse« bescheinigte Bundesforschungsminister Riesenhuber der Bundesrepublik Deutschland und ihrer Industrie, nachdem im Vorjahr für Forschung und Entwicklung in unserem Land 52 Milliarden DM aufgewendet wurden. Aber Abgrenzungsprobleme beiseite gestellt – es kommt nicht auf den Aufwand an, sondern auf den Erfolg. Wir sind in unserem Lande sicher, daß wir die »Forschungs-Mark« besser anlegen als die Amerikaner den »Forschungs-Dollar« – vor allem, weil der letztere zu einem viel größeren Prozentsatz aus den öffentlichen Haushalten stammt als die F+E-Mark. Wirtschaftsunternehmen haben im allgemeinen ihre Ausgaben besser im Griff als staatliche Stellen. Andererseits hat es den Anschein, als ob der »Forschungs-Yen« mit großer Um- und Weitsicht ausgegeben werde; nicht zuletzt sind die persönlichen Ansprüche in Japan in geradezu »schwäbischem Sinn« von Bescheidenheit gezeichnet.

Vertreten wir auf der einen Seite den Standpunkt, daß *Forschung* eine kulturelle Aufgabe ist, die nicht nur nach ihrer meßbaren Effizienz beurteilt werden darf, läßt sich doch *Entwicklung* in der Wirtschaft nur nach wirtschaftlichen Gesichtspunkten beurteilen. Wenn wir trotz aller Bedenken und Einschränkungen davon ausgehen, daß ein Vergleich des F+E-Potentials anhand der Ausgaben möglich ist, so braucht Europa sein Licht nicht unter den Scheffel zu stellen. Aus den Zahlen für 1983 ergibt sich für die fünf größten europäischen

Länder ein Forschungs- und Entwicklungsaufwand von 46 Milliarden Dollar, während Japan im gleichen Jahr etwa 30 Milliarden, die Vereinigten Staaten etwa 90 Milliarden aufgewendet haben. Die Proportionen haben sich seither nicht wesentlich verschoben, abgesehen von einer Änderung der Paritäten.

Ich habe den Eindruck, daß die etwas angestrengten Bemühungen – man könnte auch sagen: bemühten Anstrengungen –, die man in Europa macht, um gemeinsame Forschung, mehr gemeinsame Forschung zu betreiben, weder von vornherein nützlich noch eine Bedingung für eine europäische Prosperität sind. Sie sehen mich als Skeptiker, wenn ich die Chancen beurteilen soll, die man dirigistischer Gemeinschaftsforschung zuschreibt. Damit negiere ich nicht, daß auf bestimmten Gebieten Erfolge bereits erzielt wurden, auf anderen Erfolge denkbar sind. Aber ich ziehe – so »unwirtschaftlich« das aus dem Munde eines Wirtschaftlers klingen mag – den Wildwuchs der Forschung einer Forschung im Gewächshaus vor. Die europäische Chance liegt eher darin, daß wir unseren Forschern Freiheit geben, als daß wir sie in die Zwangsjacke einer Administration stecken.

*

Es gibt keine Chancen ohne Risiken. Die größten Risiken Europas im internationalen Zusammenhang sind

- auf der einen Seite die Uneinigkeit der politischen Kräfte im engeren Sinn des Wortes (und dahinter verbirgt sich objektiver und subjektiver Ehrgeiz),
- die zumindest ideologische Einigkeit der gewerkschaftlichen Bewegungen und Bemühungen auf der anderen Seite.

Die europäische Wirtschaft steht weltweit in einer Auseinandersetzung mit Wirtschaftsgebieten, die eine *andere* innere und äußere Struktur des Gewerkschaftswesen haben. Weit entfernt von der Vorstellung, das amerikanische und das japanische System unternehmens*bezogener* Gewerkschaften auf Europa übertragen zu wollen, muß man doch erkennen, daß die unternehmens*übergreifenden* Gewerkschaften (ob Einheitsgewerkschaft in der Bundesrepublik oder parteiorientierte Gewerkschaftskonkurrenz in europäischen Nachbarländern) langfristige wirtschaftliche Aspekte zurückzustellen pflegen hinter verbandspolitischen, wenn nicht überhaupt politischen Zielen.

Es genügt für heute festzustellen, daß die in Europa, vor allem aber in der Bundesrepublik in den letzten beiden Jahrzehnten durchgesetzte Lohnpolitik der internationalen Wettbewerbsfähigkeit abträglich war. Die Lohnkosten in Teilen Europas haben sich den amerikanischen rasch angenähert; im Osten liegen die Lohnkosten, qualifiziert betrachtet, noch immer weit unter den europäischen. Die gewerkschaftliche Lohnpolitik in Europa hat nicht mehr nur das Ziel, den Anteil der Arbeitnehmer an der wachsenden Wertschöpfung zu erhalten, sondern in einem Verteilungskampf zu erhöhen. Dieser trifft nicht so sehr das persönliche Unternehmereinkommen – das steht auf einem anderen Blatt. Vielmehr wird dadurch die Investitionsquote (im weitesten Sinn des Wortes: Sachanlagen, Forschung und Entwicklung, Aus- und Weiterbildung) der Unternehmungen beschnitten. Daß damit auch die Schaffung zusätzlicher Arbeitsplätze gefährdet ist, verdrängt man aus dem Bewußtsein. Hier liegt die Achillesferse Europas im internationalen Zusammenhang.

Doch zurück zu den Bedingungen unmittelbar politischer Natur: Europäische Zusammenarbeit setzt nicht nur freien Warenverkehr, sondern auch freien Kapitalverkehr über die Landesgrenzen hinaus voraus. Davon sind wir in Europa weit entfernt, auch wenn es den einen oder anderen Musterknaben gibt. Zum Kapitalverkehr gehört natürlich nicht nur die Kapitaleinfuhr, sondern insbesondere auch die Kapitalausfuhr; wie wäre sonst ein Gleichgewicht herzustellen? Über Kauf und Verkauf von Unternehmen, Aktien und Beteiligungen werde ich mich hier gar nicht auslassen: Bekanntlich sind wir in dieser Hinsicht innerhalb der Europäischen Gemeinschaft völlig frei – vorausgesetzt, daß man die Genehmigung des Landes erlangt, in dem man zu investieren bereit ist.

Ein freier Fluß von Waren, Leistungen, Geld und Kapital in Europa, aber auch anderswo – man hat sich längst prinzipiell darauf geeinigt – würde verlangen, daß man die Steuern harmonisiert, was zur Voraussetzung hätte, daß man nicht eine Reihe von Finanzministern, sondern auch den größeren Teil der Finanzbeamten vorher entließe.

Wir sind hier wieder einmal beim gleichen Problem wie bei der Schaffung des Deutschen Zollvereins. Man berichtet, daß es für viele der deutschen Länder – die ja längst einen Teil ihrer Souveränität an den Deutschen Bund abgetreten hatten – nicht um Gesicht, Ansehen, Status, Prestige ging, wenn sie zögerten, dem Zollverein beizutreten, sondern um die Zolleinnahmen.

Aber ich meine es gar nicht ironisch, sondern bitter ernst, wenn ich sage, Europa habe im internationalen Zusammenhang nur dann eine Chance, wenn wir die Steuersysteme (und möglichst auch die Steuersätze) vereinheitlichen – die andere Seite der Münze ist dann die Vereinheitlichung, möglichst die Unterdrückung der Subventionen.

Wenn ich dann schließlich noch die Vereinheitlichung der Rechtssysteme als notwendig bezeichne, fürchte ich, daß ich damit den Brüsseler Papierkrieg weiter anheize. Man hat ja im Herzen Europas weithin vergessen, daß wir zu Beginn des letzten Jahrhunderts auf der Grundlage des Code Napoléon im Westen Europas schon einmal eine Art von Rechtseinheit besaßen.

Vor allem aber muß Ordnungspolitik in den europäischen Ländern, zusammengefaßt gesagt, von kongruenter Weltanschauung getragen sein, in der für dirigistische Spekulationen kein Platz ist.

*

Arm an Energie und an Rohstoffen, kann Europa, dessen bin ich sicher, sich auch in Zukunft behaupten – möglicherweise mehr als das. Das wird den Partnern im internationalen Geschäft nicht weh tun. Die spezifischen Fähigkeiten und Begabungen Europas, in zweitausendjähriger Geschichte entstanden und im Wettbewerb weiterentwickelt, nutzen auch ihnen, den Partnern.

Wir *haben* Chancen in Europa, solange wir den amerikanischen Slogan (der freilich drüben nicht Gemeingut ist) »Small ist beautiful« nicht vergessen. Unsere Chance ist nicht die Größe, sondern die Anpassungsfähigkeit, die Beweglichkeit, die Vielseitigkeit, die Individualität und die Neutralität – und die geistige Freiheit, falls es uns gelingt, sie zu erhalten. Risiko – um das Verso nochmals zu erwähnen – wäre die Überheblichkeit.

Europa, die europäische Wirtschaft weiß sich auch in schwierigem Gelände zu bewegen, sie ist geländegängig und kommt noch im Unwegsamen zurecht. Das ist eine ihrer Chancen. Wir Europäer waren schon immer Fernhändler. Als solche waren wir angesehen. Wir haben unseren Ruf gefährdet durch den Kolonialismus, der sich letzten Endes nicht gerechnet hat. Wir haben die Chance, unser politisches und unser wirtschaftliches Ansehen wieder aufzubauen, indem wir uns als verläßliche Partner bewähren.

Marketing *ist* eine der Chancen der europäischen Industrie. Auf der Hannover-Messe im März dieses Jahres sagte der weit über die USA hinaus bekannte amerikanische Berater John Diebold: »European companies are very good at international marketing. That is one of ›their‹ strengths.« Er fuhr fort: »Only a few of our (US) corporations are international in their focus, many being more domestically oriented. We have not as much infrastructure and experience in the financing of international marketing efforts as Europe and Japan. What we (US) do have, however, are social and economic characteristics which encourage innovation and foster new enterprises. By contrast, Europe has problems in creating an entrepreneurial culture.« Das sollten wir uns nicht zweimal sagen lassen.

*

Europa kann nicht eine Politik der unkalkulierten Stärke, sondern nur eine Politik kalkulierter Schwächen betreiben. Die Frage bleibt, ob unser »kleiner Kontinent« seine Chancen im internationalen Zusammenhang nützen kann – Chancen, die, wenn ich das richtig sehe, ihre letzte Ursache in der Härte der Lebensbedingungen haben, die Europa geschichtlich auferlegt sind und die Europa, die Europäer trotz der relativen Gunst der Lage in der gemäßigten Zone seit eh und je zur Anstrengung gezwungen haben. Die Gefährdung zwischen den Blöcken verlangt ein hohes Maß an Anstrengung, wenn man überleben, wenn man nicht erdrückt oder zerrissen werden will. Dabei ist es widersprüchlich, daß, der Gefährdung zum Trotz, ein Zustand der Sättigung, wenn nicht des Überdrusses beobachtet werden muß, der kontraproduktiv ist.

Ich bin davon überzeugt, daß Europa mehr bieten muß, aber auch mehr zu bieten hat als nur wirtschaftliche Leistung. Alle Weltsprachen – ich meine: alle völkerverständigenden Sprachen – haben in Europa ihren historischen Ursprung. Davon ausgehend könnte Europa, wenn es sich als Gemeinschaft empfindet und als solche wirkt, eine Chance haben, die ich eher kulturell als wirtschaftlich sehe – dies aber von der Erkenntnis ausgehend, daß auch Wirtschaft ein Element der Kultur ist.

Früher sagte man, der Handel folge der Flagge. Wir haben keine europäische Flagge in diesem Sinne, vielleicht aber die Hoffnung auf eine europäische Kultur. Bei Jacob Burckhardt lesen wir dazu: »Was wir nicht zu wünschen brauchen, sondern schon vorhanden vorfinden, ob wir uns dessen freuen oder es beklagen, das ist Europa als alter und neuer Herd vielartigen Lebens, als Stätte der Entstehung der reichsten Gestaltungen, als Heimat aller Gegensätze, die in der einzigen Einheit aufgehen, daß eben hier alles Geistige zum Wort und zum Ausdruck kommt.« *(1986)*

Robert Bosch und sein Werk

ZUM 125. GEBURTSTAG DES GROSSEN UNTERNEHMERS UND ZUM 100JÄHRIGEN JUBILÄUM SEINER FIRMA

In diesem Gebäude, in der Stuttgarter Liederhalle, traf man sich vor 25 Jahren, am 23. September 1961. Der Geburtstag des Gründers des Hauses Bosch jährte sich zum 100. Male. Die Firma war gerade 75 Jahre alt.

Theodor Heuss, Ludwig Erhard und Hans Walz beschäftigten sich an jenem Tag in ihren Ansprachen vor allem mit der Persönlichkeit von Robert Bosch. Das werden wir heute ebenso halten. Kurt Georg Kiesinger sprach seinerzeit von der »spekulativen Phantasie« Robert Boschs. Das Wort wird uns noch beschäftigen.

Am 75. Geburtstag von Robert Bosch, im Jahre 1936, hatte der damalige Reichsbankpräsident Hjalmar Schacht – ein bedeutender Mann, in dem Größe, Irrtum und Reue zusammentrafen – gesagt: »Sie, unser Jubilar, haben durch ein langes Leben bewiesen, daß man Kapital durch Arbeit aufbauen muß und daß man ein Weltunternehmen, wie das Ihre, nicht durch Kredit und Subvention erstellt, sondern nur durch Einsetzung eines langen Lebens voll Fleiß und Beharrlichkeit.«

Was Robert Bosch getan hat und was er uns zu tun hinterließ, weist in seinen Erwartungen, seinen Forderungen an die Lebenden in die Zukunft. Wir wissen, daß ohne seine Vorstellungsgabe, ohne seine Energie und seine Ausdauer, ja, ohne seinen Glauben nicht entstehen konnte, was entstanden ist, was noch immer Bestand hat, was weiter wächst und was auch künftige Stürme überstehen wird.

Als meinen Auftrag sehe ich es an diesem Tage an, allen denen zu danken, die dazu beigetragen haben, die Aufgabe zu erfüllen, die der Gründer seinen Nachfolgern hinterlassen hat. Theodor Heuss sprach am 23. September 1961 von »der schönen Pflicht des Dankes«. Doch empfinde ich Danken heute nicht als Pflicht, sondern als Bedürfnis. Wir werden uns aber auch mit Tagesfragen beschäftigen müssen, die nicht zu einer Geburtstagsfeier zu passen scheinen. Denn von ihrer Bewältigung könnte unsere Zukunft abhängen.

Ich möchte mich zunächst an die Redner wenden, die den Gründer und das Unternehmen gewürdigt haben und die uns ihre guten Wünsche auf den Weg mitgaben. Wir können diese Wünsche brauchen; der Weg mag steinig werden. Ich bedanke mich im Namen des Hauses Bosch bei dem Bundespräsidenten, dem Bundeswirtschaftsminister, dem Ministerpräsidenten, dem Oberbürgermeister, dem Präsidenten der Industrie- und Handelskammer und dem Vorsitzenden unseres Konzern- und Gesamtbetriebsrats. Die anderen Vorredner werden es mir, wie ich hoffe, nachsehen, wenn ich auf das, was sie gesagt haben, nicht im einzelnen eingehe und mich in dieser Minute nur Herrn Rau zuwende, der auch der stellvertretende Vorsitzende unseres Aufsichtsrats ist.

Ohne daß er die Interessen der Mitarbeiter, die ihn mehrfach gewählt haben und die er zu vertreten hat, auch nur eine Sekunde vernachlässigt oder gar vergessen hätte, ist er den Notwendigkeiten des Unternehmens in vorbildlicher Weise gerecht geworden. Er verstand es, seine gewerkschaftliche Bindung, die er nie verleugnete, mit den industriellen Erfordernissen in Einklang zu bringen – eine Lebensleistung ganz besonderer Art, die wir an einem Tag wie diesem anerkennen wollen.

*

Wir befinden uns an einem historischen Platz. Die Rotebühlstraße, in deren Haus 75B Robert Bosch vor 100 Jahren seinen Betrieb eröffnete, ist von der Liederhalle nicht viel weiter entfernt als der erste Fabrikbau, der zu Beginn des Jahrhunderts drüben in der Hoppenlaustraße entstand. Gegenüber der Liederhalle, in der Breitscheidstraße (der ehemaligen Militärstraße), befand sich sieben Jahrzehnte lang die Zentrale unserer Firma, ehe sie – der Raumenge in der Innenstadt wegen – auf die Schillerhöhe im benachbarten Gerlingen verlegt wurde. In Anwesenheit des Oberbürgermeisters der Landeshauptstadt möchte ich gerne feststellen, daß der Rechtssitz der Robert Bosch GmbH nach wie vor Stuttgart ist und daß wir hier – trotz der globalen Entfaltung des Unternehmens – immerhin noch 12000 Mitarbeiter beschäftigen. Das sind, nebenbei gesagt, sechstausendmal mehr als vor hundert Jahren.

*

Es ist heute unnötig, den Lebensweg von Robert Bosch nachzuerzählen. Die Vorredner sind darauf eingegangen, und andere haben die Persönlichkeit des Gründers unseres Hauses, ihre Entwicklung und ihre Wirkung auf Zeit und Zeitgenossen eingehend geschildert. Ich denke an Theodor Heuss, der in der 1946 erschienenen Biographie alles Wesentliche gesagt hat. Kurt Georg Kiesinger sprach 1961 von der »köstlich-nahrhaften« Heuss'schen Arbeit. In neuester Zeit hat sich Hans Konradin Herdt mit Robert Bosch beschäftigt, und auch ihm ist eine große Leistung gelungen.

Ziel, Stil und Struktur unseres Unternehmens gehen unmittelbar auf Robert Bosch und auf seinen Letzten Willen zurück. Der Gründer übertrug schon 1921 einen Teil seines Besitzes an der Firma einer Verwaltungsgesellschaft, aus der dann 1964 die Robert Bosch Stiftung – dieser Name wurde erst 1969 angenommen – hervorging. Endgültige Verfügungen traf er in einem Testament, das ebenfalls auf die zwanziger Jahre zurückgeht, auch wenn es seine abschließende Form erst 1938 fand. Dieses Testament schrieb er – so hart es ihm im Alter angekommen sein mag – von Hand, um die Notarkosten zu sparen. Wirtschaftlichkeit in seinem Sinn ist unsere Devise geblieben (obwohl wir seither den Notaren manche Gelegenheit zur Rechnungsstellung gegeben haben).

Robert Bosch hatte für seine Verfügungen zwei Beweggründe: Er wollte Unabhängigkeit und Schlagkraft des Unternehmens über die Generationen hinweg sichern. Der Ertrag des Unternehmens aber sollte der Allgemeinheit zukommen. Obwohl der Wille des Erblassers eindeutig war, beschlossen die Testamentsvollstrecker, vor dem Stiftungsakt den Konsens mit seinen Nachkommen zu suchen.

Erben waren die Töchter aus erster Ehe, Dr. Margarete Fischer-Bosch und Paula Zundel, sowie deren Sohn, Robert Boschs Enkel Georg Zundel; dann die Kinder aus zweiter Ehe: Robert Bosch der Jüngere und seine Schwester Dr. Eva Madelung. Alle Erben anerkannten die Zielsetzung des Erblassers: die große Mehrheit der Anteile an der Robert Bosch GmbH endgültig gemeinnütziger Nutzung zuzuführen. Daß aus zunächst vorgesehenen 86 Prozent inzwischen ein 90prozentiger Anteil der Stiftung geworden ist, beruht auf dem Vermächtnis der Töchter aus erster Ehe, die ihre persönlichen Anteile der Stiftung hinterließen.

Stiften sei »eine weitere Dimension des Unternehmens«, sagte ich einmal bei einer Veranstaltung des Stifterverbandes für die Deutsche Wissenschaft. Heute füge ich hinzu: Die Vorbedingung einer solchen Erweiterung unternehmerischen Verhaltens ist der Verzicht. Diesen Verzicht haben die Erben geleistet. Es waren nicht etwa rechtliche Überlegungen, von denen sich die Erben bei ihrer Uneigennützigkeit leiten ließen, nicht nur der Respekt vor dem Willen des Vaters. Es war vielmehr die innere Überzeugung, daß Stiften – und damit etwas Neues bewirken – den Erben eines großen Vermögens gemäß sei.

Eine großmütige Frau muß an dieser Stelle genannt werden: Margarete Bosch, die Ehegefährtin der letzten 15 Lebensjahre des Gründers, deren gütige Hand in mancher seiner Entscheidungen spürbar geworden ist. Wenn wir jemandem Dank schulden für das, was Bosch geworden ist, so sind es die Mitglieder der Familie Bosch. Robert Bosch d.J. und Eva Madelung sind heute hier. Die beiden Töchter aus erster Ehe leben nicht mehr, und Georg Zundel ist auf eigenen Wunsch aus der Gesellschaft ausgeschieden.

Unseren Dank auszusprechen ist mir ein Herzensbedürfnis. Die Erben haben den Weg freigemacht für die eigenverantwortliche und abschließende Entscheidung der Testamentsvollstrecker. Diese verwirklichten die Vorstellungen, die der Gründer ausgearbeitet hatte, für deren Realisierung aber seine Zeit noch nicht reif war, vielleicht sogar gefährlich gewesen wäre.

Stellvertretend für jene Männer, soweit sie nicht mehr unter den Lebenden sind, erwähne ich in Dankbarkeit den Mann, der drei Jahrzehnte lang Robert Boschs engster persönlicher Mitarbeiter war und der von vornherein an die Spitze des Kollegiums trat: Hans Walz. Von unseren Freunden, die an der Schaffung der Verfassung des Hauses Bosch von 1964 beteiligt waren und die in den neuen Gremien unermüdlich mitarbeiteten, nenne ich in gleicher Dankbarkeit zwei Männer, von denen der erste hier ist, während dem zweiten die Teilnahme an unserer Feier durch Krankheit versagt bleibt: Ich spreche von Hugo Rupf und von Heinz Küppenbender. Mit ihnen betrachten wir unseren Weg nicht als Modell, auch wenn Anregungen davon ausgegangen sind.

*

Robert Bosch wußte zu rechnen, aber er war nicht berechnend. Sich nach einer Büroklammer zu bücken, ein nicht benötigtes Licht zu löschen – das drückte nicht Kleinlichkeit, sondern unbedingte Wirtschaftlichkeit aus. Das »Zusammenhalten« machte es ihm möglich, andererseits von einmaliger Großzügigkeit zu sein. Als er 1910 der Technischen Hochschule Stuttgart eine Million Mark schenkte, war das kaum weniger als die Spitzenbeträge, die zwei Jahre später zur

Gründung der Kaiser-Wilhelm-Gesellschaft (der jetzigen Max-Planck-Gesellschaft) flossen.

Die Robert Bosch Stiftung verdankt ihre Entstehung dem »Verantwortungsbewußtsein des Gründers fürs Ganze, das sich nicht mit der Hingabe von Geld allein beruhigte« – so Hans Walz am 23. September 1961. Robert Bosch wollte sicher sein, daß gespendete Mittel vernünftig verwendet würden und bereitete dafür eine Organisation vor.

Zu der politischen Aufgabe der Institution »Stiftung« sagte Bundesforschungsminister Riesenhuber im April dieses Jahres: »Denn die große Stärke der Stiftungen ... besteht in ihrer Autonomie und in ihrem Willen, ... sich nicht etwa einbeziehen zu lassen in den Mechanismus politischer Wissenschaftsplanung, sondern ihr geradezu gegenübergestellt zu sein.« Das deckt sich mit den Intentionen von Robert Bosch.

Man darf nun das Gewicht der nicht ganz 300 Millionen DM, die die deutschen Stiftungen 1985 für die Forschungsförderung aufbrachten, nicht mit den fast 55 Milliarden DM vergleichen, die im selben Jahr insgesamt für Forschung und Entwicklung in der Bundesrepublik Deutschland aufgewendet wurden. Denn nicht der absolute Betrag zählt, sondern die Erhaltung eines Freiraums.

Wir wissen, daß es Kräfte in diesem Lande gibt, die gerade einen solchen Freiraum nicht lieben, die offen aussprechen, daß sie auch die Forschung »durchplanen« wollen, ja, die so weit gehen, der Wissenschaft das Forschungsergebnis vorzugeben. Aber die im Grundgesetz verankerte Freiheit von Forschung und Lehre verlangt ein gewisses Maß an finanzieller Unabhängigkeit – Unabhängigkeit von Haushaltsausschüssen und Rechnungshöfen, die natürlich alles besser wissen, aber manches doch nicht ganz richtig. Daß die Freiheit der Wissenschaft sich ethischen Gesetzen zu unterwerfen hat, versteht sich von selbst und hat mit dem Stiftungsthema unmittelbar nichts zu tun.

Die Leistungsfähigkeit der Robert Bosch Stiftung läßt sich an der Dividende der Robert Bosch GmbH ablesen, aus der sie für 1984 rund 36 Millionen DM bekam, für 1985 (einschließlich des Jubiläumsbonus) annähernd 40 Millionen DM. Bezogen auf den Weltumsatz der Bosch-Gruppe sind das geringe Beträge. Gezielt eingesetzt läßt sich aber damit Wichtiges zumindest in Bewegung bringen.

Bekannt ist, daß die Stiftung im Sinne des Gründers einen Schwerpunkt in der Betreuung des kranken Menschen sieht. Der Anfang der siebziger Jahre mit einem Gesamtaufwand von 110 Millionen DM errichtete Neubau des Robert-Bosch-Krankenhauses in Stuttgart ist dafür ein Zeugnis. Am 10. Oktober 1986 wird dort das Kardio-Chirurgische Zentrum dem vollen Betrieb übergeben, nachdem für Ausbau und Einrichtung rund 32 Millionen DM aufgewendet wurden; damit waren auch Verbesserungen an anderen Stellen des Krankenhauses verbunden.

Einen besonderen Akzent erhielt das Robert-Bosch-Krankenhaus durch eine Schenkung von Frau Dr. Margarete Fischer-Bosch: Sie stiftete das nach ihr benannte Klinisch-Pharmakologische-Institut – eines der ersten seiner Art in der Bundesrepublik; bei wissenschaftlicher Unabhängigkeit arbeitet es eng mit dem Krankenhaus zusammen.

Doch beschränkt sich die Stiftung nicht auf Stuttgart und Baden-Württemberg. Ihr Auftrag ist viel weiter gespannt. So fördert sie mit erheblichen Mitteln Bestrebungen zur Verständigung zwischen den Nationen. Robert Bosch hatte schon während des Ersten Weltkriegs einen Anlauf dazu genommen. Verständnis der Nationen untereinander fördert die Stiftung nicht nur in *einer* Windrichtung, sondern nach West *und* nach Ost – aus der Erkenntnis heraus, daß der Osten des Kontinents geschichtlich *und* gegenwärtig zu Europa zählt. Wer derzeit westlich des Eisernen Vorhangs in Freiheit lebt und die Europäer des Ostens vergißt, ist mindestens kurzsichtig. Die kulturelle

Zusammenarbeit mit Polen gehört zu den transnationalen Schwerpunkten der Stiftung.

In Fragen der Völkerverständigung dachte und handelte Robert Bosch pragmatisch. Wenn er europäische Bewegungen unterstützte, war er mehr Idealist als Pragmatiker. Was er von sich wies – auch in seinen sozialen Bestrebungen – war jede Spielart von Ideologie. In diesen Zusammenhang gehören auch seine Beteiligungen an drei Verlagen, die politisch, nicht geschäftlich gemeint waren. Während es ihm 1920 beim Erwerb der Mehrheit an der Deutschen Verlags-Anstalt mit ihren beiden Tageszeitungen um die Unabhängigkeit des württembergischen Zeitungswesens von norddeutschen Einflüssen ging, während bei der Gründung des Hippokrates-Verlags seine homöopathischen Interessen den Ausschlag gaben, verstand er seine Beteiligung an der Gründung des Rhein-Verlags in Basel übernational. Dem Basler Unternehmen war die Rolle eines Brückenschlags über den Rhein, zwischen Deutschland und Frankreich zugedacht.

Pragmatisch – mit einem Anflug von Idealismus – versuchen auch wir Heutigen zu sein, wie man an einem Projekt sieht, das wir als einen *kleinen* Beitrag zur Befriedung im Mittleren Osten ansehen: ein Forschungsauftrag zur Züchtung von Getreidearten, die in trockenen Klimaten Ertrag bringen – züchten nicht auf dem klassischen Weg der Kreuzung, der lange Jahre erfordert, sondern auf dem Wege der Gentechnik. Das Politische an diesem Projekt ist die von uns gestellte und angenommene Bedingung, daß die Forschungsergebnisse gleichzeitig allen Nationen zugänglich gemacht werden, die in jenem Gebiet gegeneinander stehen.

Dem Brauch, anläßlich eines Jubiläums eine besondere Stiftung zu errichten, will sich auch die Robert Bosch GmbH nicht entziehen, obwohl sie ja schon weitgehend einer Stiftung dient. Sie hat beim Stifterverband für die Deutsche Wissenschaft einen Fonds begründet, der der Förderung der Wissenschaft und des wissenschaftlichen Nachwuchses dienen soll und der mit 10 Millionen DM ausgestattet ist.

Eine Stiftung braucht nicht nur Vermögen und Einkünfte, sondern auch Menschen, die in ihr wirken und die für sie eintreten. Wir sind sehr glücklich darüber, daß der Bundespräsident bis zu seiner Berufung in das hohe Amt Mitglied des Kuratoriums der Robert Bosch Stiftung war und daß sie noch immer auf seinen Rat zählen darf, wie sie auch den Beistand anderer Kuratoriumsmitglieder genießt, die heute bei uns sind.

Als Domizil der Stiftung haben wir das Haus in der Stuttgarter Heidehofstraße gewählt, in dem der Gründer unseres Hauses mehr als drei Jahrzehnte lang gewohnt hat und das, obwohl noch kein Jahrhundert alt, zum Baudenkmal geworden ist. Es hatte durch Krieg und Nachkrieg stark gelitten; wir haben es zum 125. Geburtstag seines Erbauers wiederhergestellt und wollten damit zur Erhaltung von Bausubstanz in einer Stadt beitragen, die nie reich an Baudenkmälern war und die durch Schicksal, aber auch nicht ohne eigenes Verschulden, architektonisch eher arm geworden ist. Bei der Wiederherstellung wurde das Äußere des Robert-Bosch-Hauses in seiner alten Form respektiert, das Hauptgeschoß nach bestem Wissen und Können im Stil der Bauepoche eingerichtet, die anderen Stockwerke als Domizil der Robert Bosch Stiftung neuzeitlich ausgebaut.

Das Erhalten kultureller Werte gehört zu unserer Tradition, wie ein Beispiel zeigt: Robert Bosch erwarb 1938 das in den Jahren 1910 bis 1912 von Bernhard Pankok entworfene und gebaute Haus Rosenfeld am Herdweg 63 in Stuttgart, um es vor dem drohenden Abbruch zu bewahren.

*

Bevor wir das Stiftungsthema verlassen, drängt sich uns noch eine recht substantielle Frage auf: Stiftungen erhalten, nach dem Körperschaftsteuergesetz, das in den siebziger Jahren neu gefaßt wurde, keine Steuergutschrift – im Gegensatz zu den »normalen« inländischen Anteilseignern. Dadurch entgehen der Bosch-Stiftung jährlich rund 20 Millionen DM, die als Körperschaftsteuer *vor* der Ausschüttung zu zahlen sind. Eine Geburtstagsrede soll gewiß keine politische Rede sein – so gut es den Unternehmern anstünde, politisch zu denken, zu sprechen und zu handeln. Aber vielleicht steht es dem Sprecher des Geburtstagskindes zu, *einen* Wunsch zu äußern – und sei es nur den, daß der Gesetzgeber oder der heilige Bürokratius den Mut aufbringe, eine einmal getroffene Entscheidung ohne Angst vor dem Präjudiz – womit man ja jeden Fortschritt im Keim ersticken kann – nochmals selbstkritisch zu prüfen.

Wenn wir aber schon bei den Steuern sind: Was Robert Bosch als Unternehmer und dann als Stifter erreicht hat, wäre unter dem Regime einer fast 50prozentigen »Staatsquote« nicht möglich gewesen.

Ein hoher, in Ehren ergrauter württembergischer Finanzbeamter, der längst das Zeitliche gesegnet hat und nicht mehr wegen Verrats eines Steuergeheimnisses belangt werden könnte, erzählte mir in den sechziger Jahren, daß Robert Bosch sich vor dem Ersten Weltkrieg beharrlich weigerte, eine Einkommensteuererklärung abzugeben. Weil das seinen Unabhängigkeitssinn verletzt hätte, seinen Bürgerstolz – nicht etwa, weil er keine Steuern zahlen wollte; bei dem damaligen Einkommensteuergesetz von rund 5 Prozent (eine Vermögensteuer gab es überhaupt nicht) fühlte er sich nicht überfordert. Man einigte sich schließlich auf eine Pauschale, die er in so unerwarteter Höhe anbot, daß der Finanzminister meinte, das hätten seine Beamten nie herausgeholt.

Eine *gute* Geschichte braucht nicht wahr zu sein. Aber mein Gewährsmann bürgte für die Wahrheit dieses Vorgangs aus der guten alten Zeit. In ihr begann der Aufstieg einer großen, einer eigenwilligen Persönlichkeit, die sich weder beeinflußt sah durch staatliche Fördermaßnahmen noch geschröpft durch substanzverzehrende Steuern.

*

In der Bosch-Biographie von Theodor Heuss kommt Konrad Adenauer nicht vor. Aber es gab in seinen letzten Lebensjahren kaum eine Begegnung zwischen Adenauer und mir, ohne daß er davon gesprochen hätte, wie oft er als Schuljunge an dem »Elektrogeschäft« von Karl Bosch in der Kölner Schildergasse vorübergegangen sei – Karl Bosch, das war der beinahe zwanzig Jahre ältere Bruder von Robert Bosch.

Sein Sohn gleichen Vornamens rückte später an die Spitze der IG Farben-Industrie auf und erhielt nicht nur den Nobelpreis für Chemie, sondern wurde auch Präsident der Kaiser-Wilhelm-Gesellschaft. In jenem Kölner Geschäft arbeitete Robert Bosch eine Zeitlang; was die Elektrizität angeht, täuschte sich Adenauer. Denn es war ein Fachgeschäft für Wasser und Gas. Aber Robert Bosch bekam es schon damals mit einer technischen Entwicklung zu tun, die später in die Elektrotechnik einmündete.

Die Elektrotechnik war jung, als Robert Bosch sie, davon fasziniert, zum Gegenstand seiner Geschäftsgründung machte – strenggenommen im Jahr 1886 noch jünger, als es heute die Elektronik, ein Teilgebiet der Elektrotechnik, ist. Die Anwendung des dynamoelektrischen Prinzips durch Werner von Siemens war gerade zwanzig Jahre alt. Vom Telefon – und damit sind wir wieder bei Robert Bosch – konnte man erst seit einem Jahrzehnt sprechen. Trügt unsere Quelle nicht, so war kurz vorher das erste Ortsfernsprechnetz im Gebiet des damaligen Deutschen Reiches in Mülhausen im Elsaß eingerichtet worden.

Wer, wie Robert Bosch, sich nur fünf Jahre später zur Einrichtung von Telefonen empfahl, bewies Weitsicht. Was er über Elektrotechnik wußte, war kein Buchwissen. Er hatte, ich sage das alphabetisch, bei Bergmann, bei Edison, bei Fein, bei Schuckert und bei Siemens gearbeitet, bevor er sich selbständig machte.

Nur vier Jahre vorher war in Deutschland der erste Lehrstuhl für Elektrotechnik errichtet worden, am damaligen Polytechnikum in

Darmstadt; kurz darauf gefolgt von einem Lehrstuhl in Stuttgart. Wir wissen ja, daß Robert Bosch dort 1883 ein Semester lang hospitierte, der theoretischen Grundlagen der Physik wegen. Auch hier gab es Menschen, die ihn mit dem Phänomen der Elektrizität vertraut machten – und so gebührt unser Dank rückblickend seinen für uns teilweise anonymen Meistern und Lehrern.

Ob es nun konsequentes Nachdenken war oder Intuition, was Robert Bosch zur Elektrotechnik hinführte, lassen wir offen. Wir wissen aber, daß er ein Sensorium für das Kommende hatte – wirtschaftlich und politisch. Rationalität war jedenfalls nicht alles, und es gehörte Vision, Imagination dazu, sich 1886 für die Elektrotechnik zu entscheiden – *so* selbstverständlich war das nicht. Und über das Allheilmittel unserer Zeit, auf das wir immer dann zurückgreifen, wenn wir nicht mehr weiter wissen: über die Innovation redete man seinerzeit nicht lange. Man krempelte die Ärmel hoch und machte sich an die Arbeit, Neues mit Altem verknüpfend.

Heerding schreibt in der Geschichte eines großen Elektro-Unternehmens, das in einem Nachbarland beheimatet ist, in der Gründungsphase seien »elektrotechnische Geschäfte« entweder von Leuten geführt worden, die von Wissenschaft, nicht aber vom Geschäft etwas verstanden, oder aber von Leuten, die ebenso geschäftstüchtig wie unwissenschaftlich waren. Das paßt auf Robert Bosch nicht ganz – ihn können wir unter die Männer einreihen, bei denen unternehmerischer Sinn, technisches Wissen und – das ist ein weiterer wichtiger Zug – ein geschärftes Gewissen zusammentrafen. Und man tut gut daran, einem so außerordentlichen Mann nachzuleben – reflektierend nachzuleben, indem man Wissen und Erfahrung mit Mut verbindet.

*

Im 100. Jahr des Automobils beansprucht Bosch nicht, an der Wiege dieses noch immer unersetzlichen, noch immer unübertroffenen

Verkehrsmittels gestanden zu haben. Aber Bosch kann für sich in Anspruch nehmen, das Automobil der Anfangsjahre verläßlicher, später noch sicherer, sauberer und sparsamer gemacht zu haben.

Wenn man folglich nicht sagen kann, Bosch habe einen Anteil daran, daß das Automobil gerade eben 100 Jahre alt geworden ist, haben wir doch einen Anteil daran, daß es 100 Jahre *jung* geblieben ist. An unserem Beitrag zur Entstehung und Entwicklung der Kraftfahrzeug-Elektronik läßt sich das beispielhaft belegen. Wenn wir Mitte der zwanziger Jahre Radioteile herzustellen begannen, wenn wir uns 1929 an der Gründung der Deutschen Fernseh AG beteiligten und wenn wir 1933 die Vorgängerin von Blaupunkt erwarben, so bewegten wir uns schon im Banne der Elektronen.

Das elektronische Zeitalter im engeren Sinn begann mit der industriellen Fertigung von Halbleiterelementen (die Transistoren waren 1948/49 erfunden worden) in den fünfziger Jahren. In der uns zukommenden Bescheidenheit möchte ich sagen, daß der erste *Serien*einsatz eines Bosch-Halbleiterelements für die Kraftfahrzeugelektronik bereits 1958 erfolgte. Seither folgten im Jahresabstand Entwicklungs- und Serienanläufe elektronischer Bauelemente und elektronischer Geräte. Signifikante Ereignisse:

- 1967 Serienanlauf des ersten elektronischen Systems im Kraftfahrzeug: die elektronisch gesteuerte Benzineinspritzung;
- ein Jahr später Freigabe des Baus unseres Halbleiterwerks in Reutlingen;
- 1973 Beginn der Vorentwicklung digitaler Elektronikgeräte;
- 1978 Serienanlauf unseres elektronisch geregelten Antiblockiersystems.

Beispiele, die deutlich machen sollen, daß wir von vornherein »am Ball« waren – und wir werden das auch bleiben.

Man könnte sogar weiter zurückgreifen: 1952 gründeten wir in Berlin die Blaupunkt Elektronik GmbH, von 1955 an Deutsche Elektronik GmbH, bis sie in den Geschäftsbereich Elektronik der

Robert Bosch GmbH umgewandelt wurde, der mit mehr als 2500 Mitarbeitern auf Elektronik-Geräte konzentriert ist – einer von vielen.

Unser gesamter »Elektronik«umsatz wird 1986 annähernd 10 Milliarden DM erreichen: 45 Prozent unseres konsolidierten Weltumsatzes. Rund 59000 Mitarbeiter, davon allein 5700 in Forschung und Entwicklung, sind zur Zeit bei uns auf den Gebieten der Elektronik beschäftigt – ohne die Gesellschaften, an denen wir eine Beteiligung von 50 Prozent oder weniger haben.

Auch das ist ein Stück von Bosch heute.

Einem Besucher aus der amerikanischen Automobilindustrie, der 1961 von uns wissen wollte, wohin der Weg auf unserem Arbeitsgebiet gehe, sagten wir – es gibt einen Zeugen dieses Gesprächs unter uns –, wir verfolgten alle Möglichkeiten, die zur Überwindung der Erdenschwere beitragen könnten, das heißt den Gesetzen der Trägheit nicht unterlägen. Damit wollten wir freilich nicht zum Ausdruck bringen – und ich sage das als Warnung –, wir erwarteten, die Elektronen würden in Zukunft unsere Arbeit tun, würden den Menschen sozusagen in den Ruhestand versetzen. Ich bin der Überzeugung, das Gegenteil wird der Fall sein. Aber wir wollten sagen, daß wir auf dem Weg zur Kraftfahrzeug-Elektronik vorangehen. Dabei werden wir eine amerikanische Warnung, die an die Messung der Zerfallszeit strahlender Elemente angelehnt ist, nicht in den Wind schlagen: Half-life of many technologies ist today only about ten years.

Wir beobachten nicht ohne Interesse, wie die Skeptiker der Kraftfahrzeugelektronik der sechziger und der siebziger Jahre sich *heute* gegenseitig zu überholen versuchen. Ich spreche, wie es sich gehört, nicht von unseren Kunden, sondern von unseren Wettbewerbern, die aber für uns dennoch ein Element des Ansporns auch auf einem Gebiet bleiben, das wir frühzeitig betraten, aber selbstverständlich nicht gepachtet haben.

Auf dem Weg von der analogen zur digitalen Signalverarbeitung sind wir uns der Gefahr bewußt, die in einer naturfernen, weil nuancenlosen Herrschaft von Null und eins, anders gesagt: in einer »digitalen Diktatur« liegen könnte. Wir befinden uns hier in einer Grenzsituation: Das binäre Zahlensystem – die erste Veröffentlichung darüber, aus dem Jahre 1703, stammt von Leibniz – ist technisch-wissenschaftlich optimal. Vom Standpunkt des Humanismus aus betrachtet wäre es aber bedenklich, wenn wir auf diesem Wege zu einer schwarz-weißen Welt kämen – ohne die Zwischentöne, die das tägliche Leben ausmachen. In einer neueren Ausgabe jenes Leibniz-Textes warnt der Philosoph Jean Gebser vor »einer durch Quantifizierung sinnentleerten Welt«.

*

Ich sage etwas zögernd, aber dennoch aus Überzeugung: Am Anfang des unternehmerischen Erfolgs steht häufig der Mißerfolg, den man ertragen muß. Der junge Unternehmer ist sicher, festen Boden unter sich zu haben. Aber in der Wirtschaftsordnung, die wir gewählt haben und die wir entschlossen sind zu behaupten – das heißt in der Marktwirtschaft –, gibt es kein Erfolgsgesetz, keine Garantien.

Den kleinen Betrieb, den der 25jährige vor einem Jahrhundert errichtete, würde man in der Sprache von heute als Technologiefabrik bezeichnen, obwohl es zunächst eher handwerklich zuging. Dabei stand der junge Bosch auf eigenen Füßen. Zwar war der Boden für unternehmerische Tätigkeit in Württemberg durch Ferdinand von Steinbeis bereitet. Seit Mitte des 19. Jahrhunderts gab es die von ihm geschaffene Zentralstelle für Gewerbe und Handel. Aber dem jungen Unternehmer nahm niemand, außer seinen Verwandten und Freunden, die Kapitalbeschaffung oder gar das Wagnis ab. Wagnisfinanzierung ist eine Errungenschaft, wenn überhaupt, unserer Zeit. Was Robert Bosch tat, *war* ein Wagnis, wie das erste Jahrzehnt der Firma zeigen sollte:

- Im ersten Geschäftsjahr (1887) betrug der Gesamtumsatz wenig mehr als 5000 Mark.
- Erst im zehnten Geschäftsjahr wurde ein Umsatz von etwas mehr als 100000 Mark erreicht, damit erste Anfänge von Gewinn.
- Von einem Durchbruch kann man frühestens nach fast zwanzig Jahren (1905) sprechen, als der Umsatz erstmals 1 Million Mark überschritt.

Robert Bosch verliert ein Jahrzehnt lang den Mut nicht, bis ihm endlich der Erfolg zuteil wird, der Lohn der Beharrlichkeit ist. So konnte er 1931, an seinem 70. Geburtstag, schreiben: »Mein Verdienst ist: In dieser Werkstätte, vor 45 Jahren gegründet, wirkt sich aus, was ich in den 45 Jahren an Charaktereigenschaften hineinsteckte.«

Das heißt: Der Erfolg, den der junge Unternehmer Bosch nach schweren Jahren verbuchen konnte, ist nicht auf ein Geheimnis zurückzuführen – und wenn schon, dann auf ein offenes: Er bürgte in seiner Person für

- den technischen Stand,
- verläßliche Lieferung,
- untadelige Qualität,
- wettbewerbsgerechten Preis,

und nicht zuletzt, dafür, daß das Menschliche in seinen Betrieben beachtet wurde.

Technologiefabrik sagte ich: Was Bosch machte, war zu seiner Zeit Hochtechnologie, Spitzentechnik. Und was Bosch heute macht, ist es noch immer. Wenn Robert Bosch in jenen Jahren eine Telefonanlage für das Hotel Marquardt – alte Stuttgarter wissen, was dieser Name bedeutete – baute, so beschäftigte er sich mit Kommunikation. Was wir heute bei Bosch tun, kann man als die Erfüllung einer Vision betrachten, die er damals gehabt haben könnte, ohne darüber zu reden. So abwegig ist es also nicht, davon zu sprechen, daß wir uns zurückbesinnen auf Zukunftsvorstellungen, die in diesem Hause – wenn nicht stetig, so doch immer wieder – gepflogen wurden, aber – und ich sage das in voller Übereinstimmung mit meinem jüngeren Kollegen – ein Rückweg ist das nicht, geschweige denn ein Rückzug. Eher könnte man sagen, daß sich hier ein Kreis schließt. Denn Kommunikation, ob auf Rädern, und damit der Schwerkraft ausgesetzt, oder unbeschwert im Äther, bringt Menschen zusammen.

Kraftfahrzeugausrüstung bleibt unser Kerngebiet. Kommunikation ist im Laufe vieler Jahre wieder hinzugetreten, die anderen großen Arbeitsgebiete behalten ihr Gewicht. An dem vom Gründer souverän gehandhabten *Grundsatz*, das Unternehmen nach mehreren Seiten abzustützen, hat sich nichts geändert, auch wenn das Erscheinungsbild einer Evolution unterworfen ist. Diversifikation um ihrer selbst willen haben wir nie betrieben. Es ging immer um das, was man heute Synergie heißt – freilich im weiten Sinne dieses Begriffs: Schritte in technisches Neuland wirken sich positiv auf das Ganze aus.

*

Robert Bosch fuhr 22jährig in die Vereinigten Staaten, nicht als Auswanderer, sondern um zu lernen und, reifer geworden, zurückzukehren.

Wenn der Auslandsanteil an unserem Umsatz seit langem mehr als die Hälfte ausmacht – 1985 waren es 54 Prozent –, wenn rund ein Drittel aller Bosch-Mitarbeiter außerhalb der Bundesrepublik tätig ist, folgen wir einer Leitlinie, die uns Robert Bosch gab. 1931 schrieb er im *Bosch-Zünder*, für Deutschland gäbe es nur Weltwirtschaft. Damals überstieg der Export schon seit mehr als drei Jahrzehnten den Inlandsumsatz. Bereits vor dem Ersten Weltkrieg setzte Bosch in den Vereinigten Staaten mehr um als in Deutschland, und längst stand dort eine bedeutende eigene Fabrik, und im Februar 1987 können wir die 75jährige Anwesenheit von Bosch in Japan festlich begehen.

Gewiß, Robert Bosch hatte Vorbilder – Werner von Siemens etwa, der schon fünfzig Jahre vorher begonnen hatte im Ausland zu produzieren. Heute geht es einfach um die Feststellung, daß unsere globale Politik auf den Gründer zurückzuführen ist. Für ihn waren die Vereinigten Staaten ein Teil seiner Welt, und »Weltläufigkeit des Denkens« bescheinigte ihm auch Theodor Heuss. Wir bemühen uns, diese kosmopolitische Grundhaltung zu bewahren und mit den Eierschalen des Provinziellen fertig zu werden, die uns manchmal bei der jüngeren Generation Kummer bereiten, wenn wir Mitarbeiter nach draußen schicken wollen.

Ein international tätiges Unternehmen braucht internationalen Rat. Seit einer Reihe von Jahren steht uns ein Beraterkreis zur Seite, der aus ebenso vorzüglichen wie weitschauenden Persönlichkeiten besteht. Stellvertretend für diese Gruppe nenne ich einen dieser Männer, der es sich nicht nehmen ließ, über Nacht aus New York hierherzukommen und der am Ende dieses Festaktes dorthin zurückfliegen muß. Wir danken in seiner Person dem gesamten Beraterkreis: Dr. Henry Kissinger – herzlichen Dank für die freundschaftliche Zusammenarbeit und für Ihr Kommen.

*

Was wären wir ohne unsere Kunden! Wir haben es ihnen nicht immer leichtgemacht – aber es war auch nicht immer leicht mit unseren Kunden. Oft genug glaubten wir, es besser zu wissen als sie. Und nicht in jedem Fall waren wir taktvoll genug zu schweigen, wenn das bessere Wissen auf unserer Seite zu sein schien – während wir natürlich den Mund gehalten haben, wenn wir uns vertan hatten. Und großzügig haben oft genug unsere Kunden über Unzulänglichkeiten auf unserer Seite hinweggesehen – vielleicht weil wir stets bemüht waren, sie durch frühen technischen Fortschritt, durch Verläßlichkeit zu entschädigen. Wir versprechen, daß wir uns weiterhin mit großem Ernst bemühen werden, der Aufgabe gerecht zu werden, die uns als Marktführer auf manchem Gebiet gestellt ist.

Einstweilen bleibt uns, für das Vertrauen zu danken, das uns selbst dann entgegengebracht wurde, wenn wir nicht immer in der Lage waren, rechtzeitig das Richtige in der geforderten Menge zu liefern. Das lag meist an unserem Unvermögen, nie aber an Mangel an gutem Willen. Einen Kundenstamm zu haben, der sich auf uns verläßt und auf den wir uns verlassen können, empfinden wir als eine Verpflichtung.

Wir betrachten uns im strengen Sinne des Wortes als Treuhänder unserer Kunden und folglich unsere Arbeit als Nobile Officium, wobei wir von dem antiken Wortsinn insoweit abweichen, als wir nicht honoris causa arbeiten, sondern unseren Lohn, unseren Preis, unseren Gewinn nicht nur fordern, sondern auch benötigen. Aber unsere Kunden wissen, daß wir den Grundsatz von Robert Bosch hochhalten: den Gewinn weitgehend unterzupflügen, das heißt zu reinvestieren in Form von Forschung und Entwicklung, von Aus- und Weiterbildung unserer Mitarbeiter und von Investitionen, um die Kapazität – damit die Liefersicherheit –, die Wirtschaftlichkeit und die Qualität zu erhöhen.

*

Wettbewerb ist für uns immer ein Ansporn gewesen und wird es bleiben. Wir lernen vom Wettbewerb, und so gesehen, wollen wir heute auch unseren Konkurrenten Dankeschön sagen.

Wettbewerb hat freilich längst einen globalen Aspekt. Wenn japanische Wettbewerber, die seit vielen Jahrzehnten unsere Lizenznehmer sind, in *unserem* Lande mit *unserem* Namen werben, so ist das ein bedenkenswerter Aspekt. Wir sind – als Anhänger und Nutznießer eines freien Welthandels – die letzten, die nach Protektionismus rufen. Das schließt die Forderung nach gleichen Startbedingungen nicht aus.

*

Wer seinen Kunden dankt, sollte den Dank an die Lieferer nicht vergessen. Im Laufe langer Jahre haben wir unsere Produktionstiefe planvoll verringert. Dieser Prozeß ist noch im Gange. Was von uns an Voraussicht, gleichbleibender Qualität, verläßlicher Lieferung und Wirtschaftlichkeit erwartet wird, können wir unseren Lieferern in unseren Anforderungen nicht ersparen.

Geld, Kredit und folglich Banken *nach* den Lieferern zu nennen – man sehe mir das nach –, ist keine Rangfolge. Robert Bosch hatte, wie ihm Theodor Heuss heute vor 25 Jahren bescheinigte, »zu den Gelddingen ein völlig souveränes Verhältnis«. Er habe darauf gehalten, von Banken unabhängig zu bleiben. Unabhängig: ja. Aber das heißt nicht, daß ihm an der Zusammenarbeit nicht gelegen hätte. Vor allem kam es ihm darauf an, das Vertrauen der Finanzwelt zu erhalten.

Im April 1926, zur Finanzierung des Wiederaufbaus der Auslandspositionen, begab Bosch eine Anleihe über 5 Millionen US-Dollar. Für die Rückzahlung war der Wert des Golddollars »heutigen Gewichts und Feingehalts« festgelegt. Nach Einführung der Devisenbewirtschaftung (1933) beantragte Bosch, die Anleihe zum Wert des Golddollars tilgen zu dürfen, was vom Reichswirtschaftsminister »aus grundsätzlichen Erwägungen« abgelehnt wurde; der Transfer mußte folglich zum inzwischen verringerten Tageswert des Dollars erfolgen. Bosch hatte den Vertrag korrekt erfüllen wollen.

Wurde dann 1953 eine der ersten deutschen Industrieanleihen, eine Bosch-Obligation über 20 Millionen DM, zum Erfolg, so vielleicht, weil die Bedingungen zeitgemäß waren, ja, der Zeit vorauseilten. Man sprach vom Bosch-Typ, und das Vertrauen mag zum Durchbruch beigetragen haben. Die Bosch-Anleihe von 1959 über 50 Millionen DM fiel mit einem Zinssatz von 5 Prozent auf den Tiefpunkt der Zinsentwicklung. Wir waren dankbar für den Rat, den man uns seinerzeit gab; einer der Ratgeber ist heute hier. Von 1960 an haben wir diese Anleihe *freiwillig* mit 5½ Prozent und von 1965 an, wiederum freiwillig, mit 6 Prozent verzinst. Fast muß man heute bedauern, daß die Zeit der klassischen Industrieanleihen vorüber ist, in der Schuldner beweisen konnten, daß sie den Kapitalmarkt zu pflegen wissen.

Schon vorher aber, als es für deutsche Schuldner noch nicht leicht war, Hartwährungskredite zu bekommen, hatte uns ein Schweizer Bankier einen langfristigen Kredit in zweistelliger Millionenhöhe zur Verfügung gestellt. Finanziert wurde damit die Rückgewinnung internationalen Terrains. Der Kreditgeber hatte keine Sicherheit außer dem persönlichen Wort, und in einer Phase der Anonymisierung internationaler Finanzbeziehungen erinnert man sich gerne jener souveränen Entscheidung. Der Bankier war Alfred Schaefer; er starb vor zwei Wochen.

*

In der gegenwärtigen politischen Auseinandersetzung über den richtigen Schwerpunkt der Bildungspolitik spielt das Zielproblem eine Rolle.

Dabei setzt Spitzenförderung die Breitenförderung als Fundament voraus. Kommen wir in der Bundesrepublik Deutschland nicht zu dem Konsens, daß wir beides brauchen, marschieren unterdessen draußen die anderen an uns vorbei.

Auch hier teilen wir die Überzeugungen Robert Boschs: *Alle* Begabungen müssen ihrem Potential gemäß aufgespürt und gefördert werden, ohne Rücksicht auf einen Richtungsstreit. Er hat gesagt, Demokratie ohne Führer sei der sicherste Weg zur Diktatur, und 1916 mit einer Dotation von 2 Millionen Mark den Verein zur Förderung der Begabten gegründet, um »Hochbegabte aller Kreise« in begrenzter Zahl zu fördern, hat aber auch den Verein für Volksbildung (Volkshochschule) ins Leben gerufen.

Mit diesem Ziel fördern wir bei Bosch weltweit die Aus- und Weiterbildung unserer Mitarbeiter und den Aufstieg innerhalb unseres Unternehmens. So führten wir vor 25 Jahren, der Zeit vorauseilend, den Status des »Werkangestellten« ein, der Facharbeiter im Rahmen der rechtlichen Möglichkeiten in wichtigen Arbeitsbedingungen den Angestellten gleichstellt. Seit 1973 sprechen wir von »Fachangestellten«, deren Bezüge seither monatlich gezahlt werden. Mehr als zwanzig vom Hundert (genauer 22 Prozent) unserer Mitarbeiter haben diesen Status.

Schon damals machten wir bei den betrieblichen Sozialleistungen keinen Unterschied zwischen Arbeitern und Angestellten. Es gibt aber aufgrund gesetzlicher und tarifvertraglicher Regelung Unterschiede in anderer Hinsicht zwischen Arbeitern und Angestellten, was wir für unbefriedigend halten. Seit längerem verhandeln wir deshalb mit dem Gesamtbetriebsrat über eine Anpassung der Entlohnungsgrundsätze an geänderte Fertigungstechniken und an neue Arbeitsabläufe. Als Ergebnis stellen wir uns vor, daß in nicht allzu ferner Zeit alle Arbeiter ein monatliches Entgelt erhalten werden; wir wollen den Kreis der Fachangestellten erweitern; wir werden unseren Mitarbeitern zusätzliche Schulungs- und Weiterbildungswege öffnen und ihnen damit die Chance geben, sich für höhere Aufgaben zu qualifizieren. Dabei haben wir rechtliche und tarifvertragliche Schranken zu respektieren. Robert Boschs Konzeption von Menschlichkeit ist für uns ein Ansporn, der Chancengerechtigkeit im Betrieb weiteren Raum zu verschaffen.

Man muß von Zeit zu Zeit darauf aufmerksam machen, daß sich der wirtschaftspolitische Erfolg der letzten Jahre nicht an der Zahl der Arbeitslosen ablesen läßt. Denn diese wird durch die stetige Zunahme der Zahl jener erhöht, die Beschäftigung suchen. Ein richtigeres Bild gibt das Arbeitsplatzvolumen: Die Zahl der Beschäftigten hat von Anfang 1984 bis Mitte 1986 um 530000 oder 2 Prozent zugenommen, und sie steigt weiter.

Mittelstandspolitiker wollen wissen, daß die Zunahme nicht etwa in den Großunternehmen, sondern in den Klein- und Mittelbetrieben eingetreten ist. Aber die Zahl der Mitarbeiter in der Bosch-Gruppe hat während der letzten drei Jahre weltweit um 21 300, in der Bundesrepublik allein um 14 200 (17 Prozent) zugenommen. Dies bestätigt – wenn die erwähnten Mittelstandspolitiker recht haben – die von mir aufgestellte Behauptung, Bosch gehöre dem oberen Mittelstand an, was mir meist ein Lächeln einbringt. Aber ich lege Wert auf die Feststellung, daß wir bei Bosch die Erhaltung und die Förderung des Mittelstandes, wie immer man ihn abgrenzt, für eine essentielle politische Aufgabe halten.

Den Vereinigten Staaten – bei aller Skepsis gegenüber ihrer wirtschaftlichen Entwicklung – muß man zumindest *eines* gutschreiben: Die Zahl der Erwerbstätigen steigt seit einer Reihe von Jahren steil an – um eine zweistellige Prozentzahl. Die Millionen zusätzlich Beschäftigter rekrutieren sich zu einem großen Teil aus Neugründungen und Erweiterungen kleiner und mittlerer Unternehmen, was die Beobachtung der deutschen Mittelstandspolitiker bestätigt. Ein Zeichen also unternehmerischen Wagemuts, der in der noch immer Neuen Welt in viel höherem Maß vorhanden ist als bei uns.

Dieser lebendige Prozeß ist, wie wir hoffen, ein glückliches Gegengewicht gegen die in den Vereinigten Staaten – aber neuerdings auch in Europa – um sich greifende Verschmelzung großer Unternehmen zu immer größeren Einheiten, die erst noch beweisen müssen, daß Größe auch Stärke bedeutet, die erst noch mit wachsender innerer Reibung fertig werden müssen, die erst erkennen müssen, daß sich die Geschwindigkeit, und das heißt die Beweglichkeit, eines Körpers bei gegebener Energie umgekehrt proportional zu der Quadratwurzel der Masse verhält – also bei Vergrößerung der Masse abnimmt.

*

Robert Bosch war weder sentimental noch ein Sozialromantiker. Zeitlebens hat er jede seiner Sozialmaßnahmen als Produktivitätssteigerung verstanden, auch den Achtstundentag, den er 1906 einführte. In den zwanziger und den frühen dreißiger Jahren bezeichnete er zwar die Verkürzung der Arbeitszeit – damals 48 Wochenstunden – nicht nur als betriebswirtschaftlich möglich und sogar nützlich, sondern auch als volkswirtschaftlich notwendig. Doch ließ er nie das Wirtschaftliche aus den Augen. Er war davon überzeugt, daß der Mensch in acht Stunden täglich mindestens gleich viel schaffen könne wie in neun oder zehn; denn die Ermüdung würde geringer sein. Sein Rat wurde seinerzeit nicht befolgt.

Inzwischen – unter essentiell anderen Voraussetzungen – ist die 35-Stunden-Woche mit vollem Lohnausgleich ein erklärtes politisches Ziel der Linken. Man glaubt, die Arbeitslosigkeit damit verringern zu können. Doch kann man sich dabei nicht auf Robert Bosch beziehen. Denn einerseits hat er *nie* einen Lohnausgleich angeboten. Vielmehr ging er von gleichbleibenden, nicht etwa erhöhten Lohnstückkosten aus. Zum anderen aber hat sich seither – es ist immerhin mehr als ein halbes Jahrhundert verflossen – der Investitionsaufwand je Arbeitsplatz auf das Zehnfache und mehr erhöht. Unsere zur Zeit laufenden Sachanlageinvestitionen für neue, hochtechnische Produkte erfordern einen Aufwand von mehr als 300000 DM je Arbeitsplatz. Das verlangt *heute* eine prinzipiell andere Betrachtungsweise. Wenn die Investition nicht teilweise vergeudet sein soll, ist ein sehr viel höherer Grad der Betriebsnutzung notwendig – notwendig im engen Sinne dieses Wortes. Zumindest wird also Flexibilität erforderlich.

Zu warnen ist dringend vor dem gefährlichen Gedanken, eine kostenwirksame, das heißt mit Lohnausgleich verbundene Arbeitszeitverkürzung sei geeignet, neue Arbeitsplätze zu schaffen. Das Gegenteil würde eintreten: nämlich eine Verringerung der Zahl der Arbeitsplätze wegen geminderter internationaler Wettbewerbsfähigkeit, die in einem offenen Markt zudem die nationale Wettbewerbsfähigkeit beeinträchtigen müßte.

*

Robert Bosch sprach nicht nur einmal dankbar aus, sein Unternehmen ruhe nicht auf zwei Augen und er hätte den Weg nach oben nicht ohne ausgezeichnete Mitarbeiter geschafft. Wir sprachen bereits von Hans Walz. Ohne ihn, der den Weg des Gründers von 1912 bis 1942 begleitet hat und der dann weitere zwanzig Jahre – bis zu seinem 80. Geburtstag im März 1963 – an der Spitze des Unternehmens stand, ist unser Haus in seiner heutigen Bedeutung nicht vorstellbar. Theodor Heuss hat geschrieben, Hans Walz zu gewinnen, sei eine der wichtigsten Entscheidungen gewesen, die Robert Bosch je getroffen habe. Als Hans Walz aus der Geschäftsführung ausschied, wählten ihn die Gesellschafter zum Ehrenvorsitzenden des Hauses Bosch.

In Israel und darüber hinaus ist nicht vergessen, was Hans Walz von 1933 an für viele jüdische Mitbürger getan hat, indem er ihren Aufenthalt erträglicher machte, ihre Ausreise ermöglichte und sie vor dem Schlimmsten bewahrte. Robert Bosch stellte sich bis zu seinem Tode hinter Hans Walz; sie beide nahmen die persönliche Gefahr auf sich, die mit dem Eintreten für Menschlichkeit und Gerechtigkeit verbunden war.

Im Jahr 1970 wurde Hans Walz in den Kreis der »Gerechten der Völker« aufgenommen, die in Yad Vashem in Jerusalem einen Baum pflanzen dürfen – als Symbol selbstlosen, opferbereiten Handelns. Hans Walz fühlte sich einer Reise nach Israel nicht mehr gewachsen. Vor einem Monat wurde der feierliche Akt nachgeholt. Auch das ist ein Stück Bosch.

Aus der früheren Geschäftsführung trat nach dem Kriege, außer Hans Walz, nur noch der begnadete Techniker Karl Martin Wild wieder in die Leitung des Unternehmens ein, starb aber bald danach. Er hatte sich von vornherein in den internationalen Zuschnitt des Hauses eingefügt, als er 1909 die technische Leitung der amerikanischen Fabrik übernahm.

Lassen Sie uns noch einiger anderer Männer der »ersten Stunde« gedenken, die, von vielen Mitarbeitern und unzähligen Helfern unterstützt, 1945 die Trümmer beiseite räumten und die den Wiederaufbau einleiteten. Ich nenne stellvertretend für viele andere Otto Fischer, Alfred Knoerzer und Walter Lippart. Sie alle haben in dunklen Jahren die von Robert Bosch entfachte Flamme weitergetragen. Das verlangt unseren Dank.

Noch ein Name ist zu nennen – nicht ohne an die Formulierung von Theodor Heuss aus dem Jahr 1931 zu denken, »Pflicht und Leistung« seien bei Bosch eine »Selbstverständlichkeit«. Der, den ich – und wiederum stellvertretend – nennen will, ist Hans Bacher, der am Wiederaufbau ein Vierteljahrhundert lang wesentlichen Anteil hatte und der seine Pflicht bis zuletzt tat – bis vor wenigen Jahren der Tod dem 57jährigen den weiteren Weg, der ihm bestimmt war, abschnitt.

*

Von sich selbst sagte Robert Bosch, er »habe nie eine Erfindung gemacht im landläufigen Sinne des Wortes«. Aber er verstand es, erfinderischem Geist den Rahmen zu geben, der es möglich machte, Ideen in marktgängige Erzeugnisse und Leistungen umzusetzen.

Es ist ein grundlegender Irrtum anzunehmen, Erfolg und Mißerfolg eines Unternehmens liege in der Hand eines einzelnen. In Wirklichkeit ist Erfolg immer eine Gemeinschaftsleistung. Nur der Mißerfolg kann und darf einem einzelnen zur Last gelegt werden. Gemeinschaftsleistung setzt Mannschaftsgeist voraus, die Bereitschaft, Verantwortung für die persönliche Aufgabe zu tragen, ohne daß man sich von der Gesamtverantwortung freimachen könnte.

Ich will hier und heute meinen früheren Kollegen, meinen früheren Mitarbeitern aus vollem Herzen – und verbunden mit dem Dank der Gesellschafter – bestätigen, daß sich in diesem Hause in vielen Jahrzehnten keiner dem Ruf entzogen hat zu größerer Verantwortung, zu mehr Arbeit, zu mehr Last und zu höherem Risiko – ohne daß ihm damit eine sichere Chance in Aussicht gestellt werden konnte.

Keiner hat sich dem Ruf entzogen, auch der nicht, der heute an der Spitze der Führungsmannschaft steht, obwohl er die Sorgen, die mit der Übernahme seines Amtes verbunden sind und die nicht kleiner, sondern größer werden, voraussah. Ich bin sicher, daß diese Mannschaft Bosch weiterhin erfolgreich – und nun verwende ich bewußt dieses Wort – führen wird.

*

Letztlich steht und fällt die Bosch-Gruppe mit der Leistung *aller* ihrer Mitarbeiter. Ich will anhand einiger Zahlen veranschaulichen, wer Bosch in Wirklichkeit verkörpert: Das sind 100000 Mitarbeiter in der Bundesrepublik Deutschland und annähernd 50000 Mitarbeiter in anderen europäischen Staaten, in beiden Teilen Amerikas, in Afrika, in Asien und in Australien – soweit der Konsolidierungskreis; darüber hinaus rund 20000 Mitarbeiter in Unternehmungen, an denen wir maßgeblich, aber nicht mehrheitlich beteiligt sind. Vor allem aber rechnen wir 90000 Mitarbeiter in unserer nationalen und internationalen Kundendienst-Organisation zu unserer Stärke. Alles in allem spüren und tragen wir Verantwortung für mehr als eine Viertelmillion Menschen – Menschen, die Bosch ausmachen, die bisher zu uns gestanden haben und auch in Zukunft zu uns stehen werden. Sie alle verdienen Dank – wo immer ihr Platz ist.

Es ist Recht und Pflicht, in diesem Dank ausdrücklich auch die vielen Männer und Frauen einzuschließen, die in Betriebsräten und Ausschüssen tätig sind. Wir blicken auf Spannungen und Entspannungen zurück, meist siegte die Vernunft, immer letzten Endes der Friedenswille.

*

Robert Bosch verlangte ausdrücklich, daß wir seine Unternehmung »nicht bloß erhalten, sondern kraftvoll weiterentwickeln«. In den Richtlinien, die er auf seine Vermächtnisse angewandt wissen wollte, schrieb er vor fünfzig Jahren: »Ich bin mir bewußt, daß die wirtschaftlichen und kulturellen Zustände und Bedürfnisse immerwährenden Wandlungen unterworfen sind. Daraus ergibt sich die Notwendigkeit, diese Richtlinien auf dem Wege der Fortentwicklung den Veränderungen der Verhältnisse ständig anzupassen.«

Wir sind uns bei Bosch darüber im klaren, daß nicht nur die Technik, sondern auch die Gesellschaft in Bewegung ist. Dabei handelt es sich, im Gegensatz zur Meinung des Gleichmuts ermangelnder Zeitgenossen, um einen langfristigen, einen säkularen Prozeß. Er hat sich sicherlich beschleunigt, bleibt aber beherrschbar, wenn wir die Nerven nicht verlieren.

So nötig es ist, spekulativ die Möglichkeiten und die Unmöglichkeiten zu durchdenken – mehr als jede Spekulation wird uns der gesunde Menschenverstand weiterhelfen, der uns zur Verständigung zwingt, und damit bin ich beim Ausgangspunkt: Panta rhei – alles ist im Fluß. Aber alles läßt sich eindämmen. Dämme bauen war immer eine Gemeinschaftsarbeit.

Wir wissen bei Bosch, was wir wert sind. Aber gerade dieses Bewußtsein ist Voraussetzung dafür, daß wir bescheiden bleiben und daß wir uns nicht etwa satt zurücklehnen, sondern nach Neuem Ausschau halten. So sehen wir unsere Aufgabe nicht darin, das zu ernten, was wir gestern gesät haben, sondern zu säen, was wir morgen ernten. *(1986)*

Führung durch Manager

DEMOKRATIE IM UNTERNEHMEN?

Fünfzig Jahre Erfahrung als Geführter und als Führender haben dem Autor den Glauben daran nicht genommen, daß in jedem Menschen, wenn auch graduell verschieden, sowohl die Bereitschaft steckt, sich einer Führung anzuvertrauen, soweit von besseren Argumenten getragen, als auch die Befähigung, andere zu führen, wenn die Zeit dazu gekommen ist. Das letztere unterliegt der Entwicklung und verlangt Geduld des sich Entwickelnden. Dieser Artikel ist folglich ein Erfahrungsbericht, nicht aber eine Führungslehre.

*

Führung setzt voraus, daß das Unternehmensziel für jeden im Unternehmen klar ist, wobei Tiefe und Breite der Information dem Verantwortungsbereich entsprechen müssen, den der Betriebsangehörige hat.

Es ist eine alte Beobachtung, daß aus den verschiedenen Stufen und Rängen des Unternehmens die Klage kommt, man kenne das Unternehmensziel nicht oder nicht ausreichend. Jedoch weiß in Wirklichkeit jeder zumindest so viel, daß das Unternehmen die ihm innerhalb des Ganzen zugewiesene Rolle nur ausfüllen kann, wenn es Erlöse erzielt, die höher sind als die Kosten, also einen Überschuß, den wir uns nicht scheuen, Gewinn zu nennen. Daß diese grundsätzlich unabdingbare Zielsetzung durch das Festlegen von Randbedingungen ergänzt werden muß, ergibt sich aus den jeweils im Vordergrund stehenden Teilzielen, die nur bezüglich weniger Parameter auf längere Sicht, wenn überhaupt, bestimmt werden können und müssen. Schon die Fragen nach der angestrebten Unternehmensgröße, dem ins Auge gefaßten Marktgebiet, den bevorzugten Sektoren und den Schwerpunktprodukten entziehen sich – wenn die Antwort weder evident ist noch trivial sein soll – einer Festlegung über längere Zeiträume.

Ein Unternehmen ist keine Weltanschauungsgemeinschaft, die sich ein Lehrgebäude schaffen müßte, sondern ein Zweckorganismus mit Zielen und Bedürfnissen, die sich im Zuge seiner Entwicklung und mit seinem Wachstum ändern.

*

Spricht man von Führung und läßt zunächst den unternehmerischen Aspekt beiseite, drängt sich der Vergleich mit militärischer Führung auf. Diese kann aber wegen ihrer in der Regel politisch eingeschränkten Zielsetzung auf der einen Seite, ihrer geschichtlich gewachsenen und aus der Sache heraus notwendigen hierarchischen Ordnung kein Vorbild und keine Richtschnur für die unternehmerischen Führung sein.

Autoritärer Führungsstil – sollte er je über längere Zeitläufe hinweg angewandt worden sein – ist im Begriff, überwunden zu werden durch eine neue Auffassung, worin das Kooperative, das Partizipative in den Vordergrund tritt. Kooperation bedeutet aber nicht etwa Führung von unten; jedoch tritt gerade dann, wenn hergebrachte Autorität nicht mehr ausreicht, um zu überzeugen, in der Gruppe ein neues Bewußtsein für die Notwendigkeit struktureller Ordnung und geregelter Verantwortung auf. Das Management hat dann die Chance, das Unternehmen gemeinsam weiterzubewegen, was der Forderung nach der Aufgabenteilung nicht widerspricht. Das Ziehen, das man gegenüber dem Schieben vorziehen muß, wird durch freiwilligen, auf Überzeugung beruhendem Konsensus überhaupt erst möglich. Der von den Unternehmen anzustrebende Führungsstil beruht folglich auf Zusammenarbeit bei der Vorbereitung, beim Treffen und beim Verwirklichen von Entscheidungen. Wenn Übereinstimmung der Auffassungen, Gemeinsamkeit der Willensbildung erreicht wird, kann, freilich nur für den Außenstehenden, der Eindruck autoritärer Führung entstehen. Aber Selbstzucht und Fingerspitzengefühl können der Außenwelt beweisen, daß wir es heute nicht mehr mit Anspruch auf Führung, sondern mit Ansprüchen an die Führung zu tun haben.

*

Führung ist auch eine moralische Kategorie. Man kann nicht führen ohne festen Willen, der nicht primär von Intelligenz, sondern von Charakter getragen wird. Führen ist Teilnehmenlassen an einem Ziel, das der Geführte als sein eigenes annehmen und empfinden muß, also Übertragen des eigenen Willens auf einen anderen, Motivieren, Mitreißen.

Führung enthält also auch irrationale Elemente. Die spezifischen Aufgaben, die der Führung im Unternehmen gestellt sind, verlangen aber vom Manager professionelles, pragmatisches Vorgehen, das heißt, daß man auf charismatische Deutung seiner Stellung verzichtet, indem man von ihm konsequentes und konsistentes Handeln verlangt. Autorität entwickelt sich, wenn der Manager berechenbar handelt, wie das der Mitarbeiter seiner Bereitschaft zur Einordnung zugrunde legt. Doch gehört zur Führung auch der Mut zum Gegensatz, falls er nicht auf dem Bedürfnis beruht, recht zu haben, sondern auf größerem Weitblick, auf weiterreichender Zusammenschau.

*

Der Gemeinplatz, jede Entscheidung sei besser als keine, ist durch bittere Erfahrung längst ad absurdum geführt; die Neigung einzelner zu rascher Entscheidung wird aber hin und wieder noch immer als Kriterium der Qualifikation gewertet. Daß die Verzögerung oder die

Unterlassung einer Entscheidung im beobachteten Einzelfall erfolgreich war, ist kein Beweis für eine Gesetzmäßigkeit und spricht auf keinen Fall gegen ein System sorgfältiger Entscheidungsvorbereitung, das alle Kriterien erfaßt und bewertet, ohne intuitiver Entscheidung den Spielraum zu nehmen; auch sie geht auf das – häufig unbewußte – Abwägen des Pro und Kontra zurück.

Durch frühzeitige Entscheidungsvorbereitung, die häufig »auf Vorrat« unternommen werden kann, läßt sich jedenfalls die Zahl jener »blitzschnellen Fehlentscheidungen« verringern, von denen die Rede ist. Entscheidungsvorbereitung ist in der Regel Stabsarbeit, auch wenn sie in der Linie vorgenommen wird. Die polemische Redensart: Wer etwas auf sich hält, hält sich einen Stab, trifft nicht ins Schwarze, wenn »Stab« und »Linie« wohlabgewogene Potentiale sind. Wer nur mit Stäben arbeitet, verliert den Kontakt zur Front, vergibt also die Führungsmöglichkeiten, die in der Unmittelbarkeit liegen. Wer auf Stäbe verzichtet, die hin und wieder den Blick verstellen und die Papierflut eher vergrößern, kann »vor Ort« führen – jedoch mit dem Nachteil, daß geringer Abstand zu den Tatsachen den Blick nicht schärft. Es ist ein nützlicher Kompromiß, wenn sich die Führung der Spannung bedient, die sich zwischen Stab und Linie einzustellen pflegt.

Entscheidungen müssen begründbar sein und begründet werden. Es geht nicht darum, Entscheidungen, die bereits getroffen sind, zu »verkaufen«, sondern den Mitarbeiter an der Entscheidung zu beteiligen, so daß er sie sich zu eigen macht.

*

Es ist sehr einfach, deckt sich aber nicht mit der Wirklichkeit, zu sagen, Verantwortung sei unteilbar. Diese Fassung ist im Ernstfall – wenn es nämlich darum geht, Verantwortung für einen Vorgang oder für eine Unterlassung zu *tragen* – nicht anwendbar.

Klarer ist es zu sagen, daß innerhalb einer Gruppe jedem das bestimmte Maß an Verantwortung zufällt, das seinem Anteil an der Lösung der Gesamtaufgabe entspricht. Diesen Anteil hat jeder, der eine Aufgabe übernimmt, zu tragen; er kann ihm nicht abgenommen werden. Übernähme eine Gruppe gemeinsame Verantwortung, könnte sich einer hinter dem anderen verstecken. Sanktionen für das Nicht-Gelingen gingen ins Leere. Unteilbar ist dann freilich die Verantwortung des Managers für das, was insgesamt in der Gruppe erreicht und was nicht erreicht wurde. Dies bezieht sich auf die Verantwortung jeweils nach oben, also auf die Verantwortungslinien, die der Führungsaufbau vorzeichnet.

Verantwortung ist ein Wagnis. Wer sich einem Auftrag stellt, ob er ihn allein oder als Mitglied einer Gruppe übernimmt, muß den Kopf hinhalten, wobei es mit der Erklärung: »Ich übernehme die Verantwortung« nicht getan ist.

Immer wieder stellt sich die Frage, ob Führung durch Gruppen, also institutionelle Führung statt individueller Führung, der Abgrenzung der Verantwortung genügt, mit Akzeptanz seitens der Geführten rechnen kann, Erfolg verspricht und schließlich, unter gesellschaftspolitischem Aspekt, sogar den Vorzug vor höchstpersönlicher Führung verdient. Doch ist das insofern eine Scheinfrage, als auch Führungsgruppen durch Individuen zu handeln pflegen, indem sich innerhalb einer Gruppe klar herauskristallisiert, wer führt. Gruppen sind wertvoll für die Entscheidungsvorbereitung, sie können Entscheidungen einmütig oder mehrheitlich treffen – sie durchzusetzen bleibt die Rolle des einzelnen Managers, der nach Funktion oder Sparte die Verwirklichung der Entscheidung verantwortet.

*

Informationsfluß in beiden, in allen Richtungen, ohne Zeitverlust, ist Arbeitsbedingung des Unternehmens und Bedingung für den Führungserfolg. Nur vom informierten Mitarbeiter kann der Manager Selbständigkeit erwarten.

Durch Information wird dem Entstehen von »Herrschaftswissen« vorgebeugt. Obwohl dieser Begriff polemisch übersteigert ist, existiert die Erscheinung doch, und sie beschränkt sich nicht auf bestimmte Schichten, sondern kommt auf allen Ebenen vor und mindert das Vertrauen.

Information muß zeitgerecht sein und die Zusammenhänge innerhalb des Unternehmens in ihrer organisierten Wirklichkeit: horizontal, vertikal, lateral, diagonal darstellen. Der Begriff des Zusammenhangs umgreift beispielhaft sowohl das Produkt (seine Entwicklung, seine Herstellung, seine Verteilung und seine Verwendung) als auch das Unternehmen in seiner Gesamtheit, in seiner Stellung in der Öffentlichkeit und in seinen Rechten und Pflichten gegenüber der Gemeinschaft. Zeitgerechte Information ist eines der Werkzeuge erfolgreicher Führung und der erste Schritt zur Kommunikation: die Zweibahnstraße der Information.

*

Der Gliederungsplan des Unternehmens wird nicht in erster Linie von seiner Größe, sondern von seiner Charakteristik bestimmt.

Bei der wirtschaftlich notwendigen optimalen Nutzung aller Fähigkeiten werden in der Regel jedem Mitarbeiter bestimmte, wenn auch zunächst weitgefaßte Aufgaben zugewiesen, das heißt, eine Mindestgliederung wird vorgenommen. Sie läßt bereits erkennen, ob eine vertikale oder horizontale Organisation vorgezogen wird. Jedoch entspricht eine kategorische Entscheidung nicht immer den betrieblichen Notwendigkeiten. Häufig werden beide Bindungsrichtungen verknüpft: zu einer Organisationsform, die vertikale und horizontale Züge enthält und oft als Matrixorganisation bezeichnet wird. Je stärker die Vernetzung – die sich über das zweidimensionale Bild hinaus weitere Dimensionen erschließt –, desto höher der Anspruch an die Führung, die um so differenzierter vorgehen muß, je tiefer gestaffelt die Organisation ist. Führung ist also nicht eine Funktion der Größe, sondern der Freiheitsgrade der Organisation.

Ob zentrale oder dezentrale Organisation, ist eine Frage, deren Bedeutung gemeinhin überschätzt wird; in der betrieblichen Wirklichkeit überschneiden sich beide Formen. Maßgebend für das Schwergewicht, das auf die eine oder andere Seite gelegt wird, sind Faktoren unterschiedlicher Natur; dazu gehören die quantitative und qualitative Führungskapazität, aber auch das Vertrauen, das die Führung in die Kompetenz ihrer Mitarbeiter setzt und in ihre eigene Fähigkeit, diese Kompetenz systematisch zu erhöhen. Der dezentralen Organisation kommt oft schon deshalb der Vorzug zu, weil sie zur Erhöhung der Kompetenz führt – nicht als bürokratisch zugewiesene Entscheidungsbefugnis, sondern als Entscheidungskraft. Die Organisationslehre muß also vor allem Optionen anbieten, bevor sie Lösungen empfiehlt.

Der mit der Führung betraute Manager muß die Organisation als Werkzeug, nicht als Wert an sich oder als Ziel ansehen. Er muß also jede überkommene Organisationsform in Frage stellen, neuen Organisationsformen gegenüber aufgeschlossen sein, Organisation als eine immer neue Aufgabenstellung betrachten.

Gemeinhin wird, fast in der Form eines Lehrsatzes, gefordert, in einer wirkungsvollen Organisation dürfe jeder Mitarbeiter nur *einen* Vorgesetzten haben. Diese Regel entspricht nicht der betrieblichen Wirklichkeit. Ein großer Teil der Vorgänge in einem Unternehmen läuft nicht nach einen starren Gliederungsplan ab, er beruht vielmehr auf lateralen und diagonalen Querverbindungen. Daraus ergeben sich in der Praxis Zuordnungen, die in vielen Fällen der Organisationstheorie widersprechen. Trägt man der betrieblichen Mannigfaltigkeit durch die oben erwähnte Matrixstruktur Rechnung, führt das fast immer dazu, daß ein Mitarbeiter mehr als eine Funktion auszuüben hat, auch wenn Schwerpunkte der Tätigkeit festgelegt sind. Daraus ergibt sich, daß er Weisungen von verschiedener Seite zu entsprechen hat. Prinzip bleibt aber, daß jeder wissen muß, wer sein unmittelbarer und für ihn verantwortlicher Vorgesetzter ist.

Über die »Tiefe« der Gliederung läßt sich eine allgemeingültige Aussage nicht machen; für sie gilt, daß die Zahl der Schichten nicht nur aus wirtschaftlichen, sondern vor allem aus personellen Gründen begrenzt bleiben sollte. Bürokratische Auswüchse pflegen mit der Zahl der Stufen zuzunehmen, wenn auch dem menschlichen Bedürfnis auf immer neue Bestätigung durch eine Leiter mit vielen Sprossen besser Rechnung getragen wird als mit einer zu flachen Schichtung des Gliederungsplans.

*

Hat die Idee der Demokratie einen Platz in der Unternehmensführung? Da auch die Staatsform der Demokratie konkreter Führung bedarf (vielleicht mehr noch als jede autoritäre Staatsform), bezieht sich diese Frage nicht auf die etwaige demokratische Kontrolle der Führungshandlungen, sondern allenfalls auf die demokratische Legitimierung der Führenden. Damit nähert sich die Überlegung für das Gebiet der Bundesrepublik Deutschland dem noch zu erörternden Komplex der (erweiterten) Mitbestimmung.

Streng zu trennen von der unbestrittenen Verantwortung der Führenden für den Unternehmenserfolg gegenüber der Betriebsöffentlichkeit – und in übertragenem Sinne gegenüber der Gesellschaft – ist ihre Entscheidungsfreiheit. Deren Einschränkung würde nicht nur die Grenzen der Verantwortung verrücken, sondern die Vorstufe einer Führungslosigkeit sein.

Der Führung sind Grenzen gezogen durch den politischen Grundsatz von Freiheit und Gleichheit, der jedem Mitarbeiter die Entfaltung seiner Persönlichkeit zusichert und nicht nur die Gleichbehandlung, sondern, menschlich gesehen, auch die Gleichstellung aller Mitarbeiter verlangt. Die Notwendigkeit, Ziele zu setzen, Aufträge zu erteilen und Wege zu weisen, steht diesen fundamentalen

Vorstellungen nicht entgegen, den freien Willen zur Einfügung in den Arbeitsprozeß vorausgesetzt.

Die Differenzierung der persönlichen Gewichte im sozialen Zusammenspiel wird in dem Maße anerkannt, in dem eine Gruppenautorität zustande kommt, an der jedes Mitglied nach innen und vor allem nach außen teilhat. Dies zustande zu bringen, verlangt von den Führungskräften sowohl Einfühlung als auch persönliche Zurückhaltung. Die Grenzen der Führung lassen sich ausdehnen und überwinden durch Autorität, die man ausübt, aber auch zu teilen bereit ist. Die Teilung des Arbeitserfolges führt nicht in die Anonymität, sie bedeutet vielmehr, daß das Heranziehen aller menschlichen Energien die wesentliche Führungsaufgabe ist.

Führungsbegabung über Können und Erfahrung hinaus, das heißt als Charaktereigenschaft, wird von den Mitarbeitern nicht etwa nur hingenommen, sondern, ob ausgesprochen oder nicht, gefordert. Es kommt entscheidend darauf an, daß der Manager nicht etwa Führungsrechte fordert, sondern Führung gibt.

*

In einer Reihe europäischer Länder wirken aufgrund von Gesetzen Belegschaftsmitglieder bei unternehmerischen Entscheidungen mit, teils nur beratend, teils mitbestimmend. Soweit sich diese Mitwirkung auf die Kontrollorgane eines Unternehmens – in der Bundesrepublik Deutschland also auf den gesetzlichen Aufsichtsrat – beschränkt, bleibt es umstritten, ob man einen Durchgriff dieser Mitwirkung auf die Führungsebene annehmen kann und muß. Obwohl dies im allgemeinen eher mittel- und langfristiger Einfluß sein wird, muß man für das Gebiet der Bundesrepublik Deutschland davon ausgehen, daß nicht nur die Rechte der Anteilseigner, sondern auch die Autonomie der Führung durch das Mitbestimmungsrecht beschnitten sind. Daß dem Willen der Anteilseigner über das Zweitstimmrecht des von ihnen zu wählenden Vorsitzenden des Aufsichtsrats ein gewisses Übergewicht zukommt, mildert diese Besorgnis, beseitigt sie aber nicht: Der Manager im mitbestimmten Unternehmen kann seine Position durch unternehmensbezogene, unter Umständen auf den ersten Blick aber Interessen der Mitarbeiter beeinträchtigende Entscheidungen schwächen und erschüttern.

Daß bisher Führungsmängel als Folge der erweiterten Mitbestimmung noch nicht an die Oberfläche gekommen sind, beweist nicht, daß sie führungsneutral wäre – und ihre geistigen Väter haben sie so auch gar nicht gemeint.

*

Die Befähigung zum Führen hängt weniger, wenn überhaupt, von der Fachrichtung ab, in der ein Mensch ausgebildet wurde – wenn auch konkretes Handwerk und exakte Wissenschaft jedem abstrakten Lehrgang vorzuziehen sind –, als vielmehr davon, daß er gelernt hat zu lernen, aus Erfahrung und Nachdenken. Bildung im weitesten Sinne des Wortes ist wichtiger als jede spezielle Ausbildung, als jeder mehr oder weniger bürokratische Befähigungsnachweis. Wir verzichten also darauf, bestimmten Ausbildungsgängen den Vorzug zu geben, die, natürlich, der speziellen Aufgabe angemessen sein müssen, deren Kategorie aber um so weniger wiegt, je höher die Führungsstufe.

Die Beobachtung und Förderung des Nachwuchses auf dem Wege nach oben ist eine der wichtigsten Führungsaufgaben. Der Manager muß Begabungen frühzeitig erkennen und ihnen den Weg ebnen (obwohl es gerade ein Kennzeichen des Talentes ist, daß es selbst seinen Weg findet und die Last auf sich nimmt, diesen Weg zu gehen). Wer sich im Unternehmen durch die Neigung zu lernen (und Erfahrungen zu machen ist eine Art des Lernens), durch Vorstellungsvermögen, durch zukunftsorientiertes Denken, durch die Bereitschaft, Verantwortung zu tragen, eben durch die Befähigung zu führen, auszeichnet, wird nicht nach Familie und Nation, nicht nach seinen Vermögensverhältnissen gefragt. Für ihn gilt der Grundsatz, daß jeder die gleiche Chance hat, wenn er sich an seinem Platz bewährt, Verläßlichkeit und festen Willen mitbringt, sich nicht durch Äußerlichkeiten aus der Bahn werfen läßt; kurzum, wenn seine charakterlichen und intellektuellen Eigenschaften sich die Waage halten.

Da Führung nicht als statische, vielmehr als dynamische Aufgabe betrachtet werden muß, ist es notwendig, sowohl die Führungseigenschaften fortzuentwickeln als auch die Fähigkeit der Mitarbeiter, auf Führung aktiv zu antworten. Richtig verstanden wird Führung damit zur Zweibahnstraße und schließt Geben und Nehmen ein. Im eingespielten Zustand resultiert eine optimale Gemeinschaftsleistung, die eher auf Erkenntnis und Verständnis beruht als auf Weisung im Einzelfall.

Mitarbeit dieser Qualität kann nur erwartet werden, wenn grundsätzlich jedem Mitarbeiter der Aufstieg freisteht, was ein Angebot an Aus- und Fortbildung bedingt, das die Beförderung zu einem realistischen Ziel macht, wenn der Wille dazu besteht. Auch der Führende darf nicht stehenbleiben, sondern muß sich weiterentwickeln. Über die Disziplin des Mitarbeiters hinaus ist Disziplin der Führenden eine Erfolgsbedingung, und solche Disziplin ist eher das Produkt von Selbsterziehung als von Aus- und Fortbildung.

Dynamik in der Führung des Unternehmens drückt sich nicht zuletzt in der Forderung nach Job Rotation aus. Nur dadurch kann den Erwartungen aufstiegswilliger Mitarbeiter entsprochen und nur dadurch jene betriebliche Reserve an vielseitigen Mitarbeitern geschaffen werden, die es dem Unternehmen erlaubt, dem technischen, dem wirtschaftlichen und dem politischen Wandel zu folgen – oder ihm voranzugehen.

Für die Loyalität, die von einem Mitarbeiter erwartet wird, sind Ausbildung, Fortbildung und Aufstieg wesentliche Vorbedingungen, und die berufliche Förderung ist für ihn eine Bestätigung.

*

Bemühung und Gelingen, Anstrengung und Erfolg verdienen Anerkennung, ob materieller oder immaterieller Natur. Vom Mitarbeiter kann nicht erwartet werden, daß ihn das bloße Bewußtsein, eine Leistung erbracht zu haben, befriedigt. Geht man davon aus, daß der Mensch in der Regel die Bestätigung der Mitwelt als Antrieb braucht, unterschätzt man zwar diejenigen, die ihre Maßstäbe in sich selbst finden. Man wird aber guttun, die letzteren für die Minderheit zu halten. Generell gesehen verdient der um Leistung bemühte Mitarbeiter zumindest Aufmerksamkeit, die sich in Lob und persönlicher Fürsorge ausdrücken kann, ohne daß die geldliche Komponente vernachlässigt werden darf.

Das weite Gebiet der Erfolgsbeteiligung wird hier ausgespart, aber erwähnt.

Bei der Messung von Leistung und Erfolg sind sowohl die Identifikation des Mitarbeiters mit der gestellten Aufgabe zu berücksichtigen als auch das Maß der Erfüllung. Dabei ist greifbarer Erfolg meist eine Gemeinschaftsleistung; Dezentralisierung, Divisionalisierung und die Einrichtung von »Profit Centers« erleichtern die Erfolgsabgrenzung quantitativ, können aber die qualitative Beurteilung erschweren.

Kluge Manager schmücken sich nicht mit fremden Federn, sondern sorgen dafür, daß der Erfolg auch nach außen denjenigen zukommt, die ihn intern vorbereitet und errungen haben. Die Anonymität einer vergangenen Zeit wird überwunden. Der kluge Manager gewinnt an Profil, wenn er den Anteil seiner Mitarbeiter am Erfolg sichtbar macht.

Zur persönlichen Fürsorge gehört, daß der Führende den Aufstieg seiner Mitarbeiter nicht etwa egoistisch erschwert, sondern altruistisch fördert. Die Weiterbildung des Mitarbeiters möglich zu machen, ist oft Voraussetzung für Laufbahnschritte. Die Ebnung des Weges ist die letzten Endes angemessene Anerkennung von Leistungsbereitschaft und erfüllter Leistung. Thomas Mann sagt zu diesem Komplex: »Niemand kann andere Menschen gut führen, wenn er sich nicht ehrlich an deren Erfolgen zu freuen vermag.«

*

Die Pflichten des Staatsbürgers, untrennbar mit seinen Rechten verknüpft, sind politischer Natur und stehen neben der bloßen Erfüllung der Arbeitsaufgabe, deren Rolle im kulturellen Beziehungsgeflecht freilich häufig unterschätzt wird. Denn Wirtschaft *ist* ein Element der Kultur, auch der politischen Kultur. Hier liegt eine Führungsaufgabe des Managers, der sein Teil dazu beitragen sollte, daß, auf freiem Willen beruhend, ein Ausgleich zustande kommt, er den verschiedenartigen und sich dennoch überlappenden Sphären genügt. Eine Führungsaufgabe, die, wenn sie weithin erkannt und anerkannt würde, dem Unternehmen zugute käme, ist so gesehen kein Kostenpunkt, sondern eine Investition. Für den Wirtschaftsbürger, der sich als Staatsbürger versteht, ist der Grundsatz der Legalität in seinem wirtschaftlichen Handeln nicht fremd, und er entzieht dem politisch aufgezäumten, theoretisierenden Begriff der Entfremdung den Boden, wenn er gestaltbare Arbeit anbietet, die eigener Verantwortung Spielraum läßt. *(1987)*

Erziehungssystem und Arbeitswelt

MITWIRKEN, MITDENKEN UND MITGESTALTEN IM BETRIEB

Innerhalb technischer Systeme liegen die Schnittstellen an der Grenze des jeweiligen Teilsystems, dienen aber gerade dem Grenzübergang. Der Schnittstelle zwischen Schul- und Arbeitswelt kommt eine wesentlich andere und vor allem schwerer wiegende Bedeutung zu als der technischen Schnittstelle. Auch zwischen diesen beiden Welten soll ein Grenzübergang hergestellt, eine Brücke gebaut werden. Technisch gesprochen, haben wir es aber hier mit unterschiedlichen Stromarten, Spannungen und Stromstärken zu tun, und daraus resultiert, daß es sorgfältigsten Nachdenkens sowie sorgfältigster Vorbereitung bedarf, wenn es an der Schnittstelle zwischen Schule und Arbeit nicht zu Spannungs- und Stromverlusten oder gar zum Kurzschluß kommen soll.

Hier liegt eine Forderung an den Lehrer, der seiner Aufgabe nur gerecht werden kann, wenn er selbst die Arbeitswelt kennt, wenn er dort tätig war und wenn er sich ihren Gesetzen ohne ideologische Scheuklappen öffnet. Dies macht es nötig zu erkennen, daß wir nicht in einer Welt leben, in der die Berufsarbeit nur eine Unterbrechung der Freizeit ist, sondern in einer Welt, in der der Beruf das Gerüst der menschlichen Existenz im unmittelbaren und im übertragenen Sinn ist.

Die grundsätzliche Frage kann nicht lauten, ob zweckfreie Bildung *oder* berufsgerechte, auf den Beruf zielende Ausbildung. Sie lautet vielmehr: Wie kann Bildung in den größeren Zusammenhang menschlicher Bezüge gestellt werden – auf der Erfahrung vieler vorangegangener Generationen fußend, daß die Ausübung eines Berufs insbesondere dann eine über das materielle Minimum hinausreichende Lebenserfüllung ist, wenn die Vorbereitung auf diesen Beruf sorgfältig war?

Wir schlagen uns zumindest seit Wilhelm von Humboldt mit dem Problem herum, ob die Schule – aufsteigend vom Kindergarten bis zur Hochschule – den jungen Menschen auf das Leben oder auf den Beruf vorbereiten soll. Wir sehen – vielleicht konstruieren wir nur – einen Gegensatz zwischen Bildung und Ausbildung.

Ebenso problematisch ist für uns das Begriffspaar Forschung und Lehre. Ich sage bewußt Paar, weil ich hier keinen Gegensatz sehe, sondern eine notwendige Verknüpfung: Lehre auf der Ebene der Hochschule setzt forschendes Denken und Handeln voraus; die höchste Vollendung des letzteren aber ist es, die Methoden des Forschens einer nachwachsenden Generation zu vermitteln.

An dieser Stelle sollte man zunächst einen Blick in die Humboldtschen Denkschriften zur Gründung der Universität Berlin werfen. Im Auftrag, der dem Königlichen Erlaß vom 16. August 1809 (aus Königsberg!) voranging, heißt es »Einrichtung einer allgemeinen und hohen Lehranstalt in Berlin«. Sie sollte dazu dienen, »der deutschen Wissenschaft eine ... Freistatt« zu eröffnen. Der Erlaß geht dann ein Stück weiter: Diese Lehranstalt solle der »höhere(n) Geistesbildung im Staat und über die Grenzen dessen hinaus« dienen. Erst ein Humboldtscher Entwurf aus dem Jahr 1810 spricht davon, in dieser Anstalt komme »alles, was unmittelbar für die moralische Cultur der Nation geschehe« zusammen; sie habe der »geistigen und sittlichen Bildung« zu dienen. Humboldt hatte vorher mehr über die Finanzierung der neuen Hochschule geschrieben als über deren »moralische« Aufgabe.

Ein Jahrhundert später schrieb der Historiker Franz Schnabel, es sei die Überzeugung der idealistischen Generation, der Wilhelm von Humboldt angehörte, gewesen, »daß die Beschäftigung mit dem Geistigen um seiner selbst willen die Menschen edler und besser und hingebungsvoller machen würde, daß also auch der Staat, indem er der Wissenschaft Freiheit und Raum der Betätigung gebe, doch zu gleicher Zeit damit auch für seine eigene innere Kraft am besten sorge«.

Das ist keine Abwertung des deutschen Idealismus, keine Abwertung von Humboldt. Aber aus jenen Akten ergibt sich, daß die Kräfte, die der Befreiung und dem Wiederaufbau nach der Niederlage Preußens gegen Napoleon dienten, auf dem (Um)Weg über die Philosophie aktiviert werden sollten, und die Berliner Universität diente eben nicht einer abstrakten Bildung, sondern der ganz konkreten Heranführung einer Generation an den – zunächst geistigen und sittlichen – Wiederaufbau.

Das höhere deutsche Schulwesen im 19. Jahrhundert und tief in das 20. Jahrhundert hinein wurde beeinflußt durch den Aufbruch von 1809. Das humanistische Gymnasium dominierte (wobei ich einmal beiseite lasse, wie klein der Anteil der deutschen Jugend war, der diesen Bildungsweg wählen konnte). Es ist ein immer wieder ausgesprochener Vorwurf gegen dieses Gymnasium, daß die Idealisierung der altgriechischen Welt uns nicht vor dem Sturz in die Barbarei bewahrt habe – ein Vorwurf, der nicht standhält; denn ein großer Teil dessen, was an Widerstand geleistet wurde, läßt sich zurückführen auf einen Humanismus, der sich an der Vorstellung der Unabhängigkeit, der Freiheit orientierte und der im Widerspruch stand zu Despotie, Tyrannei und Diktatur.

Nachdem ich Humboldt unterstellt habe, sein Idealismus sei pragmatischer gewesen, als dies in den Jahren der Fremdherrschaft sichtbar werden durfte, wird ein Schritt ins Konkrete notwendig. Es scheint praxisorientiert zu sein, trägt man der Schule auf, dem Schüler Schreiben, Lesen und das Einmaleins beizubringen. Aber so berufs- und lebensunfähig einer wäre, wenn er nicht lesen könnte oder die Grundrechenarten nicht beherrschte: Hier geht es nicht um die

Ausbildung zu bestimmten Berufen, sondern um Grundlagen unserer Kultur. Lesen, Schreiben, Rechnen sind nicht Werkzeuge des Arbeitslebens, sondern Bedingungen für die Teilnahme am kulturellen Leben.

Damit ist freilich der Fächerkanon, der mir vorschwebt, ohne daß man die Schule zum Erfüllungsgehilfen des Unternehmens macht, noch lange nicht umrissen, um so weniger, als sich eine fast beliebig große Zahl verschiedener Kanons denken ließe, deren konsequente Nutzung im Unterricht zur Bildung im Wortsinn führen könnte.

Immerhin setze ich voraus, daß wir uns nach Jahren des Zögerns und der Unsicherheit darauf geeinigt haben, eine Gesellschaft sei ohne bewußte Pflege des sprachlichen Ausdrucks nicht denkbar. Die Ausbildung des Gedankens ist die Voraussetzung jeder Wissenschaft, seine verständliche Übermittlung eine Lebensbedingung jeder menschlichen Gemeinschaft. Nur durch Sprache kann auch Geschichtsbewußtsein vermittelt werden, ohne das es kein Gegenwartsbewußtsein, folglich keine Politik gibt. Beherrschte Sprache ist nicht allein Mittel der Verständigung, sondern ebensosehr des Verständnisses, und sie ist auch Voraussetzung für die Entwicklung des sittlichen Bewußtseins.

Gemeint ist hier nicht bloß unsere eigene Sprache, ich gehe vielmehr davon aus, daß zumindest eine Fremdsprache jeden Schüler ins Leben begleiten sollte. Schwörten Humboldt auf Griechisch und Napoleon auf Lateinisch, so war in meiner Jugend Französisch die erste moderne Fremdsprache, heute ist es Englisch. Vieles spricht dafür, daß man bei der Wahl der (ersten) Fremdsprache nicht die Anwendung in den Vordergrund stellt, sondern den Bildungsgehalt einer Sprache, und dies wiederum verlangt vom Schüler oft mehr Weitsicht, als er gerne aufbringt.

Jedes Bildungssystem muß dynamisch, nach vorn gerichtet sein und darf nicht etwa statisch werden. Es genügt nicht, einem Schülerjahrgang das Wissen von heute zu vermitteln, das morgen schon überholt sein mag; vielmehr müssen wir dem Schüler helfen, die Werkzeuge zu handhaben, mit denen man Wissen erarbeitet, auf dem laufenden hält und nutzt.

So unverzichtbar ein Grundbestand an Wissen ist – die Vermittlung der Methoden für die Gewinnung von Wissen, für die Aneignung von Erfahrung und für die gedankliche Verknüpfung von Wissen und Erfahrung zur Erkenntnis bleibt eine notwendige Aufgabe jeder Bildungsstätte. Wir müssen lehren, wie man lernt, und die *Einübung des Denkens* muß Bildungsziel sein.

Die Problematik liegt ja darin, daß nicht derjenige mit den Lebensproblemen der Zukunft am besten fertig wird, der das meiste Wissen hat, sondern derjenige, der am besten gelernt hat, wie man mit dem Wissen fertig wird. Kurz derjenige, der nicht dem Stoff unterlegen ist, sondern über dem Stoff steht.

Nun verlangt richtiges Abwägen zwischen eigenem und gesamthaftem Interesse mehr als Wissen und Können, nämlich Disziplin. Damit sind wir bei der Charakterbildung angelangt, einer Erziehungsfrage also, und so wenig es dem »Zeitgeist« entsprechen mag: Von der Schule muß erwartet werden, daß sie sich über ihre wissenschaftliche Aufgabe hinaus mit dem Problem beschäftigt, welchen Beitrag sie zu der Entwicklung der Persönlichkeit ihrer Schüler leisten kann und muß. Selbstverwirklichung ist nicht in individualistischer Unbegrenztheit denkbar, sie bedingt vielmehr Selbsterkenntnis, das heißt Erkenntnis der Grenzen, die uns gesetzt sind und die in uns selbst liegen. Schließlich entsteht die Vision einer Bildung, in der Fähigkeiten einen höheren Rang haben als Kenntnisse, in der Eigenschaften wichtiger sind als Fähigkeiten, in der Charakter vor Wissen steht.

Es kommt ein weiteres Element hinzu: Der Staatsbürger von heute, der ein Element der Arbeitswelt ist, bedarf in einer freiheitlichen Welt eines vollen Maßes an Kritikfähigkeit; aber es muß in ihm von vornherein das Bewußtsein entwickelt werden, daß Kritik ein positives Vorzeichen zu haben hat und daß Bessermachen vor Besserwissen kommt.

Ich gerate damit von der Arbeitswelt hinüber in die Welt der Politik; beide haben – neben vielem Gegensätzlichen – gemeinsam, daß Erfolg von der Heranbildung und von der Auswahl der zur Führung Bestimmten abhängt. Haben wir doch nur die Wahl zwischen gebändigter und ungebändigter Führung, zwischen gezügelter und ungezügelter Macht und ihrer Ausübung. Diese Zügelung ist ein Element des Erziehungsprozesses, und es muß die Erkenntnis wachsen, daß keiner führen darf, aber auch nicht führen kann, der nicht zu dienen gelernt hat und der nicht zu dienen bereit ist.

Nach meiner Vorstellung soll »Bildung« zwar den jungen Menschen vielseitig auf das Leben vorbereiten – dies darf aber nicht auf eine Polyvalenz hinauslaufen, das heißt nicht auf die Vorbereitung zu mehreren definierten Berufen. Es geht mir also um die (Vor)Bildung des Menschen, die ihn befähigen soll, mit der Situation, in die er im weiteren Verlauf seines Lebens gestellt werden wird, geistig und seelisch – also charakterlich – fertig zu werden. Der Schulabschluß muß folglich berufsoffen sein und bleiben – was nebenbei auch ein Licht wirft auf die Bedeutung, die man der Abiturdurchschnittsnote für die Eignung zum Arztberuf zumißt.

*

Die Neigung des Schülers, aus Position (mangelnder Einsicht) oder aus Opposition (auf alle Fälle) Widerstand zu leisten, hat die positive Note, daß sie im Zeitverlauf zu einer Glättung der Spannungen führt, die zwischen Lehr(er)- und Schülermeinung unvermeidlich sind. Extreme, sagen die Franzosen, berühren sich. Die Aussicht besteht, daß die Wellenberge und die Wellentäler der aufeinanderprallenden Meinungen einem Ausgleich, wenn auch nicht unbedingt einer Harmonie zustreben.

In der letzten Zeit freilich schlagen die Wogen hoch. Eine »internationale Schülerstudie« zeigt, daß zwar die Grundschüler gerne, die Schüler der weiterführenden Schulen aber angeblich nicht nur ungerne den Unterricht besuchen, sondern der Auffassung sind, Lehre, Lehrstoff und Lehrmethode seien lebensfremd und falsch.

Das ist nicht mein Thema. Wenn aber hier der Standpunkt der Wirtschaft sichtbar werden soll: Welche Fächer, welche Lehrgegenstände notwendig seien, um den jungen Menschen auf das Arbeitsleben, auf das Leben überhaupt vorzubereiten, kann man – so meine Meinung – der Frage nicht ausweichen, welche Fächer, welche Lehrgegenstände, welche Lehrweisen der Schüler wählen würde, wenn er wählen dürfte. Diesen Standpunkt zu vertreten heißt nicht, das Pferd von hinten aufzuzäumen oder gar den Weg des geringsten Widerstandes zu gehen. Vielmehr heißt es, daß Motivation von innen besser ist als Motivation von außen, von oben, von unten.

Daß Schüler später nicht immer ungerne an die Schulzeit zurückdenken, hat viele Belege, von denen ich einen erwähne. Carlo Schmid schreibt in seinen 1979 erschienenen »Erinnerungen«: »Obwohl ich in meiner Schule nicht alles bekam, was eine gute Schule lernwilligen Schülern vermitteln könnte und auch sollte, bin ich meiner Schule dankbar; sie hatte mich gelehrt, zu arbeiten und auch dort, wo mir das Brett nicht gefiel, so lange zu bohren, bis ich durch war.«

*

Neue Techniken, neue Technologien verlangen höher befähigte, besser ausgebildete Mitarbeiter – freilich nicht unbedingt mehr. Führt die ökonomisch induzierte Rationalisierung zu einer Verringerung der Zahl der Arbeitsstunden, steigt das Anforderungsprofil.

Neue Techniken machen den Fachmann nicht überflüssig. Sie verändern, das heißt: sie erhöhen jedoch die Anforderungen an sein Können, an Ausbildung und Fortbildung. Der Roboter wird nicht das Wahrzeichen unserer Werkhallen der Zukunft sein. Der Kampf gegen ihn wäre ein Kampf an der falschen Front. Er ist ein Werkzeug zur Erleichterung der Arbeit; er schafft Arbeitsverknüpfungen und damit Arbeit.

Auch weiterhin wird der schaffende Mensch das treibende und das bestimmende Element sein, zwar nicht mehr in der Dichte, die in vergangenen Jahren zu dem falschen Begriff der »Humanisierung der Arbeitswelt« führte, sondern in der Individualisierung, in der sich der denkende Mensch die Arbeit untertan machen kann und machen wird, sofern wir ihn darauf vorbereiten. »Flexible Automatisierung« führt zu neuen Arbeitsstrukturen, zu einem weiteren Rückgang der physischen Arbeit, zu einer Vertiefung der Vorbereitung, die der Ausführung vorangehen muß, und damit in der Tat zu einem menschengerechten Ablauf.

Erhöhter Anforderung werden wir nicht allein dadurch gerecht, daß wir Bildung und Ausbildung verbessern. Wir müssen vielmehr alle Begabungen – mehr Begabungen als bisher – aufspüren und fördern, ohne Rücksicht auf einen Richtungsstreit.

Eliten sind eine Lebenstatsache. Ihre Negation gehört zu den Prvilegien jener, die es anderen überlassen, mit den Lebenstatsachen fertig zu werden. Gleichheit vor dem Gesetz verbürgt noch nicht Gleichheit der Begabung. Bestimmte Grundanlagen können nur entwickelt, aber nicht etwa hervorgerufen werden. Doch liegt es in unserer Hand – genauer gesagt: es ist unsere Pflicht –, für Chancengleichheit zu sorgen. Wirklichkeitsnäher müßte man sagen: Chancengerechtigkeit.

Freilich gehört zu dem Begriff der Chance nicht nur dialektisch, sondern ganz realistisch auch der Begriff des Risikos. Es wäre deshalb eine Art von Falschmünzerei, wenn man unter dem Titel Chancengleichheit eine Art von Zahlungsversprechen aushändigte, ohne daß man klar darauf aufmerksam machte, daß die Einlösung nicht in jedem Fall gesichert ist – vor allem aber, daß eine Nachzahlungspflicht in Form eigener Leistung darauf ruht.

*

Die Geringschätzung wirtschaftlicher Aufgabenstellung, die sich in unserem Land vor allem im Vorraum der Politik breitmacht – wobei die Anhänger dieser wirtschaftskritischen Richtung die Teilnahme am Genuß der erreichten Erfolge nicht durchweg verschmähen –, befreit die Einsichtigen nicht davon, immer wieder deutlich zu sagen, was unerläßlich ist.

Das Urteilsvermögen der Gesellschaft wächst nicht unbedingt proportional zu ihrem Volumen. Unerläßlich ist es deshalb – und es wäre eine gute und wichtige Aufgabe für die Schulen –, dieser Gesellschaft die wirtschaftlichen Zusammenhänge immer wieder vor Augen zu führen: wirtschaftliche Tatsachen und Zusammenhänge, die es unmöglich machen, allen kollektiven und individuellen Forderungen zu entsprechen. Es ist eben kein Lehrsatz, den die Wirtschaft aufgestellt hätte, sondern bittere Erfahrung, daß unser Dasein dem Gesetz der Knappheit unterliegt und daß das Überleben auf dieser Erde von dem erfolgreichen Kampf gegen den Mangel abhängt.

Durch Umfragen wird stets aufs neue festgestellt, daß der »Mann auf der Straße« illusionäre Vorstellungen von der Gewinnlage der Industrie hat. Es ist nicht selten, daß der Befragte den Wirtschaftsunternehmen unterstellt, sie »verdienten« zwanzig und mehr Prozent vom Umsatz. Das ist, grob gesprochen, das Zehnfache dessen, was deutschen Unternehmungen im Mittel verbleibt. Offenbar liegt diesen irrigen Vorstellungen nicht nur ein Defizit an wirtschaftlicher Urteilskraft, sondern vor allem ein Defizit an verläßlicher Information und schließlich auch ein irreführender Sprachgebrauch zugrunde: Man verwechselt die Vertriebskosten mit dem, was dem Unternehmen unter dem Strich übrigbleibt. Vermutet er überhöhte »Profite« oder glaubt er gar daran, ist der »Mann auf der Straße« schnell bei der Hand, von der Macht der »Wirtschaft« zu sprechen. Die Medien klären ihn nicht auf, oder sie verwirren ihn noch mehr.

Die Neigung zur Simplifizierung der sehr viel komplizierteren Wirklichkeit müßte eine sehr sorgfältige und verständliche Aufklärung über die Tatsachen und Zahlen gegenübergestellt werden. Denn bei Bereitschaft zu nüchterner Betrachtungsweise bleibt für den bewußt abwertenden Begriff des Profits kein Platz. Ertrag und Kapital sind volkswirtschaftliche Wertbegriffe, die sich gegenseitig bedingen, und Kapital ist die Voraussetzung für die Erneuerung der Produktionsanlagen, für deren Anpassung an die technische Weiterentwicklung und somit für die Erhöhung der Produktivität – abgesehen von der Anpassung an die wachsenden Weltmaßstäbe.

Technik ist also ohne Kapitalbildung gar nicht denkbar. Das heißt, daß die Herstellung eines Werkzeugs – wir blicken für einen Augenblick Jahrtausende zurück in vorgeschichtliche Zeit – gar nichts anderes ist als Kapitalbildung (wie auch das Zurücklegen von Saatgut aus der jährlichen Ernte oder das Aufziehen von Vieh). Damit ist noch nichts ausgesagt über das Eigentum an den Produktionsmitteln, sondern nur darüber, daß jeglicher menschliche Fortschritt – es wäre ein Fortschritt, wenn in unserer Welt, dank richtig verstandener und angewandter Technik keiner hungern und frieren müßte –, daß also jegliches menschliche Weiterschreiten aus dem Urzustand des Homo heidelbergensis zum Homo faber Kapitalbildung durch Verbrauchsverzicht voraussetzt.

Es ist vielleicht ein Vorurteil, wenn ich sage, die Schule mache sich weiterhin von der Wirtschaft ein falsches Bild und sie gäbe ihre unzureichende Einsicht in die Wirklichkeit an ihre Schüler weiter. Die Vermutung aber, daß Fehlurteile zumindest in das Unterbewußtsein der Schüler einsickern und dort nur schwer, wenn überhaupt, berichtigt werden können, läßt sich kaum widerlegen. Die Vorstellungen des Schülers von Arbeitswelt und Wirtschaft können nicht wirklichkeitsgetreuer sein als die Vorstellungen, die die Schule selbst hat.

*

Die Bundesrepublik Deutschland ist keine Insel; sie steht im Weltwettbewerb. Exporterfolge bis gestern bürgen nicht dafür, daß es uns auch in Zukunft möglich sein wird, ein Drittel unserer industriellen Produktion zu exportieren. Die deutsche Wirtschaft – die Wirtschaft, das sind wir alle – steht im Wettbewerb mit Nationen und Regionen, die im internationalen Vergleich leistungsfähiger sind, weil deren Angehörige bereit sind, mehr zu leisten als wir selbst. Das ist eine bittere Erkenntnis, die man nicht mit dem abgegriffenen Schlagwort »Standort Bundesrepublik« abtun kann, die man vielmehr von der Wurzel her untersuchen muß.

Dabei liegen die individuellen und die gesellschaftlichen Verhältnisse in den Wettbewerbsländern so unterschiedlich, daß man keine umfassende, allgemeingültige Wurzel feststellen und folglich auch kein generell wirksames Heilmittel ausfindig machen kann. Jeder, der den Fernen Osten kennt und mit ihm zu tun hat, weiß, daß dort – ich spreche einmal nur von Japan – Kulturwerte gepflegt werden, die der menschlichen Produktivität zuträglich sind. Ob es nun die Schule ist, die diese Werte hervorruft und fördert, oder ob sie nicht sehr viel tiefer, geradezu kollektiv-historisch angelegt sind: Sie existieren in der Form von Disziplin, Harmonie, Konsens und folglich Lernbereitschaft, Arbeitsbereitschaft und Selbstbescheidung.

Während dort Kollektivität und Egalität zur geschichtlichen Bedingung für das Zusammenleben auf engem Raum geworden sind, leben wir in einer Welt der Individualität, der Originalität und, nochmals, des Drangs zur Selbstverwirklichung. Ich lasse bewußt den Begriff der Kreativität beiseite, weil Grund zu dem Zweifel besteht, ob die Angriffswellen, die aus Fernost auf die westliche Welt in fast regelmäßigen Abständen zukommen, noch immer auf der den Japanern zugeschriebenen Begabung zur Nachahmung beruhen – oder ob nicht doch inzwischen kreative Kräfte an die Stelle der Imitation getreten sind.

Die deutsche Schule darf nicht an der inneren Einstellung und an den Methoden der japanischen Schule vorübergehen, ohne zumindest die Unterschiede herauszuarbeiten, um dann die Werte bevorzugt zu entwickeln, die unsere Stärke sind oder sein könnten. Sie muß daran denken, daß wir im Fernen Osten unerbittliche Wettbewerber haben, deren Fairneß nicht in Zweifel gezogen werden soll, deren Hartnäckigkeit in der Heranbildung von Einzel- und Gruppenkämpfern aber auch nicht übersehen werden darf.

*

Worauf es vor diesem Hintergrund in der Schule ankommt, ist die in die Tat umgesetzte Erkenntnis, daß Arbeit ein Element des Lebens ist – nicht als Fron, sondern als ein Stück Lebens*inhalt.*

Ich sprach vom Menschen, versuchte ihn in den Mittelpunkt der betrieblichen Überlegungen zu stellen. Der Betrieb braucht den Menschen, er ist das tragende Element. Das Unternehmen hat ein ureigenes Interesse daran, mitdenkende Mitarbeiter zu haben, seine Mitarbeiter zum Mitgestalten zu gewinnen. Denn Erfolg ist immer eine Gemeinschaftsleistung. Mitwirken, Mitdenken und Mitgestalten sind die Stufen, die dem Menschen im Betrieb offenstehen, wenn er willens ist, mehr zu sein als nur Lohn- oder Gehaltsempfänger. Doch gehört zu seinem Willen das Rüstzeug, das ihm Bildung bietet, wenn sie vielseitig genug, aber dennoch auf ein gemeinsames Ziel gerichtet ist. *(1988)*

Wirtschaft als Element unserer Kultur

UNSER VERSTÄNDNIS MANCHER BEGRIFFE IST VERKÜRZT

Wer immer die wirtschaftliche Entwicklung einer Region erklären will, greift zu Max Weber und zu seinen Arbeiten über Religionssoziologie, vor allem zu seinem Aufsatz »Die protestantische Ethik und der Geist des Kapitalismus«. Ich vermute allerdings, daß wir am Ende jeder Bemühung kapitulieren müssen, das wirtschaftliche Verhalten der Menschen monokausal zu verstehen. Denn die konfessionelle Einstellung der Menschen ist nicht immer ein tief innerlicher Prozeß, sondern häufig nur soziale Adaptation. Diese kann zwar zu einer Anpassung auch des wirtschaftlichen Verhaltens führen. Dann aber ist die Konfession, die ein Mensch annimmt, für sein wirtschaftliches Verhalten nicht kausal.

Ich finde jedenfalls bei Max Weber keine überzeugende Erklärung des spezifisch schwäbischen Aufschwungs. Denn er hat, wenigstens im ersten Teil seines Aufsatzes, ein anderes Kapitalismus-Verständnis als wir Heutigen: Er sieht den Kapitalismus in der »Rechenhaftigkeit«, in der »planmäßigen Verwendung sachlicher oder persönlicher Nutzleistungen als Erwerbsmittel«, in der rationalen Arbeitsteilung. Die letztere gibt es jedoch auch in anderen Wirtschaftsformen. Vor allem aber übersieht er zunächst (vielleicht bewußt) einen für uns bedeutsam gewordenen Charakterzug des Kapitalismus: die Kapitalbildung.

Erklärt er dann die Kapitalbildung durch asketischen, also in seinem Sinn ethischen Sparzwang (und sagen wir: Kapitalbildung durch Konsumverzicht), so sind wir in der Tat bei einem schwäbischen

Spezifikum angelangt: dem Sparwillen. Doch nennt er Württemberg nur am Rande, wenn er von Calw und seinem Pietismus spricht. Er beschäftigt sich vielmehr mit den Niederlanden, mit England und mit Frankreich in der frühkapitalistischen Phase des 16. und 17. Jahrhunderts und unter dem Einfluß von Calvinismus und Zwinglianismus. Das schließt nicht aus, daß religiös-konfessionelle Neigungen im württembergischen Kernland im letzten Jahrhundert an der Prägung seiner Wirtschaftsbürger teilhatten.

*

Ohne Zweifel hat Innovation, zur rechten Zeit, eine wesentliche Rolle für die wirtschaftliche Entwicklung in Baden-Württemberg gespielt. Ob sie im Vergleich mit anderen deutschen Bundesländern entscheidend war, lasse ich offen. Mit Recht aber geht man davon aus, daß Männer wie Benz, Daimler, Maybach, Bosch ihre zunächst einmal handwerkliche, dann ins Industrielle hinüberführende Tätigkeit weder auf Grund obrigkeitlichen Zuspruchs noch öffentlicher finanzieller Förderung begannen. Die Innovationen – daß das Automobil eine solche war, wußte man freilich seinerzeit noch nicht –, die Innovationen also, die sie in die Wege leiteten, oder die sie, diese Männer, in Atem hielten, waren weder von einer Regierung noch von ihnen selbst geplant. Sie fielen ihnen aber auch nicht etwa in den Schoß; sie wurden schlicht erarbeitet.

Vielleicht hält man es für Ironie, wenn ich frage, wieviel weitere Horizonte sich geöffnet haben würden, hätte man ihnen immer wieder, von Woche zu Woche, gesagt, der Landesvater – ich meine den König – erwarte von ihnen innovatives Handeln, kreative Phantasie und unternehmerisches Wagen. Also nicht nur »Ventures«, wie man heute sagt, sondern sogar »Adventures«. Ich frage das als Warnung vor jeder Politik, die noch tiefer in die Subventionierung führen würde. Man kann sich den alten Bosch vorstellen, den ich als junger Mann noch gekannt habe und von dem wir wissen, wie es um seinen

Untertanengeist stand ... aber lassen wir das. Es genügt zu wissen, daß jene Männer ihre eigenen Ersparnisse (und die ihrer Freunde) einsetzten, daß sie Kopf und Kragen riskierten und daß mancher von ihnen den Durchbruch, trotz aller Innovation, nicht schaffte.

Diese nüchterne Distanzierung von staatlicher Gängelei ist keine Geringschätzung des königlich württembergischen Gewerbeförderers Ferdinand von Steinbeis, der Vertrauen in die eigene Leistungsfähigkeit schuf, Anregungen gab, Ziele setzte und nicht zuletzt die Ausbildung von Fachkräften unterstützte – gerade das letztere zeichnet das Land aus: Der schwäbische Facharbeiter stellt ein Kapital sui generis dar. Seine tragende Rolle in unserer wirtschaftlichen Entwicklung darf nicht unterschlagen werden. Hätten diese Industriellen freilich den Beistand heutiger Unternehmensberater gehabt, kann man sich gar nicht vorstellen, wie steil dann ihr wirtschaftlicher Aufstieg gewesen wäre!

*

Unsere Nachbarn – vor allem die ans Mittelmeer angrenzenden, aber auch die alten Seefahrer im Westen, Nordwesten und Norden – haben zur Kultur ein unbefangeneres Verhältnis als wir. Sie *haben* Kultur, sie genießen sie. Für uns ist sie häufig angestrengte Bemühung. Das deutsche Kulturverständnis ist verkürzt, was Überheblichkeit nicht ausschließt, obwohl wir wissen, daß ein Teil unseres guten Geschmacks nur aus dem Leihhaus der europäischen Geschichte stammt. Und wir übersehen, daß uns die auf das Geistige reduzierten deutschen Kulturvorstellungen des letzten Jahrhunderts nicht vor dem Rückfall in die Barbarei bewahrten.

Die weite Auffassung dessen, was Kultur dem Menschen bedeutet, finden wir nicht nur bei unseren Nachbarn. Auch bei Max Weber lesen wir von der »Kapitalistischen Kultur«, also von einer Kultur, die gedanklich nicht nur das Wirtschaftliche meint, vielmehr die menschlichen Kraftlinien darüber hinaus einschließt. Eine Kultur, die umfassend ist, die die Gesamtheit menschlicher Lebensäußerungen umgreift, sobald und soweit sich diese einem abgrenzbaren Stilbegriff unterwerfen.

Das bringt uns zu Oswald Spengler und zu der Schwäche unseres Jahrhunderts: dem Kulturpessimismus. Die These vom Leben und Sterben der Kulturen setzt ja einen Kulturbegriff voraus, der weit über das hinausgeht, was Kulturpromotoren von heute einschränkend darunter verstehen. Wir adoptieren nicht etwa Spenglers dem digitalen Zeitalter vorgreifende Schematisierung der Kulturen nach runden Millennien, um so weniger, als wir längst bei Toynbee gelernt haben, daß Kulturen viel differenzierter abgegrenzt werden müssen, als sein Vorläufer das tat, der als Mathematiker dem Charme der Zehnerpotenzen verfallen war, wobei ihm die Natur durch die Maschen seines Zahlengitters schlüpfte.

Wie immer wir den Kulturbegriff ansehen: bei allem (durchaus zu begründenden) Stolz auf das kulturelle Leistungsbild, ja auf die frühen Leistungen des Südwestens, die bis zu den Kelten zurückreichen, sollten wir den wirtschaftlichen Vorsprung unserer Region nicht mit geistig-kulturellem Vorsprung begründen.

Gibt es aber nicht doch eine spezifisch »Schwäbische Kultur«? Allen ist jener Vers bekannt, der, indem er einige große Namen mißbraucht, eine ganze Genielandschaft zum württembergischen Besitzstand erklärt. Aber man weiß ja, Hegel – auf den Stuttgart sich gerne etwas zugute hält, obwohl man ihn nicht so versteht, wie er gerne verstanden werden wollte, wenn wir das richtig verstehen –, Hegel wurde erst jenseits der Landesgrenzen wirklich berühmt, als ihm in der Humboldtschen Universität im fernen Berlin Fürsten und Staatsmänner zu Füßen saßen. Und Schiller: Natürlich haben wir nicht vergessen, daß er seinen Freunden »Die Räuber« im Stuttgarter Bopserwald vorlas. Doch fand die Uraufführung im seinerzeit kurpfälzischen Mannheim statt, und vielleicht stimmt es, daß sein Stern erst im thüringischen Jena richtig aufging, bevor Schwaben ihn für sich in Anspruch nahm. Aber Hölderlin! Gewiß, am Neckar geboren, aufgewachsen, verdämmert. Aber wäre Hölderlin Hölderlin geworden ohne jene Hamburgerin im hessischen Bad Homburg, ohne diese Diotima, die vielleicht aus Frankreich stammte? Ohne seinen Marsch von Bordeaux zurück, im glühenden Sommer durch Frankreich ... Hölderlin, ein Europäer?

Beispiele sind kein Beweis – weder pro noch contra. Aber wir wollen nicht versuchen, Literatur und wirtschaftlichen Aufstieg in einem Atemzug zu nennen oder kausal zu betrachten. Doch schlage ich, nach diesem Intermezzo, keineswegs vor, das kulturelle Licht Baden-Württembergs unter den Scheffel zu stellen. Denn: was die spontane, absichtslose Hervorbringung kultureller Werte, »unnötiger« Werte angeht, müssen wir vielleicht anderen den Vortritt lassen – denken wir an manche Versäumnisse des letzten Jahrhunderts. So läßt sich wohl aus unseren kulturellen Beiträgen, im engeren Sinn des Worts, die wirtschaftliche Leistungskraft des Landes nicht herleiten. Wenn wir jedoch den Begriff der Kultur ausdehnen auf jedwedes menschliche Denken und Handeln, können wir versuchen, unsere wirtschaftliche Tätigkeit kultureller Evolution zuzuordnen.

Voraussetzung ist, daß wir uns darauf einigen, nicht etwa eingegrenzte Kulturphänomene zu betrachten, sondern unter Kultur alles zu verstehen, was der Mensch aus der Natur gemacht hat: Kultur im Wortsinn – vom indoeuropäischen bis auf den heutigen Sprachgebrauch in den romanischen und den germanischen Sprachen. Wirtschaften des Menschen als Beginn seines Wirkens als Kulturwesen, das sich von der Natur abhebt.

Industrielle Produktion wird und ist dann, in der weiten Auslegung des Begriffs, ein ganz bestimmter Ausdruck, ein ganz bestimmtes Element der Kultur. Verstehen wir das Wort »industriell« nicht eng, ist das schon seit der Steinzeit so. Der Mensch als »Industrieller« formt die Natur um – ein fließender Übergang zum Künstler, der sich für ihren Schöpfer halten mag. Das ist anspruchsvoll und im Zweifel jenseits unseres Bewußtseins, aber nicht jenseits einer unbewußten Realität.

Der Mensch, der »industrielle« vorzeitliche Mensch, der Werkzeuge herzustellen und zu verwenden gelernt hat, wird zum Zoon politikon, zum politischen Lebewesen, womit das beginnt, was »Politische Kultur« heißt und den weiten Gedankensprung in unser Zeitalter erlaubt – erlaubt und notwendig macht, wenn wir die Hoffnung nicht aufgeben wollen, wenigstens *einen* Hinweis für die bevorzugte Entwicklung Baden-Württembergs zu finden – obwohl wir letzten Endes im Bezirk des Unwägbaren bleiben.

Dem Himmel sei Dank dafür. Denn: so unwidersprochen Kultur von des Menschen Hand stammt, so sehr bedarf sie der Gestaltungsfreiheit, so schädlich ist für sie der Aktenstaub. Kulturbudgets jedenfalls, obwohl unerläßlich, sind nicht der Keim des Wachstums, nicht, im übertragenen Sinn, der Keim des Wohlstands, vielleicht nur die Folge. Nährboden unseres wirtschaftlichen Gleichgewichts ist meiner Meinung nach nicht ein kulturelles Niveau im allgemeinen Wortsinn – das etwa mehr Impulse ausströmte, als wir das aus anderen Bundesländern kennen –, sondern eine geschichtliche und noch immer gegenwärtige Geisteshaltung und Bewußtseinslage: eine »Politische Kultur« besonderer Art.

Mit »Politischer Kultur« meine ich nicht die politischen Institutionen selbst, den Staat, die Parteien, die Verbände, auch nicht die »Gesellschaft« (die letztere ein so diffuses Etwas, daß man sie besser nicht Institution nennte). Ich meine vielmehr, wie die Staatsbürger im politischen, im öffentlichen und im persönlichen Leben miteinander umgehen.

Politik ist in diesem Zusammenhang für mich nicht die Staatskunst oder das Staatshandwerk allein. Denn der Staat verkörpert für uns nur *eine* der Einrichtungen, womit – aber nicht wozu – die öffentliche Sache (res publica) betrieben wird. Wir teilen hier nicht die Auffassung eines unserer vielen schwäbischen Auswanderer – Hegel ist gemeint –, »die höchste Form des objektiven Geistes sei der Staat«. Wir sind vielmehr der Meinung, daß wir den Staat als Ordnungsfaktor brauchen – als die Instanz, die Ordnungen setzt, aber nicht Handlungen vorschreibt. Deshalb müssen wir, bei dieser Gelegenheit gesagt, nach wie vor das Ziel weitgehender »Deregulation« vertreten, auch wenn wir uns in der Wirtschaft damit selbst einmal den Weg verbauen oder erschweren mögen.

Es gibt Stimmen der zu Hause Gebliebenen oder Zurückgewanderten, die unserer freiheitlicheren Meinung näherkommen, wenn – ein Beispiel – Theodor Heuss schreibt, bei uns habe der Stammtisch immer mit der Souveränität der Monarchen gestritten. Von Reinhold Maier ist die Aussage überliefert, die Demokratie verständen wir »hier unten doch etwas besser«. Mit »unten« meinte er natürlich den Südwesten, und ich beginne zu verstehen, warum man von Nord-Süd-Gefälle und von oben und unten spricht: Norden ist auf den Landkarten oben, wir sind folglich unten, obwohl wir doch – jedenfalls nach landläufiger Meinung – inzwischen oben sitzen.

Man kann *unsere* Demokratie – aber damit sage ich nichts Neues – auf den Anfang des 16. Jahrhunderts zurückverlegen, das heißt auf den Tübinger Vertrag von 1514. Durch ihn unterwarf sich der Herzog von Württemberg, in heutiger Sprache gesagt, der Budgetkontrolle der »Stände«. Wenn das nicht der Ausdruck althergebrachter Sparsamkeit war, so hat doch spätestens damit das ökonomische Gewissen der Kernschwaben in öffentlichen Dingen erstmals geschlagen.

Es bedurfte also nicht des Merkspruches, den Friedrich II., nachmals der Große genannt, dem jungen Herzog Carl Eugen (1741–1744 zum Erziehungsaufenthalt nach Preußen geschickt) beim Abschied in einem »Fürstenspiegel« mitgab: »Die Finanzen sind der Nerv eines Landes.« Ob die Neigung unserer Landsleute, jede Mark zweimal umzudrehen, dadurch beeinflußt wurde, bleibe für heute beiseite.

Wir sind ein Land – ich wiederhole: nicht etwa Hegels Staat –, in dem die einstige Monarchie von der Sozialdemokratie mitgetragen wurde, in dem man seinen Militärdienst machte, ohne mit dem Säbel zu rasseln, ein Land, das 1871 konservativ wählte, um das soeben zustande gekommene Deutsche Reich zu legitimieren, dann aber zu liberaler Denkweise überging – ein im Sinne der »Kapitalbildung durch Sparen« kapitalistisches Land, kein sozialistisches, wohl aber ein soziales.

Werfen wir einen Blick auf den »Historischen Atlas von Baden-Württemberg«, der unter vielem anderen drei Karten mit den Ergebnissen repräsentativer Reichstagswahlen und Bundestagswahlen von 1871–1972 enthält. Die Herausgeber erläutern, in diesen Darstellungen komme »ein gutes Stück Kontinuität der jüngeren deutschen Geschichte zum Ausdruck« und an ihr (dieser Kontinuität) habe »der deutsche Südwesten mehr als den nur statistisch meßbaren Anteil«. Das politische Leben sei »im Vergleich zum übrigen Deutschland hier sehr früh regsam« geworden.

Die Karten zeigen zwar, daß auch in Baden-Württemberg schon 1930 das alte Parteigefüge zerstört war, daß sich aber dieser Prozeß im Reich wesentlich intensiver vollzogen hatte als im Südwesten. Noch im Juni 1932 gewannen hier die gemäßigten Parteien gegenüber den links- und rechtsextremistischen Richtungen eine klare Mehrheit, während im Reich die Extremen das Übergewicht erreichten. Zwar kamen die Nationalsozialisten auch in unserem Land bei der Reichstagswahl 1932 an die Spitze aller Parteien (in Baden noch stärker als in Württemberg). Aber die erwähnten Kommentatoren stellen doch fest, daß noch 1932 »in den meisten Gebieten des Landes die Feinde der Demokratie in der Minderheit waren«. Daß sich dies 1933 änderte, beruhte nicht mehr auf freien Wahlen, hatte nichts mehr mit politischer Kultur zu tun.

Ich verstehe unter dem Begriff der politischen Kultur weder eine vorbehaltlose Solidarität – die weniger auf Vernunft, geschweige denn auf Mitgefühl beruht, sondern auf die Ausübung gemeinsamer Stärke hinausläuft – noch die bedingungslose Konfrontation, die gar keine Einigung will. Solidarität und Konfrontation sind in diesem Sinn Werkzeug und Ausdruck politischen Machtwillens – und die Ausübung von Macht darf kein Element der politischen Kultur eines neuen Jahrhunderts werden.

Damit schildere ich nicht einen etwa schon bestehenden Zustand, so sehr es mir darauf ankommt, zu sagen, daß im Südwesten seit eh und je Voraussetzungen gegeben sind, die uns geholfen haben, mit unseren wirtschaftlichen Problemen fertig zu werden – nicht nur in der norddeutschen Tiefebene gibt es solche. Was ich sagen will, ist vielmehr, daß die Zukunft, das heißt der Fortbestand unseres materiellen Wohlergehens, damit zusammenhängen, ja davon abhängen wird, ob wir wenigstens in diesem Land bereit sind, den Karren gemeinsam zu ziehen. Von politischer Kultur zu sprechen, meint nicht etwas, was wir in seiner möglichen Ausprägung schon erreicht hätten – auch wenn wir auf dem Weg dazu sind –, sondern einen Appell an unsere Friedensbereitschaft als die Voraussetzung für eine Zukunft in der Zukunft.

*

Zur politischen Kultur im Gegensatz stünde eine »Gesellschaftpolitik des Ellenbogens«. Es fällt mir schwer, darunter nur die Beziehungen unter den Vertragspartnern zu sehen. Vielmehr gibt es auch Strömungen innerhalb der Organisationen, vielleicht durchaus unbewußte, die zur Bevorzugung der beati possidentes führen. Die Sicherung von Arbeitsplätzen, die Schaffung neuer Arbeitsplätze durch weitsichtige Tarifpolitik ist ein noch nicht von allen erkannter Weg zur Überwindung der Arbeitslosigkeit, die in ihrem Zusammenhang, über die Grenzen unseres Landes hinaus, gesehen werden muß.

Die Überzeugung, daß wir es in unserem Land mit den Ansätzen einer politischen Kultur zu tun haben, die unbewußt auf den Konsens hinsteuert, hat im übrigen nichts mit Romantik zu tun, nichts mit der idealistischen Vorstellung einer ständestaatlichen Harmonie. Im Gegenteil, hier stehen sich wohlverstandene Interessen gegenüber, und handfeste Auseinandersetzungen gehören dazu. Erst die Erkenntnis dessen, was pragmatisch erreichbar ist, führt die Parteien zueinander. Die gegenseitige Achtung bleibt aber letzten Endes erhalten, und die Überzeugung regiert, daß beide Teile ihren Nutzen haben müssen. Politische Kultur folglich als Toleranz und Respekt voreinander.

Zur politischen Kultur besonders in Baden-Württemberg gehörte es, daß es sich gehört zu arbeiten. Doch sind wir in dieser Hinsicht möglicherweise an einem Scheideweg angelangt. Meine Sorge gilt nicht allein (und vielleicht weniger) dem spürbaren Nachlassen der individuellen Leistungsbereitschaft. Sie gilt vielmehr, und zunehmend, dem kollektiven, politischen und intellektuellen Angriff auf den Komplex Arbeit. Dabei steckt gerade hinter den intellektuellen Bemühungen eine persönliche Arbeitsleistung, die im Widerspruch steht zu dem, was nach außen angestrebt wird. Das Motiv – Verringerung der Arbeitslosigkeit und Schaffung weiterer Arbeitsplätze – übersehe ich keineswegs. Ich sorge mich aber um die internationale Wettbewerbsfähigkeit unserer Industrie, die fast ein Drittel ihrer Produktion exportiert und mit fast einem Fünftel an der Gesamtausfuhr der Bundesrepublik beteiligt ist.

*

Spricht man der unternehmerischen Tätigkeit von vornherein kulturelle Qualität zu, entlastet man den Unternehmer zunächst; er leistet ja, so gesehen, seinen Beitrag. Das befriedigt uns aus zwei Gründen nicht, wobei der eine aus dem anderen folgt: Im Zweifel hat der Unternehmer, trotz steuerlicher Progression, einen größeren Anteil am Volkseinkommen als der Bürger im Mittel. Deshalb werden von ihm eigene Beiträge, unmittelbare kulturelle Betätigungen erwartet, die – worauf schon hingewiesen worden ist – weder seiner Öffentlichkeitsarbeit dienen noch als reines Opfer erscheinen sollten. Denn sie kommen dem Unternehmer durch Rückkopplung wieder zugute – ich wiederhole: nicht quantitativ feststellbar, aber tendenziell.

Unterstellt wird dabei, daß wir Bildung und Kultur nicht als »Genußmittel«, sondern als Verpflichtung des einzelnen betrachten. Das legt, in der umgekehrten Richtung, die Verpflichtung der Unternehmer fest. Unternehmer dürfen nicht daran vorbeigehen, daß die kulturelle Charakteristik einer Landschaft untrennbar ist von ihrer wirtschaftlichen Struktur – und umgekehrt. Das heißt, wir haben es hier mit einer Kausalität zu tun, von der wir nicht immer wissen, in welcher Richtung sie primär wirkt – für den weitsichtigen Unternehmer ist das eine sekundäre Frage.

*

Die Zukunft bleibt fragwürdig, aber, um mit Heidegger zu sprechen, »des Fragens würdig«. Doch gibt es nicht für jede Frage eine Antwort. Vor allem dürfen wir den Blick nicht zurückwenden. Gewiß, morgen geschieht nichts, was sich nicht heute vorbereitet hat. Aber wir müssen, mit der geschichtlichen Gewißheit, nach vorne blicken, nicht weil wir an den »Fortschritt« glauben, sondern weil wir Vertrauen in die Zukunft setzen, Vertrauen zu mehr als nur zu uns selbst.

Das »verschlossene Buch der Zukunft« gibt es nicht. Niemand kennt die Zukunft, auch wenn er von Ahnungen erfüllt ist, und vor allem kann niemand sie errechnen. Schlagen wir uns ein für allemal die Vorstellung aus dem Kopf, man könne über die Zukunft mehr sagen, als daß sie sich vom Heute unterscheiden wird. Es trifft nicht zu, daß alles schon dagewesen ist, und es wird in Zukunft Ereignisse geben, die es noch nie gab, Geräte, die noch keiner sich vorgestellt hat, Verfahren, für die es kein Vorbild gibt. Die Grenzen verläßlicher Vorhersage sind gezogen.

Vertrauen wäre um so mehr berechtigt, wenn wir uns leiten ließen von der Sparsamkeit ohne Kleinlichkeit, von Großzügigkeit ohne Verschwendung, von Wissensdurst ohne Vorurteile, von Wagemut in Abwägung der Wagnisse, von Sachehrgeiz statt von Karriereplanung, von der bedingungslosen Bereitschaft, uns dem Markt zu unterwerfen.

Daß die Zukunft der Marktwirtschaft (er sagte: des Kapitalismus) durch die Bürokratie gefährdet ist, schrieb übrigens Max Scheler schon 1914. Er sprach damals von dem »steigenden Übergewicht des ›Sicherung‹ fordernden Bürgergeistes über die Komponente des aktiven Unternehmergeistes«. Bisher hat er zwar mit der von ihm damals formulierten Erwartung des »Niedergangs des Kapitalismus« nicht recht behalten. Aber es wäre bedenklich, wenn wir die Gefahr nicht sähen – in der öffentlichen Bürokratie, aber auch in der Bürokratie von Unternehmungen.

Es ist vielleicht weit hergeholt, wenn ich die Meinung eines Unbekannten wiedergebe, die Bürokratie gehe auf die Erfindung des Schreibens und Lesens zurück. Hätte es damals schon eine »Kommission zur Technologiefolgenabschätzung« gegeben, wäre möglicherweise jene Innovation – des Schreibens und Lesens – untersagt worden. Man war ja im übrigen klug genug, diese Kunst über Jahrtausende den »Schriftgelehrten« vorzubehalten. Die breite Einführung ist die Folge einer »Emanzipation«, der ein Gegengewicht guttäte.

Und nochmals zur Marktwirtschaft: Es wäre zu begrüßen, würden sich die Regierenden leiten lassen von der Tatsache, daß Millionen und Abermillionen von Staatsbürgern besser wissen und als Marktteilnehmer zum Ausdruck bringen, was ihnen frommt – besser wissen als die Planer ... und daß öffentliche Planung folglich in die Sackgasse geführt hat – nicht nur im Osten?

*

Sollte es uns hierzulande bessergehen als den anderen: Nehmen wir das gelassen in dem Bewußtsein hin, daß es den Menschen noch nie auf Dauer gutgegangen ist, wenn es ihnen zu lange zu gut ging. Vielleicht sind die an sich nüchternen Schwaben dem Heute zu sehr verhaftet, vielleicht als Kinder des Wohlstandes zu selbstsicher geworden, und vielleicht vergessen wir alle über dem Heute das Morgen und das Übermorgen. Es wäre jedenfalls gut für die Zukunft, wenn wir uns nicht zu sehr in einem Erfolg sonnten, den die Natur nicht vorgegeben hat und dessen Basis wir unseren Vorfahren verdanken.

(1988)

Die Tugend des Vertrauens

ÜBER EINE DER GROSSEN MENSCHLICHEN KATEGORIEN

Alas! my lord,
Your wisdom is consum'd
in confidence.
Do not go forth to-day …

läßt Shakespeare Calpurnia sagen, die Gemahlin Julius Cäsars, am Morgen des Tags, an dem er unter den Händen seiner Mörder stirbt. August Wilhelm Schlegel übersetzt »…in Zuversicht geht Eure Weisheit unter…«. Wir wissen nicht, was in Cäsar vorgeht. Vieles spricht dafür, daß er nicht etwa die Gefahr verkennt, die ihm droht, sondern daß er sich ihr bewußt aussetzt.

Nur der zeigt Mut, der die Gefahr erkennt und ihr dennoch nicht ausweicht. Aber es kam Julius Cäsar nicht darauf an, Mut zu zeigen, sondern sich zum Vertrauen zu bekennen. Cäsar geht allen Warnungen zum Trotz ins Capitol. War er von allen guten Geistern verlassen, als er noch immer vertraute? Glaubte er noch immer an seinen guten Stern? War er sich seiner Sache so sicher? Wir vermuten: nichts von alledem. Vertrauen zeigen war für ihn die höhere Tugend.

Wir übergehen hier die Thematik von Schuld und Sühne. Das Schicksal mag nicht ungerecht gewesen sein. Von Thornton Wilder stammen die Zeilen: »Wäre ich nicht Cäsar, wäre ich Cäsars Mörder!« Die politischen Folgen jenes Mordes – es war die Vorwegnahme anderer schrecklicher Visionen jener Zeit – sind bekannt. Das mißbrauchte Vertrauen forderte seine Opfer.

»Wir« ist kein »pluralis maiestatis«. Denn wir haben von Pascal gelernt, es sei anmaßend, eine Wahrheit für sich selbst zu beanspruchen, wenn sie dem allgemeinen Stand der Erkenntnis und nicht nur dem Gedankengang eines einzelnen entspricht.

Wir bezweifeln nicht, daß Shakespeare mit »confidence« nichts anderes im Sinn hatte als das lateinische Confidentia, das – man muß das in die Überlegung einbeziehen – nicht nur »festes Vertrauen«, »Zuversicht« im allgemeinen bedeutet, sondern auch »Selbstvertrauen«.

Das letztere war bei Shakespeares Cäsar mit im Spiel; deshalb meine Frage, ob »er sich seiner Sache so sicher« war. Aber im Sinne der These, auf die ich hinaus will – daß Vertrauen die Grundlage, ja die unerläßliche Voraussetzung menschlichen Zusammenlebens sei –, betrachten wir Vertrauen und Selbstvertrauen als einen Komplex. Vertrauen auf andere setzt eben voraus, daß man sich selbst vertraut, und wer in sich selbst ruht, kann anderen vertrauen. Daß für die Alten »Vertrauen« den gleichen Sinn hatte wie für uns, wissen wir. Bei Cäsar selbst: Confido maximis legionibus – ich vertraue den stärksten Legionen. Shakespeare kannte dieses Zitat wohl nicht, griff aber doch zum richtigen Wort: confidence.

Daß Vertrauen und Selbstvertrauen ineinandergehen, war auch die Meinung Goethes, wenn er Mephisto sagen läßt:

Und wenn Ihr Euch nur selbst vertraut,
Vertrauen Euch die anderen Seelen,

oder wenn es im Gedicht »Seefahrt« heißt:

Doch er stehet männlich am Steuer.
Mit dem Schiffe spielen Wind und Wellen,
Wind und Wellen nicht mit seinem Herzen.
Herrschend blickt er auf die grimme Tiefe
Und vertrauet, scheiternd oder landend,
Seinen Göttern.

Ich zitiere Goethe zweimal, weil man bei Mephisto den Weg vom Selbstvertrauen zum Vertrauen erkennen kann – im Gedicht ist das umgekehrt. Vielleicht ist der Grund dieser Zitate ein tieferer: Wer zu Vertrauen rät, zu Zuversicht, schreibt damit keine Erfolgslehre. Vertrauen schützt nicht vor Mißerfolg, nicht vor dem Scheitern.

*

Vertrauen, Zuversicht, Glaube – was läge näher, als heute auch ein Gebiet zu betreten, das sich letzter wissenschaftlicher Ergründung widersetzt; das der Religion, der Religionen. Alle beschäftigen sich damit, und alle müssen die Waffen strecken, wenn sie im Hebräerbrief lesen – ich zitiere wörtlich nach dem griechischen Originaltext: Glaube sei »gehofft werdender Dinge Wirklichkeit«. An diesem Wort »Wirklichkeit« scheiden sich die Geister. Wir sind hier mit unserem Griechisch am Ende.

»God is great«, war das erste, was ich von einem Inder – es war vor dem Krieg – hörte. Für ihn war, wenn ich richtig verstand, das Gotteserlebnis die entscheidende Begegnung mit dem Westen. Doch ist unser Gott kein europäischer, er ist ein Gott aus der Wüste. Ob wir das glauben, ob wir das wissen, ob wir das zugeben, ob wir das ertragen können: Der Durchbruch zu dem Glauben an einen Gott vollzog sich nicht im Norden unseres Erdteils.

Noch heute müssen wir uns, wenn es – ein Beispiel aus einem anderen Bezirk unseres Denkens – um das wahre Wesen der Stadt, der Urbs, geht, von Südländern sagen lassen, mit unserer Manie für »grün« lebten wir noch immer in den dunklen Wäldern jenseits der Alpen, mit ihrer Vielzahl von Göttern, von Götzen.

Es mag unser Selbstgefühl treffen, daß das Christentum die Vollendung des jüdischen Glaubens an einen Gott ist. Unser Gott kommt nicht aus dem Dunkel, er ist ein Gott des Lichtes – des Vertrauens. Wir kennen die mannigfachen tiefernsten Bemühungen eines Gottesbeweises – und die ebenso ernstgemeinten Bemühungen, das Gegenteil zu beweisen – seine, Gottes, Nicht-Existenz. Alles müßige Arbeit.

Kant wischt die fünf Gottesbeweise des Thomas von Aquin (die Quinque viae) weg, zeigt die Unmöglichkeit eines Gottesbeweises, um dann aus praktischen Gründen – nämlich um seine Ethik zu stützen – einen Gott zu postulieren. Seine Kritiker sind nicht viel weiter als der Philosoph selbst, der seinen Gott »schafft«. Aber ist nicht ein bewiesener Gott ein toter Gott?· Und doch geht Friedrich Dürrenmatt so weit zu sagen: »Nicht Gott hat uns geschaffen, sondern wir haben Gott geschaffen.« Das heißt, der Mensch, wir selbst haben den Gegenstand unseres Vertrauens entworfen.

Das ist alles andere als Anmaßung oder gar Gotteslästerung, sondern »Glauben an sich«. Und doch könnte es sein, daß wir damit auf unsicherem Grund sind. Woran halten wir uns, wenn der Boden unter unseren Füßen zu weichen droht? Kehren wir dann, wie im Mai 1945, trostbedürftig in die Arme der Kirche zurück und zu ihren Gottesbeweisen? Wenn Skepsis der Anfang allen Erkennens ist, müssen wir Descartes recht geben: »De omnibus dubitandum est.« Sagt der Cartesianer dann »... que, pour être philosophe, il ne suffit pas de croire, mais qu'il fallait penser«, können wir ihm nur entgegnen: Ist die Existenz Gottes nicht rational zu beweisen, glauben wir aber, daß es ihn gibt, »schaffen« wir ihn. Und wir verzichten dann darauf, Philosophen zu sein – nicht weil wir nicht denken wollten, sondern weil es uns darum geht, jenseits des Denkens im Vertrauen einen Halt zu haben.

José Ortega y Gasset meint nicht die »allein seligmachende Kirche«, wenn er in »Gott in Sicht« schreibt: »Der Mensch ist im Grunde gläubig, oder was das gleiche ist: die tiefste Schicht unseres Lebens, die alle übrigen stützt und trägt, ist aus Glaubensgewißheiten gebildet.« Ortega weiß aber auch, daß, im Sinne Jacob Burckhardts, »alle Macht böse ist«. Damit auch die Macht jeder Kirche, die sich vom Spirituellen mehr oder weniger entfernt hat oder dabei ist, das zu tun. Was ist aus dem Friedensgebot der Bibel geworden? Montesquieu darf in den »Lettres Persanes« sagen, ohne daß man ihm widerspricht, kein weltliches Königreich habe so viele Bürgerkriege erlebt, wie das Königreich Christi.

Die Beobachtung der Alten hat sich im Laufe der Geschichte als richtig erwiesen: Homo homini lupus – der Mensch ist des Menschen Wolf. Und wir erwarten alle »Frieden auf Erden« gerade von der christlichen Kirche.

Friede ist nicht nur die Sehnsucht der Schwachen, sondern auch der Mächtigen. Man verzeihe mir, wenn ich an dieser Stelle einfüge – nicht aus Sarkasmus, sondern aus begründeter Sorge –, daß für den Starken die Friedensliebe des Schwächeren schon mehr ist als der halbe Sieg. So sucht auch der Stärkere den Frieden – nachher.

Blindheit hat mit Vertrauen wenig zu tun. Die Gefahr nicht zu sehen, befreit, wie die Geschichte meiner Generation zeigt, kaum von Schuld und keinesfalls von Verantwortung. Gefahr, nicht nur von außen, sondern auch in uns selbst. Die Gefahr, daß man sich der Seelen bemächtigt und damit Macht über den jungen Menschen gewinnt. Die Gefahr der Überheblichkeit: Der Mensch hebt sich über den Menschen hinweg und damit auch über Gott. Denn Gott zu vertrauen verlangt ein hohes Gottvertrauen.

Dabei handelt es sich nicht nur um unseren Gott. Wir sollen keine anderen Götter neben ihm haben – was heißt hier »andere« Götter; ist das nicht verräterisch? Die Philosophen abstrahieren; sie sprechen von »Summum Bonum« und meinen damit das höchste Gut – den Gott.

Es gibt in der Seele anderer Menschen andere Götter. Auch über ihnen steht ein Gott, dem genehm zu sein scheint, daß es eine Kriegskunst gibt, daß Schlachten geschlagen werden, in denen Menschen umkommen und Feldherren Ruhm ernten.

Meine Überlegungen ufern aus, und es liegt auf der Hand, warum. Auf den Beweis der Existenz Gottes zu verzichten, die Fehlschläge seines Wirkens auf Erden darzustellen, um dann doch Gottvertrauen zu fordern, ist eine Wanderung auf eisigem Grat.

Sich seiner Gnade anzuvertrauen, unser Schicksal in seine Hand zu legen – man denke an Kirchenlieder des Barock –, grenzt an die besorgte Frage, ob das Schicksal denn unabwendbar sei. So weit aber geht unsere Bereitschaft, unsere Fähigkeit nicht, uns in den Fatalismus der Wüstenvölker hineinzufinden. Francis Bacon hilft uns vielleicht weiter:

> So gewinnt auch der Mensch,
> wenn er sich dem göttlichen Schutz
> anheimstellt und sich seiner Gnade
> versichert, eine Stärke und einen
> Glauben, deren die Menschennatur
> aus sich nicht fähig wäre.

Überwindung der Zukunftsangst – in der Sprache von heute, die freilich nichts von der Tapferkeit des Herzens erkennen läßt, die uns bisher durch die Fährnisse getragen hat.

In der Politik ist Vertrauen das A und O – nicht nur, weil es bekanntlich in den Parlamenten die »Vertrauensfrage« gibt, die meist das Gegenteil von Vertrauen ausdrückt.

Wir haben uns darauf geeinigt, die Demokratie als die beste aller Staatsformen anzusehen (Churchill, freimütig wie immer: die beste aller schlechtesten Staatsformen). Im Laufe unseres Jahrhunderts scheint es möglich geworden zu sein, diese Staatsform über sich selbst hinaus zu entwickeln: Aus der »Herrschaft des Volkes« in der Demokratie wurde die Volksdemokratie. Da »res publica« die »öffentliche Sache« heißt, sind wir von der schlichten Demokratie, zum Beispiel im Fall der Deutschen Demokratischen Republik, etwas abgekommen.

Demokratie also. In ihr werden Majoritäten angestrebt. Tatsächlich regieren aber Minoritäten. Doch funktionieren sie nur, wenn Vertrauen herrscht.

Bei uns – vielleicht auch anderswo – wurden und werden Freunde zur Kasse, zur Parteikasse gebeten; die Rede war von der Erfüllung staatspolitischer Aufgaben. Wenn man sie dann, nach branchenüblicher Vorverurteilung und psychischer Tortur, den Raubtieren zum Fraß vorwirft, geht Vertrauen in Scherben. Ich stehe hier im übrigen zu der Übung amerikanischer Autoren: Ähnlichkeiten mit natürlichen Personen sind rein zufällig.

Die – wie gesagt minoritären – Machthaber halten sich dabei, von wenigen erfreulichen Ausnahmen und ausdrücklich zu erwähnenden Ausnahmen abgesehen, vornehm zurück. Die sich zurückhalten, verletzen ein ungeschriebenes Gesetz: Vertrauen gibt es nur gegen Vertrauen. Das heißt nicht, daß wir, vertrauend, einen Gegenwert, eine Belohnung fordern oder auch nur erwarten dürften. Man liest zwar bei Scipio dem Jüngeren:

> Habita fides ipsam
> Plerumque obligat fidem
> Gehegtes Vertrauen verpflichtet
> meistens das Vertrauen selbst.

Scipio mußte es wissen. Er hatte Catos stetige Forderung verwirklicht (»... Cartaginem delendam esse«) – und Vertrauen zerschlagen. Im täglichen Leben mag Scipio recht haben, und selbst das »meistens« sehen wir ihm nach. Und doch dürfen wir nicht an »do ut des«, an »Gegengeschäfte« denken: Wer Vertrauen schenkt, schenkt!

Noch sprechen wir nicht von Geschäften, sondern von Politik. Fairneß verlangt zu sagen, daß Politik eigenen Gesetzen gehorcht und Demagogie das Schicksal jedes Politikers ist, solange politische Kultur, mit ihrem hohen Anspruch an verwirklichtem Vertrauen, keine Fortschritte macht.

Sprache ist verräterisch – nirgends mehr als in der Politik. Man spricht und schreibt dort seit einiger Zeit von »Confidence building measures«, von vertrauensbildenden Maßnahmen. Doch entsteht Vertrauen weder durch Handlungen noch durch Maßnahmen. Man täuscht sich über den Charakter dieses Begriffs – dieses Inbegriffs einer Empfindung, die sich durch Aktionen eher in die Flucht schlagen läßt, als daß man sie bewußt gewollt hervorrufen könnte.

Vertrauen braucht weniger aufklärendes Wissen als aufhellendes Bewußtsein, braucht Strömung und Gegenströmung von Sympathie und Antipathie und ist folglich nicht die Wirkung gezielter Politik, sondern eher die unbewußte Akzeptanz politischer Persönlichkeiten, deren Lauterkeit sich nicht auf verbale Erklärung gründet, sondern auf Ausstrahlung.

Ich zögere an dieser Stelle, weil man vielleicht vom Menschen, und erst recht vom Politiker, zuviel erwartet. Wir sind allemal Sünder, fehlbar, und so bin ich, was die Politik angeht, auf eine abschüssige Straße, auf einen steinigen Weg geraten; es gibt hier Links- und Rechtskurven. Aber aus lebenslanger Erfahrung weiß ich: Aus Billigung oder Anerkennung eines Machtwillens, aus Unterwerfung unter einen solchen oder auch nur aus schlichter Verkennung einer Gefahr darf nicht geschlossen werden, Vertrauen keime auf. Die Staatsidee – zumindest seit Hegel aus unserem Verständnis nicht wegzudenken – verlangt Bekenntnis und Treue auch zum nicht »hinterfragten« Gesetz.

So gesehen wird von denen, die Urteile über uns fällen, ein gerüttelt Maß an Gerechtigkeitssinn gefordert, wollen sie Verantwortung für Diktatur, Menschenverachtung, Grausamkeit und Terror richtig zuteilen. Ich meine hier auch – oder gerade – unsere Verantwortung, die Verantwortung unserer Nation, die nicht aufrechnen darf, wenn sie wieder Vertrauen gewinnen will, der es aber auch nicht verwehrt sein sollte, geschichtliche Vergleiche zu ziehen.

Die Politiker haben es schwer, unser Vertrauen zu gewinnen – so gerne wir es ihnen schenken möchten. Das ist übrigens eine nachdenkenswerte Wortwahl: Vertrauen schenken, Glauben schenken.

Sagt man schlicht »ich glaube«, so ist das viel glaubhafter als »ich schenke Glaube«. Dann wieder »ich schenke Vertrauen«; darin spürt man geradezu Großmut.

*

Bleiben wir noch einen Augenblick bei der Politik. Ich komme auf eine russische Redewendung zu sprechen, die Reagan bei seinem ersten Treffen mit Gorbatschow zum Zwischenruf machte. Jener reagierte unwirsch; man muß das verstehen. Denn Reagan sagte: »Vertrauen ist gut, Kontrolle ist besser.«

Ich halte das nicht nur für eine schlechte Übersetzung, sondern für einen schlechten Grundsatz im menschlichen Zusammenleben, der freilich für die Rüstungsbegrenzung, die wir alle befürworten, von grundlegender Bedeutung ist. Wortwörtlich sollten wir übersetzen: »Vertrauen ist gut, Nachschauen ist besser.« Darin sehe ich nicht nur einen graduellen, sonden einen essentiellen Unterschied.

Denn ich halte »Kontrolle« für einen Ausdruck einseitigen Mißtrauens; in der Unternehmenspraxis mildern wir das durch die Aufweichung »Controlling«. »Nachschauen« dagegen drückt etwas Gemeinsames aus und ist ein Teil des Vertrauens. Da ist keine Haarspalterei, sondern der schmale Pfad zwischen Vertrauen und Mißtrauen, auf dem wir uns nur mit großer Toleranz bewegen dürfen, wenn wir niemandem unrecht tun wollen.

Überlassen wir jetzt die Politiker ihrem Schicksal – freilich nicht ohne vorher die Frage zu stellen, ob die persönliche Glaubwürdigkeit der Moskauer Führung gleichzusetzen ist mit dem vollen Vertrauen in die mittel- und langfristige Friedensfähigkeit einer Großmacht. Zwei oder mehr Jahrhunderte russischer Expansion, zunächst militanten Charakters, bis gestern ideologischer Prägung – das läßt sich beweisen –, berechtigen zu bohrender Fragestellung.

Ob in diesem Zusammenhang Außenpolitik nach Art des ambulanten Gewerbes der Vertrauensbildung, trotz vertrauensbildender Maßnahmen, dient, überläßt man am besten dem nächsten Historikerstreit, zumal man die Verläßlichkeit »glaubhafter« Absichtserklärungen am besten im nachhinein prüfen kann. Glaubhaftigkeit bedeutet ja nicht etwa, daß der andere unbedingt zu seinem Wort stehen wird, sondern nur, daß es plausibel, einleuchtend wäre, wenn er zu seinem Wort stünde, falls ihm das frommt.

*

Skepsis statt Vertrauen in politischem Feld – wie stellt sich das in der Wirtschaft dar? Die Frage des Vertrauens erhebt sich immer wieder für den Bankier. Ich gehörte lange Zeit dem Kreditausschuß einer großen Bank an. Mir fiel die Zustimmung zu einem unbesicherten Kredit an einen Unternehmer, der sich Vertrauen, also Kredit verschafft hatte, immer leichter als zu einem »anonymen«Kreditbegehren, auch wenn es besichert war.

Auf den Computer sollten wir uns, wenn es um Vertrauen zwischen Menschen geht, nicht verlassen. Von ihm ist nicht zu erwarten, daß er menschliche Kreativität, Phantasie, Fähigkeit der Gedankenverknüpfung, menschliche Wärme, und damit das Potential an Vertrauen ablösen, geschweige denn überwinden könnte.

Wir wollen nicht idealisieren. Die Ausdehnung des Geschäfts – ich spreche hier nicht etwa nur vom Bankwesen – über den Inlandsmarkt hinaus, die Europäisierung, die Globalisierung der wirtschaftlichen Beziehungen, der international zunehmende Eigentümerwechsel, haben den persönlichen Charakter und damit das überkommene und gewachsene Vertrauensgeflecht an mehr als einer Stelle aufgebrochen. Und dennoch kann gerade das internationale Geschäft ohne den persönlichen »touch« nicht gedacht werden.

»Personal touch« – es gibt den amerikanischen Terminus, den wir hier nur mit Zurückhaltung verwenden: »People factor«. Er betrifft nicht nur das Vertrauen, das ein Unternehmen nach außen genießt, sondern, und vor allem, das Vertrauen zueinander, das in einem Unternehmen existiert – oder nicht. Peter F. Drucker faßt das in die

Worte zusammen: »The final requirement of leadership is to earn trust. Trust is the conviction that the leader means what he says.«

Ungeachtet der Belastung des Unternehmers durch die Führung seines Unternehmens sieht er vor sich die Aufgabe, das Vertrauen der Öffentlichkeit zu erhalten oder wiederzugewinnen – Vertrauen in die Notwendigkeit und Nützlichkeit der unternehmerischen Struktur unserer Wirtschaft, die eine Martkwirtschaft ist und bleiben muß, wenn wir dem Verbraucher auch in Zukunft das Optimum bieten wollen. Das verlangt mehr als nur die Bereitschaft zum Gespräch, es verlangt Aufrichtigkeit und Offenheit – hin und wieder sogar die Preisgabe von Terrain.

Ein Brückenschlag ist um so unerläßlicher, als viele unserer Zeitgenossen durch Schlagworte beunruhigt sind – denken wir an »Raubbau«. Begriffe dieser Art ziehen immer. Denn viele von uns verzagen, wenn sie der immer wieder, in immer neuer Form ausgesprochenen Behauptung begegnen, wir lebten in einer Welt, die – angesichts knapper, schrumpfender Ressourcen – den wachsenden objektiven und subjektiven Ansprüchen nicht gewachsen sei.

Es hat Raubbau an dieser Erde gegeben, und es gibt noch immer Raubbau. In der Wohlstandsgesellschaft ist Maßhalten in mancher Hinsicht zum hohlen Begriff geworden. Und dennoch vertrete ich, was die Ressourcen angeht, aus innerer Überzeugung, die geradezu weltanschaulich ist, einen gegenteiligen Standpunkt: Ich glaube, daß unsere Möglichkeiten zur Energiegewinnung, zur Energiewandlung unerschöpflich sind. Damit aber auch unsere Möglichkeiten zur Gewinnung von Nahrungsmitteln und Rohstoffen.

Lassen wir offen, ob ich mich vom Vertrauen zu dem Schöpfer, vom Glauben an die Vorsehung – oder aber bloß von nüchternem Kalkül leiten lasse. Doch bitte ich darum, sich weder von Politikern noch von den Medien ins Bockshorn jagen zu lassen und den geradezu unendlichen Kräften zu vertrauen, die dem schöpferischen Menschengeist anvertraut sind.

Die Medien, die ich soeben erwähnte, haben ihren Anteil an entstandener Unruhe – ich meine das nicht nur negativ. Denn wir wissen, daß es auch schöpferische Unruhe gibt. Wesentlich ist nun nicht, ob Medien gelegentlich Eigentore schießen. Vielmehr, daß Demokratie nur auf der Basis des Vertrauens bestehen kann – Vertrauen in die Verläßlichkeit und in die Vollständigkeit der Information – Vertrauen darauf, daß Überschrift und Inhalt eines Artikels deckungsgleich sind – Vertrauen darin, daß nur dann Alarm gegeben wird, wenn objektiv Gefahr besteht (subjektiv ist das Leben allemal gefährlich).

Das Wort »Katastrophe« muß dem »schweren Unglück großen Ausmaßes« vorbehalten bleiben, wenn Irreführung der Öffentlichkeit und damit ein Vertrauensschaden vermieden werden soll.

*

Es sind nur Spielarten des Vertrauens, von denen wir bisher sprechen, während es uns doch um Vertrauen als eine der großen menschlichen Kategorien geht. Mit ihnen muß man sich auseinandersetzen – angesichts aller Risiken. Aber das Wagnis des Mißtrauens ist nicht kleiner.

Ich war betroffen – und bin es noch immer – von einer Zeile von Alfred Tennyson:

And trust me not at all
or all in all

Zehn Wörter genügen ihm , dem Viktorianer, um zu sagen, daß Vertrauen ein unbedingter Begriff ist, auf den es keinen Abschlag gibt. Vertrauen und Vernunft stehen in Opposition, wenn man Vertrauen, Zuversicht, Glaube gleichsetzt.

Einer meiner Freunde, der lange schon diese Welt verlassen hat, sagte einmal, Glaube sei die Gewißheit des Unbeweisbaren. Das mag man als Tautologie abtun. Wesentlich daran ist, daß wir uns jenseits der Vernunft bewegen, wenn wir vorbehaltlos vertrauen. Vertrauen unter Vorbehalt ist aber – wir sprachen über Bankgeschäfte – ein besicherter Kredit und folglich kein Vertrauenskredit mehr. Vertrauen – als eine der wenigen grundlegenden menschlichen Kategorien, Möglichkeiten – ist im Prinzip unteilbar.

Mit dem, was die technische Statistik »Vertrauensbereich« nennt, kommen wir hier nicht zurecht. Dieser Terminus betrifft Wahrscheinlichkeiten, während wir Gewißheiten suchen. Es bleibt bei der Ambivalenz zwischen Gefühl und Empfinden auf der einen Seite, Vernunft auf der anderen. Es bleibt bei dem uns auferlegten Dilemma, wofür es keine rationale Lösung gibt: zwischen Glaube oder Verzicht.

Dem Menschen nun, den man davon überzeugt hat, daß er auf den anderen zugehen muß, werden immer wieder Entscheidungen abverlangt, deren Konsequenzen kaum zu übersehen sind. Intuitive Entscheidungen, wobei wir unter Intuition nicht phantastische Eingebung, sondern den Ertrag unbewußter Erfahrung verstehen wollen.

Schopenhauer darf uns nicht entmutigen. Wir bezweifeln, bei aller sonstigen Hochachtung für ihn die Richtigkeit seiner misanthropischen Vermutung, »an unserem Zutrauen zu Anderen« hätten »oft Trägheit, Selbstsucht und Eitelkeit den größten Anteil«. Dennoch müssen wir auf der Hut sein. Die Wölfe schleichen um das Haus. Blindes Vertrauen wird nicht von uns verlangt. Wir dürfen konkrete Warnungen nicht in den Wind schlagen: Trau, schau, wem! Und doch müssen wir, des Zusammenlebens wegen, so lange vertrauen, bis wir eines Besseren belehrt werden.

Niemand kann uns folglich jene Entscheidung abnehmen, von der ich sprach. Immer werden wir vor dem Dilemma stehen, das ich erwähnte: Ob es sich bewähren wird, dem anderen zu glauben, ob er sich bewähren wird. Vielleicht wird seine Vertrauenswürdigkeit gestärkt, wenn wir ihm Vertrauen entgegenbringen. Niemand vergibt sich etwas, wenn er den ersten Schritt tut.

Vertrauen in die Gegenwart entsteht also aus der »Welt«, die wir um uns herum schaffen, und aus dem Vertrauen, das man uns entgegenbringt und das wir durch unsere Handlungen rechtfertigen müssen. Dies ist leicht und schwer zugleich. Denn es geht nicht ohne Enttäuschungen ab – und man kann auch Vertrauen verspielen. Das darf uns nicht zu Kontrolleuren machen.

Vertrauen – diese »vertu des âmes«, um mit unseren französischen Freunden zu sprechen –, Vertrauen in die Zukunft muß man jeden Tag neu erarbeiten. Es ist mit dem Vertrauen ein Kommen und Gehen – und darüber, so hoffen wir, manchmal das Lächeln eines Gottes, der uns für den steinigen Weg trösten will. *(1988)*

Ein Europäisches Haus

DIE DEUTSCHE WIRTSCHAFT UND FRANKREICH IN DER NACHKRIEGSPERIODE – AM BEISPIEL DER BOSCH-GRUPPE

Der deutsche Historiker Ranke schrieb in der Vorrede seines Erstlingswerks (1824), er wolle bloß erzählen, wie es »eigentlich gewesen«. Den Versuch, Geschichte in ihrer »Eigentlichkeit« zu erfassen, überlasse ich den Fachgelehrten. Ich muß bei dem bleiben, was ich erlebt habe und was sich mir davon eingeprägt hat. Mehr als ein Baustein zu einem Versuch, die große Linie zu finden, die sich durch unsere Geschichte hindurchzieht, ist das nicht. Doch zweifeln wohl auch Historiker, ob alles »eigentlich« so war, wie es in den Akten steht.

Den zeitlichen Rahmen, der mir hier gesetzt worden ist, muß ich nach beiden Seiten überschreiten, wenn man von mir erwartet, daß ich mehr vorlege als nur Momentaufnahmen. Die Zeitspanne, die dem Kolloquium zugrunde liegt, sind die Jahre 1945 bis 1960. Aber die deutsch-französischen Beziehungen des Hauses, dem ich angehöre, des Hauses Bosch, gewinnen Kontur vor allem dann, wenn man die Geschichte vor 1945 kennt. Und was nach 1960 kam und zu dem Stand von heute führt, wurzelt in der so wichtigen Zeitspanne, die das zentrale Thema der Veranstaltung ist. Das heißt, ich könnte keinen wesentlichen Beitrag zu seiner Arbeit leisten, wenn ich mich streng auf die 15 Jahre von 1945 bis 1960 beschränkte.

Das Kriegsende als Startpunkt für eine Untersuchung scheint mir eine gute Wahl zu sein. Für Franzosen und Deutsche, für die freie Welt überhaupt, war 1945 ein Neuanfang. Aber in der Geschichte steht jeder auf den Schultern seines Vorgängers, und der Versuch, die eigene Vergangenheit abzuschütteln, scheitert nicht nur am Tatsächlichen, sondern nicht zuletzt auch am Moralischen. Ich spreche damit eher zu meiner eigenen Nation als zu unseren Nachbarn, und ich will niemandem den Spiegel vorhalten, solange ich mich nicht selbstkritisch darin betrachtet habe.

Eher zufällig ist freilich das Jahr 1960 ein für Bosch durchaus markanter Zeitpunkt; denn in diesem Jahr konnten wir Geschäftsteile zurückerwerben, die 1947 unter Besatzungsrecht aus Württemberg in das Saarland »verlagert« worden waren – später mehr darüber.

Erlauben Sie mir also, die Zeitgrenzen, die mir gesetzt sind, nach beiden Seiten zu erweitern und zunächst einmal zusammenzutragen, wie der Gründer unseres Hauses, Robert Bosch der Ältere, das Frankreich der neunziger Jahre des letzten Jahrhunderts gesehen haben muß. Denn der Aufbau – genauer gesagt: der Wiederaufbau – der Beziehungen des Hauses Bosch zwischen Frankreich und Deutschland wird deutlich sichtbar, wenn man den Anfang dieser Beziehungen – sie begannen vor rund einem Jahrhundert – kennt.

Die Geschichte des Hauses Bosch war mit der Entstehung der französischen Automobilindustrie von Anfang an verbunden. Die Idee des Kraftwagens, in Deutschland erstmals industriell verwirklicht, setzte sich in Frankreich seit 1890 schneller durch als in Deutschland, wo es an der Vision mangelte, die unsere westlichen Nachbarn auszeichnete. Anfang des Jahrhunderts gab es, wenn man der Überlieferung glauben darf, in Frankreich einige hundert – wenn auch meist kleine – Betriebe, die »Automobile« herstellten. Wir vermuten, wohl zu Recht, daß es eher Equipagen waren, nicht mehr von Pferden gezogen, sondern von Verbrennungsmotoren angetrieben.

Robert Bosch hatte schon wenige Jahre nach seiner Rückkehr aus amerikanischen Lehrjahren den Weg nach Frankreich gefunden, nachdem es in seinem anfänglich handwerklichen Betrieb gelungen war, das Problem der Zündung des Verbrennungsmotors zu lösen: Im

Jahr 1899 wurde unter seiner Beteiligung in Paris die Cie des Magnétos Simms-Bosch gegründet. Magnétos, das waren die Zündgeräte, mit denen der Einstieg von Bosch in die Kraftfahrzeugindustrie begonnen hatte, und der Engländer Simms war ein Unternehmer, der eine Witterung für die Zukunft besaß.

Die »Ehe« mit Simms war nicht glücklich; es kam zur Scheidung, und 1906 entstand die »Société des Magnétos Bosch«, die eine eigene Fertigung aufnahm. Nach dem Ersten Weltkrieg – die Pariser Firma war enteignet worden – exportierte Bosch zunächst deutsche Produkte nach Frankreich und vertrieb sie durch eine Werksvertretung. Auf französische Anregung hin konnte er sich 1928 hälftig, später zu 100 Prozent an den Atéliers de Construction Lavalette beteiligen, einer Gründung des Comte de la Valette, die der Automobiltechnik diente. In den Jahren 1929/30 wurde eine Fabrik für Bosch-Produkte in St. Ouen errichtet.

Lavalette bekam Zugriff auf Produkte und Produktionsmethoden des Stammhauses. Erfahrungen wurden durch Entsendung von Fachkräften aus Stuttgart nach St. Ouen übertragen; einer der deutschen Ingenieure wurde mit der Fabrikleitung beauftragt. Das ging nicht ohne Rückschläge ab, als politische Spannungen zwischen Frankreich und Deutschland auftraten, die in den Zweiten Weltkrieg einmündeten. Kriege haben in der Regel eine lange Inkubationszeit, und von Mitte der dreißiger Jahre an verließen die deutschen Fachleute einer nach dem anderen Paris (den letzten hielt seine Pflicht jedoch bis Juli 1939), nachdem Schwierigkeiten bei der Vergabe von Rüstungsaufträgen an das von Deutschen »kontrollierte« Unternehmen aufgetreten waren.

Über die Kriegsjahre liegen uns keine Aufzeichnungen vor, und es gibt auch keine persönlichen Erinnerungen auf unserer Seite. Doch sprach man bei Lavalette, als ich nach dem Kriege das Unternehmen erstmals besuchte, gut von den Bosch-Mitarbeitern, die von der deutschen Militärverwaltung während des Kriegs dort eingesetzt worden waren. Robert Bosch und seine leitenden Mitarbeiter hätten auch ein unkorrektes Verhalten nicht geduldet.

Nach der Befreiung von Paris im August 1944 wurde Lavalette unter Sequester gestellt. Diese Maßnahme traf ein Werk, das noch am 26. August jenes Jahres bei einem deutschen Luftangriff auf den Norden von Paris schwer gelitten hatte. Die Schäden wurden rasch behoben; die Produktion des Werks – Ausrüstung von Dieselmotoren – wurde für den Wiederaufbau des französischen Transportwesens dringend benötigt.

Die später folgende Enteignung, die auch die Schutzrechte umfaßte, traf Bosch nicht unerwartet: Die Beteiligung an Lavalette war bilanziell längst abgeschrieben – in Gedanken freilich nicht. Und auch bei Lavalette war die Erinnerung an die fruchtbare Zusammenarbeit lebendig geblieben. In unserem Archiv findet sich als ältestes »Dokument« ein Briefwechsel aus dem Jahre 1947/48, der den Vertrieb von Lavalette-Produkten in der Schweiz durch die Robert Bosch SA in Genf betraf. Aus 1948 finden wir Preisanfragen von Lavalette bei Bosch in Stuttgart sowie Unterlagen darüber, daß seit Beginn 1948 für damalige Begriffe nennenswerte Exportlieferungen nach Frankreich gingen, die über die von der französischen Militärverwaltung eingesetzte Exportagentur Officomex liefen. Der erste Besuch der Lavalette-Geschäftsleitung in Stuttgart fand 1948 statt.

Die frühen fünfziger Jahre – ich verkürze hier die Darstellung – brachten zunächst keine weitere Annäherung von Lavalette an Bosch. Aber die privaten Investoren, an die der französische Staat das Unternehmen in St. Ouen inzwischen verkauft hatte, nahmen schon 1954 Verbindung zu Bosch auf. Ich komme später auf den Rückkauf durch uns – um einen solchen handelte es sich faktisch – zurück.

*

Auf den Wiederanlauf der deutschen Wirtschaft nach Kriegsschluß war die Aufteilung Deutschlands in Besatzungszonen von großem Einfluß. Die wirtschaftliche Struktur der Zonen, der Grad der kriegsbedingten Zerstörung dort einerseits, die politische Zielsetzung, die wirtschaftliche Lage, die Mentalität der Besatzungsmächte andererseits waren wesentlich verschieden. Sie führten in der ersten Nachkriegsphase zu einem Auseinanderleben der Zonen. Man hatte ihre Grenzen teilweise recht willkürlich festgelegt, ohne Rücksicht auf geographische Gegebenheiten, wirtschaftliche und verwaltungsmäßige Zusammenhänge und landsmannschaftliche Bindungen. Diese kritische Bemerkung gilt insbesondere für die Grenzziehung zwischen der amerikanischen und der französischen Zone in Baden und Württemberg, die von Westen nach Osten verlief, während die Anfang des letzten Jahrhunderts geschaffene Grenze zwischen Baden und Württemberg von Nord nach Süd gezogen worden war.

Bei aller Vergleichbarkeit der Unternehmensschicksale in den verschiedenen Zonen führte das für Bosch zu einer zusätzlichen Belastung – über die Zerstörung des größten Teils der Stammwerke, die Verluste im Osten und im Ausland hinaus. Denn Bosch war während des Krieges gezwungen worden, im Süden Württembergs eine große Zahl von Ausweichbetrieben – es handelte sich insgesamt um 45 kleinere und größere Standorte – zu errichten, um die Produktion vor den Luftangriffen auf den Raum Stuttgart, den industriellen Kern des Unternehmens, zu schützen. Und dieses große Verlagerungpotential lag nun von Stuttgart aus gesehen jenseits der Demarkationslinie zwischen der amerikanischen und der französischen Zone – dem Zugriff der Zentrale fast völlig entzogen.

Die rechtlichen Verhältnisse, insbesondere aber die politischen Ziele der Besatzungsmächte, deckten sich ebensowenig wie deren Denk- und Handlungsweise. Nicht nur der Personen- und Warenverkehr über die Zonengrenze war für Monate und Jahre erschwert – auch die Beziehungen zwischen den Besatzungsmächten, die Baden und Württemberg mit einem lebensfremden, unlogischen Schnitt unter sich geteilt hatten, waren, soweit für Deutsche erkennbar, nicht störungsfrei.

Daß bei allem der kleine Grenzverkehr, der private Einfallsreichtum blühte – von französischer Seite eher toleriert als von amerikanischer –, erwähne ich nur am Rande. Bosch jedenfalls blieb die Zusammenführung seiner industriellen Kapazitäten, die Rückführung von Rohstoffen und Fertigungseinrichtungen verwehrt, und das war nicht nur Willkür einer lokalen Besatzungsbürokratie, sondern zentral geleitete Requisition, Reparationsvorbereitung – wir kommen zum Thema Saar.

Im November 1946 wurde Bosch mitgeteilt, der Befehlshaber der französischen Besatzungszone habe den sofortigen »Abtransport« der in den südwürttembergischen Bosch-Betrieben beschlagnahmten Betriebseinrichtungen nach Homburg an der Saar angeordnet. Ein Jahr später verfügte die französische Militärregierung die »Ausgliederung« dieses Besitzes. Begründet wurde diese Entscheidung mit der Dekartellisierung, die im Prinzip von der amerikanischen Besatzungsmacht ausging, inzwischen aber auch von französischer Seite, in die »Verordnung 97«, übernommen worden war. Der von uns vermutete innere Grund, den ich *sine ira et studio* nenne, war die französische Politik der Stärkung des industriellen Gefüges im Saargebiet – eine Parallele zu früheren Bestrebungen Frankreichs, die außerhalb meines Urteils liegen.

Vorangegangen war dem Abtransport die Anfrage des französischen Zwangsverwalters, unter welchen Bedingungen Bosch dieser Maßnahme zustimmen könne. Die Antwort von Bosch wurde nicht abgewartet, die Anlagen vielmehr verkauft, unter anderem auch an Investoren, die möglicherweise der saarländischen Verwaltung nahestanden. Aus den Akten läßt sich schließen, daß die Käufer einen von ihnen selbst errechneten Kaufpreis in entwerteter Reichsmark gezahlt haben – wenige Tage bevor im Saargebiet die französische

Währung eingeführt wurde. Als wir nach der Rückgliederung des Saargebiets in die zwischenzeitlich entstandene Bundesrepublik Deutschland den Homburger Betrieb zurückerwerben konnten, zahlten wir in Deutscher Mark. Das tut uns, von heute her gesehen, nicht mehr weh. Aus dem nicht nach unseren industriellen Maßstäben in einer früheren Kaserne in Homburg eingerichteten »Verlagerungs«betrieb, der den Namen Feintechnik AG angenommen hatte, ist seit Anfang der sechziger Jahre eines unserer neuzeitlichsten Werke geworden.

Ein Vorteil erwuchs der Bosch-Gruppe aus dem unfreiwilligen Transfer eines Teils ihrer Kapazitäten in das für eine Reihe von Jahren dem französischen Wirtschaftsgebiet angeschlossene Saarland: Lavalette nahm Kontakt mit der Feintechnik AG auf, hielt zeitweise eine Minderheitsbeteiligung an dieser Firma, und nicht nur Warenlieferungen fanden ihren Weg, sondern auch Informationen.

*

Ich sagte eingangs, was ich vortragen wolle, beruhe auf persönlichem Erleben. Das Unternehmen, dem ich bei Kriegsende angehörte, wurde durch die Zonengrenze buchstäblich in zwei Teile zerrissen. So konnte ich Franzosen und Amerikaner als Besatzer am Werk sehen – und ich erfuhr ihr Werk am eigenen Leib.

Wie ich schon sagte, war die Ausgangslage für die Besatzungspolitik der Amerikaner einerseits, der Franzosen andererseits sowohl nach Motiven als auch nach eigenen wirtschaftlichen Bedürfnissen grundlegend verschieden. Interessant war es, daß Amerika anfänglich dogmatischer vorging als Frankreich, doch dann schon bald pragmatischer wurde. Das war nach der Rede von Churchill in Zürich, vor allem aber nach der Stuttgarter Rede des amerikanischen Außenministers Byrnes am 6. September 1946 zu beobachten. Es ging jetzt den Amerikanern offenbar nicht mehr in erster Linie um »reeducation« der Deutschen, sondern eher um »containment« der

Sowjets. Der Durchbruch kam dann mit der Rede George Marshalls am 5. Juni 1947 in der Harvard University. Politische Machtverschiebungen, die zu der Erkenntnis geführt haben dürften, die Wiedereingliederung des deutschen Potentials sei vordringlicher als die Maßregelung der Deutschen.

Frankreich ging von vornherein pragmatischer vor als die USA. Die Deckung des eigenen Bedarfs stand im Vordergrund. Allenfalls rhetorisch bezog man sich auf Prinzipien – so zum Beispiel bei der erwähnten Verlagerung von Bosch-Vermögen in das Saarland –, wenn es um greifbare materielle Interessen ging. Nur deren »Verpackung« enthielt noch die Doktrin von der Dekartellisierung.

Es konnte wohl von den Deutschen 1945 nicht erwartet werden, daß sie – im eigenen Wiederaufbau steckend – die Probleme des Wiederaufbaus im teilweise verwüsteten Frankreich erkennen würden. Das heißt, daß sie manche Härte des Besatzungsregimes nicht verstanden und daß sie die Meinungskämpfe in Paris über die unter den gegebenen Umständen »richtige« Wirtschaftspolitik nicht kannten. Heute wissen wir darüber mehr; ich denke zum Beispiel an die »Histoire de France«, deren deutsche Übersetzung seit 1988 bei der Deutschen Verlags-Anstalt in Stuttgart erscheint, betreut von Professor Karl Ferdinand Werner, dem früheren Direktor des Instituts, das uns heute eingeladen hat. Damals war die französische Besatzungspolitik für die Deutschen nicht transparent – zumindest nicht für die Geschäftsleitung von Bosch in Stuttgart, die sich während des Kriegs unter Lebensgefahr exponiert hatte, indem sie Mitglieder des deutschen Widerstands gegen Hitler nachdrücklich unterstützte.

Die Rigidität der französischen Besatzungspolitik dauerte jedenfalls länger als die der Amerikaner. Und doch bin ich der Meinung, daß spätestens mit dem Einsetzen des Marshall-Plans eine neue Phase begann, die dann in die verschiedenen Formen europäischer Zusammenarbeit einmündete. 1949 schloß sich die französische

Zone der schon 1947 zwischen amerikanischer und britischer Besatzungszone gebildeten Bizone an. Die Trizone war damit entstanden, gewann aber keine große Bedeutung mehr, weil kurz danach die Bundesrepublik Deutschland ins Leben trat.

In den fünfziger Jahren kam es, nicht zuletzt dank französischer Initiative, zur Montan-Union und zum Vertrag von Rom – Ereignisse, die auf ein industrielles Unternehmen wie die Bosch-Gruppe zunächst nicht unmittelbar einwirkten. Doch belebte sich der Handelsverkehr zwischen Deutschland und Frankreich in jenem Zeitraum spürbar, was nicht ausschloß, daß die französische Neigung zu, »industriepolitischem« Denken einerseits, das deutsche Bekenntnis zur marktwirtschaftlichen Ordnung andererseits sich nicht immer auf *einen* Nenner bringen ließen (was sich übrigens bis in den Vertrag von Maastricht hinzieht).

Ich eile mit dieser Bemerkung der Entwicklung etwas voraus. Zuvor wollte ich sagen, daß Schritt für Schritt menschliche Kontakte entstanden. Es waren Kontaktfähigkeit, Kontaktbereitschaft auf französischer Seite, die dazu beitrugen, daß allmählich kooperative Tendenzen spürbar wurden. Wenn man an die früheste Zeit der Besatzung zurückdenkt, gab es ja in der französischen Zone keine »non-fraternization«, wie sie in der amerikanischen Zone geboten war. Und als persönliche Reminiszenz erwähne ich an dieser Stelle, wie gleichberechtigt ich schon wenige Jahre nach dem Kriege aufgenommen wurde, als man mich, Mitglied der ersten Delegation der französischen Zone, zu den Marshall-Plan-Sitzungen (European Recovery Program) nach Paris sandte.

Zu Bosch zurück: Ich berichte hier von einem Fund, den ich in Morgenthaus Tagebüchern gemacht habe, als ich die Frage klären wollte, warum wohl Bosch von den Amerikanern in die Dekartellisierung einbezogen wurde. Morgenthau beschäftigte sich darin immer wieder mit der von ihm als übermächtig beurteilten IG Farbenindustrie und auch mit Carl Bosch, der bis zu seinem Tode 1940

Vorsitzender des Aufsichtsrats dieses deutschen Chemiekonzerns war. Dieser Carl Bosch war zwar ein Neffe Robert Boschs, hatte aber mit dem Unternehmen Bosch, entgegen dem Fehlschluß Morgenthaus, nicht das Geringste zu tun. Die Bosch-Gruppe mußte dann zwar bei der Entflechtung nicht so viel Federn lassen wie eine Reihe anderer deutscher Unternehmen, verlor aber die amerikanische Niederlassung, die seit 1908 in den Vereinigten Staaten produzierte. Wir haben sie, im Gegensatz zu Lavalette, nicht zurückgekauft, sind aber heute in USA, nach neuem Start, stärker denn je.

In unserer Beziehung zu Frankreich war der Vorgang Morgenthau unwichtig. In Paris erinnerte man sich noch während der Besatungszeit der alten, für Frankreich nützlichen Verbindung von Bosch zu Lavalette, wie der erwähnte Homburger Vorgang zeigt. Und als Bosch schon im Jahre 1950 wieder einen Stand auf dem »Salon de l'Automobile« hatte, schrieb die französische Auto- und Sportzeitschrift *L'Equipe:*

»›Un grand nom de retour en France‹ La mécanique, comme l'art, n'a pas de partrie. Aussi le nom du grand Robert Bosch fait-il partie de l'histoire mondiale de l'industrie automobile. C'est donc un évènement important, au point de vue industriel et commercial, que le fait de retrouver cette année, au Grand Palais, un stand Robert Bosch.«

Ungeachtet noch bestehender Hemmnisse im Verhältnis zwischen unseren Ländern – die fortdauernde Beschlagnahme des Bosch-Vermögens in Frankreich ist nur ein Beispiel – war Deutschland schon ein Jahrzehnt nach dem Neubeginn Frankreichs größter Auslandskunde geworden – und sein erster Lieferant. Bosch war an diesem für beide Teile wichtigen Warenverkehr, einer Zweibahnstraße, beteiligt, und in Frankreich waren schon wieder Bosch-Verkaufsgesellschaften entstanden, die sich 1953 zusammenschlossen.

*

Die Jahre bis 1960 waren Jahre der Vorbereitung des Bodens, Jahre der Aussaat. In unseren Büchern findet sich für 1960 ein Umsatz der französischen Vertriebsgesellschaft, die inzwischen in unseren Firmenverband zurückgekehrt war, von rund 15 Millionen DM (die Angabe in DM ist hier vorzuziehen, weil Denomination und Kurs der französischen Währung während des betrachteten Zeitraums Veränderungen erfuhren). Ein Jahrzehnt später war dieser Wert auf das Fünfzehnfache angewachsen. Im laufenden Jahr erwarten wir in Frankreich einen Umsatz mit Dritten in Höhe von rund 2,4 Milliarden DM – mit steigender Tendenz.

Ich will das nicht als Vielfaches des Ausgangswertes darstellen, zumal für uns Umsatz allein kein Wertmaß für das unternehmerisch Erreichte ist. Immerhin steht Frankreich unter allen Ländern, in denen wir fertigen, mit an der Spitze, und daß mehr als die Hälfte der französischen Bosch-Produktion exportiert wird, ist für Frankreich gesamtwirtschaftlich bedeutsam. Das gilt insbesondere auch für die Zahl der Arbeitsplätze: Am 1. Oktober 1994 hatten wir in Frankreich 5300 Mitarbeiter, darunter 250 Ingenieure, Techniker und weitere Arbeitskräfte, die der Forschung und Entwicklung dienen. Es entspricht dem Bosch-Prinzip, dort, wo wir produzieren, fertigungsnah auch zu entwickeln und die Erzeugnisse an die Kundenanforderungen anzupassen. Mehr als 80 Prozent dieser Arbeitsplätze sind seit Kriegsende geschaffen worden, überwiegend in Gebieten, die für die französische Regionalpolitik wichtig sind – ich werde ein Beispiel nennen.

Gerade der genannte Ausfuhranteil zeigt, daß hier nicht sozusagen »inselhaft« über Bosch in Frankreich berichtet wird, sondern über die wirtschaftlichen Beziehungen zwischen den Ländern Deutschland und Frankreich, soweit sie unser Haus betreffen. Man muß dabei sehen, daß die Masse der erwähnten Exporte unserer französischen Fabriken nach Deutschland geht, daß die deutschen Bosch-Werke im Verbund mit ihren französischen »Nachbar«-Werken arbeiten und daß bestimmte Bosch-Produkte europaweit nur in Frankreich hergestellt werden. Schließlich auch, daß die deutschen Bosch-Werke jährlich für rund 2,5 Milliarden FF Produkte aus Frankreich beziehen. Ein nachbarliches Verhältnis also, in der Tat.

Die Entwicklung unseres Potentials in Frankreich seit 1960 setzte nun eine Reihe von Schritten voraus, die ich umreißen will – mit grobem Stift, um meine Zuhörer nicht über Gebühr zu ermüden. Keiner dieser Schritte ließ sich »autonom« tun. Es bedurfte vielmehr der Mitarbeit der französischen Seite, und ich bitte darum, mich nicht von vornherein als einseitig frankophil einzuschätzen. Was immer wir in Frankreich realisieren konnten, beruhte auf einer Synthese unternehmerischen Willens auf unserer Seite, andererseits aber der französischen Bereitschaft, Lösungen zu finden, die wirtschaftlich ebenso rational wie legal waren, gleichzeitig aber auch emotional vertretbar.

Ohne in Einzelheiten zu gehen, will ich wenigstens sagen, daß die Wiedereingliederung von Lavalette in die Bosch-Gruppe ohne weitsichtiges, aufgeschlossenes Denken und Handeln des zuständigen französischen Ministeriums nicht möglich gewesen wäre. Dabei wurde dem Gesetz Rechnung getragen, so daß es Bosch vorläufig verwehrt blieb, Lavalette als ganzes Unternehmen zurückzukaufen – nicht aber verwehrt, den Geschäftsbetrieb zu erwerben. 1962 schlossen wir dann Lavalette mit der »SA Précision Mécanique Labinal« zusammen, deren einschlägige Abteilungen inzwischen in unseren Einflußbereich gekommen waren.

Die Verbindung mit Labinal brachte uns in den Besitz eines Betriebs in Rodez, der heute unser größtes Werk in Frankreich ist, gleichzeitig auch der größte Arbeitgeber im Département Aveyron, das mit Industrie nicht sehr gesegnet ist. Der damalige Bürgermeister unseres neuen Standortes, Boscary-Monservin, förderte unsere Ansiedlung in seiner Stadt, und er hatte dabei auch die Unterstützung von Paris. Französische Banken standen uns in der Aufbauzeit zur Seite. Ihre Flexibilität half ihnen und auch uns in den Zeiten der Kreditregulation und -restriktion.

St. Ouen, der Stammsitz von Lavalette, ist heute, nach der Verlegung der Produktion aus der Enge der Banlieue hinaus in weiträumigere Regionen, unser Zentrum in Paris – ein »Europäisches Haus«.

*

Es gibt, über das Thema hinausgreifend, Beziehungen von Bosch zu Frankreich, die nicht wirtschaftlicher Natur sind. Das Interesse, das Robert Bosch an Frankreich nahm, war umfassend. Gewiß, er war Industrieller von Grund auf. Aber als er einmal im Meldezettel eines Hotels die Spalte »Beruf« ausfüllen sollte, schrieb er »Mensch«. Wie wir gehört haben, hatte der Industrielle den geschäftlichen Weg nach Frankreich schon wenige Jahre nach der Gründung seines damals noch kleinen Unternehmens gefunden. In dem Menschen Robert Bosch entstand während des Ersten Weltkriegs die Idee, dazu beizutragen, eine Brücke zwischen den lange verfeindeten Ländern zu schlagen. Denn er sah im Verhältnis zwischen Deutschland und Frankreich den Schlüssel zur zukünftigen Einigung Europas.

Noch während des damaligen Krieges traf er Anstalten zur Verwirklichung seines Gedankens – die Gründung eines im neutralen Land, in der Schweiz, ansässigen Verlags. Die wirtschaftlichen, zunehmend auch die politischen Umstände stellten sich ihm entgegen. Aber in seinem Vermächtnis legte er den Grund dafür, daß seit 1964 mehr als 80 Prozent, heute mehr als 90 Prozent des Unternehmens der Robert Bosch Stiftung gehören, und er legte fest, daß die Erträge daraus gemeinnützig zu verwenden seien. Mehr noch, er bestimmte, daß insbesondere die Völkerverständigung zu fördern sei – Frankreich dabei im Vordergrund.

Die bisherigen Aufwendungen der Robert Bosch Stiftung für den Brückenschlag nach Frankreich nähern sich dem Betrag von 30 Millionen DM – Prioritäten sind Information, Bildung und Fortbildung, wissenschaftliche Beziehungen, kurz, der geistige und kulturelle Austausch. Dabei kommt dem Spracherwerb, in beiden Richtungen, ein besonderes Gewicht zu – Sprachkenntnis als Voraussetzung für das Verständnis von Land und Leuten, als Voraussetzung bleibenden politischen Verständnisses. Die Zusammenarbeit mit Medien, Verlagen, Hochschulen spielt hier eine Rolle. Ein Beispiel ist die Errichtung des Alfred-Grosser-Lehrstuhls am Pariser Institut d'études politiques durch unsere Stiftung. Politik über das Unternehmen hinaus.

*

Von dem deutschen Industriellen Walther Rathenau stammt das Wort, die Politik sei unser Schicksal. Am Ende seiner Laufbahn – und seines Lebens – hatte sich Rathenau dem Primat der Politik unterworfen; er übernahm in spannungsreicher Zeit das Amt des deutschen Außenministers. Wir schließen aus seiner Tätigkeit in der deutschen Regierung auf seine Erkenntnis, daß Politik, erfolgreiche Politik, wirtschaftliche Voraussetzungen hat. Auf beiden Seiten – in Deutschland und in Frankreich – haben die Unternehmen seit 1945 dazu beigetragen, die wirtschaftlichen Voraussetzungen für eine europäische Politik zu schaffen. *(1994)*

Bürgerengagement und Stiftungsidee

WER GEGEN DIE ALLGEGENWART DES STAATES IST, DARF NICHT BEISEITE STEHEN

Wenn ich gleich zu Beginn festhalte, daß Schenken und Stiften zweierlei sind, nehme ich – einer aktuellen Frage wegen, auf die wir zurückkommen werden – meine Auffassung vorweg: Der zum Engagement bereite Staatsbürger – durch die konfiskatorische Staatsquote über Gebühr belastet – dürfe nicht dazu überredet werden, weitere Teile seines Einkommens oder seines Vermögens wegzugeben, ohne daß ein Gegenwert, ohne daß etwas Neues entstehe.

Vor Jahren sagte ich in einem Vortrag zu den Begriffen »unternehmerische Initiative« und »gesellschaftspolitische Verantwortung«, daß Stiften seiner Wortgeschichte nach die Bedeutung hat: gründen, ins Werk setzen, erbauen, einrichten, in Ordnung bringen. Und die französischen und englischen Wörter für Stiftung »fondation« und »foundation« weisen zurück auf das lateinische fundo: den Grund zu etwas legen. Damit gehört der Begriff »Stiften«, die Errichtung einer Stiftung von vornherein nicht in die passive Sphäre des Schenkens, des bloßen Entäußerns.

Setzt auch der Entschluß, eine Stiftung zu errichten, großmütigen Verzicht voraus, überwiegt doch das Element des Handelns. Die Institution der Stiftung gehört damit ihrem Wesen nach in das Umfeld gestaltender Denkweise. Dieses unternehmerische Element des Stiftens, des Errichtens einer Stiftung verlangt von jeher aber auch staatsbürgerliches Bewußtsein des Stifters; bürgerschaftliches Engagement heißt das in der Überschrift dessen, was ich heute zu sagen versuche.

Vita activa also – im Sinne von Hannah Arendt –, eingebunden in die Gesellschaft, die unsere Existenzgrundlage nicht nur in materieller, sondern vor allem auch in ideeller Hinsicht ausmacht. Immer geht es bei der Errichtung einer Stiftung um mehr als eine Schenkung, es geht um eine Aktion, und wenn wir über bürgerschaftliches Engagement sprechen, ist das entscheidend: Wer eine Stiftung errichtet, gestaltet, mehr noch, er gestaltet mit.

Nicht jede Institution, die sich des Namens einer Stiftung bedient, erfüllt die Voraussetzung, daß ihr eine Vermögensmasse zugrunde liegen muß. Wir kennen viele solcher Einrichtungen; sie liegen am Rande unseres Themas. Damit stelle ich die Tendenz in Frage, das Ansehen, das die »Stiftung« sich in Jahrhunderten erworben hat, auf Einrichtungen zu übertragen, die weitab von unserer Vorstellung liegen. In den letzten Jahren waren es vor allem politische Schritte, die zur Annexion des Namens Stiftung führten – ohne Überlassung einer Vermögensmasse. Partei-Stiftungen, um ein Beispiel zu nennen, haben, im engeren Sinn, mit einem Engagement des Staatsbürgers nichts zu tun.

Stiftungen, die kein eigenes Vermögen haben, deren Tätigkeit folglich auf Zuwendungen beruht, müssen Jahr für Jahr auf Entscheidungen warten, die von außerhalb getroffen werden – oft von der Bürokratie. Das Gesetz der Unabhängigkeit, das für die Institution Stiftung gelten muß, wird hier ebenso verletzt wie die Grundanschauung, daß jede Stiftung ein Individuum ist, dem Gedankenfreiheit zusteht.

In seinen Haushaltsnöten lockt der Staat den Stifter. Er spricht offen aus: Stifter, private Stifter müßten für kulturelle Aufgaben einspringen, die doch zu den Obliegenheiten des Staates gehören. Hier liegt ein Fehlschluß bei den Mächtigen – der Stifter ist nicht Lükkenbüßer. Er ist in der Stiftungswirklichkeit der Wettbewerber der Staatsgewalt. Er ist nicht berufen, Etatlöcher zu schließen. Seine

Zielvorstellung ist, die »operative« Stiftung, der er eigene Zwecke setzt, die Stiftung, die nicht als Nothelfer des Staates zu verstehen ist, sondern eher als sein Gegenpart, der sich nicht der »Tyrannis der Majorität« (Coustard de Rebeque) beugt. Durch die Stiftung in unserem Sinn soll also Spannung erzeugt werden, und der Stifter distanziert sich von einem überholten Kollektivismus.

Stiften heißt Freiraum schaffen; dieser Begriff darf nicht etwa zu einer Form zusätzlicher Besteuerung der »Besserverdienenden« deformiert werden. Damit sind wir bei einem entscheidenden Faktor neuzeitlicher Gesellschaftspolitik angelangt: der Mitwirkung des Bürgers im Staat.

Wir haben – ob wir heute oder morgen Stifter sind – ein unmittelbares, aber auch ein mittelbares Interesse an einem Staat, der seinen Aufgaben dient. Aber wir bestreiten diesem Staat das Recht, den tätigen Staatsbürger mehrfach zu besteuern. In dieser inneren Gegenposition liegt ein Ausdruck für das Gestaltungsbedürfnis des Staatsbürgers, den weniger eine Opfermentalität bewegt, wenn er stiftet, als die Chance, eigene Vorstellungen zu verwirklichen.

Das Feld der Stiftung liegt also nicht, jedenfalls nicht in erster Linie, dort, wo Mittel fehlen, sondern dort, wo es an Initiativen – auch an solchen nonkonformistischer Art – fehlt. Denn Stiftungen

- können das »Warten auf den Staat« vermeiden helfen; sie können der langen Ansprechzeit, die den Entscheidungsprozeß der öffentlichen Hand kennzeichnet, durch Phantasie und Tempo zuvorkommen,
- haben das Recht zum Wagnis, das man der Administration nicht oder nicht im gleichen Maß zugestehen kann,
- greifen Aufgaben an, bei denen ein Multiplikator- oder ein Akzeleratoreffekt erwartet werden kann.

Was das Institut der Stiftung vor allem auszeichnet, sind folglich:

- die Fähigkeit, ausgefahrene Geleise zu vermeiden, neue Wege zu gehen,

- die Bereitschaft, rasch zu handeln,
- der Mut, Wagnisse einzugehen,
- das Recht, Ziele zu setzen, die den Fächer der Initiativen über das dem Staat Mögliche hinaus erweitern.

Es gibt staatsbürgerliche Pflichten, die keinen Rechtscharakter haben, die vielmehr moralischer, ethischer Natur sind, weil es zu einem demokratischen Staat gehört, daß der Bürger im Staat mitwirkt. Der Staatsbürger, der sich dieser Pflicht zur Mitwirkung entzieht, verzichtet nicht nur auf die Chance, seine Überzeugungen, sein Können und seine Erfahrung in die Gestaltung des demokratischen Prozesses einzubinden. Vielmehr entzieht er sich der Mitverantwortung, von der Richard von Weizsäcker kürzlich gesagt hat: Eine Demokratie sei nur lebensfähig, »wenn der einzelne bereit ist, für das Ganze Verantwortung zu übernehmen«.

Sie erinnern sich an die gemeinsame Erklärung, die Bundespräsident Rau zusammen mit seinen Vorgängern Herzog, von Weizsäcker und Scheel abgegeben hat und die zur Stärkung der Bürgergesellschaft aufruft. Eine Zeitung brachte das unter der Überschrift »Vier Präsidenten wollen weniger Staat« zum Ausdruck. »Den Bürger aus seiner Gleichgültigkeit aufzustören«, verlangte ein Zeitgenosse in einem Leserbrief, der zu der Erklärung der Präsidenten Stellung nimmt. Dieser Leser hätte sich eine noch deutlichere Aussage gewünscht. Er bezog sich auf Kant, der von der »selbstverschuldeten Unmündigkeit« (des Bürgers) spricht.

Die Abwägung von Rechten und Pflichten, die sich Staat und Bürger gegenseitig schulden, hat auf den ersten Blick mit unserem Thema »Stiftung« nichts zu tun. Aber das Institut der Stiftung kann – zumindest auf wichtigen Teilgebieten – Hebel für die bürgerliche Mitwirkung sein. Ich zitiere nochmals Richard von Weizsäcker: »Stifter geben ein Beispiel für verantwortliches Handeln im demokratischen Staat.«

Bürgerengagement, zu dem aufgerufen wird, ist ein Weg, ein

Mittel, dort zu wirken, wo die Grenzen des Staats erreicht sind. Der Bürger, der sich engagiert, wird zur Stütze des Staates, den wir alle wollen, in dem Sinn, daß er Aufgaben übernimmt, die der Staat nicht erfüllen kann, darf oder will – in seinem Zuschnitt, in seinem Etatismus, in seiner begrenzten Weitsicht.

Ruhe ist nicht die »erste Bürgerpflicht«, die man den Berlinern nach der Schlacht von Jena von seiten der »Obrigkeit« zugerufen hat. Eher wäre der Begriff der »schöpferischen Unruhe« am Platz. Und vom Staat kann, in seiner Struktur, nicht erwartet werden, daß er allein die Gerechtigkeit herstellt; dazu bedarf es der Mithilfe aller.

Wir wollen den Begriff des »Kommunitarismus«, der in den Vereinigten Staaten zunehmend erörtert wird, nicht ohne weiteres auf uns übertragen. Aber in seinem Kern hat dieser Gedanke, der auf eine Fortentwicklung von Staat und Gesellschaft zur »Civil Society« hinausläuft, mit der Idee der Stiftung zu tun. Und die Teilnahme des Bürgers am Staat kann sich nicht darin erschöpfen, daß er Forderungen stellt, muß hinzugefügt werden.

Dem Unternehmer müssen wir sagen, daß die Stiftung eine neue Dimension unternehmerischen Gestaltens erschließen, Fortsetzung des Unternehmens mit anderen Zielen und auf anderer Ebene Mittel sein kann. Der Unternehmer, der die Nutzung des von ihm erwirtschafteten Produktivkapitals als Treuhandaufgabe betrachtet, für den Gewinn Maßstab und Werkzeug ist, nicht aber einen Eigenwert bedeutet, kann in der Stiftung Aufgaben angreifen, die, über das Unternehmen hinaus, auf den Nutzen des Ganzen abgestellt sind. Was man in dieser Beziehung als gestaltend ansehen kann, muß dem Fortschritt dienen, ohne daß man auf die Vereinfachung verfallen dürfte, alles Bewahrende, Erhaltende sei an sich Rückschritt, alle Änderung aber an sich Fortschritt. Der Stifter, der seinen Einsatz nicht verloren geben will, betrachtet seinen Beitrag als Saatgut. Er denkt ursprünglich. Er sieht die Früchte seines Tuns vor sich. Diese Sicht hilft über die Schwelle des Verzichts hinweg.

Kürzlich erreichte mich aus Israel, aus dem Weizmann Institute of Science in Rehovot, ein Brief, der eine Gedankenverknüpfung auslöst – von dem Sigmund Warburg Chair, der dort aus einer privaten Stuttgarter Stiftung vor mehr als einem Jahrzehnt entstand, zur Stiftung als Saatgut. Über die Aufgabenstellung dieses Stiftungslehrstuhls berichtet dieser Brief: die Entwicklung einer Getreideart, die in ariden Gebieten gedeiht. Ein bemerkenswertes Exempel dafür, wie ein materieller Einsatz zu einer geradezu politischen Zielsetzung wird: Das zu entwickelnde neue Saatgut muß nicht nur den Israeli, sondern gleichzeitig auch den Arabern zugänglich gemacht werden – so lautet die Auflage zu jener Stiftung.

Die öffentliche Diskussion kreist zur Zeit um Rechts- und Steuerfragen, die mit der Stiftung zusammenhängen. Der »Palandt«, ein Kurzkommentar zum BGB, bezeichnet die im Bürgerlichen Gesetzbuch getroffene Regelung des Stiftungsrechts als »lückenhaft«. Die meisten deutschen Länder haben zur Ergänzung eigene Gesetze erlassen, ohne daß dadurch eine grundlegende und umfassende Ordnung des Stiftungswesens geschaffen worden wäre. Seit Jahrzehnten wird deshalb eine Reformdiskussion geführt, noch ohne Ergebnis. Die bestehenden Stiftungen haben jedoch, soweit ich beobachten kann, bisher unter dem Fehlen einer systematischen Rechtsordnung nicht fühlbar gelitten – jedenfalls nicht bei der Erfüllung ihrer stiftungseigenen Ziele.

Wenn jetzt die Reformdiskussion wieder angestoßen wird, so kommt das weniger aus der Welt der Stiftung als aus dem politischen Raum. Die schon erwähnte Ursache dafür liegt auf der Hand: Der Staat, in Finanznöten, setzt, vor allem für die Verwirklichung kultureller Aufgaben, nicht nur auf bestehende, sondern auf noch zu schaffende Stiftungen. Das sieht dann in Presse-Überschriften so aus:

– »Für die gute Sache: Der Staat will an das Geld der Reichen« (*Stuttgarter Zeitung* vom 9. November 1999) oder

– »Den Mäzen wiederentdeckt« (*Frankfurter Allgemeine Zeitung* vom 5. Oktober 1999), letzteres mit der zusätzlichen Überschrift: »Auf der Museumsinsel predigt Gerhard Schröder Bürgersinn.«

In derselben Ausgabe der *Frankfurter Allgemeine Zeitung* findet man dann eine Überschrift: »Schröder stellt Reform des Stiftungswesens in Aussicht.« Seit der Veröffentlichung der so überschriebenen Artikel reißen Ankündigungen über die Vorbereitung eines neuen Stiftungsgesetzes nicht ab. Wir hören das gern, wenn auch nicht ganz ohne Ironie, da es ja ein altes Stiftungsgesetz gar nicht gibt, während das derzeitige »lückenhafte« Stiftungsrecht die Bereitschaft, Stiftungen zu errichten, nicht sichtbar gedämpft haben dürfte.

Die öffentliche, vor allem aber stiftungsinterne Erörterung betrifft nun aber nicht zuletzt einen viel wichtigeren Gegenstand: das Spendenrecht oder, genauer gesagt, die steuerliche Seite. Man würde am Leben vorübergehen, wenn man übersehen wollte, daß die Bereitschaft der Stifter – oder derjenigen, die es werden wollen oder sollen – auch davon abhängt, ob es sich steuerlich »lohnt«, eine Stiftung zu errichten. Gewiß: Jeder, der gestiftet hat, jeder, von dem erwartet wird, daß er spendet, überlegt, wieviel man durch eine Stiftung an Steuern »spart«. Aber das Wort »sparen« ist an dieser Stelle falsch. Denn jede Stiftung, auch wenn ihr Betrag steuerlich abgesetzt werden kann, verlangt vom Stifter, daß er sich eines Vermögensteiles entäußert.

Im internationalen Vergleich ist der deutsche Stifter im Nachteil. Wir sprechen noch über die amerikanische Stiftungswelt, die stärker ausgeprägt erscheint als die deutsche. Das hat nicht nur, aber auch, steuerliche Gründe, und zweifellos wäre die Bereitschaft zu stiften auch bei uns höher, wenn man die steuerlichen Anreize erhöhte. Der Steuergesetzgeber kann und muß mitziehen; es sollte ihm um so leichterfallen, als der »öffentlichen Sache« durch die Errichtung von Stiftungen neue Mittel zugeführt werden, die über den Steuerausfall weit hinausgehen.

Bei allem dürfte staatliche Überwachung der Stiftung nicht das

Thema einer Reform des Stiftungsrechts sein. Freiwillig gebotene Transparenz und Information können Kontrolle ersetzen. Das bayerische Stiftungsgesetz spricht von »Obhut« – ein guter, sachdienlicher und ausreichender Begriff. Eine Aufsicht, die sich anmaßte, Sachentscheidungen zu beurteilen, würde den Gedanken der Stiftung als einer ergänzenden, ausgleichenden Komponente zur Förderung gemeinnütziger Aufgaben gefährden.

Bedenklich für den Stiftungsgedanken wäre es auch, wenn man die von der jeweiligen Majorität angestrebten Ziele zur Richtschnur für Stiftungen machen wollte. Denn eine Majorität, die über die Rechte der Minorität hinwegginge, könnte nicht die Qualifikation echter Demokratie für sich beanspruchen. Die Macht der Demokratie bedarf des Gegengewichts. Freiheit der Forschung gehört mit zur Sicherung der Balance, und Stiftungen unterstützen die Freiheit der Forschung. Die kreative Freiheit des Instituts der Stiftung dient der Freiheit überhaupt – sofern man bereit ist, dieses pluralistische Element in einer Umgebung von Utopien nicht nur zu dulden, sondern zu fördern.

Die gemeinnützige Stiftung hat gezeigt, daß sie mit dem geltenden Recht auszukommen versteht, obwohl es förderlich wäre, wenn die Stiftungswilligen festen juristischen Grund unter sich hätten. Ich gestehe aber, daß ich es vorziehe, mit dem derzeitigen Rechtsfundament – lückenhaft und uneinheitlich – auszukommen, solange die Erfahrung in diesem Land zeigt, daß der Perfektionismus der Gesetzesmacher dem Bürger die Luft abschneidet. Und ein unvollkommenes Stiftungsrecht, in der Anwendung von Toleranz getragen, ist einem perfekten und damit fast zwingend intoleranten Stiftungsrecht vorzuziehen.

Wenn der Stifterverband in seinem Jahresbericht 1998 eine »Optimierung« des Stiftungsrechts vorschlägt, so ist das ein Begriff, der die gestellte Aufgabe gut trifft. Sind die Politiker bereit, die gesetzlichen Grundlagen des Stiftungswesens zu verbessern, wird man diesen Weg gern mitgehen. Da und dort werden bessere Gesetze die Schwellen, die vor einer Stiftungsentscheidung stehen, überwinden helfen.

Vordringlich bleibt weiterhin eine großzügige Neuregelung des Spendenrechts, also der steuerlichen Seite. Hier liegt ein Schlüssel für die Verbreitung des Stiftungsgedankens. Der Fiskus beklagt sich im übrigen zu Unrecht darüber, er trage, durch Steuerausfall, einen großen Teil der gestifteten Beträge. Tut er das doch für eine gute Sache zum halben Preis. Umgekehrt: Es würde den Fiskus das Doppelte kosten, wenn er die Stiftungsaufgaben allein auf sich nehmen müßte.

Wenn schon von Steuern die Rede ist, will ich Ihnen einen steuerlichen Leckerbissen nicht vorenthalten, der soeben auf meinen Tisch kam. Das Amts-Blatt des Königlich Württembergischen Steuer-Collegiums vom 6. November 1858 teilt mit, daß vom 1. Juli 1858 an für drei Jahre die Einkommensteuer auf vier Prozent herabgesetzt wird. Es geht aus dem schönen alten Stück, das mir zur Hand ist, nicht hervor, wie hoch der Steuersatz vorher war. Nehmen wir einmal viereinhalb oder fünf Prozent an, so war doch zu jener Zeit der steuerliche Anreiz, eine Stiftung zu errichten, nur begrenzt. Aber: 96 Prozent des Einkommens verblieben dem württembergischen Untertan, und damit war der Spielraum für eine offene Hand des Staatsbürgers um ein Vielfaches größer als bei allen Abzugsmöglichkeiten, die wir heute haben oder die man uns in Aussicht stellt.

Der Stifterverband für die Deutsche Wissenschaft, der selbst keine Stiftung ist, aber in der Nachkriegszeit zum »zentralen Ort« der Spenden- und Stiftungstätigkeit der deutschen Wirtschaft wurde, hat einen Stammvater im alten Rom: Maecenas. Über ihn schrieb Josef Eberle – selbst ein Stifter großen Stils – einen lesenswerten Aufsatz. Vor mehreren Jahren habe ich Eberles Würdigung des großen Römers – genaugenommen war er ein Etrusker aus Arezzo – für meine Freunde neu herausgegeben. Es heißt in meinem Begleitbrief: »Maecenas bekam übrigens, wie die Historiker des Stiftungsgedankens vermuten, nie eine Spendenbescheinigung.«

Das mag zwar damit zusammenhängen, daß dieser Maecenas – ein überaus wohlhabender Mann – in Rom gar keine Steuern zu zahlen hatte. Wie immer das war: Die Förderung der Kunst und der Wissenschaften war für Maecenas kein Problem der Steuerersparnis, sondern ein inneres Bedürfnis. Martial sagte über ihn ein schönes Wort: »Sint Maecenates, non deerunt, Flacce, Marones.« Schaffe Mäzene, mein Freund, so wirds an Vergilen nicht fehlen, hat Eberle das übersetzt. Martial meinte Vergil; aber auch Horaz genoß den »maecenatischen Großmut«.

Der Stifterverband hat nicht nur die Aufgabe, die Spendenbereitschaft der deutschen Wirtschaft für wissenschaftliche Zwecke anzuregen. Vielmehr ist er auch – vorbildlich und anspornend – der Verwalter einer großen Zahl treuhänderischer und selbständiger Stiftungen. Deren Aufzählung macht im Jahresbericht elf Seiten aus: mehr als 250 deutsche private Stiftungen mit einem Vermögen Ende 1998 von fast 1,7 Milliarden Mark. Die Erträge aus der Vermögensanlage betrugen 1998 annähernd 90 Millionen Mark, die zur Förderung der Stiftungszwecke, in der Regel also für bestimmte Aufgaben ausgegeben wurden.

Während der Umfang im Rahmen der Aufwendungen, die in der Bundesrepublik Deutschland für wissenschaftliche Zwecke insgesamt gemacht werden, gering erscheinen mag, ist die Wirkung nicht zu unterschätzen, zumal in den meisten Fällen die Leistungen nicht einfach gestreut werden, sondern scharf fokussiert sind. Bedeutsam ist die – privat getragene – Motivation der Wissenschaft, die sich nicht den öffentlichen Haushalten »ausgeliefert« fühlen muß, sondern von vielen Seiten getragen.

Eines drängt sich dem Beobachter des Stiftungswesens hier auf: die unverwechselbare Individualität der Stifter und der von ihnen festgelegten Zweckbestimmungen. Die Stiftungswelt in den Vereinigten Staaten ist in mehrerer Hinsicht reicher als unsrige. Der Amerikaner darf als Stifter mit einem größeren Entgegenkommen des Steuerfiskus rechnen, als wir das in der Bundesrepublik kennen. Es sind jedoch vermutlich nicht in erster Linie die Steuervorteile, die den amerikanischen Bürger stiftungswilliger machen, als es der Deutsche bisher ist. Vielmehr haben wir es auch mit einem Unterschied der Mentalitäten zu tun. Der Amerikaner, der ein Vermögen erarbeitet, häufig auch ein Vermögen ererbt hat, ist für die Stiftungsidee aufgeschlossener als der Deutsche.

Unter den Motiven des Amerikaners gibt es durchaus eigennützige Überlegungen, wobei die Erhaltung des Namens des Stifters für die Nachwelt keine kleine Rolle spielt; es gibt ja auch Eigennutz, der sich nicht unmittelbar in Geld ausdrücken läßt. Aber unverkennbar ist, daß die Stiftungsbereitschaft in den USA eine Wurzel in dem Gefühl staatsbürgerlicher Verpflichtung hat, das sich in der amerikanischen Demokratie stärker entwickelt zu haben scheint als auf unserem Kontinent. Für das Denken des amerikanischen Staatsbürgers halte ich eine Formulierung für charakteristisch, die sich in der Nummer der *New York Review of Books* vom 18. November 1999 findet: »Just say no: Between 1776 and 1789 Americans replaced a government over them with a government under them. They have worried ever since about keeping it under.«

Eine Nation, die über dem Staat steht, weiß, daß der Staat Grenzen hat, daß er gar nicht alle sozialen und kulturellen Bedürfnisse eines großen Landes befriedigen kann – kurzum, daß es ohne Selbsthilfe, ohne das Engagement des Staatsbürgers um die Nation schlecht bestellt wäre. Das religiöse Moment, das in manchem Fall in den USA von Einfluß gewesen sein könnte, erinnert uns daran, daß der Anfang auch unseres Stiftungswesens in einer Zeit liegt, in der die Kirche stärker als heute auf die Entscheidungen des einzelnen einwirkte.

Die amerikanische Stiftung sieht sich vor allem in der Struktur der dortigen Universitäten bestätigt, die der unsrigen in wichtigen Punkten voraus ist. Die weitgehende Unabhängigkeit der US-Universität vom Staat ist Stiftungen zu verdanken; ihre wissenschaftlichen Erfolge kann man darin begründet sehen. Man wird aber gut daran tun, die Annahme einer Ursächlichkeit nicht zu weit zu spannen – wissenschaftlicher Fortschritt liegt in weitem Feld.

Bosch arbeitet, wie man vielleicht einfügen darf, seit einer Reihe von Jahren eng mit einer der bedeutenden amerikanischen Stiftungsuniversitäten, der Carnegie Mellon University, zusammen: auf dem Campus in Pittsburgh ist, mit einem Funding der Bosch-Gruppe in Höhe eines zweistelligen Millionenbetrages, das Carnegie Bosch Institute entstanden, das in völliger wissenschaftlicher Unabhängigkeit arbeitet, frei auch von jedem Staatseinfluß.

Stiftungsuniversitäten sind Beispiele für Bürgerengagement. Sprechen wir von der Gründung der Universität Frankfurt am Main, die heute freilich staatlich ist, so steht an ihrem Anfang die »Opferwilligkeit der Frankfurter Bürger«, »die Gründung einer Hochschule aus der Kraft der Bürger einer Stadt«, wie Paul Kluge in seinem Buch über die »Stiftungsuniversität Frankfurt« schreibt. Kluge bemerkt – wir sollten das nicht übersehen –, daß zu den Zielvorstellungen der Frankfurter auch die Umwandlung »des alten Obrigkeitsstaats« gehörte, ein Argument für die Förderung der Stiftungsidee: die Unabhängigkeit des Denkens und Handelns einer Bürgergemeinschaft vom Staat, die Opfer rechtfertigt.

Vergleicht man die Frankfurter Gründung mit dem zeitgleichen Vorgang zur Aufbringung der Mittel für die Gründung der Kaiser-Wilhelm-Gesellschaft zur Förderung der Wissenschaft (heute: Max-Planck-Gesellschaft), so muß man den potentiellen Stiftern des Jahres 2000 vor Augen stellen, daß die Frankfurter Bürger seinerzeit insgesamt rund 15 Millionen Mark spendeten, das Doppelte dessen, was für die Kaiser-Wilhelm-Gesellschaft reichsweit zusammenkam.

In den Frankfurter Gründungsberichten findet sich schließlich eine Bemerkung von großem Stolz: »Die noch fehlenden 6 Millionen Mark wurden binnen kurzem von den Bürgern aufgebracht …«

Spielte in dieser Stadt vielleicht auch der »alte Frankfurter gemeinnützige Bürgersinn« mit: Es war in den Köpfen mancher Frankfurter auch die Sorge des alten Reichsstädters vor preußischer Dominanz. Dem Bürgersinn der alten Reichsstadt ist, wie man bemerken muß, auch das »Freie deutsche Hochstift« zu verdanken und nicht zuletzt das »Städel«.

Nicht vergessen dürfen wir Köln und Mannheim. Dort entstanden, dank dem Einsatz von Bürgern, »Universitäten« aus »Handelshochschulen«, die inzwischen zwar in die Staatssphäre übergingen, was aber die Erinnerung an den bürgerschaftlichen Ursprung nicht auslöschen darf. Beispiele sind keine Beweise für zukünftige Möglichkeiten, sie weisen dennoch in die Zukunft.

Dem Stifter, auch wenn man ihm Anerkennung nicht immer versagt, bleibt doch eine kritische Analyse seiner tatsächlichen oder vermeintlichen Beweggründe oft keineswegs erspart. Wo man ihm nicht ein schlechtes Gewissen unterstellt – die Hingabe eines Teils des Vermögens zur Sündentilgung, als eine Form von Ablaß –, vermutet man ein Bedürfnis zur Statusbildung. Wo man dem Stifter keine unmittelbaren materiellen Vorteile aus seiner Tat nachweisen kann, versucht man darzutun, daß die Stiftungsentscheidung der Festigung einer Position, der Abwehr eines Wandels, der Bewahrung und nicht dem Fortschritt diene.

Dem Stifter des Mittelalters winkte das Ewige Leben als Lohn für seine gute Tat. Der Begriff »Stift« – wir kennen ihn aus Tübingen, aber auch in Stuttgart haben wir eine altehrwürdige Stiftskirche – hat sich bis in unsere Zeit erhalten als geschichtlicher Ausdruck von Gemeinsinn auf Erden und dem Glauben an ein Leben nach dem Tod zugleich. Der Stifter, den wir heute gewinnen wollen, mag sich in dem einen oder anderen Fall von einem Fortleben eher irdischen Charakters bewegen lassen: die Verbindung seines Namens mit seiner Tat.

Wir kehren aber zu dem Staatsbürger zurück, dem es beschieden war, in seinem Erdenleben mehr als das Notwendige erwerben zu können und der sich einem ungeschriebenen Gesetz unterwirft, zu dem Staatsbürger also, der mehr tut als seine Pflicht, der einen Wert hingibt, um neue Werte zu schaffen. Denn darin, den Wert einer Spende nicht untergehen zu lassen, sondern einem Ziel dienlich zu machen, liegt der Sinn des Stiftens. »Errichten« – wir sind bei dem Urbegriff des Stiftens: Wer stiftet, spendet nicht nur, er schafft, er baut etwas Neues. Etwas, das ihn überlebt. Und worüber er sprechen darf.

Die heutige Robert Bosch Stiftung erhielt ihren Namen erst lange nach dem Tod ihres Gründers. Robert Bosch stand immer hinter seinem Werk zurück. Er wollte sich kein Denkmal setzen, als er entschied, daß der größte Teil des Vermögens, das er erarbeitet hatte, gemeinnützigen Zwecken zuzuführen sei. Wir wissen aus seinen mündlichen und schriftlichen Äußerungen, daß es ihm um die Früchte ging, wenn er gezielt spendete, und daß er zuletzt an die Entäußerung dachte. Es wurde zum Saatgut, was er tat; er war der Unternehmer, der, wenn er spendete, investierte. Es war Gemeinsinn, der ihn veranlaßte, der Gesellschaft zurückzugeben, was er erarbeitet hatte. Und es war Gemeinsinn, wenn er seiner Stiftung auf den Weg mitgab, ihre Erträge im Sinne der res publica zu verwenden.

Dieser Begriff steht »an Start und Ziel« der Stiftung. Das gilt nicht nur für ihre großen Arbeitsgebiete Gesundheitspflege, Völkerverständigung, vielmehr nicht zuletzt für einen Themenkreis, der in jüngster Zeit Gestalt angenommen hat: das Thema »Ehrenamt«. Geht es bei einer Stiftung um die Hingabe von Vermögen, so spendet der Träger eines Ehrenamtes persönliche Kraft, persönliche Zeit – und das ist in vielen Fällen das knappste Gut und das größte Opfer, das einer bringen kann. Und der, der Zeit schenkt, übernimmt mit dem Ehrenamt Verantwortung, wie sie einer unpersönlichen Obrigkeit nicht aufzuerlegen wäre.

Hinter jeder Stiftung in unserem Sinn, hinter jedem Ehrenamt steht ein Mensch, eine Gruppe von Menschen. Das Persönliche, das diesem Komplex anhaftet, unterscheidet ihn von aller Staatlichkeit, von aller Staatsmacht, und führt uns hinüber zu dem Begriff, den wir bei Franz Oppenheimer finden: »Freibürgerschaft«.

Ehrenämter zeichnen sich unter anderem dadurch aus, daß ehrenamtliche Tätigkeit unbezahlt bleibt. Eine kürzliche Zeitungsüberschrift trifft den Nagel auf den Kopf: »Sie sind unbezahlt, aber auch bezahlbar.« Aber vielleicht muß wieder einmal deutlich werden, welche Ehre die Übernahme eines öffentlichen Amtes, einer Tätigkeit im öffentlichen Interesse, als unmittelbare Hilfe für Menschen bedeutet; in den alten Reichsstädten wußte man das.

Wenn ich nun soeben von »Start und Ziel« sprach, so meinte ich, daß nicht nur ein Stiftungsentschluß von Gemeinsinn zeugt, daß es vielmehr auch die Zielvorstellung einer Stiftung sein kann, Gemeinsinn zu fördern. Gemeint sind hier die Bemühungen der Stiftung unseres Hauses, die sich für das »ehrenamtliche Engagement« mit Rat und Tat einsetzt. Sie hat unter diesem Stichwort bisher mehr als 1000 Projekte, vor allem in den neuen Bundesländern, initiiert und finanziert – mit einem Aufwand in zweistelliger Millionenzahl –, geleitet von dem Denken Robert Boschs: »den ehrlichen Gemeinschaftswillen und den Geist der Gemeinnützigkeit im Bürgerraum zu pflanzen und zu pflegen«.

Wir sehen gleiches Denken in unserer Stadt, die einen »Wegweiser zum Ehrenamt« herausgegeben hat. Im April des nächsten Jahres soll eine »Stuttgarter Akademie des Ehrenamts« ihre Arbeit aufnehmen – ein Zeichen zunehmenden Verständnisses für die Notwendigkeit bürgerschaftlicher Selbsthilfe. So ist auch die Überlegung zu verstehen, eine »Bürgerstiftung« in Stuttgart zu gründen, in die 44 alte Stiftungen von Bürgern, die derzeit vom Stadtkämmerer verwaltet werden, eingebracht werden könnten – als Grundlage für neuen Aufschwung.

Zum guten Ende verdichtet sich das Bild: Wer den demokratischen Staat will, muß mitmachen. Er muß sich engagieren, er muß für die Gemeinschaft eintreten. Wer dem gegenwärtigen Staat kritisch gegenübersteht, muß erst recht mitmachen. Und wer Abstand von der Allgegenwart des Staates halten will, darf nicht beiseite stehen. Stiftungen bieten einen Weg zum Ziel: dem Bürgerengagement als Voraussetzung jeder Demokratie.

Verstehen wir folglich den Wahlspruch des Stifterverbands »Maecenates voco!« als Aufruf: nicht etwa ein Vermögen ins Ungewisse zu entlassen, sondern einer Aufgabe zuzuführen. Um eine Stiftung zu schaffen, braucht es schöpferische Unzufriedenheit. Vielleicht braucht es auch – im Sinne Senecas – eine gewisse Unzufriedenheit nicht nur mit den Zuständen, sondern auch mit uns selbst, um der Idee der Stiftung den weiteren Weg zu ebnen. *(1999)*

Editorische Notiz

Die Beiträge von Hans L. Merkle beruhen auf einer Auswahl seiner Vorträge und Aufsätze aus drei Jahrzehnten. Sie sind vom Autor durchgesehen, teilweise überarbeitet und um tagesaktuelle Bezüge gekürzt worden, ohne dabei den vom Zeitpunkt der Entstehung bestimmten Charakter der Texte zu berühren. So ist erkennbar, welche der wiederholt angeschnittenen Fragen im Laufe der Zeit gelöst werden konnten und welche fortbestehen. Es ergab sich dabei von selbst, die Beiträge nicht thematisch, sondern chronologisch zu ordnen – mit Ausnahme des autobiographischen Vortrags »Beruf als Erfahrung«, gehalten am 12. Juli 1988 an der Universität Frankfurt am Main und erstmals in dem Band Hans L. Merkle, »Der steinige Weg« 1993 im Zürcher Manesse-Verlag veröffentlicht.

Die Rede »Über die Kunst der Prognose« auf einer Veranstaltung des Verbands der Pfälzischen Industrie am 15. März 1972 in Bad Dürkheim, die Ansprache »Dämonie der Macht« anläßlich der Verleihung der Freiherr-vom-Stein-Medaille in Gold der Stiftung F. V. S. am 23. Oktober 1973 in Stuttgart, die Rede »Inflation und öffentliche Finanzen« in einer Reihe des Presseausschusses Kammern/Verbände von Baden-Württemberg am 20. Februar 1975 in Stuttgart und der Vortrag »Bruchzonen der Gegenwart« zum 75. Geburtstag von Ernst Schneider am 6. Oktober 1975 in München stammen ebenso wie die folgenden Texte aus dem 1982 in Stuttgart bei der Deutschen Verlags-Anstalt (DVA) erschienenen Band Hans L. Merkle, »Bruchzonen der Gegenwart«.

Der Beitrag »Die Ordnung des Wettbewerbs« ist 1976 für die Festschrift »Wettbewerb im Wandel« zum 65. Geburtstag von Eberhard Günther geschrieben worden. Die Rede »Die Kräfte der unbelebten Natur« wurde zur Eröffnung der 109. Versammlung der Gesellschaft Deutscher Naturforscher und Ärzte am 19. September 1976 in Stuttgart gehalten, der Vortrag »Der staatsfreie Raum des Unternehmens« zum 70. Geburtstag von Max Schmidheiny am 9. Mai 1978 in St. Gallen. Der Kommentar »Rechte und Pflichten in der Republik« wurde in der Reihe »Reden auf die Republik« des Süddeutschen Rundfunks am 4. Februar 1979 gesendet. Die Ansprache »Dienen und Führen« wurde zum 60. Geburtstag von Wilfried Guth am 10. Juli 1979 in Frankfurt am Main gehalten, der Vortrag »Eliten und ihre Förderung« am 24. April 1982 vor dem Rotary Club Stuttgart.

Aus dem 1988 in der DVA herausgegebenen Band von Hans L. Merkle, »Kultur der Wirtschaft« sind für diese Auswahl entnommen worden: Die Vorträge »Führung im multinationalen Unternehmen« vor der Statistisch-volkswirtschaftlichen Gesellschaft in Basel am 14. März 1983, »Die Seele der Wirtschaft« zum 30jährigen Bestehen der Baden-Badener Unternehmergespräche am 29. September 1984, »Über die deutsch-französischen Beziehungen« vor der Offiziellen Deutsch-Französischen Industrie- und Handelskammer am 12. Juni 1985 in Paris und »Die Chancen Europas« vor der Friedrich-List-Gesellschaft am 25. April 1986 in München. Die im selben Band enthaltene Ansprache »Robert Bosch und sein Werk«, gehalten auf der Jubiläumsveranstaltung 100 Jahre Bosch am 23. September 1986 in Stuttgart, wurde um einige Passagen erweitert und um manche tagesbezogenen Bemerkungen gekürzt. Aus diesem Band stammt auch der Beitrag »Führung durch Manager« für das »Handwörterbuch der Führung«, Stuttgart 1987.

Die Vorträge »Erziehungssystem und Arbeitswelt« am 17. Februar 1988 vor der Pädagogischen Hochschule Kiel, »Wirtschaft als Element unserer Kultur« vor Gästen der Robert Bosch Stiftung am

7. Juli 1988 in Stuttgart und »Die Tugend des Vertrauens« am 1. Oktober 1988 vor Mitgliedern der Rotary Clubs Graz, Lausanne, Lyon und Stuttgart wurden in dem oben erwähnten Band »Der steinige Weg« veröffentlicht.

Der Diskussionsbeitrag »Die deutsche Wirtschaft und Frankreich – am Beispiel der Bosch-Gruppe« auf dem Kolloquium über »Deutsch-französische Wirtschaftsbeziehungen 1945–1960« des Deutschen Historischen Instituts am 8. Dezember 1994 in Paris liegt bisher nicht in Buchform vor; die Rede »Bürgerengagement und Stiftungsidee« auf dem Stuttgarter Stiftungstag am 26. November 1999 erscheint parallel in dem von Wolfgang Schuster und Warnfried Dettling beim Hohenheim Verlag herausgegebenen Band »Zukunft Stadt«.

Bei den einführenden Beiträgen von Henry A. Kissinger und Hermann Scholl handelt es sich um Vorträge in englischer Sprache, die am 4. und 5. Oktober 2001 in Berlin auf dem Hans L. Merkle Symposium on the Practice of International Management des Carnegie Bosch Institute for Applied Studies in International Management der Carnegie Mellon University in Pittsburgh, Pennsylvania/USA, gehalten wurden.

Ulrich Frank-Planitz

Die Deutsche Bibliothek – CIP-Einheitsaufnahme
Ein Titeldatensatz für diese Publikation ist bei der Deutschen Bibliothek erhältlich

2001 Hohenheim Verlag GmbH, Stuttgart · Leipzig

Satz: Hahn Medien GmbH, Kornwestheim
Druck- und Bindearbeiten: Ludwig Auer GmbH, Donauwörth
Printed in Germany
ISBN 3-89850-058-6